THE CURRENT STATE OF THE COHERENCE THEORY

PHILOSOPHICAL STUDIES SERIES

VOLUME 44

THE CURRENT STATE OF THE COHERENCE THEORY

Critical Essays on the Epistemic Theories
of Keith Lehrer and Laurence BonJour,
with Replies

Edited by John W. Bender

KLUWER ACADEMIC PUBLISHERS
DORDRECHT / BOSTON / LONDON

ISBN 0-7923-0220-6

Published by Kluwer Academic Publishers,
P.O. Box 17, 3300 AA Dordrecht, The Netherlands.

Kluwer Academic Publishers incorporates
the publishing programmes of
D. Reidel, Martinus Nijhoff, Dr W. Junk and MTP Press.

Sold and distributed in the U.S.A. and Canada
by Kluwer Academic Publishers,
101 Philip Drive, Norwell, MA 02061, U.S.A.

In all other countries, sold and distributed
by Kluwer Academic Publishers Group,
P.O. Box 322, 3300 AH Dordrecht, The Netherlands.

printed on acid free paper

Printed in The Netherlands

contents

preface

The subtitle of this book should be read as a qualification as much as an elaboration of the title. If the goal were completeness, then this book would have included essays on the work of other philosophers such as Wilfrid Sellars, Nicholas Rescher, Donald Davidson, Gilbert Harman and Michael Williams. Although it would be incorrect to say that each of these writers has set forth a version of the coherence theory of justification and knowledge, it is clear that their work is directly relevant, and reaction to it could easily fill a companion volume.

This book concentrates, however, on the theories of Keith Lehrer and Laurence BonJour, and I doubt that any epistemologist would deny that they are presently the two leading proponents of coherentism. A sure indication of this was the ease with which the papers in this volume were solicited and delivered. The many authors represented here were willing, prepared, and excited to join in the discussion of BonJour's and Lehrer's recent writings. I thank each one personally for agreeing so freely to contribute.

All of the essays but two are published for the first time here. Marshall Swain's and Alvin Goldman's papers were originally presented at a symposium on BonJour's *The Structure of Empirical Knowledge* at the annual meeting of the Central Division of the American Philosophical Association, Chicago, Illinois, in April, 1987.

With few exceptions, the contributors were involved in one or the other (or both) of two summer programs sponsored by the National Endowment for the Humanities. These were the 1986 Summer Institute in the Theory of Knowledge, at the University of Colorado, Boulder, headed by Alvin Goldman and Keith Lehrer, and the 1987 Summer Seminar, "Reasons, Justification and Rationality," run by Robert Audi at the University of Nebraska, Lincoln. This book is a not-so-indirect result of these programs, and I know I speak for all of the contributors to this volume who participated in them when I appreciatively thank the Endowment as well as the directors for conducting these marvelous activities. The field is richer and more warmly collegial as a result of them.

It is only through the willingness of Keith Lehrer and Larry BonJour to commit the very considerable amount of time necessary to studying and replying to the numerous essays (many of which passed through draft versions) that the dialogical intent of this book was realized. Their philosophical openness and admirable encouragement of current debate and interchange directly benefits the future state of the coherence theory. I must offer a special thanks to Keith Lehrer for the time he gave to extended philosophical correspondence with me, from which I learned very much, and for his enthusiastic support of this project.

The Ohio University Research Committee provided funds to assist in the preparation of this book, and Ms. Julia Houdashelt, her friendly and welcome secretarial and proof-reading assistance.

introduction

coherence, justification, and knowledge:
the current debate

Coherence, Justification, and Knowledge:
The Current Debate

John W. Bender
Ohio University

   Despite Emerson's maxim associating consistency with little minds, no philosopher champions incoherence, and this is how it should be. Since the most basic virtue of a belief is that it be knowledge, and since no belief stands alone, but is held in the context of other things believed, sound relations among beliefs are bound to be epistemically important.

   Reasons-giving, explanation, and inference, for example, generally require that one's background beliefs possess a degree of interconnection and cohesion. When we refer to an individual's belief *system* or to a conceptual *scheme* or *framework*, the words we use indicate our presumption or hope that a reasonably high level of coherence characterizes what we believe.

   Coherence obviously is both a normative and an epistemic concept: it concerns the goodness of "fit" among beliefs, and it is plausible to think that the degree of this fit may well measure the degree to which we are *justified* in believing what we do, and ultimately, may determine what we can be said to *know*.

   Coherence also is an abstract and generic concept. Inferential, evidential, explanatory, and probabilistic relations of various sorts are either partially constitutive of the concept or at least affect the degree of coherence. Now, it is an embarrassing fact of philosophy that the canons of induction, confirmation, explanation, and probability are at best only incompletely and darkly comprehended, and to lay all of these core problems at the doorstep of the coherence theorist and await the solutions would be philosophically unrealistic and unfair. But what, then, is meant by "the coherence theory"?

   "The" coherence theory is a *type* of epistemological theory - a type whose instances can vary in many details, as will become obvious in what follows. It is committed to the thesis that the conditions of empirical justification and knowledge can be expressed in terms of the complex, holistic relations that obtain among what we believe or accept, and that these relations are ultimately reciprocal or cyclical in some sense.

   The idea of mutual support or the reciprocity of justification-conferring relations is a denial of the primary tenet of *foundationalism*, viz., that justification is transmitted from one belief (or small set of beliefs) to another belief in a strongly directional or linear manner, and that all such lines of transmission find their source in one or another form of *basic* belief, a belief characterized by a kind of epistemic priority, in that its own justification is not, in turn, transmitted to it from other beliefs. In short, then, the coherence theory claims that no empirical beliefs enjoy epistemic priority, and all rely for their justification on their connection to, or membership in, the body of other things believed or accepted.

   Even at this extremely sketchy level, it is possible to see that promulgation of the central ideas of the coherence theory needs to advance on two broad fronts. First, offering a general rationale for the theory, as well as arguments for its basic cogency and adequacy, take up the task of sufficiently defusing or neutralizing the well-known principled objections to such a view so that traditional foundationalists, or other contending theorists such as the reliabilists, cannot claim victory by default. Second, in order to move from mere "theory-sketch" to actual theory, an elaboration of the details and the dynamics of coherence, and the working out of the account of justification and knowledge within those terms, is clearly necessary.

   These goals have been forcefully taken up in the work of Keith Lehrer and of Laurence BonJour. Generally speaking (and perhaps *only* generally speaking), BonJour

1

J.W. Bender (ed.), The Current State of the Coherence Theory, 1–14.
© 1989 by Kluwer Academic Publishers.

has focussed somewhat more on the general structure and defense of a coherence theory while Lehrer has developed and revised a detailed instrument which can be applied to actual cases for testing. Taken as a whole, the essays in this volume examine every nook and cranny of these two theories with impressive critical acumen, and BonJour and Lehrer, in their turn, have responded in a careful and quite particular way to these contributions. It is not my intention to repeat or systematically summarize this dialogue here.

Rather, I hope to accomplish something a bit more synthetic that may push the debate forward another step or two. Lehrer's and BonJour's original work, as well as the critical essays and the replies contained here, suggest a set of questions, questions to some degree, perhaps, still open, that express the current state of the discussion, and organize the problems. Interestingly, although there are many significant differences between BonJour's and Lehrer's work, the questions I will propose apply to both, and give us a framework for appreciating important similarities as well as the differences.

I. Is coherence a property or a relation, and in what sense is it holistic?
A large part of the initial, intuitive appeal of the coherence theory is traceable to the metaphor involved in the idea that a body of beliefs should "hang together" or "mesh", the threads of the fabric of knowledge being, as they are, interwoven. Thus envisioned, coherence is a *holistic* (and not obviously relational) property, ascribable, presumably in varying degrees, to the system as a whole, much as the property of strength applies to fabric.

Coherence in this sense is very probably an important epistemic virtue of a belief system, and specifying the elements of this coherence an important philosophical project. BonJour, in fact, offers an outline of this concept (1985, 93-101). But while a list of the symptoms of coherence or incoherence may answer the question of when a system possesses this virtue, it does not, at least directly, answer another question, and one which may be logically prior,*viz.*, what it is for a particular empirical belief to cohere with a system.

Coherence here is being conceived in way subtly different from the "strength of the fabric" metaphor above. It has now become a *relation* between a given belief and a system of other beliefs, rather than a property of the whole system. Perhaps this distinction is not viewed as important, since the coherence of the system may simply be a function of the strength with which each member coheres with the rest, but I think there are at least two reasons for keeping the "relational" and the "systemic" notions of coherence clear.[1]

First, consider BonJour's theory, which places primary focus on systemic coherence. What justifies a particular empirical belief, in BonJour's view, is (at least in part) its *membership* in a system possessing a high degree of coherence (as well as certain other characteristics) (92,154). Overall coherence of the system is (at least in part) determined by its logical consistency, degree of probabilistic consistency, the number and strength of inferential interconnections among its members, its unity or lack of isolated subsystems, and its freedom from unexplained anomalies (95-99).

What are the conditions for the membership of a particular belief in such a system? The mere fact of a person's *holding* that belief is not sufficient, since held beliefs can be unjustified, and since, for BonJour, justification requires membership in a system which is stable and remains coherent over the long run (153,169). So membership must involve contributing to (or at least not disrupting) coherence. Perhaps BonJour means us to infer that the conditions for the (relational) coherence of a particular belief with a certain system are exactly those which he stipulates for systemic coherence: a belief, then, coheres with a system to the degree it is logically and probabilistically consistent with it, has strong and numerous inferential connections to other beliefs in the system, does not promote the subdivision of the system, and is not explanatorily anomalous in relation to the system.

Although some serious questions may be raised about these conditions for membership, my point is not to suggest that they are implausible, but to suggest that the nature, interpretation, and implementation of these conditions are matters far too difficult and important to a coherence theory for us to be "extrapolating" them from BonJour's general remarks about systemic coherence. There are interesting and difficult questions concerning the connections between the two concepts of coherence that remain unaddressed, in part, I think, because univocality has been implicitly assumed. For instance, is a system coherent just in case each of its members coheres in its turn with the remaining members, or are there further constraints, or possible undermining circumstances? Is there a certain order in which the coherence of particular beliefs must be tested? Might *groups* of beliefs cohere with a system in some Quinean way not reducible to the coherence of individual group-members to the system?

A clear and unified coherence theory must acknowledge all of this complexity, and it may be initially helpful in this effort to utilize the distinction between systemic and relational coherence.

The second reason for making the distinction is that Lehrer's theory, which is primarily a theory of relational coherence, provides us with another sense in which coherence can be called *holistic*. The coherence of a certain proposition to a background system of acceptances is a relation that does not depend on inference, according to Lehrer (1986, 21), and is a measure of the relative reasonableness of the proposition, in comparison to any competing proposition, given the background system. An important determinant of a proposition's reasonableness on a person's acceptance system is its probability relative to that system.

In principle, the probability of a proposition can be affected by the probability assignments given to any or all of the other propositions accepted, and it is this interaction of probabilities that makes it significant for Lehrer to claim that coherence of a proposition to an acceptance system is a holistic relation the proposition has to the entire system, and is distinct from the inferability of the proposition from some small set of premise beliefs. The distinction between the systemic and relational senses of coherence allows us, then, to identify two somewhat different claims made in favor of holism.

Moreover, it may now occur to us to ask whether it is a component of Lehrer's view, as it is of BonJour's, that (systemic) coherence is required of the system to which an empirically justified belief or acceptance coheres (relationally). It is clear that an individual's acceptance system, i.e., the system of acceptances the person holds given that her objective is to obtain truth and avoid error, does not have to exhibit systemic coherence in order for the individual to be what Lehrer calls "personally justified" in accepting a certain proposition (1988). But personal justification is only a "subjective" sense of justification (1986, 8) and inadequate for the role that epistemic justification plays in the analysis of knowledge. For a person to know a proposition, that proposition must also cohere relationally with the numerous systems that can be generated from a person's original acceptance system through various corrections of that system in the direction of greater truth.

Whether such corrected systems are more coherent as a result of these adjustments toward truth, and whether a judgment that a proposition is indeed more reasonable than its competitors, relative to one of these corrected systems, in some indirect way implies that the system exhibits high coherence are, indeed, interesting questions whose answers are not obvious at this time.

II. What is the extent of coherence's role in the analyses of justification and knowledge?

Simply stated, the coherence theory is the view that justification is a matter of the relations among beliefs, but as the theory is developed and elaborated, we might find it illuminating to ask two questions: are the conditions for coherence sufficient for epistemic justification; and, in addition to the traditional truth and belief or acceptance conditions, are coherence requirements all that is necessary for knowledge? On these matters we find significant divergence between Lehrer and BonJour.

Over the years, Lehrer's view has become more simplified and elegant on these points. In its present form (1988), maintenance of the coherence of an accepted proposition throughout the systems constituting the ultrasystem of the subject is sufficient for that subject's knowing the proposition. Likewise, being completely justified in accepting a proposition is a matter of the coherence of that proposition to a specified subset of the systems constituting the ultrasystem (*viz.*, the acceptance and the verific systems). Lehrer's theory, therefore, attempts a unified handling of the problems of epistemic justification as well as the so-called Gettier problem.

One general worry worth considering is whether Lehrer's analysis tells us when a person is completely justified in believing what she does. Complete justification is intended to be tracked in Lehrer's theory by the coherence of the accepted proposition within both the acceptance system and the verific system of the subject. Such dual coherence reflects the fact that whatever it is that makes the proposition subjectively more reasonable than its competitors for the person is not dependent upon any false belief in her acceptance system. One might wonder if this idea is coextensive with the notion of complete epistemic justification.

On one hand, if individuals can be justified in believing something that is false, can they not also be fully justified in believing something on the basis of some falsity, provided that belief in that falsity is itself justified? On the other hand, is it not possible that a person may believe herself to be justified when she is in fact not, and the situation be such that the true acceptances which carry over into the verific system are sufficient to maintain coherence of the proposition to that system?

Other potential difficulties with Lehrer's unified treatment, many surrounding the Gettier problem, have been canvassed in a number of the essays of this volume.

In contrast to Lehrer, and despite his claim that a coherence theory of the sort he offers is "the leading candidate for a correct theory of empirical knowledge" (1985, 188), BonJour for the most part ignores the Gettier problem, and furthermore, on his view, coherence alone, whether construed systemically or relationally, is insufficient for justification. Therefore, while we await further treatment of the Gettier problem from BonJour, it is best to view his theory as one of epistemic justification, rather than of knowledge.

As a justification theory, BonJour's view relies heavily on the concept of coherence, but augments this with a number of substantive additional conditions. I believe that our distinction between relational and systemic coherence suggests a particularly clear way of organizing and exhibiting BonJour's theory.

Beginning with the concept of systemic coherence, and adding to it certain further conditions which a system must meet for it to confer justification on member beliefs, we can characterize a "justification-conferring coherent system." We may then state the conditions for the justification of a particular empirical belief in terms of its membership in such a system, along with certain additional constraints suggested by BonJour.[2]

A system of beliefs is a justification-conferring, coherent system iff:

(i)   It is logically consistent,

(ii)   It has a high degree of probabilistic consistency,

(iii)   It has a significant number of relatively strong inferential connections among component beliefs,

(iv)   It is relatively unified, i.e., does not divide into relatively unconnected subsystems,

(v)   It contains few unexplained anomalies,

(vi)   It provides a relatively stable conception of the world and remains coherent (i.e. satisfies (i) - (v) in the long run) and

(viii)   It satisfies the Observation Requirement, i.e., it must contain laws attributing a high degree of reliability to a reasonable variety of cognitively spontaneous beliefs, including introspective beliefs.

S is empirically justified in his belief B iff:

(i)   S's system of empirical beliefs is a justification-conferring, coherent system,

(ii)   B is a member of this system,

(iii)   S believes that B coheres with the other beliefs of his system and that the system is coherent to a high degree,

(iv)   S bases his belief (or continued acceptance of B) on the fact that B is a member of his highly coherent system,

(v)   S has at least implicit access to the metajustification for his system of beliefs, *viz.*, that the coherence and stability of the system is best explained by the fact that the epistemic standards embodied in his system are highly likely to yield truth in the long run. Satisfaction of this condition involves a metabelief (or at least an implicit understanding) that B is a belief of a certain type F, as well as an (*apriori* justified) belief that beliefs of type F are likely to be true.

I will be remarking on a number of the features contained in this analysis in the remainder of this introduction, and at this point mention only two things. In clear contrast to Lehrer's theory, more than coherence is involved in empirical justification for BonJour. At one point, BonJour makes this explicit by saying that "[c]oherence is not the sole basis for justification" (1985, 148). Many of the other conditions enumerated express the uncompromising *internalism* of his view, the idea that the conditions of justification must be within the cognitive grasp or access of the believer. For BonJour, conditions to which the subject has no access or about which he has no belief or grasp cannot be justification-determining conditions. I will focus on the matter of access in section III below.

Second, if our earlier discussion of relational and systemic coherence is correct, then the second condition for the justification of a particular belief, *viz.*, that the belief be a member of a coherent system believed by S, would need to be fleshed out in terms of the relational coherence of the belief to the system, the details of which account we have already found somewhat wanting.

III. How accessible to the subject must the facts of coherence be?

BonJour leaves no doubt about his answer to this question: an actually justified believer must have a grasp of his overall belief system, must have "cognitive access to the fact of coherence," and must have metabeliefs regarding the nature of his first-order beliefs and about their likelihood of being true (1985, 102-3; 118-9). BonJour admits that, in actuality, our grasp of these matters may be no better than tacit or implicit, but he holds to these demands nonetheless. Kornblith and BonJour carry on an interesting discussion of the possibility of having this required access, in their contributions to this volume .

The matter is more complex when we turn to Lehrer. Certain sorts of metabeliefs or "meta-acceptances" have a vital function in his theory, but on the other hand, having no access to the "corrected" systems of her ultrasystem (after all, a person does not have knowledge of which among her acceptances are false), the facts of coherence relative to those systems are not generally available to the subject, and such availability is not a condition for either epistemic justification or knowledge, in Lehrer's view.

This said, it must be stressed, however, that the coherence of a proposition with an acceptance system, and therefore the justified acceptance and knowledge of that proposition, depends on the subject's evaluation of the information, the circumstances, and indeed, himself, as being epistemically trustworthy. Hence, acceptance systems that are justification- and knowledge-supporting must contain numerous metabeliefs or, more precisely, meta-acceptances, and this is a feature shared with BonJour's theory. Lehrer has recently expressed this requirement by saying that knowledge is "metaknowledge" (1988). The meta-evaluations involved must be true for the coherence of a given proposition to be maintained within the ultrasystem, so although it is incorrect to say that the facts of coherence must be accessible to the knowing subject according to Lehrer, the subject must have the true meta-acceptances which partially determine the facts of coherence by preserving the reasonableness of the accepted proposition in the face of its competitors.

But are there not difficulties with postulating that knowing subjects must accept that they are trustworthy evaluators of certain kinds of information in certain kinds of circumstances? There is the straightforward question, similar to the one mentioned in BonJour's case, namely, whether subjects can realistically be claimed to have such meta-acceptances. But I set this aside for the most part (although I will make a later comment) for there is another, more interesting problem, which is similar in spirit to a difficulty Richard Feldman has posed for process reliabilism, called "the generality problem" (Feldman, 1985. Cf. also Pollock 1984).

Beliefs about one's trustworthiness in present circumstances can vary in their scope and truth value, depending on how generally or specifically the "present circumstances" are understood or defined. In a perceptual example, for instance, the present circumstances may be conceived as those of observing something on my living room wall, as observing something on my wall in certain kinds of lighting conditions, as observing something in these lighting conditions on a certain part of my wall, as observing something on this part of my wall at a certain time, and so forth. By adjusting the scope of the description, we can change the truth value of my acceptance that I am a trustworthy perceiver in these circumstances. I may be trustworthy in general about things on my living room wall, but not trustworthy in observations I make during a certain time period at a certain part of the wall. Which of these possible acceptances must I have and which must be true on Lehrer's theory? Notice that things can't be made too specific without running the risk of turning the meta-acceptance into nothing more than the first-order acceptance of the particular proposition in question as true. Then again, setting the circumstances too broadly risks the possibility that one is *not* trustworthy in circumstances so generally described.

Provided that we do not go to such extremes, it might be that Lehrer is willing to say that we in fact hold acceptances at each of the various levels, and that justification fails whenever, for any true acceptance about our trustworthiness, there is a false acceptance at a more specific level of description. Hence, if there is unusual lighting in part of my living room and I accept that something in that part of the room is red, my belief that I am generally trustworthy about the colors of things in my living room will not be capable of "putting down" or beating the challenge to my belief that the thing is red which comes from the competing claim, "I am not trustworthy about colors in this unusual lighting." I would not be justified in my color-belief in this case, and this is the result Lehrer wants. To be justified, I must accept that I am trustworthy about things' colors in this unusual lighting, and this must be true. (See the Mattey and the Davis and Bender papers for related discussions.)

This is the sense in which our evaluations of our trustworthiness must be correct if we are to be completely justified and have knowledge. This discussion leads, however, to a number of other questions about metabeliefs and meta-acceptances, especially about their nature and their own justification.

IV. What is the nature or psychological status of meta-acceptances and metabeliefs?

We have seen that, according to Lehrer, the acceptance system of the human knower must contain higher-order acceptances to the effect that the person is trustworthy in accepting a certain proposition. If one were not to accept that one is trustworthy in the particular case, certain competitors of the accepted first-order proposition could not be beaten, and coherence of the proposition with one's acceptance system would fail.

If our acceptances about our trustworthiness were construed as *beliefs*, and, even more forcefully, if they were construed as conscious beliefs of the knower, then Lehrer's position would surely be open to the objection that such a requirement is too stringent to be met by most non-reflective knowers. Yet Lehrer is clear (and perhaps clearest on this point in his reply in this volume) that acceptances are not beliefs or judgments, but rather are a kind of functional state whose role is exhibited in thought, inference, and action. An acceptance that p is a state which can, but does not always, arise from a reflective judgment that p, and influences how we think about the fact that p, how we draw inferences about matters related to p, and how we act as a result. Acceptances, then, are functional states which we as epistemic beings actually realize, rather than beliefs which are only tacitly, or in some dispositional sense, true of us.

Lehrer admits that a fully articulated version of this functional theory of acceptance remains to be worked out, and prior to this working out, I think it must be conceded that it is difficult to be fully at ease with his wielding of the concept. It is particularly difficult to clarify the conditions for ascribing a certain acceptance to someone. Lehrer is happy to say that we accept that 57 is a odd number even if we have never considered it, but denies that, in a case where Smith truly believes that he has seen Tom steal a book, Smith accepts that no one who knows Tom has said that he was out of town at the time, even though Smith acts and makes inferences as though he believes that there is no evidence which undermines his observation. (See Russell's article in this volume.) If acceptance is "weaker" than belief, it is apparently "stronger" than what we might be said to presume, assume, or presuppose is true, but clearly, more needs to be said.

Whether BonJour ultimately bites the bullet when it comes to metabeliefs or hedges at the last moment is somewhat harder to decipher. Although he asserts that one of the main conditions of empirical justification is that the person have a *reflective grasp* of the fact that his system of beliefs is coherent to a high degree and more coherent than alternative systems (1985, 154), only two pages earlier, he says this :

> Thus the basic claim of my coherentist position...must be that careful reflection on actual cases will reveal that these elements [the inferences appealed to in the account of justification, and awareness of the entire system of beliefs] are tacitly or implicitly involved in the actual cognitive state of a person who has empirical knowledge, even though he does not bring them explicitly to mind and indeed

would normally be unable to do so even if explicitly challenged. Such a claim is obviously difficult to establish. (152)

It is unclear what tacit involvement amounts to when explicit challenge cannot bring the involved elements to mind. Perhaps BonJour would appeal to a functionalistic understanding of these elements much as Lehrer opts for a functional construal of acceptance. It might be claimed that the actual cognitive states of a knower must include some functional equivalent to the justificatory inferences and grasp of the entire system which BonJour finds crucial.

However this story is developed, it does appear that ultimately there is more bullet-biting than hedging on BonJour's part here, for he is willing to interpret the degree to which we fail to instantiate the accessibility conditions he has placed on epistemic justification as the degree to which we merely approximate optimal epistemic rationality, rather than as a grounds for concluding that his conditions are unrealistic and overly stringent. I will return to the element of idealization in BonJour's theory in section VIII.

V. Mustn't metabeliefs and acceptances of trustworthiness themselves be justified?

Evaluations of trustworthiness, Lehrer says, must be part of a person's acceptance system and must be true if justification and knowledge are to be attained. But must not our acceptances of our own trustworthiness in the given present circumstances also be *justified* as well as true if they are to play a role in justifying our first-order acceptances? If the answer to this is yes, then isn't the coherentist one step away from infinite regress, vicious circularity, or foundationalism?

Lehrer's answer is that, yes, evaluations of trustworthiness must be justified if they are to be of any epistemic use, but, no, this does not place coherentism within the squeeze of its three lethal enemies. The question of my justification for accepting that I am trustworthy in the present situation surrounding my acceptance that p is, like all matters of justification, one of coherence. An acceptance of current trustworthiness must be able to beat competitors, just as is required of any acceptance, if it is to be justified. Lehrer claims (in his reply in this volume and in Lehrer 1988) that the coherence of such particular evaluations of trustworthiness is at least partially dependent upon our acceptance of a general principle of trustworthiness, roughly the principle that our faculties are trustworthy and that we are, in general, trustworthy evaluators of truth.

Although this general principle seemed to be acknowledged as a *foundational* principle in Lehrer (1988), his current view is more interesting and provocative. Challenges to the general trustworthiness principle are beaten on the basis of what the subject accepts about his or her past successes and failures in the pursuit of truth and avoidance of error. Coherence cycles but is not circular. The justification for particular acceptances may rely upon the acceptance of a general trustworthiness principle, while acceptance of that principle may depend on what is accepted about past successes.

Lehrer does not address the question of the justification of the prior acceptances whose successes help to establish the trustworthiness principle, in particular, how they manage to beat *their* competitors without the help of this principle. The threat of circularity certainly exists at this juncture, but let me suggest a more promising avenue that opens up if we begin to think of the coherence theory *dynamically* rather than purely structurally.

Perhaps part of the what is implied by the idea that coherence "cycles" is that each subject or believer must "bootstrap" his or her way to complete justification and knowledge. Our original acceptances, though not fully justified, suffer through a certain process of confirmation and disconfirmation, some of which we experience or eventually become aware of. As past successes build, there comes a point when we accept that we are generally trustworthy. With enough successes in place, competitors to the general principle are beaten. The principle can then assume its role in the justification of new acceptances.[3] Circularity is avoided by the admission that there must be an "ascent" to justification and knowledge from a more impoverished original position.

I cannot say that Lehrer endorses this interpretation, but in addition to providing some response to the threats of circularity and company, this suggestion has the advantage of highlighting a fact often ignored by epistemologists, *viz.*, that our epistemic theories must become more sensitive to the dynamics of justification.[4]

Turning to BonJour, we come to what is probably the most-discussed claim of his book, *viz.*, the assertion that empirical justification is conditional in nature, and rests upon the so-called "Doxastic Presumption". The general point expressed by the Doxastic Presumption is that

> ...the essential starting point for epistemological investigation is the *presumption* that the believer has a certain specific belief, the issue being whether or not the belief thus presumed to exist is justified. (81)
>
> When this claim is applied to a coherence theory, whose basic unit of justification is the entire system of beliefs, the issue of empirical justification presupposes that a system approximately the same as what the subject takes himself to hold does exist. Therefore, one's metabeliefs to the effect that one has certain beliefs may be presumed to be true. (104)

BonJour admits that a believer's grasp of his own system consists of a set of empirical metabeliefs which are themselves in need of justification.(102) During his anti-foundationalist arguments, BonJour considers the suggestion that certain foundational beliefs are justified in virtue of some property they possess, and says this:

> But how exactly is the possession of this property (call it ø) supposed to confer epistemic justification or warrant upon some particular belief B of the relevant sort? ...First, I must believe, with justification, that beliefs which have property ø are likely, to the appropriate degree, to be true; it is this belief which the envisaged position claims to be justified *apriori*. ...But, second, I must apparently believe, again with justification, that belief B does have property ø ...and that it is accepted by me now. And the immediate problem is that whatever may be the case concerning the status of the first of these beliefs, it seems undeniable that the second conjunct of the second belief, the claim that I presently accept a certain specific belief B, is itself an *empirical* claim requiring *empirical* justification. (80-81)

But he eschews the position that we saw Lehrer willing to accept regarding meta-acceptances, *viz.*, that they too are justified by coherence with the rest of the acceptance system. BonJour finds this answer "unacceptable" and "beyond any doubt viciously circular" (102). The Doxastic Presumption fills the breach by reminding us of our primary epistemological focus - the justification of first-order empirical beliefs:

> ...the primary justificatory issue is whether or not, under the presumption that I do indeed hold approximately the system of beliefs which I believe myself to hold, those beliefs are justified. And thus the suggested solution to the problem raised...is that the grasp of my system of beliefs which is required if I am to have cognitive access to the fact of coherence is dependent...on this *Doxastic*

Presumption, as I will call it, rather than requiring further justification. (103)

I confess to a lack of understanding how a principle which is tantamount to the presumption of the *truth* of certain metabeliefs is supposed to silence a challenge about their *justification,* but I put aside this general point to focus on a more specific one.

BonJour admits that reliance on the Doxastic Presumption not only makes the justification deriving from a coherence theory *conditional* in nature, but also leaves it uninsulated from a certain kind of skepticism - a skepticism about one's metabeliefs. He downplays skepticism of this form, saying:

> Certainly it would be a very unusual brand of skepticism which would challenge whether my belief B is justified by raising the issue of whether I do in fact accept B, the normal skeptical claim being precisely that certain beliefs which are in fact held are nonetheless unjustified. (81)

I grant that a skepticism which doubts the truth of the metabelief, 'I accept belief B,' is not a very interesting or gripping form of skepticism, and see little that keeps us from agreeing that the Doxastic Presumption rightly sidesteps this quibble. There are, however, other metabeliefs whose justification is a prime target of serious skepticism, and which cannot, I think, be legitimately protected by the Doxastic Presumption. It is BonJour's position that empirical justification requires that the person have a reflective grasp of the fact that his system of beliefs is highly coherent. If I understand BonJour on this matter, this grasp will involve, in the case of a particular first-order belief, B, whose justification is of interest, a metabelief that B coheres (relationally) with the person's system. Such a metabelief is analogous to those of the form, 'B has feature ø' to which BonJour refers in his anti-foundationalist discussion and which I have cited above. Since skeptical alternatives are precisely challenges to B's coherence, a presumption that *these* metabeliefs are justified seems to be just that - presumptuous.

It appears, then, that even if we are willing to presume the truth of the metabeliefs that assert that certain beliefs are *held* by the subject, and also are willing to agree with BonJour's claim of *apriori* justification for the metabeliefs (involved in the metajustificatory argument) to the effect that beliefs of certain kinds are *likely to be true,* the metabeliefs about *coherence* stand in need of justification. BonJour may, then, be forced to consider a response along the lines suggested above in connection with Lehrer, and retract the claim that such a response is irrevocably circular. Handling this issue is, in my estimation, absolutely crucial to the future of the coherence theory.

VI. Are BonJour's endorsement of the Doxastic Presumption and Lehrer's reliance on the principle of general trustworthiness significant qualifications of their coherentism and serious concessions to foundationalism?

Having questioned the power of the Doxastic Presumption, I nonetheless think that it can be saved from the further charge of being, at bottom, a foundationalist strategy which has the effect of turning the metabeliefs under its jurisdiction into *basic* beliefs. A few writers have suggested this (see Alvin Goldman's essay), but I think that BonJour has now made it clear that the Presumption is no form of justification-conferring principle, and, in particular, its operation does not provide metabeliefs with any form of self-warrant. What its implementation does do, however, is make BonJour's coherence account of justification seriously *conditional* and I have indicated above that this may not be a very happy stopping place for the coherence theory. In other words, BonJour may be more comfortable with this consequence than he should be.

Similarly, it is already clear from the discussion in the above section that an acceptance about our general epistemic trustworthiness does not amount to a foundational tenet in Lehrer's view, but receives its justification from its relations of coherence to the rest of the acceptance system.[5] New foundationalist lures may well arise when an attempt is made to elaborate the idea that coherence cycles, but I do not think that Lehrer has succumbed as of present.

VII. Is the coherence theory an implicitly *inferential* theory?

There is clearcut disagreement between BonJour and Lehrer over the answer to this question, at least in regard to relational coherence. Justification of a particular belief involves, on BonJour's view, at least the implicit instantiation by the believer of an *argument* - the metajustificatory argument (1985,10,92,169-172). Premise beliefs involved in this argument include the beliefs of the subject that she presently holds a belief of a certain type; that beliefs of that type satisfy one of the standards for coherence to the belief system; and that the best explanation of the coherence of beliefs satisfying such standards is that they are likely true (or that the long-run coherence of a system governed by such standards is best explained by the fact that the member beliefs are true).

Lehrer, on the other hand, has consistently touted as a virtue of his coherence theory the fact that coherence relations, i.e., relations of comparative reasonableness of a proposition, over its competitors, on a given acceptance system, are distinct from the actual or implicit inferences performed by the subject. It might be asked, though, whether the subject's acceptances about her own trustworthiness do not perform their justificatory function by being premises in implicit arguments or inferences which the subject performs. The answer, however, is "no." Evaluations of one's trustworthiness must be part of one's acceptance system in order that certain competitors to what one accepts are beaten or "neutralized". But what one accepts is not the conclusion of an inference which involves meta-acceptances as premises. Lehrer reiterates this in his reply in this volume:

> My being justified in accepting that I have a headache does not directly depend on my accepting that my belief that I have a headache is an introspective belief and that introspective beliefs are likely to be true. It depends, instead, on my accepting that I can tell that I have a headache when I have one. My accepting that I can tell a headache when I have one is also justified on the coherence theory. The justification for that depends on something else I accept which I might put by saying that I would not accept that I can tell a headache when I have one unless I could. None of this justification involves using one statement as a premise for inferring a conclusion, however.

The independence of coherence from inference in this sense raises the hard question whether it is necessary that an adequate theory of *being justified in believing that p* be sensitive to the actual inferential structure of one's belief system. Might it be that Lehrer's theory captures only the conditions for a belief's *being justifiable for a person*, on his acceptance system?[6] Since this point is considered in the article of Davis and Bender, I will not pursue it here.

It is safe to say, I believe, that there is no similar disagreement between Lehrer and BonJour when it comes to systemic coherence. As a property of a belief system as a whole, coherence is determined in part by the inferential connections obtaining among the system's members, but these connections are commonly understood as quasi-logical relations among propositions, and not as a psychological "map" or record of past inferences of the believer.

VIII. Does the coherence theory express an epistemic ideal or a realistic state of human knowers?

This question uncovers another rift in the ranks of coherentists. A number of contributors (Kornblith and Bogen at greatest lengths) have objected that BonJour's conditions for epistemically justified belief either are not met in the preponderance of actual cases, or in principle cannot be met, due to the nature of the accessibility requirements that are central to his internalistic coherentism.

It is to BonJour's credit, and a mark of the exceptional candor with which he carries on the philosophical argument of his book, that he explicitly takes up this kind of objection, at least in its general outlines (151-3). As mentioned above in section IV, BonJour is confident that his conceptual analysis of justification is on the mark and not overly stringent and, consequently, he concludes that a grasp of one's system and of the inferences necessary for justification must be at least tacitly involved in the actual cognitive state of the believer, *and*, to the extent that this is not the case, commonsense instances of knowledge must be accepted as only loose approximations of an epistemic ideal.

BonJour seems to be suggesting, then, that his coherence theory either presents an idealized picture or a picture of an ideal. As a picture of the actual cognitive architecture of justified belief, it is an idealization in the sense of being an abstract model, a model, say, of the *functional* structure of justified belief. So, for example, the actual cognitive state of the justified believer involves, on this picture, an access operation on one's belief system that is functionally similar to an explicit grasp or conscious awareness of that system. As a picture of an epistemic ideal, on the other hand, it gives us a view of what it would be like to be a kind of epistemic *saint*, what it would be like to be more consciously "virtuous" - if the limitations and hidden machinations of human belief fixation were not so powerful.

Kornblith has offered some strong reasons for doubting that BonJour's theory gives us a model of the justified believer's actual cognitive state, and BonJour has responded. It is not an unattractive alternative to regroup from this debate behind the notion that justification and coherence are epistemic ideals, for insofar as they are positive normative concepts, they obviously are. But the pressing question clearly is whether we often or at least sometimes come up to these ideals of belief-formation. I suggest that it would be easier to accept BonJour's conditions as a statement of an ideal (rather than as an overstatement or misstatement of the "facts" of justification) if it were easier to see how it is that we can be said to *approximate* rather than blatantly *violate* those conditions.

Doxastic ascent, or more accurately, the ascent to second-order acceptances may seem to drive Lehrer's theory, too, further from "the real" and closer to the ideal. But Lehrer resists this on the grounds that what a person does not consciously believe he might nevertheless actually *accept*.

One reason the notion of acceptance was originally introduced by Lehrer was that acceptance is a notion "essentially relative to some purpose" and it is "acceptance of something for the purposes of obtaining truth and eschewing error" with respect to the thing one accepts that is a condition of knowledge (1986, 6). Beliefs, on the other hand, can be held for a variety of reasons having nothing to do with the pursuit of truth. This distinction, however, in no way explains how "most of what we accept...we accept without ever having considered it" (this volume). And it is clear that it is this latter feature of acceptance that allows Lehrer to posit acceptances of certain sorts when the posit of an analogous belief would be dubious, or at least debatable. Deciding whether Lehrer's coherence theory is or can be as realistic as he wants and claims requires what we at present do not have, *viz.*, clearcut ascription conditions for the idea of an acceptance.

IX. How does coherence effect the "truth connection"?

The virtue of epistemic justification is not, as it were, an intrinsic good, and is worth such extensive theorizing as we see in Lehrer's and BonJour's work only if it ultimately connects itself - and us - to truth. As BonJour puts it, "The basic role of justification is that of a *means* to truth, a more directly attainable mediating link between our subjective starting point and our objective goal" (1985, 7). Lehrer echoes this thought when he says that, "Justification is the intersection of the subjective, the mental operations of the knower, and the objective, the truth about reality" (1986, 5). Both Lehrer and BonJour would agree that coherence effects the truth connection because coherent beliefs *must* be likely to be true, but their different theories give different interpretations of this 'must'.

BonJour's theory connects to truth *via* the metajustificatory argument (169-178). A system of beliefs that remains coherent and stable over the long run while satisfying the Observation Requirement *must* be at least approximately true in the sense that the system's approximation to independent reality provides the *best explanation* for its continuing coherence and stability in the face of always-new observational input. This "best-explanation" defense of the truth connection is discussed and criticized in the essays by Swain and Alan Goldman, which, in turn, have provoked an interesting rebuttal by BonJour.[7]

Lehrer draws the truth connection even more tightly, though like BonJour, it is drawn at the meta-level. It follows *conceptually* from Lehrer's analysis of coherence that if a person is completely justified in accepting something then it is probable that that acceptance is true.

To be *personally* justified in accepting something, a person must accept that she is trustworthy about such matters, and her acceptance system must make it probable/reasonable that she is so reliable. The acceptance of her trustworthiness must, in addition, be true, if that acceptance is to pass into the corrected systems of her "ultrasystem"; and the probability that she is trustworthy in the matter must remain high within the corrected systems if coherence is to be maintained therein. Only when all of these conditions are satisfied is the person's acceptance of something *justified in a way that is undefeated*. (Lehrer identifies *complete* justification with coherence in one of the corrected systems, *viz.*, the verific system; the same implication holds between complete justification and the probable truth of the acceptance as holds between undefeated justification and probable truth. The notion of undefeated justification is now more central to Lehrer's theory than that of complete justification.) A cryptic expression of this position is given in these two passages from earlier articles:

> The coherence theory incorporates the idea that one must believe that one is trustworthy with respect to what one accepts and be right in that belief in order to be completely justified in accepting what one does. (1986, 23)
> [T]he connection between justification and truth lies in what one accepts about the probability of both the truth and the reliability of the belief. The truth connection is attained through doxastic ascent. (1983, 194)

It is this rather intricate position about the truth connection that underpins Lehrer's characterization of his coherence theory as part internalistic and part externalistic, and which prompts his recent claim that human knowledge is "metaknowledge".

X. Conclusion

Questioning could easily continue in the same vein, with more affinities and differences between Lehrer's and BonJour's work coming to light. I have not mentioned some issues that confront both of these theories, such as the so-called "isolation problem", because these have been extensively treated in the essays which follow. Other interesting and difficult matters that are to a degree more parochial to one or the other theory, such as the interpretation and assignment of probabilities within belief systems (something of a problem for Lehrer), I have thought best saved for elsewhere.

The questions we *have* examined have, I think, provided a means of organizing many of the details of these two thinkers' complex work around common issues which it is likely any version of the coherence theory would need to address. It is in the process of asking and answering questions of this sort - a process taken up in greater length and detail in the essays and responses that follow - that we get the best measure of the current state of the coherence theory.

NOTES

1. As will become clearer when I take up Lehrer's view of coherence, the distinction between relational and systemic coherence that I am suggesting here is not the same as BonJour's distinction between the local and global levels of justification, even though global justification involves systemic coherence. The difference is this. Local justification, for BonJour, is a nonholistic, inferential matter of the connection of a belief to other, premise, beliefs. It is the linear nature of local justification that, according to BonJour, has obscured the fact that justification at the global level is a nonlinear matter of mutual and reciprocal support, a matter of the overall coherence of the system (91). Relational coherence, on the other hand, can be conceived as a holistic and noninferential relation of a particular belief to the whole system of background beliefs, not to a few premise beliefs. In fact, as we will see, Lehrer holds just such a holistic and noninferential view of relational coherence.
2. I have assembled these conditions from the various remarks BonJour makes in his (1985). See 9,10,92, 102-3,106,116,123-4,141,151-4,170,191.
3. It is legitimate to wonder at this point whether the work of the general principle of trustworthiness could not be fully absorbed by the more specific claims of trustworthiness, and those specific claims themselves be justified on the basis of one's past successes in similar circumstances. On this alternative, coherence and justification become a form of reflective equilibrium between first order and second order acceptances. For more on reflective equilibrium and coherence, see Sosa's paper in this volume.
4. We see some increase in the awareness of epistemic dynamics in the recent work of Gilbert Harman, which focuses on change in belief. See Harman (1986). Also see Castañeda's essay in this volume.
5. This point is clearer now, given Lehrer's reply in this volume, than it was when Davis and I insinuated that his theory might contain foundational elements. See our article contained herein.
6. Pollock argues this point in *Contemporary Theories of Knowledge,* (1986, 81).
7. The concept of best explanation has recently been put to heavy use but for different purposes in Alan Goldman's *Empirical Knowledge* (Berkeley: University of California Press, 1988) and Paul Moser's *Knowledge and Evidence* (Cambridge: Cambridge University Press, 1989).

REFERENCES

BonJour, Laurence. *The Structure of Empirical Knowledge.* Cambridge, MA: Harvard University Press, 1985.
Feldman, Richard. "Reliability and Justification." *Monist* 68 (1985), 159-74.
Harman, Gilbert. *Change in View.* Cambridge, Mass.: MIT Press, 1986.
Lehrer, Keith. "The Coherence Theory of Knowledge." *Philosophical Topics* 14 (1986), 5-25.
-----. "Metaknowledge: Undefeated Justification." *Synthese* 74 (1988), 329-347.
-----, and Cohen, Stewart. "Justification, Truth, and Coherence." *Synthese* 55 (1983), 191-207.
Pollock, John. *Contemporary Theories of Knowledge.* Towata: Roman and Littlefield, 1986.
----. "Reliability and Justified Belief." *Canadian Journal of Philosophy* 14 (1984), 103-114.

i. abstracts of contributed essays

Lehrer's Coherentism and the Isolation Objection

Paul K. Moser
Loyola University of Chicago

Among coherence theories of epistemic justification, Keith Lehrer's version is second to none in its originality, detail, and precision. It is, without a doubt, the most refined coherence theory in circulation. In this paper I ask whether Lehrer's coherentism withstands the familiar isolation objection to epistemic coherentism. Part 1 outlines Lehrer's coherentism in its most recent garb. Part 2 states the isolation objection to coherentism without relying on the troublesome metaphor of "cutting off" empirical justification from the world. And Part 3 argues that Lehrer's coherentism falls prey to the isolation objection because of a deficiency shared by all versions of epistemic coherentism.

Personal Coherence, Objectivity, and Reliability

G. J. Mattey
University of California, Davis

The isolation argument purports to show that the existence of a relation of coherence among what one accepts need not reflect the structure of the world, and hence is inadequate as a criterion of justification. Lehrer defends his coherence theory by claiming that complete justification involves the reliability of the acceptance system and the acceptance of that reliability. This is supposed to establish the connection between justification and truth. I argue that Lehrer's defense is only partially successful, applying to reflective acceptance alone. His coherence theory is too permissive to establish the truth connection for unreflective belief.

Fundamental Troubles With The Coherence Theory

Wayne A. Davis, Georgetown University, and
John W. Bender, Ohio University

Coherence of a belief to the body of other beliefs a person holds is neither a necessary nor sufficient condition for the empirical justification of that belief, we argue.

We make the non-necessity claim in discussing the question of basic beliefs. The more interesting debate, however, concerns whether coherence is ever sufficient for epistemic justification.

The paper offers two arguments for the insufficiency thesis. The first argues that a coherence measure fails to capture the inferential structure of a set of beliefs and that that structure is important to justification. The second argument claims that coherence will not yield justification even if the background system is entirely true - because the system might be a set of lucky guesses. (This should not be confused with the "isolation argument" which objects that purely fictitious systems can be coherent.)

These arguments are directed primarily toward Keith Lehrer's version of the coherence theory; however, certain suggestions of Laurence BonJour also are considered.

Lehrer's Coherence Theory of Knowledge

Richard Feldman
University of Rochester

In two recent papers Keith Lehrer has developed the coherence theory of knowledge and justification that he originally proposed in *Knowledge*. The current theory is that a person knows a proposition if and only if the proposition is justified relative to the person's actual acceptance system and relative to every acceptance system that can be constructed out of the actual system by eliminating falsehoods and replacing them by their true denials. Justification relative to a system is spelled out in terms of coherence with that system, and a proposition coheres with a system provided it is more reasonable to believe that proposition than its competitors on the basis of that system. However, Lehrer says rather little about comparative reasonability, particularly about what determines the comparative reasonability of propositions in non-actual acceptance systems. As a result, although it is difficult to assess the merits of his theory, it appears that the theory avoids skeptical implications only by making it too easy to have knowledge and justification and it also appears that the theory does not avoid some variations on standard Gettier-style counterexamples. Finally, the theory has the incorrect implication that people lack knowledge in cases in which there are misleading defeaters.

How Reasonable is Lehrer's Coherence Theory?   Beats Me.

Philip Peterson
Syracuse University

Keith Lehrer offers a probablistic approach to a coherence theory of *justification* (where the more-probable-than relation is the basis for explaining the more-reasonable-than relation). For S to know that p, for Lehrer, is all and only for S to accept that p when p is true and undefeated, where also for each competitor X of p, p is more probable for S (personally and verifically) than X is given S's background system of beliefs, A. Very recently, Lehrer has slightly modified this conception of knowledge possession by substituting so-called ultra-system justification for personal and verific justification and undefeatedness.

A requirement that any theory of knowledge should satisfy is *non-iteration* (that knowing that p does not require knowing that one knows that p). The mere possibility of knowing that one knows that p, however, does not violate *non-iteration*. On Lehrer's account (with Wagner), *a priori* knowledge (e.g., *a priori* intuition) - i.e., an empiricistic account of and/or substitute for it - is explained through the notion of rational consent (via convergence of aggregated probabilities). One's acceptance of something is "intuitive" only if the appropriate form of rational consent holds. But any case of rational consent is *not* easy to observe or determine, so that conscious knowledge that an acceptance *is* intuitive is difficult. As a result, knowing that one knows that p wherein acceptance of p is an intuition is practically (though not theoretically) impossible.

The same kind of result carries over to Lehrer's general account; i.e., it is not practically possible that anyone ever does know that he knows that p (for ordinary non-intuitions like that it's raining here today). This is *not* because knowing it's raining here today requires conscious awareness of that proposition's beating or neutralizing all its competitors (such knowledge is not a requirement of Lehrer's). However, Lehrer's notion of simply *being* justified is sufficiently complicated to make knowing that one is (and hence ever knowing that one knows that p) practically impossible. Fodorizing (with Cohen) his theory could help Lehrer to fashion a distant substitute for knowing that one knows that p. However, his recent introduction of ultrajustification makes fodorization less plausible.

When Can What You Don't Know Hurt You?

Bruce Russell
Wayne State University

It looks as though certain Gettier cases that do not involve any false *beliefs* count against the view that knowledge is undefeated, justified true belief. To save the view one might require that both beliefs *and assumptions* be considered and argue that such Gettier cases involve false assumptions that *do* defeat the subject's belief. But modifying the view in that way will create problems in cases involving misleading, unpossessed evidence, for it seems that in such cases assumptions must be attributed to the subject that defeat his belief, and so destroy his knowledge, according to the modified account.

The dilemma cannot be avoided for knowledge (I argue) is justified, non-accidentally held true belief and an accidentally held true belief may be justified but undefeated by any of the subject's *beliefs* while a non-accidentally held true belief may be justified but defeated by some misleading or remote piece of evidence. There seems to be no way to give an account of assuming that ensures that in cases of the first sort the target belief is defeated by what the subject *assumes* that does not also imply that the target belief is defeated by assumptions about the misleading or remote piece of evidence in cases of the second type.

BonJour's *The Structure of Empirical Knowledge*

Alvin I. Goldman
University of Arizona

Despite the sophistication of BonJour's defense of coherentism, the book faces a number of serious problems. First, it is difficult to see how his notion of a "standard" of justification is compatible with his metajustification requirement. Second, the metajustification requirement creates an objectionable circularity in the theory. Third, BonJour's arguments for the metajustification requirement seem to rest, ultimately, on level-confusions. The metajustification requirement is central to BonJour's conception of internalism. But, as Brueckner has shown, BonJour's attempt to defend coherentist internalism has insuperable problems. Although BonJour denies the existence of basic empirical beliefs, his Doxastic Presumption in effect creates a class of beliefs that qualify as basic. There are also some technical problems in BonJour's formulation of coherentism. More serious yet is the fact that BonJour has no *unified* theory of justification. Since *a priori* justification requires neither coherence nor metajustification, the account is badly bifurcated.

BonJour's Coherence Theory of Justification

Marshall Swain
Ohio State University

Some of the core arguments in *The Structure of Empirical Knowledge* are examined here and found inconclusive. BonJour's arguments against externalism fail against certain forms of externalism which are able to handle BonJour's alleged conterexamples. It also is argued that the "accessibility" requirement BonJour suggests is too stringent, and that BonJour's "metajustificatory" argument fails, because theoretical beliefs can satisfy coherence criteria and in the long run still not enjoy a high likelihood of truth. An example of this point is provided.

Bonjour's Coherentism

Alan H. Goldman
University of Miami

This paper argues that Bonjour's requirement of internal coherence of belief systems is both not necessary for knowledge and insufficient when added to true belief. It is not sufficient because the problem of incompatible but fully coherent belief systems still looms despite the addition of a requirement for continuous observational input. An example that illustrates the problem is provided.

The same example shows that Bonjour's criterion of justification does not indicate probable truth. In order to demonstrate truth and knowledge, epistemologists begin with foundational beliefs (shown to be possible despite Bonjour's argument to the contrary). They then infer to an external relation (in addition to truth) as the source of knowledge. To validate this source, they must adopt an interpersonal viewpoint missing from Bonjour's internalist picture.

Circularity, Non-Linear Justification and Holistic Coherentism

Timothy Joseph Day
Indiana University

The coherence theory is sometimes accused of circularity in its response to the regress problem. To answer this charge coherentists have appealed to a non-linear theory of inferential justification. This is in contrast to a linear theory that treats inferential justification as imposing an ordering relation on a set of beliefs. In this paper, I consider the response to the charge of circularity that Laurence BonJour gives in his book *The Sturcture of Empirical Knowledge*. I argue that the coherentist response to regressive circularity does not depend on any non-linear theory of inferential justification. Instead the coherence theory uses inference in a way that the issue of circularity does not arise. BonJour himself actually develops such a theory. The coherence theory can make use of the same sorts of inferences as any theory of justification. Hence, there is no reason for BonJour to introduce a non-linear theory of inferential justification. The real issue is whether there is inferential justification (linear or not) in the sense required to generate the regress.

Coherentist Theories of Knowledge
Don't Apply to Enough Outside of Science and
Don't Give the Right Results When
Applied to Science.

James Bogen
Pitzer College

Coherentist theories of the kind advocated by Bonjour fail to give an adequate account of epistemic responsibility in two kinds of cases for which an epistemological theory should provide an account. The first includes a wide variety or ordinary, non-scientific beliefs (e.g., my belief that my name is 'Bogen', and that Thelonius Monk composed 'I Mean You' after 1935, and a cook's belief that his sauce needs more cheese). Here coherentist tests for epistemic responsibility require access to a belief system whose specification makes the requirement psychologically realistic. The second class includes scientific beliefs (e.g., Newton's belief that gravitation is a universal force which acts uniformly). Here there are accessible systems which approximate to those coherentism requires. But the application of coherentist tests leads typically to the conclusion that scientists are epistemically irresponsible - an unacceptable result. The paper concludes with some methodological remarks about how to pursue a more plausible sort of coherentism.

The Saint Elizabethan World

Joseph Thomas Tolliver
University of Arizona

I take the following to be a platitude about knowledge: there would be no problem of knowledge if everything always had been, were, and always would be just as we believe it to be. A world were all beliefs are always true I call "an incorrigible world." One might hope that our best account of the nature of knowledge might explain why this platitude is platitudinous. If not, one would at least hope for the preferred account to be compatible with it. Unfortunately, coherence accounts of knowledge do not fulfill this hope, for they imply that there are some incorrigible worlds that are epistemically inaccessible. One such world I call "the St. Elizabethan World." It is the world that is the content of the beliefs of a deranged patient, John H., at St. Elizabeth's Hospital. John's beliefs are so unsystematic that the only standard of coherence that they meet is consistency. Yet, I argue, at the St. Elizabethan World John knows everything he believes to be true. I consider the coherence analysis offered in *The Structure of Empirical Knowledge*, by Laurence BonJour as a representative case, showing why that analysis is inconsistent with the above judgment, and suggest why this is general problem for coherence theories. I end by suggesting that a solution to the problem is to abandon the presupposition present in many coherence theories that coherence properties are world-invariant.

Coherence, Observation, and the Justification of Empirical Beliefs

Stuart Silvers
Tilburg University, The Netherlands

Coherence theories of justification for empirical knowledge and belief all confront the problem of getting empirical content somehow into the doxastic systems they characterize. On the one hand, the justification proceeds holistically in terms of the (proper) relations among the beliefs constituent of the system. On the other hand, empirical beliefs must satisfy conditions of (sensory) observation. In this paper, BonJour's (1985) coherence theory of knowledge is examined and found to lack arguments strong enough to make the appropriate connections between belief justification in virtue of (the degree of) coherence of the doxastic system and the required content for the system to have empirical content. It is also suggested that coherence theories of belief justification perhaps shouldn't bother with trying to connect what is conceptually disjoint.

Epistemic Priority and Coherence

Noah M. Lemos
University of Texas at Austin

There are two related topics considered in this paper. The first concerns the status of basic beliefs and the thesis of epistemic priority, and the second concerns the justification of observational and introspective beliefs within a coherentist approach to justification. These issues are related since the proponents of coherence theories typically deny the thesis of epistemic priority and the existence of basic beliefs, and since those sympathetic to the thesis typically maintain that our introspective beliefs are among the clearest examples of basic beliefs. In the first section I consider an argument by Laurence BonJour against the existence of basic beliefs and the thesis of epistemic priority. This argument presupposes a certain view of what is required for justification. In the second section I argue that this view of justification presents problems for BonJour's positive account of the warrant of observational and introspective beliefs. In the third section I consider a brief proposal by Roderick Firth in response to the objection that coherence theories cut off justification from the world.

BonJour's Anti-Foundationalist Argument

Matthias Steup
Univerity of Wyoming

In *The Structure of Empirical Knowledge*, Laurence BonJour presents a refutation of foundationalism which rests on the presupposition that metajustification is a necessary condition of first level justification: a belief B is justified for a subject A only if A believes that B has a feature f such that most beliefs that have this feature are true. If this were correct, then there could not be any basic beliefs - beliefs that do not depend for their justification on other beliefs. Hence, foundationalism, affirming that knowledge rests on a foundation of basic beliefs, would be wrong. However, BonJour's presupposition is problematic because it makes skepticism inevitable. Furthermore, because of the specific way BonJour construes his conception of metajustification, he faces the same difficulty as do proponents of reliabilism: the problem of generality. In order to handle this problem, BonJour would have either to revise his account of metajustification or to countenance epistemic principles of foundational status, which would undermine the purity of his coherentist approach to the analysis of knowledge.

Foundations

Carolyn Black
San Jose State University

The thesis is that some recent coherentist criticism of the purportedly basic elements of foundationalism, notably that of Laurence BonJour in *The Structure of Empirical Knowledge,* fails to apply to a certain type of foundation. After describing some of the criticism I examine an account of grounds in the later philosophy of Wittgenstein which I then modify so as to suggest what we take to be the case as basic. One of BonJour's central claims against foundationalism is that the only justification for empirical belief is other empirical belief. I contend that this is false and that we can initiate a sound foundationalism with bases which are neither true nor false nor simply empirical.

The Unattainability of Coherence

Hilary Kornblith
The University of Vermont

I argue in this paper that the ideal of belief acquisition which coherence theorists propose is unattainable. In section I, I discuss Laurence BonJour's internalist coherence theory and argue that it fails on its own terms: the ideal which BonJour proposes cannot be met. In section II, I discuss Gilbert Harman's externalist coherence theory and argue that it proposes an ideal which is beyond the powers of any human being to realize; indeed, it proposes an ideal which cannot be realized by any information processing device whatsoever. I conclude that human beings do not and cannot arrive at their beliefs by determining whether they cohere with beliefs already held. In section III, I discuss an argument due to Jerry Fodor which suggests that the only alternative to a holistic account of the fixation of belief is skepticism. I propose a way to elude the horns of this dilemma.

Epistemically Justified Opinion

Bruce Aune
University of Massachusetts

The theories of epistemic justification offered in recent years are generally developed as contributions to a theory of knowledge. It is argued here that such theories exaggerate the importance of knowledge for a sound epistemology and also, perhaps as a consequence, take an ill-advised foundational or coherentist form. A new concept of epistemic justification is, accordingly, introduced. Since the new concept has interesting affinities with the coherentist conception of epistemic justification recently proposed by Laurence BonJour, the latter is critically discussed. Critical remarks are also directed to a Bayesian theory that provides another, increasingly popular alternative.

The Multiple Faces of Knowing:
The Hierarchies of Epistemic Species

Hector-Neri Castañeda
Indiana University

Knowledge is coherence, of course. It is hierarchical and it must have a base. This need not be an absolute foundation. In any case each particular state of knowing or of justified belief must have a base consisting of a relevant hierarchy of background assumptions and, especially, takens-for-granted. These are non-justified justifiers. No local epistemic base need be an absolute foundation. This view is called *(local) foundationism* to stress its differences with (absolute) foundationalism.

The next major claims are these: Each epistemic base determines a species of justified believing or knowing, and perhaps species fall under different types; perhaps the species are determinates and they and their determinables are captured only schematically in definition schemata. A crude analogy is with colors. There is a generic green and its subordinate species down to the determinate shades of green.

In support of this Multiple-Species View of knowledge a family of diverse humdrum-type cases of knowing is marshaled. The hypothesis that debates in epistemology involve arguments from different species of knowledge is corroborated by a well known dispute between Keith Lehrer and Alvin Goldman. Further evidence is garnered from Lawrence Powers's connection between knowledge and powers to answer questions.

The outcome is a proposal to consider species of knowledge determined by six parameters, some of which are actional and take us outside the circle of beliefs. These are: (i) believing, (ii) methodological constraints and epistemic goals, (iii) epistemic powers (to answer questions), (iv) inferential powers, (v) standardness or normality condition, (vi) evidence condition. A theory of questions developed elsewhere forms an appropriate pedestal.

Equilibrium in Coherence?

Ernest Sosa
Brown University

The method of reflective equilibrium aims to maximize two factors in one's beliefs: harmonious coherence, and plausibility of content. Analytic philosophy has long paid deference to these factors, for instance in its ubiquitous use of the counterexample, which attacks a principle as *incoherent with the plausible* (by one's lights). A severe critique of this tradition has recently appeared, and it shall be my main objective here to assess its merits. An appendix shall apply our results to issues of moral relativism and rationality.

ii. focus: the work of keith lehrer

Lehrer's Coherentism and the Isolation Objection

Paul K. Moser
Loyola University of Chicago

Among coherence theories of epistemic justification, Keith Lehrer's version is second to none in its originality, detail, and precision. It is, without a doubt, the most refined coherence theory in circulation. In this paper I ask whether Lehrer's coherentism withstands the familiar isolation objection to epistemic coherentism. Part 1 outlines Lehrer's coherentism in its most recent garb. Part 2 states the isolation objection to coherentism without relying on the troublesome metaphor of "cutting off" empirical justification from the world. And Part 3 argues that Lehrer's coherentism falls prey to the isolation objection because of a deficiency shared by all versions of epistemic coherentism.[1]

1. Lehrer's Coherentism

Epistemic coherentism, put simply, is the view that the epistemic justification of any proposition, P, for a person, S, is a function solely of P's coherence relations to certain other propositions, such as other propositions believed or accepted by S. Lehrer's own general statement of coherentism basically agrees with this characterization:

> According to the coherence theory, ...a belief is justified if and only if it coheres with other beliefs in a specified system of beliefs... . The coherence theory might well be renamed the *relation* theory, for the fundamental conception is that some *relation* between beliefs is what determines whether or not a belief is justified.[2]

In its most recent garb, Lehrer's coherentism focuses on one's "acceptance system" instead of one's belief system; for acceptance, being an action rather than a state, seems to be more easily controllable than believing, and seems to be essentially relative to a purpose, such as the epistemically relevant purpose of obtaining truth and avoiding error.[3]

One distinctive thesis of Lehrer's coherentism is that epistemic justification is based on one's subjective probability assignments when one's only goal is to obtain truth and avoid error. In opposition to certain versions of foundationalism, Lehrer denies that justification derives from nonbelief perceptual and sensory experiences. Instead, he holds that all epistemic justification is a function only of coherence relations between propositions concerning what one accepts. Two basic questions for Lehrer's coherentism, then, are these: what sort of acceptance system underlies all justification, and what exactly is the relation of coherence? Lehrer has provided answers to both questions, and they now demand our attention. I shall focus mainly on Lehrer's very recent detailed statement of his theory in his (1986). The account in Lehrer (1988) is not relevantly different, at least for purposes of this paper, from his (1986).

A person's (S's) acceptance system is a set of propositions having the form 'S accepts that P', 'S accepts that Q', and so on. One's acceptance system is defined not by the propositions one accepts, but by the propositions stating that one accepts the various propositions one actually accepts. There is, however, an important qualification: one's acceptance system describes only one's acceptance of the propositions one accepts "in the attempt to accept something true and [to] eschew accepting what is false with respect to just the thing one accepts" (1986, 8). Lehrer is thus concerned with one's *epistemically motivated* acceptance system, i.e., the acceptance system resulting from one's aim to acquire truth and to avoid error.

Lehrer uses his notion of an acceptance system to provide the following notion of personal, or subjective, justification:

J.W. Bender (ed.), The Current State of the Coherence Theory, 29–37.
© *1989 by Kluwer Academic Publishers.*

D1. S is personally justified in accepting that P iff P coheres with S's acceptance system.

Thus, on Lehrer's view, to determine whether S is personally justified in accepting that P, we must determine whether P coheres with S's acceptance system that articulates what S accepts in an attempt to acquire truth and to avoid error.

Lehrer explicates his notion of coherence by means of this undefined locution: it is more reasonable for S, on the basis of his acceptance system, to accept that P than to accept that Q. Given this primitive notion, Lehrer introduces the following notion of propositional competition:

D2. P competes with Q for S on the basis of his acceptance system A iff on the basis of A it is more reasonable for S to accept that P on the assumption that not-Q than on the assumption that Q.[4]

In light of familiar lottery-style cases, Lehrer denies that epistemically relevant competition can be restricted to contradictories and contraries. His notion of competition is presupposed by the two notions he uses to define coherence. The first notion, that of beating a competitor, is quite straightforward:

D3. P beats Q for S on the basis of his acceptance system A iff (i) P competes with Q for S on the basis of A, and (ii) on the basis of A it is more reasonable for S to accept that P than to accept that Q.

Lehrer claims that a proposition's beating all its competitors is sufficient for personal justification, but denies that this is necessary. He holds that competitors that are not beaten can be eliminated by being neutralized, in the following sense:

D4. R neutralizes Q as a competitor of P for S on the basis of his acceptance system A iff (i) Q competes with P for S on the basis of A, and (ii) on the basis of A, the conjunction (R & Q) does not compete with P for S when, on the basis of A, it is as reasonable for S to accept that (R & Q) as to accept that Q.

Following Lehrer (1986, 11), we can illustrate this notion via the skeptic who challenges, on the ground that people sometimes hallucinate, my claim that I see a monitor. The way to neutralize the skeptic's ground, on Lehrer's view, is for me to affirm that I am not hallucinating. For, on the basis of my acceptance system, it is as reasonable for me to accept the conjunctive claim that (people sometimes hallucinate, and I am not now hallucinating) as to accept the claim that people sometimes hallucinate. Thus, Lehrer denies that the foregoing conjunctive claim competes with the claim that I see a monitor.

We now can introduce Lehrer's notion of coherence:

D5. P coheres with S's acceptance system A iff, for every proposition, Q, that competes with P for S on the basis of A, Q is either beaten or neutralized for S on the basis of A.

Lehrer resists defining the notions of coherence and reasonableness via the notion of probability, but he does take probability to be the primary determinant of coherence: "If something is more probable than its competitors with respect to the acceptance system, then it coheres with the acceptance system and they do not."[5] This raises the question of what sort of probability Lehrer has in mind.

Regarding personal justification, according to Lehrer (1982, 205), "the notion of probability that is appropriate is [the notion of one's] estimate of the probability of propositions conditional on what one accepts." Thus, on Lehrer's account, a central determinant of personal justification for a person is how probable that person thinks a proposition is on the basis of his acceptance system. In fact, given D1, the previous quotation concerning the primary determinant of coherence implies this principle:

PJ. S is personally justified in accepting that P if S accepts that P is, on the basis of his acceptance system, more likely to be true than not-P and any other competitors.

This principle clearly illustrates the subjectivist component of Lehrer's account of justification.

However, Lehrer holds that we need to supplement the notion of personal justification to obtain a complete analysis of epistemic justification. He worries about the possibility that all but one of the propositions a person accepts in his acceptance system is false; for we might be inclined to deny that one is justified in accepting such a single true proposition when it coheres with a system full of errors. This worry, in conjunction with the notorious Gettier problem, leads Lehrer to introduce the notion of a person's *verific* acceptance system. A verific system is a subsystem of a person's acceptance system; it results simply from the omission of all acceptance of false propositions from the person's acceptance system. In his 1988 (343-44), Lehrer replaces the notion of a verific system with the notion of an *ultrasystem*. One's ultrasystem is formed by correcting errors in one's acceptance system in two ways: (a) by *weak* correction where we simply delete any error in the acceptance system and any error it entails, and (b) by *strong* correction where we replace any error in the system with the acceptance of its denial, and make such replacements for any error entailed by it. However, we shall see that, for purposes of this paper, Lehrer's notion of an ultrasystem is not relevantly different from the notion of a verific system.)

Given the notion of a verific system, Lehrer introduces this notion of verific justification (1986, 8):

D6. S is verifically justified in accepting that P iff P coheres with S's verific system.

We have seen that probability is the primary determinant of coherence on Lehrer's view. This raises the question whether the sort of coherence relevant to D6 can arise simply from one's subjective, personal probability estimates. Lehrer answers no, on the ground that the contrary view "would undermine some advantage of deleting error from the [acceptance] system" (1981a, 89; cf. 1982, 207). Lehrer claims that we need some sort of objective probability, such as propensity probability, for verific justification, but (so far as I know) he has not provided a developed account of such probability.

Given the notions of personal and verific justification, we now can introduce Lehrer's analysis of complete epistemic justification:

D7. S is completely justified in accepting that P iff S is personally and verifically justified in accepting that P.

Lehrer requires both personal and verific justification for complete justification to insure (a) that one's justification is based on what one antecedently accepts, and (b) that one's does not lose one's justification via the omission of error.

Armed with this outline of Lehrer's coherentism, then, let us turn to a consideration of the familiar isolation objection to epistemic coherentism.

2. The Isolation Objection Formulated

A crude early suggestion of the isolation objection can be found in an essay by Moritz Schlick (1934, 215-16):

> If one is to take coherence seriously as a general criterion of truth, then one must consider arbitrary fairy stories to be as true as a historical report, or as statements in a textbook of chemistry, provided the story is constructed in such a way that no contradiction ever arises. I can depict by help of fantasy a grotesque world full of bizarre adventures: the coherence philosopher must believe in the truth of my account provided only I take care of the mutual compatibility of my statements. . . [A]ccording to the coherence theory, there is no question of observations, but only of the compatibility of statements.

Unfortunately, Schlick does not consider sorts of coherence other than consistency; nor does he adequately distinguish considerations about the *definition* of truth from considerations about the *criteria* for discerning truth. Thus, it is not obvious that he is criticizing coherence theories of *justification*. However, Schlick clearly is worried about the significance of observation, or perceptual experience, in a coherence theory; and this worry does pertain to coherence theories of justification.[6] Or, at least, I shall support this point, especially with respect to Lehrer's coherentism.

The isolation objection to epistemic coherentism was revived recently by John Pollock in connection with his criticism of a "nebula theory" stating that there can be infinite regresses of justification. Pollock's version of the isolation objection is:

> The nebula theory commits us to what is essentially a coherence theory of justification... . The basic difficulty with this is that it cuts justification off from the world. A person could be justified in believing anything. All that would be required would be a sufficiently outlandish but coherent set of beliefs... [B]ut the beliefs are nowhere tied down in any way to the evidence of [the] senses. As long as a person's beliefs form such a coherent set, he could hold any beliefs at all regarding the colors, shapes, sizes, etc., of things, regardless of how they look or feel to him.[7]

This statement of the isolation objection improves considerably on the version suggested by Schlick. It avoids confusion of the definition and the criteria of truth, and it is directed at a coherence theory of justification. But Pollock now finds the isolation objection to be a "very bad argument" against epistemic coherentism, on the ground that (a) according to coherentism justification is a function of coherence with the propositions one believes, and not of coherence with all propositions, and (b) what one believes is causally influenced by the world. On this basis, Pollock now denies that epistemic coherentism "cuts justification off from the world."[8]

However, Pollock's abandonment of the isolation objection is much too quick; it fails to show that the objection is harmless against coherentism. Part of the problem with Pollock's treatment of the isolation objection is that it relies on the unclear metaphor of "cutting justification off from the world." Perhaps there is a sense in which epistemic coherentism does not cut justification off from the world, because of causal relations between beliefs and the world. Yet there still might be another sense in which the isolation objection does apply to coherentism. I believe there is.

The relevant isolation objection is not that epistemic coherentism entails that any, or at least virtually any, contingent proposition can be justified for a person under certain circumstances. Such an objection not only seems to apply equally well to various alternatives to coherentism, but also seems to be harmless. If the circumstances in question involve one's having a certain sort of unusual evidence, one might very well be justified in accepting bizarre propositions. More generally, relative to certain changes in one's evidence, one might be justified in accepting virtually any contingent proposition. Since it is possible for one to have radical changes in evidence, it is also possible for one to be justified in accepting propositions radically different from what one is now justified in accepting. Thus, I doubt that the objection at hand is effective.

I also doubt that the relevant isolation objection is that coherentism entails that all one's justified beliefs can be false. Such an objection, like the foregoing version, applies equally well to various alternatives to coherentism, and is ultimately harmless. Given that justified belief does not require truth, we have no reason to think that some of one's justified beliefs must be true. It seems to be a conceptually live option that all one's justified beliefs are false. At the same time, we should recognize that the contingent members of some belief systems cannot all be false, such as a belief system including the proposition that some physical objects are transparent and the proposition that my body is not transparent. Yet there is no reason to think that justified belief requires such a belief system.

Another ineffective version of the isolation objection claims that according to coherentism all one's justified empirical beliefs can be unrelated to the empirical world. This version is ineffective because of the unclarity of the phrase 'unrelated to the empirical world'. Coherentism can require that one's empirical beliefs be *causally* related to the empirical world. Thus, the current objection must be supplemented with an account of the relation to the world that is neglected by coherentism, i.e., an account of how a justified empirical belief must be related to the empirical world. Without such an account, this objection is too vague to pose a threat to coherentism.

My own version of the isolation objection aims to avoid the defects of the foregoing versions. It can be summarized as follows:

> IO. Epistemic coherentism entails that one can be epistemically justified in accepting a contingent empirical proposition that is incompatible with, or at least improbable given, one's total empirical evidence.[9]

The talk of *total empirical evidence* in IO demands some clarification. Obviously the proponent of IO does not restrict empirical evidence to empirical propositions believed or accepted by a person. Given such a restriction, IO will be ineffective against any version of coherentism that places a consistency requirement on one's evidence, and requires that a justified belief be highly probable relative to all one's other justified beliefs.

However, IO becomes universally applicable to coherence theories of justification once we expand the scope of empirical evidence beyond the propositions believed or accepted by a person. Suppose, for instance, that the subjective nonpropositional contents of one's *non* belief sensory and perceptual awareness-states (such as one's state of feeling a pain or of seeming to perceive something) are part of one's empirical evidence.[10] For now we can remain neutral on the ontological status of such contents, allowing for adverbial or sense-datum accounts of apparently presented items. However, being nonpropositional, such contents are not among what one believes or accepts. One might accept *the proposition* that one is presented with certain subjective perceptual contents, but of course this does not mean that the contents themselves are a proposition one accepts. Once we include such contents of nonbelief sensory and perceptual states in one's empirical evidence-base, IO bears directly on all coherence theories of justification. For, by definition, coherence theories make epistemic justification a function solely of coherence relations between propositions, such as propositions one believes or accepts. Thus, they neglect the *epistemic* or *evidential* relevance of the nonpropositional contents of nonbelief sensory and perceptual states.

Let us now return to Lehrer's coherentism to illustrate the effectiveness of my proposed isolation objection.

3. The Isolation Objection Applied

Our main question now is whether Lehrer's coherentism, as outlined in Part 1, entails that one can be epistemically justified in accepting an empirical proposition that is incompatible with, or at least improbable given, one's total empirical evidence. An example will help us answer this question.

Suppose that eliminative materialism about pains is true, and thus that there are no pains, certainly no throbbing pains. And consider the beginning, truth-seeking philosophy student, California Jones, who accepts eliminative materialism about pains as a result of hearing some of Paul Churchland's introductory supporting lectures. One night Jones, while eating his own homegrown popcorn, bites into a rusty bolt that had fallen into his cornfield from his old tractor. Jones, as would be expected, apparently experiences a throbbing toothache, since the bolt cracked one of his teeth. (Note that eliminative materialism about pains is, by hypothesis, true, and thus that, by hypothesis, there are no throbbing toothaches; accordingly, one's *apparently* experiencing a throbbing toothache does not entail that there is a throbbing toothache.) However, Jones, let us suppose, does not believe or even accept that he has a throbbing toothache, because he has been convinced by Churchland's eloquent presentation of eliminative materialism about pains.

Jones, accordingly, accepts various true propositions indicating that he does not get throbbing toothaches, and this acceptance is the result of Jones's aiming to obtain truth and avoid error. Further, the proposition that Jones does not get throbbing toothaches coheres (in Lehrer's sense of D5) with his acceptance system. Yet, as suggested, Jones is acutely aware of his apparent throbbing toothache; it definitely attracts his attention, and it prevents him from finishing his popcorn. Unfortunately, however, Jones, being a beginner at philosophy, has not absorbed enough of Churchland's lectures to account for his apparent throbbing toothache in terms of eliminativism. What, then, should we say about what Jones is justified in accepting - aside from obvious lessons about the risks of homegrown popcorn and the dangers of but a little philosophy?

Let's make some of the example's assumptions more explicit. We are assuming that the proposition that N [=There are no throbbing toothaches] coheres with Jones's acceptance system in the sense of D5 from Part 1. Or, more specifically, we can assume, in light of principle PJ from Part 1, that Jones accepts that N is, on the basis of his acceptance system, more likely to be true than all its competitors. Given such assumptions, we can assume that Jones is personally justified in accepting that N, in the sense of D1. But is N also *verifically* justified for Jones? Suppose, as my example suggests, that the propositions providing personal justification for N for Jones are true. Suppose also that N coheres with Jones's verific system in the required sense, and thus that the probabilities determining this coherence are objective in the relevant sense. Roughly characterized, these probabilities, according to Lehrer (1981b, 237), are the probabilities that Jones, given his verific acceptance system, "would be right" about N. Given these suppositions, we can assume that Jones is verifically justified in accepting that N, in the sense of D6. (Similarly, to consider Lehrer (1988), we can suppose that Jones is justified in accepting that N on the basis of his ultrasystem, the system formed by weak and strong corrections in his acceptance system.) We now can assume also that Jones is *completely* justified in accepting that N, in the sense of D7.

But something has gone wrong. For Jones's apparent throbbing toothache is directly relevant to the justification of his accepting that N. We may call this apparent toothache a *potential underminer* of that justification, since if Jones cannot account for it via an explanation that can incorporate N, then (a) his justification for N will be evidentially defective, and thus (b) he epistemically should refrain from accepting that N. That is, Jones epistemically needs an explanation of his apparent toothache in accord with his eliminative materialism; and if he lacks such an explanation, he epistemically should not accept that N, since his justification for N will then be defective. Jones's accepting that N without such an explanation would be evidentially defective and epistemically irresponsible in the sense that it would be to disregard gratuitously a potential underminer. Epistemically justified acceptance is incompatible with such defectiveness and irresponsibility. Hence, the implication of Lehrer's coherentism that Jones is justified in accepting that N seems wrong.

Put positively, my point is that epistemic justification is a function of, but not only of, what one apparently experiences. That is, the subjectivenonpropositional contents of one's sensory and perceptual experiences are part of one's total empirical evidence, and thereby place constraints on what one is justified in accepting. My California Jones example illustrates just this point. Thus, a coherence theory, such as Lehrer's, that makes justification a function *only* of coherence relations between accepted propositions, even accepted propositions in a verific system or an ultrasystem, neglects a key constraint on justification. To return to the language of my isolation objection, such a coherence theory allows that one can be justified in accepting an empirical proposition that is improbable relative to one's total empirical evidence. Relative to the subjective contents of Jones's nonbelief experiences, Jones's eliminative materialism (specifically its component N) is not sufficiently probable to be justified, since Jones has no account of how his eliminativism can accommodate the potential underminer due to those experiential contents. Thus, so far as I can tell, my isolation objection applies straightforwardly to Lehrer's coherentism.

In reply, Lehrer apparently would object that the nonpropositional contents of one's nonbelief sensory and perceptual experiences are not part of one's evidence, and thus do not determine what is probable for one. (See, for instance, Lehrer 1982, 208.) Lehrer grants, quite plausibly, that one can be in a sensory or perceptual state while not accepting that one is, and he grants that such a state can play a causal role in justified acceptance. But he holds that the nonpropositional contents of such a state are *epistemically* relevant for one only if one accepts that one is presented with those contents. The motivation for this view, expressed in Lehrer (1981b, 238), is that "until I form some opinion of what I experience, until I have some belief on the matter, I cannot ascertain probability."

I accept Lehrer's claim about ascertaining probabilities, but I doubt that it is relevant to my isolation objection. For there surely is a pertinent distinction between (a) a proposition's *being* probable for one and (b) one's *ascertaining* that a proposition is probable for one. And I know of no compelling reason to think that an empirical proposition's being justified for one requires one's *ascertaining* that it is probable. Rather, what is required is that the proposition *be* probable for one. The alternative view obscures the basic distinction between (c) conditions for an empirical proposition's being justified for one and (d) conditions for one's being justified in accepting that an empirical proposition is justified for one.

Lehrer does hold that first-order justification requires higher-order justification, and that "knowledge without metaknowledge is an impossibility" (1986, 24; 1988, 331-32). This view might seem obviously excessive. Since metajustification and metaknowledge apparently require one's having the concepts of justification and knowledge, Lehrer's view apparently implies that one has justification and knowledge only if one has the concepts of justification and knowledge. The latter implication should be rejected, it seems, on the ground that it precludes knowers such as very young children and certain animals outside our species.[11] Thus, one might automatically reject Lehrer's view of the epistemic significance of experiential contents.

However, Lehrer (1988, 331-32) denies that the sorts of metajustification and metaknowledge relevant to his view entail iterative justification and knowledge. Rather, they require only evaluation of information as trustworthy or untrustworthy; and such evaluation need not be evaluation of the claim that one knows, or is justified in accepting, a proposition. Perhaps this denial saves Lehrer from the standard sorts of epistemic level-confusion, but I doubt that it contributes to a plausible reply to my isolation objection. For Lehrer (1988, 332) restricts epistemically relevant information to "truth-claims," which of course are propositional, and thus he fails to accommodate the potential underminers due to one's nonpropositional sensory and perceptual contents.

Lehrer might reply (as John Bender suggested to me) that his account can accommodate nonpropositional potential underminers in virtue of the fact that people accept propositions concerning what they *apparently experience*. On this reply, Jones accepts that he has an apparent toothache, and this acceptance provides an unneutralized competitor for Jones's view that there are no pains. I am not convinced that this acceptance provides a relevant competitor in Lehrer's sense, but this is not my main problem with the anticipated reply. The main problem is that there is no reason to think that in my example Jones must accept that he has an apparent toothache. As Pollock (1979, 1986) and others have suggested, people rarely even consider propositions about what they *apparently* experience (e.g., what they *seem* to see); and thus it is plausible to suppose that in my example Jones does *not* accept the proposition that he has an apparent toothache. Yet Jones still has the potential underminer due to his nonpropositional sensory contents.

A final challenge to my use of the California Jones example claims that Jones's acceptance of eliminative materialism is defective given Lehrer's notion of a truth-seeker. The key claim is that (a) Jones's accepting eliminative materialism is epistemically faulty relative to the goal of obtaining truth and avoiding error, and thus that (b) Jones's acceptance of eliminative materialism has no place in his epistemically motivated acceptance system. However, I fail to find any compelling basis for such a claim. Clearly, Jones can be a *beginning* truth-seeker, and thus have serious explanatory gaps in his epistemically motivated acceptance system. One's being epistemically motivated does not entail one's having a highly sophisticated explanatory belief system. So, Jones can be a truth-seeking eliminativist who cannot account for his throbbing toothache in accord with eliminativism. Accordingly, the current challenge fails.

4. Conclusion

Overall, then, we have reason to believe that Lehrer's coherentism falls prey to a version of the isolation objection. So long as an epistemology fails to acknowledge the *evidential* significance of the subjective nonpropositional contents of one's sensory and perceptual states, it will face serious problems from the isolation objection. And this means that epistemic coherentism, by definition, will always be haunted by the isolation objection.

NOTES

1. Because of space limitations, I shall not discuss versions of coherentism other than Lehrer's. I have critically discussed the versions of Nicholas Rescher and Laurence BonJour in Moser (1985, Chapter 3). My more recent criticisms of BonJour's version can be found in my (1987) and (1988).
2. See Lehrer (1977), 18. Similar characterizations by Lehrer can be found in *Knowledge*, 154 and (1980b, 234) and Lehrer and Cohen (1983), 193.
3. On this change in Lehrer's coherentism, see Lehrer (1980a, 79-80) (1983, 172-83) and 1986, 6-7).
4. This definition comes from Lehrer (1986, 10). For Lehrer's earlier characterizations of competition, see (1974, 192-97), (1980c, 188f.), and (1980a, 86f).
5. Lehrer, (1987, 98). Lehrer, (1982, 204f) and Lehrer and Cohen (1983, 193f).
6. Such a worry, accompanied by a fairly clear distinction between the definition and the criteria of truth, can also be found, for example, in H. H. Price (1936, 19); Ayer (1936, 228-43); Russell (1940, Chapters 8-11); Lewis (1946, 338-43). For a useful discussion of the distinction between the definition and the criteria of truth, see Nicholas Rescher, (1973, 12-22).
7. Pollock, (1974, 27-28). For a related recent statement of the isolation objection, see Ernest Sosa (1980, 18-20).
8. See Pollock, (1979, 102). Cf. Pollock, (1986, 76f.)
9. I first introduced this version of the isolation objection in Moser (1985), 85. I also argued there, very briefly, that Lehrer's statement of coherentism in *Knowledge* does not adequately handle this objection.
10. For extensive argument for this supposition, and for clarification of the relevant notion of awareness, see my (1985) and (1989, forthcoming). See also James Van Cleve, (1985, 90-104). The operative assumption of my account, put very broadly, is that we need to acknowledge the evidential role of experiential contents to provide a nonarbitrary basis for empirical justification and to solve the notorious epistemic regress problem.

I also claim that such contents provide needed constraints on epistemically relevant inference to the best explanation. On the need for such constraints, see Lehrer, (1974, 170-78).
11. For elaboration on this point, see William Alston, (1980, 135-50) and Alston, (1983, 84-86).

REFERENCES

Alston, W. P. "Level Confusions in Epistemology," in Peter French, T. E. Uehling, and H. K. Wettstein, eds., *Midwest Studies in Philosophy, Vol. 5: Studies in Epistemology,* Minneapolis: University of Minnesota Press, 1980,135-150.
-----. "What's Wrong With Immediate Knowledge?" *Synthese* 55 (1983), 73-95.
Ayer, A. J. "Verification and Experience," (1936), in Ayer, ed., *Logical Positivism,* New York: The Free Press, 1957, 228-43.
Bender, John. "The Ins and Outs of 'Metaknowledge'." *Analysis* 48 (1988).
BonJour, Laurence. *The Structure of Empirical Knowledge.* Cambridge, Mass.: Harvard University Press, 1985.
Lehrer, Keith. *Knowledge.* Oxford: Clarendon Press, 1974.
-----. "The Knowledge Cycle." *Nous* 11 (1977), 17-25.
-----. "Self-Profile." (1981a) In R. J. Bogdan, ed., *Keith Lehrer,* Dordrecht: D. Reidel, 1981, 3-104
-----. "Reply to Pastin." (1981b) In R. J. Bogdan, ed., *Keith Lehrer,* Dordrecht: D. Reidel., 233-41.
-----. "Coherence and the Racehorse Paradox." (1980c) In Peter French, T. E. Uehling, and H. K. Wettstein, eds., *Midwest Studies in Philosophy, Vol. 5: Studies in Epistemology,* Minneapolis: University of Minnesota Press, 233-41.
-----. "Knowledge, Truth, and Ontology," in Werner Leinfellner, ed., *Language and Ontology: Proceedings of the 6th International Wittgenstein Symposium,* Vienna: Holder-Pichler-Tempsky, 1982, 201-211.
-----. "Belief, Acceptance, and Cognition," in Herman Parret, ed., *On Believing ,* Berlin: Walter de Gruyter, 1983, 172-83.
-----. "The Coherence Theory of Knowledge." *Philosophical Topics* 14 (1986), 5-25.
-----. "Personal and Social Knowledge." *Synthese* 73 (1987), 87-107.
-----. "Metaknowledge: Undefeated Justification." *Synthese* 74 (1988), 329-47.
-----, and Cohen, Stewart. "Justification, Truth, and Coherence." *Synthese* 55 (1983), 191-207.
Lewis, C. I. *An Analysis of Knowledge and Valuation.* La Salle, Ill.: Open Court, 1946.
Moser, Paul. *Empirical Justification.* Dordrecht: D. Reidel, 1985.
-----. "Critical Notice of *The Structure of Empirical Knowledge,* by L. BonJour." *Philosophy and Phenomenological Research* 47 (1987), 670-73.
-----. "Internalism and Coherentism: A Dilemma." *Analysis* 48, (1988).
-----. *Knowledge and Evidence.* New York/Cambridge: Cambridge University Press, 1989.
Pollock, John. *Knowledge and Justification.* Princeton: Princeton University Press, 1974.
-----. "A Plethora of Epistemological Theories," in G. S. Pappas, ed., *Justification and Knowledge,* Dordrecht: D. Reidel, 1979, 93-113.
-----. *Contemporary Theories of Knowledge.* Totowa, NJ: Rowman & Littlefield, 1986.
Price, H. H. *Truth and Corrigibility.* Oxford: Clarendon Press, 1936.
Rescher, Nicholas. *The Coherence Theory of Truth.* Oxford: Clarendon Press, 1973.
Russell, Bertrand. *An Inquiry into Meaning and Truth.* London: Allen & Unwin, 1940.
Schlick, Moritz. "The Foundation of Knowledge," (1934), in A. J. Ayer, ed., *Logical Positivism.* New York: The Free Press, 1957.
Sosa, Ernest."The Raft and the Pyramid: Coherence versus Foundations in the Theory of Knowledge," in Peter French, T. E. Uehling, and H. K. Wettstein, eds., *Midwest Studies in Philosophy, Vol. 5: Studies in Epistemology,* Minneapolis: University of Minnesota Press, 1980, 3-25.
Van Cleve, James. "Epistemic Supervenience and the Circle of Belief." *The Monist* 68 (1985), 90-104.

Personal Coherence, Objectivity, and Reliability

G. J. Mattey
University of California at Davis

1. Coherence Theories and Objectivity

The most troubling criticism of coherence theories of justification is that coherence within a system has no apparent connection with the truth. Johnathan Dancy claims that coherence theories leave us with a "mystery," insofar as "it would be difficult to find a reason for thinking that where the internal relation of justification is present, the external relation of truth is present also" (117). John Pollock calls this the "isolation argument." "According to coherence theories, justification is ultimately a matter of relations between propositions one believes, and has nothing to do with the way the world is. But our objective in seeking knowledge is to find out the way the world is. Thus coherence theories are inadequate" (76).[1]

The isolation problem is a limiting case of a more general problem of the relation between justified belief or acceptance and its object. Keith Lehrer terms this the "ontological problem."

> Knowledge is the intersection between ontology and subjectivity. It has a subjective aspect, a system of accepted propositions, and an objective aspect, a connection with reality. The ontological problem in epistemology can be stated as follows: how are we to explain the connection between acceptance and truth, between subjective states of the knower and the ontology of what is known? (1982, 201)

The isolation argument is clearly an attempt to show that on a coherence theory, the connection with reality, or "truth connection," cannot be satisfactorily explained, since it seems possible for a system of acceptances to cohere independently of any link with the world.

Although Lehrer himself does not explicitly mention the isolation argument, it has grave implications for his subjective coherence theory, according to which the relation of coherence within an individual's acceptance system determines justification. That is, it is sufficient for subjective justification that a proposition be relatively reasonable within the acceptance system. The determination of reasonableness is left almost entirely up to the individual, the only constraints imposed by the theory being consistency and the obedience of an injunction that one endeavor to believe as many true propositions and to avoid believing as many false ones as possible.[2] It is this normative character which leads him to a coherence theory.[3] There is a potential for a myriad of acceptance systems, each with its own assignments of reasonableness, and each providing subjective justification on widely diverse grounds. As Sosa states the problem:

> The view that justification is a matter of relations among beliefs is open to an objection from alternative coherent systems... . [T]he surrounding world... is held constant while the body of beliefs is allowed to vary... . [A]ccording to the coherentist, there could be no effect on the justification for any belief. (1980, 18)

If Sosa's formulation of the isolation problem is correct, it seems that the connection between justification and objectivity is at best accidental on a coherence theory.

The central issue to be addressed in this paper is whether Lehrer's theory of justification is able to overcome the isolation problem, and more generally whether it can explain how justified acceptance is related to the truth. Because Lehrer's defense of his theory is closely tied to the reliabilist response to the ontological problem, it will be useful to provide a background sketch of that highly influential approach to justification.

J.W. Bender (ed.), The Current State of the Coherence Theory, 38–51.
© 1989 by Kluwer Academic Publishers.

2. Reliability and the Truth Connection

The simplest form of the truth connection is mere true belief, which Plato rejected as knowledge on the grounds that it could come about as the result of mere persuasion (*Theaetetus* 909). This initiated a search for a way of characterizing more generally a non-fortuitous connection (which subsumes cases of mere persuasion as well as lucky guesses, etc.) between subjective and objective which could be characterized as knowledge. Historically, the search has placed the burden on the subjective side, i.e., to describe some state of the system of accepted propositions which would, by its very existence, bring about the desired intersection with the objective. Then the intersection would not be the result of luck. The primary problem with this approach is its vulnerability to the skeptical argument that the only reality with which subjective states non-accidentally intersect is a subjective one. One is faced with a choice between phenomenalism or skepticism, Berkeley or Hume.

A strategy not conducive to phenomenalism or vulnerable to skepticism would work in the opposite way. It would describe some state of the objective facts which would produce the required subjective state, as with a causal or reliabilist theory. A reliabilist theory "effects" the truth connection in the sense that the employment of reliable processes generally brings about the intersection between the subjective and objective. And it explains the connection by describing the mechanism which brings about true belief. All that remains for the theory to be completed is to refine the notion of reliability and discover the proper mechanisms.

3. Lehrer's Criticism of Reliabilism

Despite the attractiveness of this kind of approach to the truth connection, it can be charged with placing too much weight on the objective side. That is, reliablity is itself an objective relation between the subjective and the objective. As such, it ignores the fundamental rule of the subjective in justification: the truth-seeking activity which is its hallmark. A theory which does not accord the activity a central role can be charged with at best describing the functioning of a system which yields mere information, not knowledge.

> To know, one must understand and evaluate the information one receives. To do that, one must have a background system to evaluate the trustworthiness of the incoming information. It is such higher order evaluation of information that yields knowledge. There is no knowledge without such evaluation. Knowledge without metaknowledge is an impossibility. (1986, 24)

The distinction between informational and evaluational systems is central to Lehrer's theory of justification. The acceptance system of a person S is a set of propositions of the form 'S accepts that p' along with a set of propositions about the relative reasonableness of propositions based on the set of acceptances. Acceptance is distinguished from belief in three ways: (1) it is relative to the epistemic obligation mentioned above, (2) it is not dispositional, and (3) it is "more closely connected with decision and optionality" (1986, 7). Acceptance is intellectual, as opposed to belief, which is the end-product of a mechanical "Input System," an automatic processor of mere information. While systems of the second type are important for epistemology, particularly with respect to cognition in animals and small children, "I prefer a method that considers human behavior from above rather than from below. I shall present a model of an inquirer to which one might aspire rather than one to which one might descend" (1981, 37).

This well-motivated distinction enables Lehrer to preserve a conception that is appropriate for the normative theory of justification he offers. At the same time, he is not forced to intellectualize all the human cognitive systems. Lehrer claims that the reliabilist account captures a part of the human psychological makeup (the belief system) but fails to capture the intellectual side (the acceptance system) which is characterized by goal- directed activity.

To see this more clearly, suppose one modified reliabilism by claiming that in order to be justified, a person must have a reliable belief system and also believe that the system is reliable. Such a person still might lack what Lehrer would consider knowledge, because this higher-order belief might itself be the mechanical outcome of a reliable process (perhaps one which protects intelligent creatures from excessive skepticism in practical matters).[4] Such an account would be just another objective characterization of a subjective state, which does not take the intellectual nature of acceptance into account. To generalize this result, one could say that the reliabilist takes the effected truth connection as a starting point and asks what conditions would satisfy it.[5] The question is whether Lehrer's theory, which gives the evaluative component of justification the central role, provide a satisfactory response to the acute form of the ontological problem, the isolation problem.

The contrary approach, adopted by Lehrer, is to take the subjective as a starting point and ask whether it effects the connection. The task is to put certain constraints on justification and try to get the right connection from it, in a way that is not ad hoc. If the right connection is reliability (without reliabilism), then the attempt is to show that on Lehrer's theory, an acceptance of a proposition p is justified for a person S only if S is sufficiently reliable regarding p.[6]

4. Lehrer's Theory of Justification

In the initial exposition of his theory, Lehrer appeared to admit its susceptiblity to the problem of isolation. "When a man is veracious, when he is a hunter after truth, we allow that he is completely justified in believing that he killed his prey, even if, as luck would have it, his best shot has missed the mark. What a man is completely justified in believing depends only on what he would believe as a veracious man . . ." (1974, 214). However, he immediately attempted to neutralize the effect of this passage by distinguishing between subjective and objective justification and allowing that complete justification could be taken to require both.

> Those who remain unconvinced, and protest that a man cannot be completely justified in believing something on the basis of false beliefs, may be accommodated within our epistemology by some verbal modification. Such a critic may call the justification we have articulated subjective justification, and reserve the name complete justification, for what is to come later. This is a mere verbal difference we would happily countenance. If our disputant will but concede that a man may achieve some justification, if only subjective, from beliefs representing his impartial and disinterested effort to reach the truth, we can appease him. With a simple qualification for the sake of veracity, such justification, despite the subjective spring from which it runs, may be purified to yield the sweet taste of knowledge." (1974, 214)

If this gambit is accepted (and indeed it is taken up in Lehrer's later papers) the prospects for the coherence theory against the isolation argument are greatly improved.

The "simple qualification for the sake of veracity" would render the isolation at most partial. Indeed, requiring an objective component of justification might be seen as more than a verbal difference, but an abandonment of the coherence theory itself. Nonetheless, in the detailed formulation of the qualification, a substantial element of subjectivity and the formal relation of coherence are retained. So it is not altogether clear whether the kind of objectification provided is sufficient to overcome the isolation argument. A rough sketch of the objectifying qualification will suffice to show this.

Beginning from the acceptance system, Lehrer presents both a theory of justification, which consists in the articulation of the requirements for justification, and a quasi-formal model which implements the requirements. Reasonableness is taken as a primitive concept, an unspecified function of probability and content (thus the incomplete character of the formalism). Justification is the outcome of a specific mathematical relation holding between the reasonableness values of various beliefs. To be justified, a proposition p must be more reasonable than any proposition p* which "competes" with p in the sense of reducing the reasonableness of p.[7]

A person is fallible with respect to what he accepts and the reasonableness relations he posits, and the qualification of the acceptance system will purge falsehoods of both kinds from the system. Its exact character has evolved since its introduction in Knowledge; a recent version follows:

> Suppose that we delete every proposition from the acceptance system of the person affirming that the person accepts a proposition that is, in fact, false. Thus, if the person accepts that p for the purposes of obtaining truth and avoiding error, but p is false, then the proposition that the person accepts p is deleted from the acceptance system. The system thus cleansed of error will be a proper subsystem of the acceptance system. I call that the verific system of the person since it contains only propositions to the effect that the person accepts a proposition when the proposition is, in fact, true. The probability estimates of the acceptance system are replaced in the verific system with actual propensities relativized to the nonprobabilistic subsystem of the verific system. A person is objectively justified in accepting that p if and only if p coheres with the verific system of the person. (1982, 207)

Because the verific system is a subsystem of the acceptance system, much of the subjectivity of the acceptance system is preserved. No facts concerning propositions absent from the system itself has any impact on objective justification. So the theory retains its flavor as a subjective coherence theory despite its objective aspect.[8]

The subjective basis of objective justification leads to a "natural objection," i.e., that "other factors" (the etiology of acceptance or the inferential or sensory states of a person) ought to be relevant to the objectivity of justification (1982, 208). Lehrer's basic response is that such external requirements result in too broad a conception of justification, in that they could yield justification when a person does not have access to the relevant factor. This response is of value only when directed against an externalist claim that such factors as the causes of belief are sufficient for complete justification. On the other hand, reference to some such factors could prove to be be useful as necessary conditions which would strengthen verific justification so as to insure the proper kind of objectivity.

What is the proper kind of objectivity? Lehrer states that the connection is that it must be handled "appropriately" by the theory. (1983, 191, 207). Appropriateness requires explaining the truth connection and "effecting" it. "The coherence theory of justification on which the coherence theory of knowledge rests effects the truth connection and explains the intersection between the mind and the world" (1986, 5). Lehrer does not explicitly state what the word 'effect' means, but presumably, to effect the truth connection means that justification in itself brings about the intersection between the subjective and objective.

There are several possible strategies for showing that the truth connection is effected. The most direct approach is to hold that subjective justification requires an acceptance of one's own reliability, and that complete justification requires that this acceptance be correct. An approach with a less obviously satisfactory conclusion is to hold that subjective justification requires the acceptance of the probability of one's own reliability, so that a completely justified acceptance is probably reliable. Both these approaches are based on a "doxastic ascent" which is a reflection on one's own reliability in accepting propositions.

Before he formulated the doxastic ascent arguments and directly addressed the issue of the truth connection, Lehrer sketched a different approach, based on the way in which objective justification takes place, in response to a version of the isolation problem. On this view, a person who is objectively justified has a certain propensity to be right in his acceptance, and this propensity is the needed reliability component. I believe there are significant difficulties with each of these approaches, and after considering them, I shall present an alternative and argue for its superiority.

5. Reliability and Probability

The interface between reliability and coherence in an acceptance system of the kind postulated by Lehrer's coherence theory is probability. So central is probability that, "it is the notion of probability that connects with reliability and thus provides the answer to the ontological question with which we began" (1982, 205). The notion of reasonableness, the subjective side of justification, is virtually identified with probability, in that "other things being equal, the more probable a statement is, the more reasonable it is to accept it, and conversely, the less probable it is, the less reasonable it is to accept it" (1986, 12). On the objective side, reliability is a function of probability: "high probability is associated with high reliability" (1982, 205). Thus probability seems to mediate between the subjective and the objective, but the way in which it connects the two is not at all straightforward.

First, let us see what conception of probability is appropriate to the kind of reliability Lehrer needs to effect the truth connection. To say that a person is highly reliable is to say that the judgments that issue from the person's acceptance system are highly likely to be true. Although one might attempt to apply a frequency interpretation of probability here, Lehrer opts for a propensity interpretation. High reliability is a strong propensity for a person with a given acceptance system to make true judgments on the basis of that system.

Lehrer distinguishes between general reliablity and situation-specific reliablity. For example, a person may be generally reliable in judging colors of objects but unreliable under circumstances of unusual lighting (1986, 16). General reliability is associated with prior probability, while special reliability is associated with probability conditional on the circumstances. One can ask about the probability of the circumstances themselves. The low probability of special probability-lowering circumstances can increase the prior probability of a proposition. One's color judgment may be highly generally reliable, because normal circumstances for judging colors are so much more probable than abnormal circumstances. Thus in the case of situation-specific reliability, the propensities of a person to judge truly are based on two objective factors: the characteristics of the acceptance system and those of the circumstances in which the acceptance system is utilized.

Let us contrast the probabilistic nature of reliability with the probabilities which virtually constitute reasonableness. Ordinarily, such probability estimates have to do with highly specific propositions, e.g. that there is a painted red patch on the wall in front of me. These are supposed to be subjective estimates, conditional on the acceptance system, of objective probabilities. The subjective probabilities become objectified in the transition from the acceptance system to the verific system. The objectified probabilities in the verific system are relativized to the surviving members of the nonprobabilistic part of the acceptance system, that is, the true acceptances.

Because these objective probabilities will be highly variable from system to system, the related reliability will be correspondingly variable.[9] Any lacuna in the acceptance concerning the special circumstances relevant to the reliablity of a proposition is not taken into account in the assignment of probabilities in the verific system. Thus, the objective probabilities found in the verific system need not be based on the full range of circumstances in which one finds oneself. This leaves open the possibility of a divergence between the objective probability that a person is right in given circumstances (reliability) and the objectified version of the subjective probabilities in a person's acceptance system. The last point will figure heavily in what follows, in that Lehrer wants the verific system to provide the entire objective component of objective justification, yet he severely limits the truths which affect it.

6. Reliablity as Propensity

One candidate for effecting the truth connection is based on the way the probabilistic component of the verific system is constructed, and it is the basis for some of Lehrer's earlier responses to versions of the isolation argument. A way to press the isolation argument is to show a specific way in which a justified belief might be isolated from the truth. There is a potential problem, raised by Lehrer himself, which concerns a very small acceptance system, say one which consists entirely of the proposition that God exists and the estimate that it is more reasonable to believe that God exists than to believe any other proposition. The person would seem to be subjectively justified. As Cornman pointed out, Lehrer's original response to the problem, that a veracious man would not have a very small belief system, depends on an arbitrary interpretation of veraciousness (1980, 143).

In response to a similar point by Pastin, Lehrer appealed to the verific system to argue that the problem of small systems cannot arise because persons accepting few propositions would not be justified there.

> A person with an almost null doxastic system is one who would not have any better chance of being right about the truth of one proposition than another. His probability curve over propositions would be flat. Hence the few propositions he believes would be no more probable than their competitors in the verific alternative, and, therefore, would not be justified. (1981, 237)

If a person has little propensity to be right about anything, then the person would be justified about nearly nothing in the verific system. "Crudely put, one must have many ideas in order to have any significant chance of being right, and the person with very few ideas is a poor bet to obtain truth" (1981, 237).

Lehrer's response might be generalized in the sense that the notion of a "propensity to be right" could be used to explicate the notion of reliability without any recourse to doxastic ascent and its attendant problems. But this suggestion is not in accord with Lehrer's model of justification. The propensities are objective probabilities based on a person's verific acceptance system. How reliable a person is under certain circumstances depends on the objective features of the circumstances, which may not be reflected in a person's verific system. To put the matter in another way, insofar as the verific system is a subsystem of the acceptance system, the objective probabilities there virtually constitute an objective reasonableness, which is limited by the original evidence.[10]

Consider one of Lehrer's examples. A person is confronted with a white wall containing painted red patches and red patches projected by light. She is caused to believe that she sees a painted red patch by actually looking at one. Further, she has no evidence that there are any projected red patches in the room (1986, 22). Lehrer argues that the person is not objectively justified despite her subjective justification. So her purified acceptance system is not isolated from the real. "The problem is that the person assumes, incorrectly, that circumstances are those in which she can tell the real thing when she sees one" (1986, 22). Here is Lehrer's diagnosis:

> Since it is false that the circumstances are ones in which she is trustworthy in what she accepts, relative to the verific system the person does not accept that she is trustworthy in accepting that she sees a painted red patch. Hence, relative to the verific system, competitors cannot be beaten or neutralized. There is no neutralizing proposition for the competitor that says that she is seeing a white patch illuminated with red light, nor can that competitor be beaten. So the person is not completely justified in believing that she sees a red patch. (1986, 24)

But suppose that she assumes that it is probable that the circumstances are those in which she can tell the real thing when she sees one, i.e., that she does not reflect on her circumstances, but simply relies on general reliability. There is no reason that she should reflect on her circumstances, since she has no evidence of anything going wrong. It will remain probable that there are no special circumstances. Then she can still accept in the verific system that it is probable that she is trustworthy.

Because of her lack of evidence about the deceptiveness of the circumstances, there is no apparent reason to posit that the person has a false acceptance which, when purged from the acceptance system, would affect the objective probability of her being right. The contents of a person's acceptance system are determined by the person's truth-seeking strategies, and such strategies, as Lehrer recognizes, vary from person to person. To neutralize this objection, Lehrer must argue that there is some strategy- independent element of everyone's acceptance systems which will be retained in the verific system in a way that yields the objective probabilities required for reliability whenever a person is justified.

7. Accepting One's Own Reliability

Lehrer appeals to "doxastic ascent," acceptance of one's own reliability, to provide the needed element in the acceptance system. Because true acceptances are retained in the verific system, facts about one's own reliability will be relevant there, and justification in the verific system will be partially based on a person's actually being reliable. For clarity, the argument can be broken down as follows:

(1) If S is justified in accepting that p, then if S accepts that S is reliable in accepting that p then S is reliable in accepting that p.

(2) If S is justified in accepting that p, then S accepts that S is reliable in accepting that p. Therefore,

(3) If S is justified in accepting that p, then S is reliable in accepting that p.
Here is Lehrer's formulation of the argument for (1):

> Suppose that a person accepts some proposition and estimates that he is reliable about the truth of p. Imagine, moreover, that he also judges himself to be a reliable judge of his own reliability. He turns out to be personally justified in accepting that p. Now imagine, moreover, that not only is p true but that the person is also correct in accepting that he is reliable about such matters generally and that he is a reliable judge of his reliablity. In that case, the connection between justification and truth naturally results. The person is both personally and objectively justified. It is not merely that p is true, but, since the person is correct in his estimates of his own reliablity, subjective and objective probability coincide. Thus, if he is justified, personally and objectively, there is an appropriate fit between subjective conviction and ontological reality. (1982,207)

This argument is a straightforward instance of the appeal to the verific system, so let us turn to premise (2).

The argument for (2) is that if a person S is subjectively justified in accepting that p, then S accepts that S is reliable about p. Lehrer contends that this argument is not an ad hoc smuggling of the notion of reliability into an ostensible coherence theory: "as a matter of fact, people do make assumptions about when they are trustworthy. So the assumption is psychologically well-grounded. An analysis of completely justified belief should be based on a realistic psychology of belief" (1986, 24). Further, "there is . . . both common sense and scientific evidence that quite young children and adults evaluate their first order beliefs of memory and perception, and do so reliably" (1983, 199).

The theory presented in *Knowledge* makes psychological assumptions, e.g. the minimal assumption that there are minds which accept propositions (249). It also makes assumptions required for the model of justification, i.e., that we have beliefs about comparative probabilities (191). It does not require of any specific proposition that it be a part of the nonprobabilistic part of a person's acceptance system. The reason for this minimal set of commitments is the normative character of the theory of justification, which allows maximum latitude in truth-seeking.

It may be that our choice in acceptance is constrained by the evaluations of our beliefs of memory and perception, in which case there would be less latitude than there appears to be. Doxastic ascent would be inevitable, and the truth connection would be effected when we reliably evaluate our beliefs. However, if self-evaluation is automatic, then justification is given an externalist element which Lehrer apparently wanted to eschew. But he has a way out, since he allows that certain beliefs are presented for acceptance and unreflectively processed. "This acceptance, though optional, may appear automatic and thus mimic the Input System in the mode of operation. But the option is genuine" (1983, 198).

Unfortunately, the existence of such unreflectively processed beliefs would not provide support for premise (2). The processing Lehrer has in mind is the simple conversion of beliefs into acceptances, not the acceptance of higher order propositions about our own reliability. On the contrary, these acceptances, if there are any, are the result of disregarding the intricacies of reflection in the interest of computational economy (1983,199; 1981,51).[11]

So the inevitability of doxastic ascent must be secured in a different way. If it could be shown that the normative theory of justification requires assumptions people make about their own trustworthiness, that they accept that they are reliable when they are justified, then the doxastic ascent assumption is not a major departure from the original conception. The most plausible argument is that it is impossible to pursue the goal of avoiding error with respect to a proposition p without accepting that one is reliable concerning it.

If a person must indeed accept that he is reliable, this could mean one of two things. Accepting that he is generally reliable would not be sufficient to secure the truth connection, because the person might not be reliable in the present circumstances. In the color judgment example described above, the person is generally reliable but not reliable in the situation in question, so the color judgment is not objectively justified. Note that apparently automatic acceptance (e.g., "accept the beliefs formed from perception") would be of this level of generality, and thus of no help against the isolation argument.

If a person must accept that he is reliable in the circumstances, there are once more two possibilities. One might accept flat out that the circumstances are not deceptive, or one might accept that they are probably not deceptive. The first possibility is more promising from the standpoint of the truth connection, for any mistake here will show up in an altered verific system, and the verific justification would be blocked.[12] But it is far from clear that the theory of justification requires this kind of acceptance, because the theory does not place strictures on the strategies one employs in truth-seeking.

A person need not accept that the circumstances are distorting, when pursuing a bold truth-seeking strategy with respect to propositions under consideration. He could simply assume that they are probably normal, and that he is probably reliable in the present circumstances. Or one could pursue a conservative strategy with respect to the circumstances. The woman gazing at the wall has no evidence that there are red projections on the same wall, and she might therefore deem it highly probable that the circumstances are not abnormal. By their very nature, judgments about unusual circumstances call for more than usual circumspection.[13] A person might well wish to make only probabilistic judgments about circumstances, and given the nature of the model of justification, these may make it reasonable to accept, e.g., that there is a painted red spot on the wall.

My claim that on Lehrer's theory, a person can make a justified perceptual judgement without accepting that the circumstances are usual, has textual support. Lehrer's attempt to refute the reliabilist suggests that *reason to believe* , not actual belief, is all that is required.

> Justification is a normative concept. It is an evaluation of how well one has pursued one's epistemic goals. Consequently, if we have reason to believe that perception, for example, is a reliable process, then the mere fact that it turns out not to be reliable, because of some improbable contingency, does not obliterate our justification for perceptual belief. This is especially clear when we have *good reason to believe* that the contingency, which if fact, makes our cognitive processes unreliable, does not obtain. (1983, 193, emphasis mine)

Similarly, Lehrer gave examples in which justification relies only on probable judgments about circumstances, to show that there can be Gettier cases which do not involve reasoning through a false lemma (1974, 19-20). That justified perceptual judgment requires acceptance of anything but probabilities runs against the grain of Lehrer's notion of justification.

A final objection to the present approach is that the acceptance of reliablity when one is reliable is insufficient to establish the truth connection. To establish the connection, one must have accepted one's reliablity for the right reasons, i.e., reasons which are objectively responsible for one's being reliable. If this can occur, then the element of fortuitousness intrudes, and the isolation argument is not overcome.

8. Probable Reliability

To overcome this objection, it seems that Lehrer must hold that, whenever S is justified in accepting that p, S is justified in accepting that S is reliable about p (1983, 195). However, because this leads to a regress,[14] the claim is weakened to the requirement that S be probably reliable: "one is personally justified only if it is probable on one's acceptance system that one is reliable when one believes what one does in conditions of the sort in question" (1983, 194). Lehrer thus substitutes for (3) the weaker conditional: (3'): If S is justified in accepting that p, then S is probably reliable in accepting that p.

The argument for (3') might parallel the argument for (3). Justification is linked to probable reliablity through the acceptance of probable reliability: "the connection between justification and truth lies in what one accepts about the probability of both the truth and the reliability of the belief" (1983, 195). The modified premises then are:

(1') If S is justified in accepting that p, then if S accepts that S is probably reliable in accepting that p then S is probably reliable in accepting that p.

(2') If S is justified in accepting that p, then S accepts that S is probably reliable in accepting that p.

However, premise (2') is unnecessary, given that there is no real distinction in Lehrer's theory between a probability within the acceptance system and what is accepted about the probability.[15]

In fact, direct argument can be given for (3'):

> hypotheses concerning the unreliability of belief are negatively relevant to the belief and compete with it. For example, the belief that I see something red competes with the hypothesis that my beliefs about the colors I see are unreliable in present circumstances. Therefore, the probability of my belief being reliable must be sufficiently higher than the probability that this belief is unreliable. Only then is the belief justified. (1983, 193-4)

Since subjective justification requires only that in the acceptance system there must be a probability estimate about reliability, there need only be an objective probability of reliability remaining in the verific system when one is completely justified.

The question is whether being probably reliable in this way effects the truth connection. It is tempting to think that, since reliablity is itself probabilistic, the levels distinction collapses, and probable reliability is itself a kind of reliability. Lehrer maintains "that it makes perfectly good sense to talk about the probability of probabilities, the reliability of judgments about one's own reliability, and that such judgments are germane to justification" (1982, 205). If the objective probability of one's judgments about one's reliability is a measure of "the reliability of one's own judgments about reliability," a case for the truth connection could be made.

However, there is no reason to think that the higher-order objective probability is a measure of the reliability of reliability than that the lower-order probability measures reliability itself. Reliability is a function of the actual circumstances in which a person finds himself, while the objective probability of the verific system rests on a set of acceptances, which need not capture all relevant aspects of those circumstances.

There may be another way to preclude accidentally justified higher-order acceptance. Lehrer has argued that it is possible to non-circularly justify a method using the method itself (1981, 43-51). So if I use a method which I deem reliable, I may be justified in accepting that it is reliable by applying the method. Therefore, if the method is reliable, I have accepted it for a reason which establishes the truth connection.

Intriguing though it may be, this response is not sufficient to overcome the fundamental objections to the doxastic ascent approach. First, Lehrer acknowledges the possibility of cases where there is no convergence in the hierarchy of methods (1981, 52). So there is no guarantee that the possibility of isolation is ruled out in a given case. Furthermore, the theory of justification leaves it open to a person to choose whatever methods (including higher-order methods) one deems to be the best of the pursuit of truth and the avoidance of error.

In summary, all Lehrer's attempts to "effect" the truth connection fail. The fact that a person's justification holds up in the verific system is inadequate, because the system itself might not bear the right relation to the truth. The probabilities in the verific system are based on what a person actually accepts, and the range of accepted propositions may omit aspects of one's circumstances which bear on how reliable the person is, and hence on whether the truth connection is properly effected. The doxastic ascent strategy was supposed to remedy this problem by insuring that the relevant acceptances are there: if a person is justified, he must have accepted the reliability or probable reliability of his methods for seeking the truth or avoiding error. However, none of the attempts to show that justification entails an appropriate attitude toward one's reliability succeed.

9. Diagnosis

There are several possible conclusions that might be drawn from this argument. Perhaps the quasi-formal model of justification needs to be given a strengthened formulation of objective probability, or maybe it should be dropped altogether. Or it may be that the coherence theory of justification cannot cope with the isolation argument by any means. If so, this may discredit the theory, or it may cast doubt on the utility of the isolation argument.

It is tempting to blame the quasi-formal model of justification for the difficulties with effecting the truth connection. Each attempt was thwarted by the essentially subjective character of the verific system, which is not guaranteed to generate the right objective probabilities. But it is hard to see how the model could be changed without introducing an external element to provide a sure basis for objective probabilities. I argued earlier that it is possible to add this element without undermining Lehrer's attack on reliabilism, in that objective reliablity need not be considered a sufficient condition for justification. However, such a fix would have to cope with Lehrer's arguments to the effect that allowing this kind of external contamination might open up lines of justification in the verific system which were not available in the acceptance system (1974, 221-2).[16]

Yet it is not really the daunting technical difficulties posed by Gettier cases which make a technical approach to solving the isolation argument unsatisfactory.[17] I believe that the primary obstacle to Lehrer's solution to the isolation problem is the parallel he draws between two kinds of reliability, one appropriate for belief and the other for acceptance. In the former case, reliability lies in the accuracy of transmission of information, whether through perception or through memory. In the latter, reliability lies in the relative success of intellectual strategies for truth-seeking and error-avoidance.

The reliability of information transmission has already been mentioned as constituting the truth connection for externalist theories. Although Lehrer rejects this approach to the truth connection, the doxastic ascent strategy with which he replaces it merely mimics it at a higher level. Just as the interaction of the world with our input system can automatically and reliably yield beliefs, the interaction of the belief system with the acceptance system can habitually and reliably yield acceptances.

However, this picture is inimical to the motivation of the coherence theory, because, as I have argued, it denigrates the optionality built into the epistemic norms of truth-seeking and error-avoidance. There is a certain irony in Lehrer's description of his theory of justification as "an information processing model of human knowledge" (1986, 20). An information processing model is primarily concerned with the preservation of the integrity of data, while an acceptance system evaluates this reliability when required, but does much more.

To be sure, judgments about the reliability of our belief-forming systems are often important in the justification of knowledge claims or the determination of which propositions to accept. However, they are important in general only for claims which directly involve those systems: perception, memory, inference, etc.. Many of our knowledge claims go far beyond these, and their truth connection ought not to be explicated in terms of the kind of reliablity appropriate to belief-forming mechanisms. Universal generalizations, claims about the distant past, theoretical objects, abstract objects, etc. do not fit the model of information processing. Nor do the intellectual activities involved in resolving intellectual conflict, testing hypothesis by experiment, and so forth; all of which are activities undertaken in the pursuit of the truth.

10. Coherentism and Reliabilism

The upshot of my discussion of the isolation problem is that it leaves Lehrer's coherence theory with a dilemma: either reduce the optionality of the acceptance system and secure the truth connection, or retain the optionality. I believe that the primary motivation of the coherence theory would be lost if the first alternative is chosen. If we hold that reflective acceptance systems justify propositions which are beyond the pale of information processing systems, and that they often do not justify propositions which the latter systems continually produce, propositions common to both will be less plentiful than Lehrer might think desirable. He holds that when the intellectual element is absent, there is no knowledge, as in the case of young children and animals. Everyone else knows what they know because they can and do reliably evaluate their information systems. But if we need not do so, as I have argued, then it will turn out that much of what is ordinarily regarded as knowledge is really information, though it is readily convertible into knowledge.

I think that Lehrer's doxastic ascent argument is a failed attempt to preserve a large domain of knowledge, by claiming that the conversion is, if not automatic, then habitual. My suggestion is that we abandon the apparently hopeless task of finding a conception of 'knowledge' which treats both the intellectual and the informational aspects of our cognitive success univocally. I regard foundationalism as another unsuccessful attempt to combine these two notions, and in his wake the two tasks have divided between coherentism and reliabilism, respectively. The task of justifying ordinary perceptual belief falls to the reliabilist, who inherits the secure epistemic status of such beliefs. The task of justifying intellectual acceptance falls to the coherence theorist, who inherits the insecurity (and excitement) of the intellectual quest. To demand the same standard for the success of the two theories is not reasonable.[18]

The intellectual quest and the absorption of information are associated with theories of justification which have different criteria of success. Effecting the truth connection is a straightforward requirement for an epistemology of information, for the concept of information rests on the nomological connection between the world and its representation. This connection does not involve the intellectual apparatus of justification, unless it is called into question or cannot provide the required information.

Can Lehrer's strategy for effecting the truth connection succeed with respect to those propositions which are reflectively accepted? In other words, is it the case that when one is justified in reflectively accepting p, then one is justified in accepting one's own reliability with respect to p? In this case, I think that the norms of truth-seeking and error-avoidance require such an acceptance, as Lehrer has argued. All my objections so far have to do with the cases in which one is not sufficiently reflective.

It is difficult to determine how restricting the justification to reflective acceptance would affect the quasi-formal model. What is needed is a notion of reliability which is commensurate with the intellectual nature of the theory of justification. How does one measure the reliability of truth- seeking strategies, e.g., the preference for simpler hypotheses, or for more comprehensive ones? Lehrer proposes that we measure the force of such strategies in terms of prior probabilities: "If one assigns a higher probability to simpler hypotheses than complex ones that would lead us to expect the same observations, that is because we assign a higher antecedent probability to simpler hypotheses" (1981, 39). Whether these prior probabilities hold up in the verific alternative depends on whether corresponding objective probabilities can be assigned to them. If there is some objective correlate to the high probabilities assigned by methods, then their presence in the verific system would be a primary factor in establishing the truth connection.

The upshot of my argument has been that the challenge of the isolation argument emphasizes an important limitation of Lehrer's coherence theory, i.e., the absence of justification in many cases in which information is reliably received. This is due to the inherent optionality of reflective acceptance. Lehrer's response to the isolation problem, particularly the emphasis on verific justification, is original and effective in the limited domain of reflective acceptance. However, his attempt to effect an *Aufhebung* of foundationalism and reliabilism, while ingenious, founders on the heterogeneity of information and reflection.

1. Pollock does not find this argument ultimately convincing, because the coherence relation holds of beliefs, which must have a causal relation to the world (cf. 76).
2. James (276-7), cited approvingly by Chisholm (1977, 14). A difference between James' and contemporary approaches is that the latter do not in general adopt a pragmatic (or coherence) theory of truth, leaving open the possibility of isolation.
3. Lehrer and Cohen claim that Chisholm's adoption of these goals virtually commit him to a coherence theory (203), and presumably this claim could be generalized to state that the pragmatic account of justification necessitates a coherence theory.
4. This should be distinguished from what Chisholm called "particularism," which begins with paradigm instances of knowledge and looks for epistemic principles which would justify them (1982, 66).
5. Alvin Goldman's reliabilist theory (1986) distinguishes between the reliability of a process and the higher level reliability of a method for acquiring or sustaining the process and finds both essential for knowledge (52-3). He remarks that second-order methods "may be wired-in features of our cognitive architecture" (53).
6. Lehrer variously writes of the reliability of persons, of acceptances, etc. His primary notion seems to be that of a person's making reliable judgments about propositions or classes of propositions.
7. Competing propositions may also be "neutralized," but this detail does not figure in Lehrer's arguments concerning the truth connection.
8. In this respect it differs from the "hybrid" coherentist theories of Cornman (157-95) and Chisholm (1977, 82-6). Both these theories are foundationalist, with coherence providing non-foundational justification. Neither, however, employs so liberal a conception of coherence as Lehrer's.
9. This may pose a problem of determining whether the degree of reliability in the verific system is sufficient for knowledge. In particular, because the proposition need only beat the strongest competitor, which may be weak, a justified proposition may not have very high reliability. However, reliability theories are not precise about the degree of reliability required for knowledge, either.
10. Thanks to the editor for reminding me that the notion of reasonableness is retained in the description of the verific system.
11. This postulation of habitual unreflective acceptance appears to be ad hoc, despite Lehrer's assurances to the contrary. Why assume that habitual acceptance goes on, when it would do equally well to say that, when called on to make an intellectual judgment, the acceptance system retrieves the required material from the belief system? Indeed, it may be that the methods employed by the input system diverge significantly from the methods one employs reflectively, rather than being derivative from them. At any rate, this is clearly an empirical issue which cannot be settled by speculation. Lehrer does claim that it is not necessary for the defense of his theory (1983, 198), and in this he is surely right.
12. Because it is a false acceptance, it would be deleted from the verific system, and the problem of objective probability would arise. However, in the first version of his model, and in an unpublished version post-dating the published works referred to here, Lehrer makes provisions for replacing the false acceptances with true ones in a way that may avoid criticisms of his earlier attempts to avoid Gettier-type problems.
13. Hume made a similar point about miracles in Chapter X of the *Enquiry*.
14. It is unclear why Lehrer here accepted the regress argument. In *Knowledge* he outlined a pragmatic method for stopping it (16), and a fundamental motivation for a coherence theory is that it does not fall prey to the argument (155-7). He developed his response extensively in "Hierarchy" whose publication predates "Justification" by two years. This response will be considered at the end of the present section.
15. Thanks to the editor for bringing my attention to this point.
16. These are cases where misleading information one does not possess comes into play (1974, 221-3).
17. One could maintain a coherence theory of justification without the quasi- formal model. BonJour's theory not only lacks a model, but it gives a set of necessary but not sufficient conditions for justification. Chisholm's and Cornman's hybrid theories, on the other hand, provide such models. But to abandon the search for a workable model would be a mistake, in my view. Although leaving it open to counter-examples, a model enrichs a philosophical theory in several ways. It gives the theory precision that would otherwise be lacking. It provides a more or less precise context for evaluating the theory. And its modification to meet objections can strengthen the theory.
18. Of course, there are still foundationalists, and there are reliablists such as Goldman who want to account intellectual acceptance in reliabilist terms. I think they will not be successful, but I can only claim to have

given an argument against a coherentist attempt to account for justified belief in coherentist terms.

REFERENCES

BonJour, Laurence. *The Structure of Empirical Knowledge*. Cambridge: Harvard University Press, 1985.
Chisholm, Roderick. "The Problem of the Criterion," in *The Foundations of Knowing*. Minneapolis: University of Minnesota Press, 1982, 61-75.
-----. *Theory of Knowledge* . 2nd. ed. Englewood Cliffs: Prentice-Hall, 1977.
Cornman, James W. *Skepticism, Justification, and Explanation*. Philosophical Studies Series in Philosophy 18. Dordrecht: D. Reidel, 1980.
Dancy, Johnathan. *An Introduction to Contemporary Epistemology*. Oxford: Basil Blackwell, 1985.
Goldman, Alvin. *Epistemology and Cognition*. Cambridge: Harvard University Press, 1986.
Hume, David. *An Enquiry Concerning Human Understanding*. 2nd. ed. L. A. Selby-Bigge, ed., Oxford: Oxford University Press, 1966.
James, William. "The Will to Believe." *The Writings of William James: A Comprehensive Edition*. John J. McDermott., ed., Chicago: U niversity of Chicago Press, 1977, 771-735.
Lehrer, Keith. "Coherence and the Hierarchy of Method," in *Essays in Scientific Method: Dedicated to Paul Weingartner*. Edgar Morscher, Otto Neumaier, Gerhard Zecha, eds., Bad Reichendall, Austria: Comes Verlag, 1981, 25-56.
-----. "The Coherence Theory of Knowledge." *Philosophical Topics* 14 (1986), 5-25.
-----. *Knowledge*. Oxford: Oxford University Press, 1974.
-----. "The Knowledge Cycle." *Nous* 11 (1977), 17-25.
-----. "Knowledge, Truth and Ontology," in *Language and Ontology: Proceedings of the Sixth I International Wittgenstein Sumposium* , Werner Leinfellner, Eric Kraemer, and Jeffrey Schank, eds., Vienna: Hulder-Pichler-Tempsky, 1982, 201-11.
-----. "A Self Profile," in *Keith Lehrer*. Radu J. Bogdan, ed., Dordrecht: D. Reidel, 1981, 3-104.
-----, and Cohen, Stewart. "Justification, Truth, and Coherence." *Synthese* 2 (1983), 191-207.
Plato. *Theaetetus* . F. M. Cornford, tr., *The Collected Dialogues of Plato* , Edith Hamilton and Huntington Cairns, eds., Princeton: Princeton University Press, 1971, 845-919.
Pollock, John L. *Contemporary Theories of Knowledge*. Totowa, N.J.: Rowman & Littlefield, 1986.
Sosa, Ernest. "The Raft and the Pyramid: Coherence versus Foundations in the Theory of Knowledge," in *Studies in Epistemology*, Midwest Studies in Philosophy Volume 5, Minneapolis: University of Minnesota Press, 1980, 2-25.

Fundamental Troubles With The Coherence Theory

Wayne A. Davis
Georgetown University, and
John W. Bender
Ohio University

In evaluating any coherence theory, we must answer two classic questions: (A) *What is coherence* ? and (B) *Can there be several internally coherent but mutually incompatible systems of belief?* Given a plausible answer to (A), the answer to (B) must be "Yes." This dooms any coherence theory of *truth*. For trivially, there cannot be two incompatible systems of true beliefs. But a "Yes" answer to (B) is a point in *favor* of coherence theories of *justification*. For a justified belief need not be true, and it is quite possible for two individuals with incompatible beliefs to both be fully justified in their beliefs. Note that a coherence theory of justification would not entail that there may be incompatible systems of *knowledge*. For knowledge requires true as well as justified belief. Given two individuals with incompatible but fully justified beliefs, at most one can have knowledge.

Coherence theories of justification raise a third and equally pressing question, however: (C) *Can an internally coherent system of beliefs without external foundation provide any justification at all?* A coherence theory of justification must answer "Yes." But a general understanding of "coherence" makes an affirmative answer extremely implausible. A complete fantasy could have any degree of internal coherence, it would seem, without any part being the least justified. So a coherence theory of justification seems almost as unfounded as a coherence theory of truth, but for different reasons.[1]

Keith Lehrer has worked out an impressively sophisticated coherence theory of justification.[2] In our opinion, it is the first serious attempt to provide more than a vague specification of what coherence is. Nevertheless, we have argued elsewhere[3] that the letter of Lehrer's answer to (A) has major technical defects which seem irremediable. In this paper, however, we are concerned with more fundamental problems, problems which should arise for any coherence theory of justification. In section I we sketch out Lehrer's definition of coherence. In section II we observe that coherence is unnecessary for justification because of the existence of "basic beliefs." We argue in section III that coherence is insufficient for justification because it ignores the inferential structure of the subject's belief system. Lastly and most seriously, we argue in section IV that coherence is insufficient for justification because it requires no external basis. Hence the very spirit of Lehrer's answer to (A) makes a "Yes" answer to (C) unreasonable.

In the course of our argument that coherence is fundamentally neither necessary nor sufficient for justification, we show how some of Bonjour's ideas[4] can be used to help Lehrer's theory. But they too ultimately fail to the extent that they do not incorporate tenets of foundationalism.

I. The Coherence Theory of Justification

The precise notion Lehrer defines is *being completely justified in accepting that p,* which he takes to be the justification condition for knowing that p. According to Lehrer, complete justification has a subjective and an objective component. Both consist of the proposition's cohering with a body of acceptances held by the subject. The subjective component requires that the proposition cohere with the total set of S's acceptances, which Lehrer calls S's *acceptance system.* The objective component of justification requires that the proposition cohere with the set of all true acceptances of S, which Lehrer calls S's *verific system.* S's verific system is the result of deleting all false acceptances from his acceptance system. According to Lehrer, then, S is completely justified in accepting that p

J.W. Bender (ed.), The Current State of the Coherence Theory, 52–68.
© *1989 by Kluwer Academic Publishers.*

if and only if p coheres with both the acceptance and verific system of S.

Lehrer's conception of coherence does not require logical closure or explanatory coherence, for these features may be eliminated or reduced by deleting falsehoods from S's acceptance system. Instead, Lehrer's basic idea is that a proposition coheres with a given system provided that on the basis of the system it is more reasonable for the subject to accept that proposition than it is for him to accept competing propositions. In Lehrer's terminology: p *coheres* with system A for subject S iff p beats every unneutralized proposition it competes with for S on the basis of A. As Lehrer defines these notions, p *competes* with q for S on the basis of system A iff it is more reasonable for S to accept p on the assumption that not q than on the assumption that q on the basis of system A; p *beats* q for S on the basis of system A if and only if p competes with q for S on the basis of system A and it is more reasonable for S to accept p than to accept q on system A.

The idea that competitors can be neutralized is designed to rebut skeptical attacks. Lehrer wants to say, for example, that S can know that the apple he is looking at is red. But one competitor is "People sometimes hallucinate." Since this is as certain as empirical propositions get, it will be impossible to beat. S can still know that the apple is red, according to Lehrer, because "People sometimes hallucinate" is neutralized by "I am not hallucinating now." The conjunction of these two propositions is not a competitor of "The apple is red," and according to Lehrer is no less reasonable than "People sometimes hallucinate." Since neutralization will not be important in the arguments to follow, we will not present its definition.[5]

To complete our exposition of Lehrer's theory, we must indicate what his measure of comparative reasonableness is. While the full story is more complex, the basic determinant of a proposition's reasonableness is its probability of being true, relative to a given system of acceptances.

> The relation between reasonableness and probability may be articulated by saying that, other things equal, the more probable a statement is, the more reasonable it is to accept it, and, conversely, the less probable a statement is the less reasonable it is to accept it. I call this the *correspondence* principle. The reason that the qualification, other things being equal, is added is that, as noted, the risk of error is only one determinant of epistemic reasonableness (Lehrer 1986, 12).

The only other determinant Lehrer cites is "informativeness." Lehrer's subsequent use of the correspondence principle indicates that he considers other things to be equal in a wide range of cases. We believe our use of the principle below will fall within the same range.

It is important to note that a justified belief need not have a probability of 1 on the basis of the subject's verific system (see Lehrer 1986, 12-15). A justified belief need only be *more probable* than competitors. By not requiring a probability of 1, Lehrer is allowing for human fallibility. The truth of a proposition accepted today with full justification need not be logically necessitated by the evidence, which is almost never complete. Hence further evidence may require rejecting the proposition.[6]

On first reflection, it might be thought that Lehrer's concept of justification is too weak for use as the justification condition of knowledge. According to Lehrer,

> S knows that p iff
> (i)   it is true that p,
> (ii) S accepts that p,
> (iii) S is completely justified in accepting that p, and
> (iv) S is so justified in accepting that p in a way that does not depend essentially on S's acceptance of any false statement (1986, 6).

Now let L be "I will lose the state lottery." It would seem that a normal lottery entrant S is completely justified in believing L on Lehrer's view since it is so much more reasonable than its negation given a normal system of beliefs about lotteries. Furthermore, S's justification does not depend essentially on any false statement, assuming that he infers L from the true proposition that thousands of other people have an equally good chance of winning. It would follow that if L happens to be true, then S knows that he will lose the lottery, which is incorrect. Hence Lehrer's analysis of knowledge coupled with his analysis of justification appears too weak. A similar problem would arise when most other analyses of knowledge are coupled with Lehrer's theory of justification.

However, reality differs from appearance here because of Lehrer's unconventional notion of competition. On Lehrer's definition, "I will lose" competes with "Someone will win the lottery" even though the two are in no way incompatible. For the former is slightly less reasonable given the latter than given its negation. Since "I will lose the lottery" is slightly less reasonable than "Someone will win," the former does not beat all propositions it competes with. And according to Lehrer, nothing neutralizes this unbeaten competitor. Hence Lehrer's view is that S is *not* completely justified in accepting that he will lose the lottery, and consequently does not know that he will. So when competition is understood properly, Lehrer's combined analysis gives the correct ruling concerning knowledge in the lottery example. [7]

II. Coherence as Unnecessary for Justification: Basic Beliefs

We will now argue that if coherence is anything like what Lehrer's theory says it is, then coherence is neither necessary nor sufficient for justification. In this section, we shall show that coherence is fundamentally unnecessary for justification because of a relatively small but significant class of beliefs.

IIA. The Problem of Basic Beliefs.

According to the foundationalist picture of knowledge, most justified beliefs are justified because they are based on other justified beliefs. But some beliefs are justified without such a basis. These so-called "basic beliefs" provide the foundation for the entire system of beliefs. Foundationalists usually identify certain classes of beliefs as basic. These typically include beliefs about one's current conscious states, usefully called "self-presenting" states, and beliefs in certain obvious propositions, usually called "self-evident" propositions. The belief that the bird looks brown (when one is looking at it) is an example of the former sort of belief, and the belief that all men are men is an example of the latter. According to the foundationalist, these beliefs have an "external" justification, in the sense that they are justified but not by other beliefs. Instead, beliefs about self-presenting states are justified by the nature of certain psychological states, and beliefs about self-evident truths are justified by the nature of the propositions.

Many aspects of the foundationalist story are controversial. But one part seems hard to deny: beliefs about self-presenting states and self-evident propositions are prime examples of justified beliefs. Our question, then, is this: Why are such beliefs justified on a coherence theory? Why according to Lehrer's theory are we justified in believing "The bird looks brown" when we are looking at it? There must be some other beliefs in our acceptance system that make this proposition more reasonable than competitors. But what are they? We have no evidence for the proposition. And nothing can be identified as our reason for believing it. The foundationalist would say that we are justified in believing that the bird looks brown simply because the bird does look brown to us. But the bird's looking brown is not a proposition in our acceptance system.

Nevertheless, at least in our case there are propositions meeting the requirements of Lehrer's theory. For in addition to "The bird looks brown," we also accept "The bird is brown" and "The bird looks brown because it is brown." These last two propositions do make the first more probable than any competitors. If it were a plausible assumption that people always accepted an explanation of their self-presenting states (or always made an "inference to the best explanation" from them), then the coherence theory could account for the justification of beliefs about self-presenting states. But surely the assumption is dubious. When in unusual lighting conditions, someone may well accept "The bird looks brown" without accepting anything like "The bird is brown, which is why it looks the way it does." Similarly, people often know that they have a headache, or a tingling sensation in their legs, without knowing why they do. It is especially hard to see how such isolated introspective judgments could cohere with the subjects' acceptance systems in anything like Lehrer's sense.

The same problem arises for belief in self-evident truths like "All men are men." There are no reasons for which we believe such propositions, and they do not serve to explain anything else we believe to be the case. So there does not seem to be anything in our acceptance system that justifies us in believing them. Lehrer might observe that we do accept a more general self-evident truth, like "Everything is what it is." We would deny that this was our *reason* for accepting "All men are men," but that would not matter on Lehrer's theory. More tellingly, we can simply direct our question toward this further principle, and ask what propositions in our acceptance system justify us in believing it. A more general proposition will not always be available.

IIB. First Response: The Probability Function.

Lehrer has a response to the problem of self-evident truths. The reasonableness of accepting a proposition is determined in Lehrer's theory by its probability conditional on the (other) propositions in the subject's acceptance system. The conditional probability of a logical truth is 1 given any other proposition relative to which a conditional probability is defined. This means that a logical truth will automatically defeat any incompatible proposition. But it also means that a logical truth will have no competitors at all as Lehrer defines them. It would be natural, therefore, for Lehrer to stipulate that a logical truth vacuously defeats all competitors and so is justified.

This proves too much. Surely, not everyone is completely justified in believing all logical truths. Some are not self-evident. And by the same reasoning, any mathematical truth has a conditional probability of 1 given any other proposition, and so should also vacuously defeat all competitors. Yet it cannot be maintained that everyone is justified in believing all mathematical truths, including those not yet proven. The failure of this defense shows that in any theory like Lehrer's, *"The probability of p on the basis of S's acceptance system" cannot be interpreted as a conditional probability*. It must instead be interpreted as expressing the relationship intended in the familiar dictum "probability is relative to the evidence," which measures the degree to which the evidence *supports* the given proposition. Even though the conditional probability of the Pythagorean Theorem given "Roses are red" is 1, the latter proposition provides no evidential support whatsoever for the former. A complex logical or mathematical truth should have a probability of 1 relative to the evidence only if the evidence contains other propositions constituting proof of that proposition.

Similarly, the conditional probability of "All men are men" given "Roses are red" is also 1 even though the latter provides no evidence for the former. So the question remains: what in our acceptance systems supports self-evident truths and makes them more reasonable than any competitors? The answer appears to be "Nothing." A natural move at this point is to say that self-evident propositions are automatically part of "the evidence," because they are self-evident: they support themselves. Hence their probability is automatically 1 relative to the evidence. This would not mean that all logical and mathematical truths are automatically maximally reasonable, just the self-evident ones. A similar move is natural for propositions about self-presenting states. But to say anything like this is to adopt a key tenet of foundationalism. Lehrer's coherence theory would be such in name only if the existence of basic beliefs were introduced by the probability function used in the theory.

IIC. Second Response: Metaknowledge.
    Bonjour (1986, 130-31) tackles the problem of introspective knowledge head on. His suggestion - very much in the spirit of Lehrer's theory - is that something like the following will be in every knowledgeable subject's acceptance system:

> (1)   Introspective beliefs (of certain sorts) are very likely to be true.

This principle alone, however, does not suffice to make "I have a tingle in my leg" or "The bird looks brown" more probable than any competitor. Since these propositions are not about beliefs, principle (1) must be supplemented with an additional premise like the following:

> (2)   I have an introspective belief (of the proper sort) that I have a tingle in my leg.

(1) and (2) certainly support:

> (3)   I have a tingle in my leg.

Indeed, it is plausible that (1) and (2) would suffice to make (3) more probable than any (unneutralized) competitor.
    This line of reasoning shows that it is *possible* for a belief about a self-presenting state to be justified on a coherence theory like Lehrer's. But the crucial question now is Bonjour's assumption that something like (1) and (2) will be in the acceptance system of everyone who ever has a justified belief about a self-presenting state. This seems extremely implausible. In our own case, (1) is one of our standing beliefs. But what about the philosophically unsophisticated man-in-the-street? It is dubious that he even has the concept of an introspective belief. This problem can be avoided easily enough, however, by replacing (1) and (2) with something less sophisticated:

> (1')   Beliefs about one's own sensations are very likely true.
> (2')   I believe that I have a tingle in my leg.

We imagine that most adults would readily accept (1'). But does everyone who knows that they have a bodily sensation *actually* believe a generalization like (1')? We suspect that many people, especially children, have not even considered the proposition. Whether they have or not, though, seems completely irrelevant to whether they are justified in believing that they have tingles or other sensations. Moreover, there is a long line of behaviorists who would *reject* (1) and anything like it. We are nonetheless confident that they still had countless justified beliefs about their self-presenting states. As this illustrates, justified beliefs can survive in practice despite incoherence with the subject's misguided skeptical theories.
    Now what about (2)? It seems unlikely that everyone who justifiably accepts "I have a tingle in my leg" also accepts (2). With thoughts focused on one's leg, (2) may never come to mind or may come to mind only later. Perhaps it is always true that (2) would have been accepted if it had been considered; but in many instances it simply is not considered. We are not confusing belief with occurrent belief. We agree that people may

believe that p for a long time while seldom thinking the thought that p. But we also insist on maintaining the difference between actual and potential belief. There are all sorts of things we would believe if only we thought about it. But it cannot be said that we actually believe a proposition unless we have at some time considered it. "Mary believes that 3,874,462 is an even number but has never thought about the matter" is close to a contradiction in terms.[8]

Suppose now we actually did believe (2). Then "I believe (introspectively) that I have a tingle in my leg" is another proposition about a self-presenting state that we were justified in believing. Why? On Bonjour's approach, we were justified because (1) and (4) were in our acceptance system.

> (4) I believe (introspectively) that I believe (introspectively) that I have a
>   tingle in my leg.

It is even less likely that all of us believe something like (4) when thinking about how our leg feels. But if we did, then we will just have to ask what justifies believing (4). Surely for any given individual at any given time, there will be some end to this regress of beliefs about beliefs.[9] The highest order belief will be just as justified as the lowest. But nothing in the subject's acceptance system will be capable of justifying that proposition along the lines suggested.

For the record, we would strenuously deny that anything like (1) and (2) might have constituted *our reasons* for believing (3). Our reasons for believing something seldom if ever include the fact that we believe that very thing. Of course, the fact that *you* believe something may provide us with an excellent reason to believe the same thing. But after "Why do you believe p?" the answer "Because I believe p" would sound nonresponsive or irrational. At best, we would regard (1) and (2) as providing a *post hoc* rationalization for (3). And we think that any theory holding that we are justified in believing something solely in virtue of such a rationalization is *ipso facto* defective. The rationalization problem would be especially acute if Bonjour's treatment were attempted for self-evident logical truths.

Perhaps the coherence theorist will bite the bullet here and conclude that children and unreflective people do not have justified beliefs about their sensations. This concession leads to an extreme form of skepticism, however. For standard analyses of knowledge, including Lehrer's, say that knowledge requires justification. Hence the coherence theorist must further concede that children and unreflective people do not know anything about their sensations. But even the most radical skeptics, historically, have granted that we at least have knowledge of sensation. It is little consolation for the coherence theorist to observe that most people possess what is necessary to make their beliefs about sensations justified. For merely being capable of justifying ones beliefs is not sufficient for knowledge.

III. Coherence as Insufficient for Justification: Inferential Structure

Coherence is not only unnecessary for justification, it is insufficient. For coherence, at least as Lehrer defines it, ignores the inferential structure of the subject's acceptance system, and requires no justification of any kind for the subject's acceptance system itself.

IIIA. The General Problem of Inferential Structure.

The first problem is that the probability of p relative to any system of propositions depends on what propositions are in the system, but not on the inferential structure of that system. This means that on Lehrer's theory, whether S is justified in accepting p does not depend on how S reasoned in arriving at p, and indeed does not depend on whether S reasoned at all. But whether S is justified in accepting p certainly does depend in many cases on whether and how he reasoned. Lehrer (1986, 21) is surely correct in maintaining that justification does not always depend on inference. But just as surely, justification depends on inference in some cases. And when S's beliefs are based on inference, their justification depends on the nature of the inference.

The point can be expressed another way. It is commonly observed that a subject can *have* good reasons for a belief even though his belief is unjustified. For those may not be *his* reasons for believing what he does. On Lehrer's theory, though, merely having good reasons suffices for justification. As Bonjour would express it, the inferability of a belief is critical on Lehrer's theory, not its actually having been inferred. As we observed in section II, this wrongly implies that a belief can be justified in virtue of a *post hoc* rationalization. It also wrongly implies that a person can be justified even though he is "right for the wrong reason." Thus a student who bases his belief that 51 is not a prime number on the fact that it ends in 1 will be justified in his belief as long as he also believes that 51 is divisible by 3 and 17, even though he never saw the connection between "51 is divisible by 3 and 17" and "51 is not prime."

So it is important whether a belief was based on some good reasons possessed by the subject. It is equally critical whether the belief was based on those reasons in the right way. Although the basing relation is difficult to analyze satisfactorily, it is, in our view, a crucial element in a theory of justified belief. Consider a system consisting of the acceptance of each of the following propositions:

> (1) All and only those with at least a 90 on a preliminary exam get an A on it.
> (2) All and only those with an A on every prelim are exempt from the final.
> (3) I got at least a 93 on every prelim.
> (4) I got an A on every prelim.
> (5) I am exempt from the final.

Any subject holding this system has a conclusive reason to accept (5), but having a conclusive reason is not the same as being justified in one's belief. Compare Alan and Bob, for both of whom the propositions are all true. Alan inferred (4) from (1) and (3), and he inferred (5) from (2) and (4). Bob inferred (5) from (1) and (4), (1) from (2), (2) from (3) and (4), and (4) from (5). Now Alan may be justified in accepting (5). For every step of his reasoning was valid. But Bob is certainly not justified in accepting (5). His reasoning was viciously circular, and every step was idiotic. Lehrer's criterion of justification is insufficient, we argue, since it fails to consider the inferential structure of the subject's acceptance system.

Lehrer may argue that Bob accepts something that distinguishes him from Alan, *viz.* the false proposition that (5) follows from (1) and (4). Acceptance of this falsehood, Lehrer may suggest, is either not personally justified for Bob, or will be expunged, due to its falsehood, in Bob's corrected systems such as the verific system. Bob is therefore not completely justified in his acceptance of (5).

But why must Bob accept that (5) follows from (1) and (4)? Might he not simply accept what is true, *viz.*, that (5) is inferrable from (1)-(4), and *perform* the inference through invalid steps? The true belief that (5) follows from (1)-(4) carries through into Bob's corrected systems and surely coheres with his acceptance of (1)-(5).

More generally, must Bob have *any* such acceptance regarding what follows from what? Must Alan accept that (5) follows from (2) and (4) in order to be justified in believing (5) on the basis of inferring it from (2) and (4)? On pain of regress, it cannot be the case that we are justified in believing q on the basis of inferring it from p and p>q *only if* we also believe that (p & p > q) and if (p & p > q) then q.[10] Is acceptance supposedly different from belief in this regard?

IIIB. The Problem of Inferential Structure in Gettier Cases.

The fact that Lehrer's theory does not capture the inferential structure of the subject's acceptance system raises a further problem: Lehrer's analysis of knowledge may be too weak to rule out standard Gettier cases. Lehrer's fourth condition, designed to exclude such cases, requires that S's justification not depend essentially on S's acceptance of any false statement. But this seems to be entailed by Lehrer's third condition, which requires that a known proposition cohere with the subject's *verific* system as well as his acceptance system. In the standard Gettier case, S infers a true statement T ("Nogot or Havit owns a Ford") from a false but justified statement F ("Nogot owns a Ford"), which in turn is inferred from evidence E ("Nogot said he owns a Ford," etc.). It is natural to say that S's justification for believing T depends essentially on accepting a false statement, because S inferred T from F. But on Lehrer's theory, it would seem, S's justification does not depend essentially on any falsehood. For even when the acceptance of F is eliminated from S's system, that system will still contain 'S accepts E'. Given this, T should beat all competitors.[11] The fact that T coheres with S's verific system guarantees this. So given his theory of justification, Lehrer's analysis of knowledge appears to rule, *pace* Gettier, that true justified belief is sufficient for knowledge.

This problem can be solved by interpreting Lehrer's fourth condition as requiring more than that a known proposition cohere with the subject's verific system. Let us say that S's justification for accepting p does not depend essentially on any falsehood when p coheres with S's *strongly corrected acceptance system*. And let S's strongly corrected acceptance system be defined as the result of deleting all false acceptances from S's system *and replacing the acceptance of the denial of the false statement*.[12] The weaker verific system is thus a subset of the strongly corrected acceptance system, and may be thought of as a weakly corrected acceptance system, since falsehoods have been deleted without replacement. In the Gettier example, S's verific system contains neither 'S accepts F' nor 'S accepts ~F'. Since the verific system still contains 'S accepts E', T beats all competitors. But S's strongly corrected acceptance system contains 'S accepts ~F', which means that T is no longer more probable than competitors. ~F *defeats* S's justification for T. Thus we have Lehrer's familiar view that knowledge is undefeated justified true belief.

While this strong interpretation of Lehrer's fourth condition of knowledge yields the correct result in the Gettier case, it does not help us with the general problem of inferential structure. Since (1)-(4) in our example above are all true, (5) will cohere with S's strongly corrected acceptance system as well as his verific system. So Lehrer's theory will incorrectly rule that Bob as well as Alan has knowledge as well as true justified belief. And the student who infers "51 is not prime" from "51 ends in 1" will have true justified belief and knowledge that 51 is not prime as long as he happens to believe that 51 is divisible by 3 and 17.

IV. Coherence as Insufficient for Justification: External Basis

IVA. The Global "Lucky Guess" Problem.

Coherence is insufficient for justification for a second fundamental reason: the subject's verific system may itself be wholly unjustified. As Lehrer himself put it in his critique of explanatory coherence theories, "We must ask whether a man who is completely justified in his belief relative to a system B is completely justified in his belief. In other words, is system B a system to which a man may appeal to completely justify his beliefs?" (1974, 181). However, the only constraint Lehrer's 1986 theory places on the subject's verific system is that the beliefs in it be *true*. But it is well known that a subject may have a true belief that is not justified. It might be a "lucky guess," or something worse. It seems no less possible for S's entire verific system to consist of true beliefs that are unjustified. But it is hard to see how the coherence of p with a set of lucky guesses could make S justified in accepting p.

To make the problem concrete, again look at an acceptance system containing (1)-(5) of section III, and compare two cases. Chuck read (1) and (2) in the course syllabus, and heard the professor announce his grading policy in class. Chuck has all his preliminary exams in front of him, and can see the grades 93, 95, and 98 in the upper right-hand corners. He draws the conclusion that he got an A on all his exams, and that he is therefore exempt from the final. Don, on the other hand, has no reason whatsoever for accepting (1)-(3). He hasn't a shred of evidence relevant to these propositions, and does not even remember taking the exams. Nevertheless, he firmly believes (1)-(3), and purely coincidentally, they are true. He then draws the conclusion that he got an A on all his exams, and that he is therefore exempt from the final. Now Chuck may be justified in accepting (5). But surely Don is not. Nevertheless, on Lehrer's theory both Don and Chuck are completely justified in believing that they are exempt from the final. The glaring differences between the two cases are irrelevant because in both the proposition that he is exempt from the final coheres maximally with the subject's verific system.

IVB. First Response: Chains and Mutually Supporting Systems

Two possible solutions to this problem come to mind. Both involve defining subsets of the subject's verific system that contain only justified beliefs. Such a subset might be called a *justified verific system*. Then Lehrer's theory can be strengthened by requiring that a completely justified belief p must cohere with a justified verific system. The trick will be to define successfully such a system using only the coherence criterion of justification. Bonjour has identified this "global issue of the justification of the cognitive system itself" as the fundamental issue for the determination of epistemic justification (Bonjour 1986, 121).

The first possibility is to define a justified verific system as one satisfying the following condition: the propositions in the system can be enumerated in such a way that the first proposition in the system coheres with the remaining n-1 propositions; the second proposition coheres with the remaining n-2 propositions; and so on. This obviously leaves the nth member of the system without justification, however. One gets the image of a collapsing chain of dominos. Without moving in a circle, this procedure can yield a system in which every proposition is justified by some other only if the system is infinite. But it is dubious that any real human being's actual acceptance system contains an infinite number of beliefs. And it is notoriously hard to see how an infinite regress of justification provides any justification at all. This time the image is of an endless chain of falling dominos.

The second possibility, an adaptation of Bonjour's own suggestion (1986, 121), is to define a justified verific system as a subset of the verific system in which every proposition coheres with the rest of the subsystem. This suggestion will be either too strong or too weak to handle the case of Chuck and Don. It might rule that even Chuck cannot be justified in believing (5). For while (3) coheres with the other propositions, as does (4), (1) and (2) do not. (1) for example does not beat "Only those who get at least a 93 on a prelim get an A on it" relative to (2)-(5). Of course, Chuck might accept some other true propositions that make (1) and (2) more probable than competitors. But then Don might accept the same propositions totally without justification.

More seriously, the Bonjour criterion for a justified verific system is circular: if q and r are members of a justified verific system as defined, then q will be justified in relation to r and r will be justified in relation to q. Unfortunately, it is hard to see how such a circle could provide any justification for the members of such a system. To avoid the charge that we are merely begging the question by assuming a "linear" conception of justification[13], consider the system, belonging to Gus, involving the acceptance of the following propositions:

Dr. Smith shaves; Dr. Smith is a man;
Dr. Jones shaves; Dr. Jones is a man;
Dr. Johnson does not shave; Dr. Johnson is not a man;
Shaving is correlated with being a man.

Every member of this acceptance system coheres with the rest of the system. Nevertheless, the mere fact that these beliefs are "mutually supporting" gives them not the slightest degree of justification. Gus may have no evidence whatsoever for any one of these propositions. It is possible that he never saw Drs. Smith, Jones, and Johnson, never talked to anyone who knew them (although he heard their names mentioned), never read anything about them, and so on. His beliefs about them might be products of staring at tea leaves, pure articles of faith, or manifestations of dementia. His belief about the correlation might be another article of faith, or an inference from his groundless beliefs about the doctors. It might be suggested that because so many are true, Gus's beliefs about the doctors must be produced by a reliable mechanism, and therefore are justified. This idea can be dispelled by padding Gus's acceptance system with further beliefs that conform to the correlation but are false.

IVC. Second Response: Perception as External Basis

The necessity for some sort of external criterion to provide initially justified beliefs thus seems clear for the usual foundationalist reason: to avoid an infinite regress, or a circle, of justification. Perception is one of the most commonly cited sources of initially justified beliefs. Indeed, Lehrer himself says it is an "obvious truth" that "if we were all deprived of our senses, no one would be justified in believing there to be any objects of sense experience" (1974, 78). Lehrer's theory, however, implies no such thing. Consider another acceptance system, this time containing the acceptances of the following propositions, which are true.

(6) The triangle on the page is red.
(7) The rectangle on the page is red.
(8) The pentagon on the page is red.
(9) There is nothing else on the page.
(10) Every polygon on the page is red.

Both Ed and Fred accept these propositions. Both inferred (10) from (6)-(9). Ed's beliefs (6)-(9) are produced by sense-perception in the normal way: he is looking at the page in good light, has normal color vision, and can see everything on the page clearly. Fred is blind. Random misfirings of his brain have miraculously made him believe (6)-(9). Now observe that Lehrer's theory yields the absurd result that Fred is just as justified as Ed is in believing that every polygon on the page is red. Indeed, both know (10). For (10) coheres with (6)-(9) for both subjects. The fact that Ed's beliefs were the product of sense perception while Fred is blind is completely irrelevant on Lehrer's theory since it has nothing to do with their acceptance systems.

Note that it does not matter whether or not we describe either Ed or Fred as believing that he is seeing the page, as believing that the page looks a certain way, or as believing that his senses are trustworthy. First, Lehrer's theory does not require such beliefs. Lehrer says only that a belief is justified if it coheres with the subject's acceptance and verific systems, which means that the belief is more reasonable than competitors on the basis of the system. Lehrer defines the acceptance system as everything the subject accepts, and the verific system as everything true the subject accepts. None of this places any specific constraints on the contents of S's acceptance system. Second, (10) coheres with the subjects' acceptance and verific systems whether or not such beliefs are possessed. Note also that if Fred does believe (falsely) that the triangle looks red to him, it would not matter on Lehrer's theory whether or not this was any part of his reason for believing that the triangle is red. For as we observed above, the inferential structure of the subject's acceptance system is irrelevant to coherence.

IVD. Third Response: Bonjour's Observation Requirement

Bonjour concedes that "Any adequate account of empirical knowledge must *require*, not merely allow, input from the world into the cognitive system. For without such input any agreement between the system and the world would be purely fortuitous..." (1986, 133). Thus he imposes an "observation requirement." The question is how such a requirement can be imposed without producing a foundationalist theory. Bonjour first claims that a perceptual belief that the triangle is red is *"cognitively spontaneous,"* in that "it is not arrived at via any sort of conscious ratiocinative process, but simply occurs to me, strikes me, in a coercive manner over which I have no control" (Bonjour 1986, 125). He notes that introspective beliefs are similarly spontaneous. Then Bonjour formulates his observation requirement by saying that "for a cognitive system to be even a candidate for the status of empirical knowledge, it must include laws attributing a high degree of reliability to a reasonable variety of kinds of cognitively spontaneous belief..." (1986, 133).

Bonjour's observation requirement is not strong enough to help with the case of Fred. "Every polygon on the page is red" coheres with the rest of Fred's acceptance system. It will still cohere if Fred's system is augmented with principles saying that a reasonable variety of spontaneous beliefs are reliable. So Fred will remain justified in his belief even though it has no observational basis. The problem is this: insisting only that an acceptance system contain statements concerning the reliability of observation does not guarantee that those statements will be used to justify any beliefs in the system.

Bonjour must require something like this: To be justified, an empirical statement must cohere with, *and have a "spontaneous basis" in,* the subject's acceptance system and verific system. Given the general tenor of Bonjour's discussion (see 1986, 124-28), he might stipulate that p has a "direct" spontaneous basis if it can be inferred by the following schema:

> (i)   I have a spontaneous belief (of kind K) that p.
> (ii) Spontaneous beliefs (of kind K) are reliable.
> Therefore p.

That is, p will have a direct spontaneous basis in S's acceptance or verific system provided that system contains propositions of forms (i) and (ii). The parenthetical qualifications are to be activated if it is believed that only certain kinds of spontaneous beliefs are reliable. Bonjour might then offer a recursive definition of "spontaneous basis" in general: p has a spontaneous basis if it has a direct spontaneous basis or can be inferred from propositions with a spontaneous basis.

Even this proposal does not help with the case of Fred. Fred may believe (i) that he has a spontaneous belief that the triangle on the page is red. He may also believe (ii) that at least his spontaneous beliefs are reliable. Both these beliefs may be true. Nevertheless, Fred's belief that the triangle on the page is red has no observational basis because Fred is blind.

Bonjour might point out that the spontaneous belief mentioned in (i) was produced by a neural malfunction, and that spontaneous beliefs of that kind are not reliable. While this reinforces our claim that Fred is completely unjustified in his belief about the polygons, it does not help Bonjour's theory. For Fred may not know that his spontaneous belief about the triangle was produced by a malfunction. Moreover, Fred's belief about the reliability of his spontaneous beliefs in general may be true--despite the fact that his spontaneous belief about the triangle was produced by an unreliable mechanism--as long as such spontaneous beliefs are rare. That is, if 99.99% of all S's spontaneous beliefs are produced by reliable mechanisms such as (nonvisual) perception and introspection, then S's spontaneous beliefs in general will be reliable (very probably true) even though .01% are produced by unreliable mechanisms. This fact shows that it will not help for Bonjour to insist that a "kind K" be specified in every application of (i) and (ii). For spontaneous beliefs produced by perception, introspection, or Fred's rare malfunction form a kind of spontaneous belief, and a reliable kind. [14]

The basic problem is that S's acceptance and verific systems may contain propositions of form (i) and (ii) even though S's belief that p has nothing like a perceptual or introspective basis. So Bonjour should replace "spontaneous" with "observational," where this term includes both introspection and sense-perception.[15] The coherence theory will then say that an empirical statement must cohere with, and have an observational basis in, the subject's acceptance and verific systems, where a statement has a direct observational basis in a system if that system contains:

> (i')   I have an observational belief (of kind K) that p.
> (ii') Observational beliefs (of kind K) are reliable.

This observation requirement is still not strong enough to guarantee the appropriate observational basis for empirical justification. Suppose Ed tells Fran - who is blind like Fred - that the triangle is red. Fran justifiably believes him, and then infers that the triangle looks red to her. Then on Lehrer's theory, Fran may well be justified in believing that the triangle *looks* red even though she is *blind*! We need to suppose, of course, that Fran does not realize she is blind; so suppose her blindness is a temporary condition that just came over her.

Lehrer and Bonjour might insist that it is just psychologically impossible for a person to believe that something looks a certain way unless it does. First, that would not matter on Lehrer's theory, for being justified in accepting p does not require accepting p on Lehrer's theory. Second, such a belief is not impossible: all we need to imagine is that Fran is hallucinating, so that there appears to be a red triangle on the page. This would enable Fran to believe that the triangle on the page looks red even though it does not look any way to her because she is blind. Bonjour's observational requirement does not help here. True, "The triangle looks red" will not have a *direct* observational basis in Fran's verific system, since "I have an observational belief that the triangle looks red" will be false. Fran has that belief, but not on the basis of introspection or any other form of observation. However, Fran's belief that the triangle looks red may well have an *indirect* observational basis, since it is based on having heard Ed say that the triangle is red. We might solve this problem by requiring that a proposition self-ascribing a self-presenting state to S is justified only if it has a direct observational basis in S's acceptance and verific systems.

Since (i') must be in the verific system, it must be true. Thus (i'), unlike (i), represents a significant *external* constraint on justification. Indeed, the resulting version of the coherence theory incorporates the key tenet of foundationalism: an empirical belief is justified only if it is an observational belief or is inferable from an observational belief. In other words, we have a hybrid theory, part foundationalist, part coherentist. The main point distinguishing this hybrid from a pure foundationalist theory is its denial that any belief have a purely external justification. That is, Bonjour denies that any observational belief p is justified just because it is an observational belief. Rather, it is justified only if it is also inferable from beliefs (i') and (ii'). This part of Bonjour's theory was criticized in section II, when we considered introspective beliefs in particular.

IVE. Fourth Response: Metaknowledge
    A new question arises. The requirement that some beliefs be observational beliefs is *necessary* to explain, among other things, why Fred's beliefs about the polygons, and Fran's about the way they look, are not justified. This requirement also seems *sufficient* for that task. So what is the point of Bonjour's additional requirement that an observational belief be inferable from beliefs (i') and (ii')? Why not simply adopt a causal theory, according to which observation is a source of initially justified beliefs because it is one of the designated causal processes, or a reliabilist theory, according to which observation is such a source because it is a reliable process?
    Lehrer provides an answer. He criticizes causal and reliabilist theories on the grounds that a true belief can arise in circumstances that are highly deceptive, in which case they will not be justified or constitute knowledge.

> Consider a simple belief. A person sees a red patch, and her seeing a red patch causes her to believe that she sees a red patch. That is a paradigmatic instance of the appropriate etiology to yield knowledge. But does she know that she sees a red patch? Her conviction may fall short of knowledge. Suppose that she is looking at a painted red patch on a wall in a room where there appear to be several such red patches which are quite indistinguishable from each other in quality. Suppose, moreover, some of the patches are painted red patches while others are the result of projecting a red light on the wall. If the person seeing the painted red patch cannot tell a red patch from a spot that is merely illuminated with red light, then she does not know that she sees a painted red patch when she sees one, for she cannot tell a painted red patch from an illusion in this context. We may imagine, furthermore, that the person has no idea that she is confronted with any illuminated spots. The problem is that the person assumes, incorrectly, that circumstances are those in which she can tell the real thing when she sees one (Lehrer 1986, 22).

We recognize the problem here, but doubt that Lehrer's theory provides the solution. Suppose Tina accepts the following true propositions.

> (11) Things are the way they appear on *this* small part of the wall.
> (12) There appears to be a painted red patch on this part of the wall.
> (13) There is a painted red patch on this part of the wall.

Given that (11) and (12) are in Tina's acceptance and verific systems, (13) will defeat all competitors. Hence Lehrer's theory wrongly rules that Tina *does* know (13).
    Lehrer indicates in the passage just quoted that Tina does not know (13) because she incorrectly assumes (14):

> (14) Circumstances are those in which I (Tina) can tell painted red patches from
>   illuminated ones.

First of all, nothing in Lehrer's definitions of coherence, justification, or knowledge *requires* that Tina accept (14). So Lehrer would do well to modify his theory along the lines suggested by Bonjour, requiring that a justified belief p not only cohere with, but also have an observational basis in, the subject's acceptance and verific system. Moreover, to handle the problem of deceptive circumstances, the definition of direct observational basis must refer to the conditions of observation. Adapting another idea of Bonjour's (1986, 124-28), let us say that p has a direct observational basis in S's acceptance and verific systems only if they contain:

(i")   I have an observational belief (of kind K) that p.
(ii")   Observational beliefs (of kind K) are reliable in condition C.
(iii")   Condition C obtains.

In the case of Tina, the kind of belief involved consists of beliefs about painted red spots on walls. Then in order for (ii") to be in Tina's verific system, Lehrer would insist, the conditions involved must be those in which Tina can tell painted red spots from illuminated ones. But then (iii") will not be in Tina's verific system because (14) is false. So Tina's belief that there is a painted red spot on the wall will not have an observational basis, as defined, in Tina's verific system. Hence her belief will not be justified.

Thus modified, Lehrer's theory implies that anyone with any justified empirical beliefs must have what Lehrer calls "metaknowledge," knowledge about when "object beliefs" are reliable. Lehrer thinks it a "plausible psychological assumption" that every knowledgeable subject has the appropriate metaknowledge (see "Metaknowledge: Undefeated Justification"). We do not agree. While it is undeniably plausible that *some* people who know propositions like (13) also accept propositions like (14), it does not seem plausible that *all* people do. Surely a young child may know that there is a painted red patch on the wall without believing anything as sophisticated as that he can discriminate painted red patches from illuminated ones.[16] Of course, the child must be *able* to tell painted red patches from illuminated ones, and must *not* believe that he *cannot* do so. But that does not imply that he must have a positive belief about his discriminatory powers. Similarly, we ourselves have many times in our adult lives known that there were painted red patches on a wall. But the idea that they might have been illuminated red patches - or patches of blood demonically oozing through the wall, or mysterious light-emitting patches, or anything else of this sort - never entered our minds at the time. Hence we *did not believe* that we could discriminate a painted red patch from these other things (nor, or course, did we believe that we could not). It is not just that this belief was "natural" and consequently went "unnoticed," as Lehrer suggests. While we *would* have formed this belief if we had thought about the matter, we never even considered whether the paint might be light spots.

Citing Reid, Lehrer insists that it is simply part of "our natural constitution" to accept the trustworthiness of our senses, memory, and other faculties. But any such belief general enough to be possessed by every human being in any situation will not be specific enough to play the role Lehrer assigned to (14). By no stretch of the imagination is (14) part of "our natural constitution." So the idea that perceptual knowledge requires accepting something like (14) seems much too strong.[17]

It is also unclear whether our modification of Lehrer's theory is really strong enough to rule that Tina is not justified in her belief about the red spot. The problem is that S will be justified in believing p as long as there is *some* condition C such that S truly believes both (ii") and (iii"). Thus for Tina, let C be "conditions in which things are the way they appear to be on this part of the wall." Then because (11) and (12) are true, Tina may indeed have an observational basis, as defined, for her belief that there is a painted red spot on the wall. Some further restriction needs to be placed on C, but it is hard to see how to do this without making the theory impossibly restrictive.

Furthermore, the "lucky guess" problem arises anew. In order for S to be justified in believing one empirical proposition p, p must cohere with a verific system containing (ii") and (iii"). But these are significant empirical propositions themselves. What if S's beliefs that they are true are simply lucky guesses? Worse yet, what if they are the fortuitous products of completely irrational reasoning? Lehrer himself confronts the "lucky guess" problem in "Metaknowledge." He observes that a lucky guess - a belief that just happens to be true - does not suffice for justification or knowledge. He also observes that requiring one belief to cohere with another hardly helps, since the second belief itself might be a lucky guess.

Lehrer thinks there is an escape from this regress of lucky guesses. On his view, S's belief about a perceived object will be justified only if it coheres with a verific system containing S's belief that his senses are trustworthy. S's belief that his senses are trustworthy will be justified only if it coheres with a verific system containing S's belief that he is a trustworthy evaluator. This latter belief, however, will not be justified in terms of any other belief. It is essentially the *foundation* of S's justification and knowledge.

While we might wonder how Lehrer can still claim to be advocating a coherence theory, it is more important to ask what justifies S in believing that he is a trustworthy evaluator. Lehrer observes first that this belief is true: S is a trustworthy evaluator, at least assuming that he is a normal adult human being. Then Lehrer concludes that *since S's belief that he is a trustworthy evaluator is the evaluation of a trustworthy evaluator, it is not just a lucky guess.* But this conclusion does not follow. Even trustworthy evaluators may make lucky guesses on occasion. What Lehrer needs to show is that S's particular belief about his own trustworthiness is not one of his rare lucky guesses. Moreover, if as Lehrer holds, every normal adult truly believes that he is a trustworthy evaluator, and if every evaluation of a trustworthy evaluator is *ipso facto* justified, then it will follow straightforwardly that every true belief of a normal adult will be justified.

V. Conclusion

The most important question with which we began this paper was: *Can an internally coherent system of beliefs without external foundation provide any justification at all?* Our last section showed that the answer provided by a coherence theory like Lehrer's is *Yes.* The section also showed that an affirmative answer is most definitely incorrect, and that the theory can be improved only by adding key tenets of foundationalism. In addition, we have shown that Lehrer's basic conception of coherence is unnecessary for the justification of basic beliefs, and wrongly makes the inferential structure of a subject's beliefs irrelevant to justification. So Lehrer's development has not overcome the major objection to a pure coherence theory of justification. We believe that our arguments are strong enough to require a new generation of defenses from the committed coherence theorist. But given its present state of collapse, we are doubtful that any reconstruction will be successful. Indeed, we submit that the facts presented which have led to the downfall of the coherence theory show that only a foundationalist view of justification is tenable.[18]

NOTES

1. This has not always been appreciated. Many advocates of the correspondence theory of truth, for example, attempt to define "correspondence with the facts" as correspondence with the *perceptually given facts*. And many who find the correspondence theory implausible do so because they assume such a definition is required. But correspondence of beliefs with perceptually given facts is necessary (if at all) only to provide some external justification for the beliefs. Correspondence with any type of fact is sufficient for a belief to be true.
2. Our main source is "The Coherence Theory of Knowledge" (1986), which revises the theory presented in Knowledge (1974). The revised theory is also defended in "The Gettier Problem and the Analysis of Knowledge" (1979), "Justification, Truth, and Coherence" (Lehrer and Cohen 1983), and "Metaknowledge: Undefeated Justification" (1988).
3. "Technical Flaws in the Coherence Theory," *Synthese,* forthcoming.
4. In "The Coherence Theory of Empirical Knowledge" (1986).
5. We discuss problems with the concept of neutralization in "Technical Flaws in the Coherence Theory."
6. Actually, Lehrer himself excludes a probability of 1: "We, like the skeptic, admit there to be a genuine chance that any of our beliefs may be false" (1974, 240). This is surely false: The probability is 0 that our belief in "It either will or will not rain today" is false. Fortunately, Lehrer's *theory* does not exclude a probability of 1.
7. We argue in "Technical Flaws in the Coherence Theory" that this understanding of competition makes

Lehrer's analysis of justification too strong, and that as a result his analysis of knowledge rules incorrectly in other cases.

8. Cf. Audi (1982). BonJour airs a similar issue: whether the subject actually infers (3) from (1) and (2). "It is not necessary that the belief [in 3] actually originate via inference, however tacit or even unconscious; but it must be the case that a tacit grasp of the availability of the inference is the basis for the continuing acceptance of the belief and for the conviction that it is warranted" (BonJour 1986, 129). We are not sure what BonJour means, but he seems to be saying that the subject is justified in believing (3) because he believes tacitly that he could infer it from (1) and (2). We doubt that many subjects have such sophisticated beliefs even tacitly. Note that if the subject does not actually believe (1) and (2), then he could not have inferred (3) from them.

9. We are not questioning the intelligibility of endlessly iterated belief statements, only their truth. Lehrer and Cohen (1983, 198-99) thus missed the point when they answered a question about the "psychological reality" of iterated beliefs by arguing that iterated belief statements can be understood. Lehrer also argues for a "doxastic iteration principle" in *Knowledge* (1974, 229-30). There he concludes that *if S believes p then S believes he believes p* from the premise that *if S believes p then S is convinced that p and is ready to affirm p*. But we do not see how this conclusion follows, and also find the premise questionable. BonJour agrees that an endless iteration of belief is psychologically implausible (1986, 131). But apparently his argument that (1) did not need the adjective "spontaneous" led him to think that (1) without (2) would justify (3).

10. This point is also made by John Pollock in his 1986, 146.

11. Cf. Lehrer 1979, 75.

12. This is what Lehrer proposed in *Knowledge* (1974, ch. 9), except there he used the term "verific alternative" for what we have called the "strongly corrected acceptance system." (Lehrer used "corrected accepted system" in Knowledge for something different.) In "Metaknowledge," Lehrer says that S's justification for accepting p depends on no falsehood when p coheres with every member of S's "ultrasystem," which contains every system obtainable from S's acceptance system by deleting one or more falsehoods or replacing them with truths. Questions concerning complete justification are to be answered by determining p's coherence to weakly corrected members of the ultrasystem, in which falsehoods have been deleted without replacement. Questions concerning knowledge must be answered by determining p's coherence to strongly corrected members as well, in which falsehoods are deleted and replaced by truths. What we have called S's strongly corrected acceptance system will be one member of S's ultrasystem, the crucial member in our view.

13. Cf. BonJour 1986, 120-21, and Lehrer 1986, 21-22.

14. Cf. Feldman's (1985) arguments concerning the "generality problem."

15. BonJour does not want to restrict "observation" to sense-perception and introspection, though. He thinks that other processes - such as clairvoyance, telepathy, and the use of certain instruments - should count as observation if they are sufficiently reliable.

16. In "Metaknowledge," Lehrer suggests that "know" has a different sense when we say that a child knows there is a red patch than when we say that an adult does. See also Lehrer and Cohen (1983), 200. We see no such ambiguity in the word "know," though we see plenty of differences between a child's knowledge and an adult's. If Lehrer is right, a statement like "John knows there's a red patch" should have the same sort of ambiguity as "Anna Karinena is romantic." The latter is ambiguous because "Anna Karinena" can refer to a person or a work of literature, and "romantic" has very different meanings when applied to people and literary works. "John knows there's a red patch" does not seem to change meaning in the same way even though "John" can refer to an adult or a child. Hence "John Davis (a child) knows there is a red patch and John Bender (an adult) knows there is a red patch, therefore they both know there is a red patch" is a valid argument (this point is due to John Greco). Note that when "John" refers to a robot, "know" does seem to change meaning (we tend to hear scare-quotes around it), and a similar argument would be invalid.

17. Bender argues at length against the idea that justification requires such "higher-order evaluations" in "Knowledge, Justification, and Lehrer's Theory of Coherence" and in "The Ins and Outs of Metaknowledge."

18. We would like to thank Keith Lehrer, Robert Audi, Kevin Possin, and John Greco for helpful comments on an earlier version of this paper.

REFERENCES

Audi, Robert. "Believing and Affirming." *Mind* 91 (1982), 115-20.
Bender, John W. "The Ins and Outs of Metaknowledge." *Analysis*, October, 1988.
-----. "Knowledge, Justification, and Lehrer's Theory of Coherence." *Philosophical Studies* (1988), 49-75.
Bonjour, Laurence. "The Coherence Theory of Empirical Knowledge." In *Empirical Knowledge*, P. Moser, ed., Roman and Littlefield, 1986, 116-43. Reprinted from *Philosophical Studies* 30 (1976), 281-312.
Davis, Wayne and Bender, John W. "Technical Flaws in the Coherence Theory." *Synthese* (forthcoming).
Feldman, Richard. "Reliability and Justification." *Monist* 68 (1985), 159-74.
Lehrer, Keith. *Knowledge*. Oxford: Clarendon Press, 1974.
-----. "The Gettier Problem and the Analysis of Knowledge." In *Justification and Knowledge*, G. Pappas, ed.,

Dordrecht: Reidel, 1979, 65-78.
-----. "The Coherence Theory of Knowledge." *Philosophical Topics* 14 (1986), 5-25.
-----. "Metaknowledge: Undefeated Justification." *Synthese* 74 (1988), 329-347.
-----, and Cohen, Stewart. "Justification, Truth, and Coherence." *Synthese* 55 (1983), 191-207.
Pollock, John. *Contemporary Theories of Knowledge.* Totowa, New Jersey: Roman and Littlefield, 1986.

Lehrer's Coherence Theory of Knowledge

Richard Feldman
University of Rochester

In two recent papers (1986 and 1988), Keith Lehrer has developed the coherence theory of knowledge and justification that he originally proposed in *Knowledge*. In broad outline, Lehrer's new view is that one has knowledge when "the right combination of internal and external factors" are present, and this obtains when there "is a rational connection between subjective states and truth." (1988, 330) Knowledge requires the proper "evaluation of incoming information in terms of background information." (1988, 330) When a proposition coheres with one's new information and one's background information, it is justified. But this sort of justification is merely "personal justification". One's background information might be largely erroneous, so coherence with it (together with truth) is not sufficient for knowledge. What is required is also coherence with a system resulting from correcting the errors in the background system. When such coherence obtains, one has undefeated justification and, therefore, knowledge.

In my view, the abstract and general idea Lehrer advances is quite plausible. Knowledge does require the right mix of the objective and the subjective. Justification does require the proper evaluation of information in the light of background beliefs. Moreover, by requiring coherence with corrected belief systems, Lehrer is deviating from typical coherence theories in a promising way. However, I have serious reservations about the adequacy of the more precise theory Lehrer develops. Many of the questions I want to raise turn on features of the primitive notion of comparative reasonableness that he uses. In this paper I will examine a series of examples that reveal the obscurity of his primitive, and the implausibility of the supposition that the primitive can be interpreted in a way that gives the theory acceptable results.

I

Lehrer's theory is elegantly stated in a series of definitions beginning with a generic notion of justification.(1988, 341-344) He then defines some more specific notions of justification that are used in the definition of knowledge. The generic notion of justification is defined as follows:

> (D2) S is justified in accepting p at t on the basis of system X of S at t if and only if p coheres with X of S at t. [1]

The concept of coherence used here is defined this way:

> (D3) p coheres with X of S at t if and only if all competitors of p are beaten or neutralized for S on X at t.

This definition makes use of the technical notions of competition, beating a competitor, and neutralizing a competitor. These are defined as follows:

> (D4) c competes with p for S on X at t if and only if it is more reasonable for S to accept that p on the assumption that c is false than on the assumption that c is true on the basis of X at t.

> (D5) p beats c for S on X at t if and only if c competes with p for S on X at t, and it is more reasonable for S to accept p than to accept c on X at t.

69

J.W. Bender (ed.), The Current State of the Coherence Theory, 69–76.
© *1989 by Kluwer Academic Publishers.*

(D6) n neutralizes c as a competitor of p for S on X at t if and only c competes with p for S on X at t, the conjunction of c and n does not compete with p for S on X at t, and it is as reasonable for S to accept the conjunction of c and n as to accept c alone on X at t.

Definitions (D3) - (D6) provide the basis for understanding the definiens of the generic conception of justification defined in (D2). Notice that (D2) merely characterizes justification relative to a system, but no mention is made of any specific system. The theory of knowledge that Lehrer proposes requires justification relative to one's actual acceptance system as well justification relative to a series of corrected versions of that system. The actual acceptance system of a person, S, at a time is the set of all statements of the form "S accepts that p" that are true at that time. An actual acceptance system can contain numerous errors in that it may report (correctly) that a person accepts statements that are false. Acceptance systems with such errors can be corrected by simply eliminating reports of false statements that are accepted (weak corrections) and they can be corrected by replacing reports of falsehoods accepted with reports of acceptance of their denials (strong corrections). The "ultrasystem" of a person is the set of acceptance systems which "includes the [actual] acceptance system as one member and includes as other members any system resulting from making one or more weak or strong corrections in the acceptance system." (1988, 344)

With these concepts in hand we can define undefeated justification:

(D8) S is justified in accepting that p at t in a way that is undefeated if and only if S is justified in accepting p at t on the basis of every system that is a member of the ultrasystem of S at t.

Finally, Lehrer proposes defining knowledge in terms of undefeated justification:

(E) S knows that p at t if and only if S is justified in accepting p at t in a way that is undefeated.

Since undefeated justification implies both truth and acceptance, this is a version of a traditional analysis of knowledge.

A simple example will illustrate the way these seemingly complex definitions are intended to work. I accept the statement that Ronald Reagan was President of the United States in 1985. Potential competitors with this statement are statements such as that Carter was President at that time, that Nancy Reagan was President, etc.. But the statement that Ronald Reagan was President in 1985 beats all of these competitors on my actual acceptance system because, on that system, it is more reasonable for me to accept it than any of the competitors. Similarly, it beats those competitors relative to all the members of my ultrasystem since (let us assume) all the relevant pieces of evidence I accept concerning this statement are true and thus are retained in all those acceptance systems. Therefore, there is no correction of my acceptance system relative to which the statement that Reagan was President in 1985 fails to beat (or neutralize) its competitors. So, it is justified relative to all those systems. Thus, I know that Reagan was President in 1985.[2]

Contrast this with something I accept but do not know, for example that Dwight Gooden will be on the all-star team in 1994. This proposition does not beat all its competitors, such as the proposition star athletes sometimes lose their skills over a 6 year period. These brief examples illustrate the way the system is supposed to work. More details about how it is supposed to work, and some possible problems, will emerge in the sections that follow.

II

Two good ways to evaluate a theory of knowledge and justification are to consider how it deals with a range of examples that have been discussed following the publication of Edmund Gettier's "Is Justified True Belief Knowledge?" and to consider how it deals with skepticism. I will consider skepticism first.

Lehrer claims that his theory provides a satisfactory response to skepticism because, relative to our typical acceptance systems, skeptical hypotheses are beaten or neutralized by their common sense rivals. As an example of the way in which Lehrer's theory is supposed to avoid skepticism, consider the proposition that I now see a monitor. Competitors to this proposition include the proposition that I am hallucinating and the proposition that people sometimes hallucinate. According to Lehrer, the former proposition is beaten by the proposition that I see a monitor since it is more reasonable for me to believe that I see a monitor than to believe that I am hallucinating. The proposition that people sometimes hallucinate is also a competitor, but, according to Lehrer, it is neutralized by the proposition that I am not now hallucinating. In support of this claim, Lehrer asserts that the conjunction of the statements that people sometimes hallucinate and that I am not hallucinating does not compete with the statement that I see a monitor (since the second conjunct in effect disarms, or neutralizes, the first) and it is as reasonable for me to accept the conjunction as it is to accept the simple statement that people sometimes hallucinate.

This later claim, of course, is apt to arouse suspicion, and Lehrer anticipates the objection. Although the conjunction cannot be as probable the one conjunct alone, Lehrer claims that accepting the conjunction involves only negligible risk and that if "the acceptance of a more informative statement involves only a negligibly greater risk of error than accepting a less informative one, then it is as reasonable to accept the more informative as the less informative one." (1986, 11)

The obscurity of Lehrer's primitive makes this response difficult to refute, but it is unclear why it would succeed without making the theory imply that we have knowledge in cases in which we clearly do not. Consider, for example, a person who has evidence based on opinion polls early in an election campaign supporting the proposition that candidate X will win. Suppose that the evidence is strong enough to make believing this proposition more reasonable than believing its denial, but not sufficiently strong to yield knowledge. Specific competitors, such as the proposition that some other candidate will win or the proposition that most voters will change their minds, are less reasonable and therefore beaten. More general competitors, such as the proposition that candidates who are ahead in early opinion polls sometimes lose, are, apparently, neutralized in just the way described above. In this case, the competitor is neutralized provided it is as reasonable to believe the conjunction of the proposition that candidates who are ahead in early polls sometimes lose and the proposition that candidate X will not lose as it is to believe the first conjunct alone. The argument for this being the case is exactly like the one above in the hallucination example. So, Lehrer's theory apparently implies, incorrectly, that we have knowledge in some cases in which we have reasonable, but not fully justified, beliefs.

There is additional support for the view that Lehrer's theory avoids skepticism only by dealing incorrectly with propositions that are reasonable to believe without being known. A key element of his view is that comparative reasonability is a function of a combination of informativeness and risk of error. Thus, when two propositions are equally risky, but one is more informative than the other, the more informative one is more reasonable. This suggests that comparatively less well supported but highly informative propositions will be more reasonable than their competitors, and thus justified and known, while equally well supported but less informative propositions will not be. That is a highly counterintuitive result.

Although it remains possible that there is a way to assess comparative reasonableness that avoids these results, Lehrer has provided no such account and no intuitive interpretation yields the results Lehrer needs. It appears, therefore, that his theory avoids skepticism only by implying that too many propositions are justified and known.

III

A second major test for theories of knowledge and justification concerns their treatment of Gettier-style examples. It will be useful to begin discussion of this topic by considering a variation on an example first proposed by Lehrer himself. (Lehrer, 1965)

Suppose Smith works in an office with Jones. Smith has seen Jones driving a Ford, heard Jones say that he owns a Ford, seen a certificate of Ford ownership in Jones's possession, etc. Smith thus has a great deal of evidence supporting the proposition that Jones owns a Ford. We can express this evidence in the sentence:

  1. Jones, who works in the office, says he owns a Ford, etc..

Smith knows (1) to be true and this justifies him in accepting:

  2. Jones, who works in the office, owns a Ford.

On the basis of (2) he is justified in accepting its implication:

  3. Someone who works in the office owns a Ford.

In the discussion that follows it will be useful to assume that Smith also accepts the proposition:

  4. No one in the office other than Jones owns a Ford.

What makes this a Gettier case, of course, is that although (1) and (3) are true, (2) is false. Jones merely aspires to Ford ownership and pretends to own one. However, (3) is still true because someone else in the office, not known to Smith, does own a Ford. The clear and almost universal intuition is that Smith does not know (3) to be true even though it is a truth he accepts with justification.

For Lehrer's theory to deal with this case properly it must be that Smith's justification for (3) is defeated. Thus, it must fail to cohere with some member of his ultrasystem. This requires that it fail to beat or neutralize some competitor relative to some member of the ultrasystem.

Relative to Smith's actual acceptance system, it seems clear that accepting (3) is justified. Competitors of (3) are propositions such as the proposition that Jones does not own a Ford, that Jones is merely pretending to own a Ford, that no one in the office owns a Ford, etc. But it is more reasonable for Smith to believe (3), that someone in the office owns a Ford, than it is to believe any of these competitors. So, relative to his actual system, (3) is justified. In Lehrer's terminology, Smith is personally justified in accepting (3). That is the standard view about Gettier cases and there is no reason to think that Lehrer's theory goes astray at this point.

Since (3) is justified relative to Smith's actual acceptance system, for the theory to avoid the incorrect result that Smith knows (3), it must be that (3) is not justified on the basis of some other element of Smith's ultrasystem. Consider first the element of the ultrasystem in which all of Smith's false beliefs are replaced by truths. In this element of the ultrasystem, the false proposition (4) will be replaced by its true denial. So, this system will include acceptance of the proposition that someone in the office other than Jones owns a Ford. Presumably, then, relative to this system it is also more reasonable to believe (3) than its denial (or any of its other competitors), so (3) is justified relative to this completely true system. The reason (3) is justified relative to this system is that, in effect, by replacing *all* the falsehoods in Smith's actual system by their denials, the false (4) is replaced by a truth that provides a new line of support for (3).

Thus, for the theory to have the correct implications, it must be that (3) is not justified relative to a different member of Smith's ultrasystem, most likely relative to some member in which this new support for (3) is not added. The most plausible candidate is the acceptance system just like the actual one except that (2) is replaced by its denial. The idea is that in this system (3) loses the support it had from (1) via (2), but does not gain any new support. Let us call this acceptance system N. The relevant statements in N are the following:

5. Smith accepts the proposition that Jones, who works in the office, says that he owns a Ford, etc. (i.e., Smith accepts (1).)

6. Smith accepts the proposition that it is not the case that Jones, who works in the office, owns a Ford. (i.e., Smith accepts ~(2).)

7. Smith accepts the proposition that someone who works in the office owns a Ford. (i.e., Smith accepts (3).)

8. Smith accepts the proposition that no one in the office other than Jones owns a Ford. (i.e., Smith accepts (4).)

The key question, then, is whether Smith is justified in accepting (3) on the basis of N. If the theory implies that Smith is justified in accepting (3) relative to N, then Lehrer's theory does not avoid standard Gettier style examples.

According to (D2), Smith is justified in accepting (3) relative to N just in case (3) coheres with N. According to (D3), (3) coheres with N just in case it beats or neutralizes all of its competitors. One obvious and crucial competitor to (3) is its denial, the proposition that no one who works in the office owns a Ford. So let us consider whether (3) beats or neutralizes this competitor.

(3) beats ~(3) on N if it is more reasonable for Smith to accept (3) than ~(3) on N. Now, one might think that (3) does not beat ~(3) on N since N includes Smith's acceptance of (4) and ~(2) and they imply ~(3). But that surely is inadequate to show that ~(3) is more reasonable than (3) on N. This is because N also includes Smith's acceptance of (1), which supports (2) and thus (3). So, arguably, on N it is more reasonable for Smith is to accept (2) and (3) rather than ~(2) and ~(3). Indeed, there is no good reason to think that what's reasonable to accept relative to N is at all different from what's reasonable to accept relative to Smith's actual acceptance system since the basic evidence, (1), is the same in both systems. The only difference is that in N Smith fails to accept (2), which is obviously supported by (1). But the fact that he does not accept what (1) supports does not make accepting those things unreasonable.

The example under consideration is particularly troublesome partly because the conjunction of things accepted by Smith in N is inconsistent. In N, S accepts (1), the evidence concerning Jones's Ford ownership; he accepts (3), the proposition that someone in the office owns a Ford; he accepts (4), the proposition that no one in the office other than Jones owns a Ford; but he does not accept the consequence of these, (2), that Jones owns a Ford. Instead, in N, he accepts ~(2). Unless the inconsistencies accepted in N are all justified in N, something that Smith accepts in N must fail to beat or neutralize all its competitors.[3] Lehrer's assumption is that (3) is the proposition that loses out. But other alternatives are possible. My suggestion is that ~(2) fails to beat its competitors, since N includes Smith's acceptance of strong evidence for the denial of (2). The question is whether, relative to this inconsistent acceptance system, it is more reasonable for Smith to believe that Jones does own a Ford, and thus accept (2) and (3), or it is more reasonable for Smith to believe that no one in the office owns a Ford. (It is also possible, of course, that (3) and ~(3) are equally reasonable relative to N, and this would suffice to establish the desired result that (3) is not justified for S on N.)

Lehrer has said very little about how comparative reasonability is determined, about how changes in acceptance systems affect the rest of the system, and about how to deal with inconsistent acceptance systems. Without a much more elaborate account of comparative reasonableness, we have no reason at all to think that Lehrer's theory has the desired results and we therefore have no reason to think that the theory deals properly with this sort of Gettier case.

In "The Coherence Theory" Lehrer does discuss probability, conditionalization, and reasonableness. He says that "other things being equal, the more probable a statement is, the more reasonable it is to accept it" (12) and that "probability is conditional on some background system." (13) However, those remarks and the rest of his discussion do not help deal with the present problem. The present problem is caused by the fact the probability of propositions added in the corrected systems is unspecified. There is good reason to assign propositions such as ~(2), when they are added to systems such as N, very low probability. This is because the system contains strong evidence for their denials. Moreover, given Jones's background beliefs, it seems that (2) is highly probable relative to N, even though it is not accepted in N. If so, this and other standard Gettier-cases are not avoided by this theory.

Possibly Lehrer could avoid the problem just described by stipulating that propositions added to an acceptance system are given high probabilities and that other probabilities are adjusted on that basis. If so, then in N ~(2) is given a high probability and, presumably, (2) and (3) will have low probabilities. But this proposal has two serious drawbacks. For one, if ~(2) has a very high probability in N, then it would seem that (1) must have a low probability in N. If Jones doesn't own a Ford, then it is unlikely that he said he did, etc. So, it seems that, relative to N, (1) will not beat or neutralize all its competitors (especially general skeptical competitors) and thus the theory implies, on this interpretation, that (1) is not known. But that is a clear mistake. In addition, avoiding Gettier-cases in this way exacerbates the problem to be discussed in Section V.

IV

There are variations on standard Gettier cases that, I think, pose an even greater problem for Lehrer's theory than the one already considered. These are cases in which there is no falsehood that plays any direct role in supporting the justified true belief that is not knowledge. Consider a case just like the one above except that, unbeknownst to Jones, Jones does own a Ford as a result of just having won one in a lottery.[4] We may assume that in this version of the example no one else in the office owns a Ford. Thus, all of (1) - (4) are true and Smith accepts them in his actual acceptance system and in every system within his ultrasystem. Therefore, it appears that (3) remains well-supported relative to all members of the ultrasystem and thus that its justification is undefeated. So, the theory implies, incorrectly, that this is a case of knowledge.

By considering additional propositions that Smith accepts it is possible that some falsehoods will be encountered. For example, he might accept the statement that Jones owns the car he drove to work today, which is false. One might argue that in elements of the ultrasystem in which these falsehoods are corrected, (3) is not justified. However, it is not at all clear that there must be any such falsehoods that Smith actually accepts, although there surely are false statements that he would accept if he were to consider them. Thus, unless acceptance is construed rather broadly, there need not be any relevant falsehoods that Smith accepts in this sort of case. Moreover, since so much of the evidence for (2) and (3) is true and thus is retained in every element of the ultrasystem, these minor changes seem inadequate to render (3) unjustified. As a result, it is reasonable to conclude that the justification for (3) is undefeated and that Lehrer's theory implies, incorrectly, that Smith does have knowledge in this example.

V

At the end of section III I mentioned a second problem that arises when propositions added to acceptance systems are assigned high probabilities. In this section I will discuss that problem. One collection of troublesome cases discussed in the Gettier literature concerns misleading defeaters. These are true but misleading propositions that would undermine a person's knowledge if the person knew of them, but don't undermine that knowledge when the person doesn't know of them.

Probably the most discussed example concerning misleading defeaters was first proposed by Lehrer and Paxson. (1968) Suppose S sees Tom, whom he knows well, steal a book from the library. S knows that Tom stole the book. But suppose that, unbeknownst to S, Tom's mother has said that Tom's identical twin stole the book. This statement is a defeater. But if we assume further that Tom's mother is demented, that Tom has no twin brother, and that Tom did steal the book just as S thinks, then we are still inclined to think that S knows that Tom stole the book. The existence of the false statement of the demented mother does not undermine S's knowledge. Knowledge is not undermined by the existence of false counter-testimony by unreliable sources. The true statement - that the mother said these things - is a misleading defeater.

If there are misleading defeaters, it is clear that Lehrer's theory will not deal with them correctly if additions to acceptance systems are assigned high probabilities. Assume that in the example just described S accepts the false statement that no one who knows Tom has said that Tom did not steal the book. Now consider that element of S's ultrasystem in which this falsehood is replaced by its denial. Relative to that acceptance system, the statement that Tom stole the book will not beat all its competitors since relative to that system it is considerably less probable than it is relative to the actual acceptance system.

I assume here that changing the acceptance system affects comparative reasonableness in the general way that Lehrer describes in other cases. Specifically, the added truth is assigned a high probability and appropriate adjustments are made to the other statements in the system. Thus, adding the statement that someone who knows Tom has said that he didn't take the book does make the statement that he took the book less probable. It will, therefore, not beat or neutralize all its competitors relative to this system. For example, since it is less probable on this system than on the actual system, it cannot neutralize on this system the general skeptical hypotheses that it neutralizes on the actual system.

Of course, Lehrer could propose interpreting his primitive in a way that does not have this implication. But if he does interpret comparative reasonableness in a way that makes the statement that Tom stole the book beat all its competitors in this example (where all its defeaters are misleading), then the statement would also beat all its competitors in other cases in which it has a genuine, or non-misleading, defeater. For example, if it beats all competitors in this case, then it also beats all competitors in cases in which there is testimony against it by a generally reliable, but mistaken, person. More generally, there is little plausibility to the idea that a statement that has only misleading defeaters beats or neutralizes all its competitors in all members of the ultrasystem and that statements that have genuine defeaters fail to beat or neutralize all of their competitors. In other words, the truths of standard Gettier counter-examples will turn out have undefeated justifications.

The problem for Lehrer then, is to distinguish properly between misleading and genuine defeaters. Because the basic notion of comparative reasonableness is not well-developed, it is not possible to establish that the theory does not handle this distinction properly. However, consideration of examples suggests that it does not. The reason is that one's actual acceptance system will contain falsehoods that conflict with misleading defeaters. In one's ultrasystem there will be systems in which these falsehoods are replaced by their denials. But relative to such systems these misleading defeaters will be defeaters. That is, they will defeat the justification for propositions that actually are known. There appears to be no way to avoid this result without making genuine defeaters ineffective.

Lehrer's mistake, I believe, is requiring justification relative to all corrections of one's actual system. Justification relative to corrections associated with misleading defeaters ought not be required. Instead, justification should be required relative to systems formed by correcting only genuine defeaters. However, to include this condition in the theory in any precise way requires an adequate specification of what a genuine defeater is. That is something that neither Lehrer nor anyone else, to my knowledge, has been able to do in an acceptable way.

VI

I conclude that Lehrer has not provided a theory of knowledge and justification that provides the basis for a satisfactory response to skepticism or that deals adequately with Gettier-style examples. While I endorse the general ideas he mentions while broadly characterizing his view, I believe that serious problems arise in the details. In part, the problems are caused by Lehrer's reliance on an unanalyzed notion of comparative reasonableness and his unsupported claims about the comparative reasonability of propositions relative to non-actual acceptance systems. There is, of course, nothing wrong with his appealing to some primitive, nor is there anything wrong with appeal to a primitive with significant epistemic content. The problem is that a much more fully developed theory of comparative reasonableness and its application to non-actual acceptance systems is needed before we have grounds to think that his theory can avoid the consequences described above.

NOTES
1. For reasons that I will not discuss here, Lehrer develops his theory in terms of *acceptance* not belief.
2. I will discuss in section II the way Lehrer deals with competing general skeptical hypotheses.
3. It seems to be impossible for inconsistencies to be justified since they seem to compete with each other and it can't be that both beat or neutralize all their competitors. However, if they can all be justified and (3) is justified relative to N, then N isn't the element of the ultrasystem that shows the justification for (3) to be defeated. It is unlikely that any other element of the ultrasystem is the desired defeating member either.
4. Examples like this one are discussed by Paul Moser.

REFERENCES
Gettier, Edmund. "Is Justified True Belief Knowledge?" *Analysis* 23 (1963), 121-123.
Lehrer, Keith. "The Coherence Theory of Knowledge." *Philosophical Topics* 14 (1986), 5-25.
-----. *Knowledge*. Oxford: Clarendon Press, 1974.
-----. "Knowledge, Truth and Evidence." *Analysis* 25 (1965), 168-175.
-----. "Metaknowledge: Undefeated Justification." *Synthese* 74 (1988), 329-347.
-----, and Thomas D. Paxson, Jr. "Knowledge: Undefeated Justified True Belief." *The Journal of Philosophy* 66 (1968), 225-237.
Moser, Paul. "Propositional Knowledge." *Philosophical Studies* 52 (1987), 91-114.

How Reasonable is Lehrer's Coherence Theory?   Beats Me.

Philip Peterson
Syracuse University

I shall briefly review Lehrer's theory of knowledge (in Section I) and then criticize his treatment of *a priori* knowledge (Section II) and extend that criticism to his general account (Sections III and IV). My understanding of Lehrer's theory is based on Lehrer 1974, 1981a, 1981b, 1982, 1983, 1986a, 1986b, 1986c, and 1988.

This paper is extracted from a longer manuscript, "How to Evaluate Lehrer's Coherence Theory". In the manuscript, I introduced some general ideas about evaluating theories; in sum, that any theory or explanation in a field of inquiry (from physics and mathematics to history and epistemology) must apply to both recognized phenomena and established (general) facts in the field. A theory must *explain* the general facts (or some of them) and, at the very least, it must "honor" the established facts and/or treat them as "requirements" not to be violated. For the sub-field of epistemology that Lehrer is concerned with, I suggested that there are 32 basic kinds of epistemological phenomena (or, better, possibly there are), revealed by recognizing the possibility of complete cross-classification resulting from the basic five polar-dimensional concepts (basic concepts for classifying phenomena in this sub-field) - viz., +A PRIORI, +NECESSARY, +INNATE, +INDIVIDUAL, +TACIT. Also, I proposed for this sub-field that there are three totally non-controversial general facts about cognitions (1-3 below) and three possibly controversial facts (4-6 below) - as follows:

(1) Cognition Theory Facts (Requirements)

Fact/Requirement	Abbreviation	Name
1. Knowledge that p requires that p be the case (that p be true)	$Kp \rightarrow p$ (is true)	TRUTH
2. Knowledge that p is distinct from mere belief that p when p is true	$\sim(TBp \Leftrightarrow Kp)$	BELIEF/ KNOWLEDGE
3. Knowledge that p does not require knowing that one knows p	$\sim(K \rightarrow KKp)$	NON-ITERATION
4. Knowledge that p requires a belief-like relation (e.g., acceptance) to p	$K_i p \rightarrow B_j p$	WEAK-(KB)- ENTAILMENT
5. Belief (acceptance, etc.) that p requires related knowledge (e.g., what it is that is believed)	$Bp \rightarrow (Eq)Kq$	BK-ENTAILMENT
6. It is false that possession of knowledge differs from belief only in that what is known is true & what believed false.	$\sim(\sim(Bp \Leftrightarrow Kp)$ only via T-value)	ANTIMALCOLMISM

J.W. Bender (ed.), The Current State of the Coherence Theory, 77–93.
© *1989 by Kluwer Academic Publishers.*

Although I will assume all of these are facts to be explained (and/or requirements to be honored) in epistemology, and actually discuss some aspects of them, I will not further explain or justify them herein (due to space limitations).

I

Lehrer holds that the possession of knowledge crucially and centrally involves justification - that knowledge is, in part, the product of an evaluation and is, thereby, normative. At bottom, Lehrer's idea is that the kind of complete or perfect justification required for (or contained in) knowledge amounts to the coherence of what's in question (a belief that is a candidate for being known) with the rest of a knower's beliefs and knowledge. Short of Lehrer's very specific details about coherence, the idea should be understood as developing out of the proposal that justification is achieved when what's believed fits in properly with what one already knows and believes.

The sort of proper fitting-in, to start with (for Lehrer or other such coherentists), is consistency - i.e., the lack of conflict of the type which would be contradiction. However, just as believing doesn't make it so (nor does mere *true* believing constitute knowing), so *consistent* believing (when true) does not amount to knowledge. That is, I take this simple-minded coherentism to be observationally disconfirmed. We, none of us, would *call* that knowledge. Even if such fitting-in *qua* not-contradicting were necessary for knowledge, it's surely not sufficient when coupled with truth and acceptance.

Of course, Lehrer's theory is not a simple-minded theory. His theory contains a number of steps or levels of explication. At the first level (step), he holds that S (e.g., Anne above) knows that p (e.g., the hypothesis about Ronald's longevity) if and only if (i) p (is true), (ii) S accepts that p, and (iii) S is completely justified in accepting that p.[1] Then Lehrer proposes a series of embedded substitutions for what complete justification is. First, it is two-part. One is completely justified if and only if one is "personally" justified and one is also "verifically" justified. To be either one of these requires a third level analysis of being justified. This is where Lehrer introduces the word "coherence" explicitly. Being justified (either personally or verifically) with regard to a proposition - e.g., Anne's state of being justified *vis a vis* the proposition that Ronald lives to over 100 years - reduces to (or is explained as) having the proposition cohere with the rest of one's beliefs. Then at the fourth-level "coheres with" is reduced to (defined, explained as) *beating or neutralizing each competitor*. Here finally, is how Lehrer's theory crucially differs from the simple-minded one sketched above.

Justification is achieved not just when what one believes is merely consistent with the rest of one's beliefs (including genuine cognitions). That is too weak, and would lead to rejection of the analysis for reasons like those given above. Rather, Lehrer proposes that each "competitor" of the given proposition (Anne's concerning Ronald's longevity, say) must be handled in some way - e.g., each competitor that directly contradicts p must be rejected, or judged now to be false rather than true. His basic idea is that of one proposition "beating" another in that given that a choice between one and the other must be made (i.e., pretend that - parallel to being forced to choose between two contradicting propositions), a rational choice is made. One proposition can "beat" another in the game of being most worthy of being believed. Lehrer phrases it this way: "it is more reasonable for S to accept p than to accept q on the basis of system A". (System A is the background system of beliefs and cognitions that S actually possesses; i.e., it is the "system" - acknowledging thereby that it is more than just a mere set of propositions - for which p is to be considered as "cohering" or not with. And p's competitors can arise from A or just be separate from it. But if a competitor for a proposition *is* beaten by some proposition judged to be true, then it is definitely out as a present component of system A.)

Notice that "coherence" has come down to something stronger than just not conflicting with something already believed (something in system A). On the simple-minded theory, a proposition (say some true one) can be added to what one believes simply because it doesn't conflict with anything already believed. Here that is definitely not the case. Dynamically phrased, a proposition has to do something to get in (so to speak - to get in the "knowledge" labeled class). It has to beat out competitors.

Before going into how probability as a winner-making feature comes into Lehrer's theory, stop and consider the 5-level (step) analysis we have from Lehrer. We have (L) as a three-part analysis whose third component, (3), gives way to four steps or levels of analysis:[2]

(L) S knows that p =def./IFF

(1) p (is true) + (2) S accepts p + (3) S is completely justified (in accepting p)

Where (3) =def./IFF (3.1) S is personally justified + S is verifically justified

=def./IFF (3.2) p coheres with S's system of accepted beliefs A personally and verifically

=def./IFF (3.3) p beats or neutralizes each competitor for S on A personally and verifically

=def./IFF (3.4) for each competitor X, p is more reasonable to accept (personally and verifically) than X for S on A.

If we simply insert (3.4) for (3.3) and that for (3.2), etc. to (3) itself, we obtain:

(L)* S knows that p =df./IFF

(1) p (is true), and

(2) S accepts p, and

(3) for each competitor (of p) X, p is more reasonable to accept (personally and verifically) than X is for S on system A.

(L)* would seem to be Lehrer's real theory - one that does not even contain the word "coherence" (or some derivative) in it. Lehrer's idea, then, is that being more reasonable to accept than any competitors (for S given A) is a coherentist sort of notion. It's a matter of each candidate proposition being weighted or evaluated against a background of two sets of propositions. (That is, it is no simple matter of just being compatible or not with one set of propositions - say, those in A.) First, there is the general background set of propositions, those in the set A of propositions already known or believed by S.[3] Second, there is the set consisting of competitor propositions, each of which must be "beaten" or "neutralized" via (3.4)'s reasonability features. (Since it will not bear on my criticisms below, I will ignore neutralizing herein.) So, if a proposition does stand in exactly the right relationship to these two different sets of propositions, it "wins" (i.e., becomes a completely justified proposition and thus a known one). Although these relationships are peculiar and/or (as Lehrer says in another connection) "baroque", they are complicated enough to warrant the verb "coheres" when a proposition is placed just right (by Lehrer's theory) with respect to them. Certainly, the notion of "fitting-in" seems apt. If a proposition fits in in just the right way between its competitors and the system of propositions already accepted, then that is by Lehrer's lights - and not implausibly, I too maintain - a kind of justification. That is, p is justified via "fitting in" *vis a vis* (i) other propositions that might be believed (accepted), the competitors, and (ii) the other propositions already fitted-in (or assumed to be, or simultaneously fitting-in - i.e., fitting together, since foundationalism is rejected), the system of accepted propositions.

This is not Lehrer's final step, however. He goes on to add that one proposition *is* (or can be) more reasonable than another in virtue of its probabilistic features. Roughly, the idea is that being more probable than a competitor[4] is good evidence, support, and (even) explication of what it is to be more reasonable than a competitor; i.e., more-probable-than is sufficient for and somehow helps explain more-reasonable-than. For example, if the proposition p above (that Ronald Reagan lives to over 100 years) were to be judged correctly by Anne to be more probable than a competitor like (say) q, that no U.S. president ever lives to be 100 years old (since none ever have), then p would be for Anne (given her system of beliefs A) more reasonable than q would be. Now it is very important to consider whether Anne has to actually make this judgment (concerning relative probability, to support reasonableness) for p to be completely justified for Anne (i.e., p be probable in a certain respect for Anne aside from whether she ever does or can judge p to be probable given everything she knows or believes). The answer is "no". But before detailing that consequence (and, more importantly, going on to assess it), consider the following final collapsing of Lehrer's definitions:

> (L)**   S knows that p =df./IFF
> (1)   p (is true)
> (2)   S accepts p
> (3)   for each competitor X of p, p is more probable for S (personally
>   and verifically) than X is given S's background system of beliefs A.

(L)** must be understood in a certain way, for Lehrer does not hold that being-more-probable-than is either a definition of more-reasonable-than (or, for short, that probability defines reasonableness) or that it is necessary and sufficient for being-more-reasonable-than. Rather, he just holds that it *is* sufficient (probability sufficient for reasonability) - "criteriological conditions, sufficient conditions, for the application of [reasonableness]" (1986a,12). The important point, to me, is that Lehrer is reversing Chisholm's position. Chisholm holds that reasonability must be at the bottom of probability. (Note that Chisholm's 1977 D6.6 rests on D4.1 which is in turn rests on D1.2 which is a basic definition utilizing "more-reasonable-than" as basic and undefined. Clearly, Lehrer reverses this order of dependency.) Lehrer also expresses the dependence (e.g., explanatory dependence, as I would put it, in that probability being sufficient for reasonability importantly helps to explain what relative reasonability is) as a "correspondence" (the "correspondence principle", Lehrer 1986a,12). Thus, if reasonability judgments aren't exactly probability judgments, they are very like them. Understanding how probability judgments work contributes a lot (perhaps the whole story) to understanding how one thing is more reasonable than another for an individual .

One of Lehrer's significant achievements has been to marshal the arguments for the efficacy of higher-ordered probabilities (e.g., probability judgments about other probabilities) to (i) counter Hume's observation that such iterations will eventually lead to lower or zero probabilities (cf. Lehrer 1983,195) and (ii) reveal how such complexities could serve to explain (via the above-mentioned "correspondence") how reasonability judgments (*qua*, e.g., weighted probability judgments) could play a role in being the heart of justification conditions which, in fact, involved truth. One natural way to look at Lehrer's further extension of his investigations into probability - with Wagner, applying his approach to the question of social consensus (beyond just individual judgments) - is that he realized that some of these facts about his particular kind of coherentist theory of justification for individuals could be re-applied to questions about what groups of individuals believed (e.g., about what the consensus, and/or shared beliefs are).

Lehrer's theory, as I understand it, satisfies straightforwardly the three fundamental requirements for such knowledge theories - viz., TRUTH, BELIEF/KNOWLEDGE, and NON-ITERATION.[5] However, a couple of matters may need mentioning to make this perfectly clear. First, Lehrer can be interpreted as asserting that truth is not a component of knowledge - due to his adoption of the "absolute" theory of truth. I would relabel this theory the "elimination" theory. In stating the truth requirement, I put the words "is true" in parentheses - e.g., "S's knowing that p requires that p (is true)" abbreviated "Kp -> p (is true)" - thereby suggesting that the requirement (general fact) about so-called "truth" could be expressed either way - with or without the word "true". On Lehrer's view, it is only the fact that p (expressed without using "fact") that is a necessary condition for knowing that p (cf. Chapter 2 of Lehrer 1974). Now he might have gone on to say that this component is independent of the truth that is generated via his complete justification component. But really this would be unpersuasive. For even if the concept of truth is eliminable as he says, still it is re-introducible at that point; i.e., reversing Lehrer's direction of analysis, we can substitute "p is true" on the basis of his elimination hypothesis "it is true that p if and only if p". So, I claim, truth is essentially involved in or related to Lehrer's first condition, so that his "truth connection" does involve more than just his complete-justification component.

Secondly, given what I have published before on Lehrer (Peterson 1983), it might be predicted that I would attack Lehrer's acceptance condition for knowledge. I won't. For one thing, if it's rejected, it would be impossible (as far as I can tell) to discuss or evaluate the rest of his theory (especially, its "coherence" part). And although I do still believe knowledge can't be proved to entail belief unqualifiedly (as Lehrer attempted in 1974 and I refuted in my 1983), I also believe it can't be (or hasn't yet been) proved to prohibit belief (especially in the usual way that is claimed, cf. Peterson 1977). But Lehrer does not speak of "beliefs" anymore, but rather "acceptances". Acceptance is appropriately belief-like in the sense in which something is needed to label the state we were in when we discover (say now) that it was not knowledge (since what was thought to be known to be true is false). Of course, we could just label it the state of "thinking-I-know". Two things then arise. Maybe it's not that knowledge that p entails some sort of belief-like relation (adoption, acceptance, judgment, etc.) to p, but rather it entails believing (or otherwise thinking) that you know - where it's possible both to believe that you know and also not know. Well, maybe. This seems to me to be more complicated and problematic than my belief-related state B_jp vis a vis K_ip (e.g., "B_j" representing judging). The iteration of cognitive states (KKp, BBp, BKp, etc.) is daunting in every case. I will discuss some aspects of it below, but I will herein simply ignore the possibility (leaving it for another time) that rather than K_ip -> B_jp we want Kp -> BKp. One thing in favor of this new wrinkle, however, is that it reduces to Kp -> (Eq)Bq, where ~(q=p) - which is the converse of fact/requirement BK-ENTAILMENT.

Although Lehrer's theory appears to satisfy transparently NON-ITERATION, problems arise with respect to a so-called "corollary" of this fact. To this feature I now turn.

II

NON-ITERATION - the falsity of (Kp entails KKp) - is logically equivalent to the possibility of Kp and not-KKp. I want to raise now the other side of this last coin. Granted it is possible to know a proposition to be true and not know that you know it, but should it be possible to know it and also know that you know it? (At least for some propositions? For all? For many?) Granted we do not want to violate NON-ITERATION on pain of everyone's having to be an epistemologist (indeed, one who knows which theory of knowledge is correct) to know anything at all. However, do we want to prohibit absolutely knowing that one has knowledge? It seems to me this is what Lehrer does (or almost does).

Consider what are traditionally referred to as "intuitions" because they are allegedly cases of so-called *a priori* certainties. Lehrer doesn't think there are any such infallibilities, but he does have a theory about what the intuitions that are candidates for that lofty status really are. They are certain of the products of rational social consensus.

> ...the appeal to intuition is, rather clearly, an appeal to consensus. When some philosopher claims that something is intuitive, or, on the contrary that something is counter-intuitive, these claims rest on implicit reference to the consensual opinion of some group. (Lehrer 1981a, 9)

Consider such a case where a Lehrer-ish intuition is known - say, my knowing that (4), where:

(2) One proposition (p) contradicts another (q) if and only if the truth of the one (p) requires the falsity of the other (q) and *vice versa*.

(3) Contradiction is the relationship between two propositions such that the one contradicts the other, and "a contradiction" refers to any proposition, C, (often called a "self-contradiction") which contains two propositions which contradict each other where C entails each of the two.

(4) All contradictions (or self-contradictions) are false.

It's not merely that I believe (4) because it is rationally consented to (though that is somehow crucially involved in the explanation of the genesis of the acceptance), but I also satisfy the other knowledge requirements (truth & complete undefeated justification). Now is it possible for me to know as well that this cognition is of an intuition? That is, can (b) be true for "p" taken to be (4) above (or (c) be true, which is the same thing for Lehrer [6])?

> (a) I know that p
> (b) I know that (p is intuitively true)
> (c) I know that (p is rationally consented to)
> (d) I know that (I know that p is rationally consented to)

You should first reply that this is not knowing that you know that p, but merely knowing a quality of p (its intuitiveness). Thus, it is not a case of both knowing that p and knowing that you know. Right! But it is certainly on the way to that case, isn't it? And if I am really going to know that I know that p - where p is an intuition like (4) - I have to achieve this by knowing the kind of truth p is, using that as a basis for achieving knowledge that I do know it. That is, in this kind of (*a priori* -ish) case, something like (b) (or (c) to be clear for Lehrer) is definitely required to be true prior to, or simultaneously with, KKp.

How could I know that p is rationally consented to (appropriately) without checking out the details which would make it so? (And doing that would produce simultaneously or subsequently, I contend, knowledge that they did obtain. If you are inclined to quibble here - concerning maybe only having beliefs about the details, etc. - please drop that quibble for the sake of continuous argument. In the long run, it won't make any difference.) Now think about what checking out those details would be. The kind of project it would be is the exact opposite of what the traditionalist proposes it is for the same thing (his intuitions). For only cool and calm intellectual gaze is apparently required to see that a non-demonstrative *a priori* truth is an intuition for a traditionalist. It is the paradigm of self-evidence. The reason the proposition that contradictions are false is a true one is because contradictions - those things I have now a clear mental grasp of - directly have the property of falsity. Such intuitions from the traditionalist's point of view are not extremely difficult to notice, but fairly easy to recognize - which causes them to be thought unimportant by some, and the possibility of them to be severely abused by others (some fans of God's goodness, for example).

But on Lehrer's view, establishing that a cognition is his kind of "intuition" - e.g., my establishing the truth of (b) via (c) - is fantastically complicated. Notice what I would have to do. I would have to carry out a large-scale social-psychological observational study to somehow, at the end, reach a conclusion about whether (4) does satisfy the requirements for rational consensus (not just mere consensus, which would be difficult enough). My suspicion is that Lehrer's model for determining rational consensus has never been applied seriously in any social-psychological study (controlled, scientifically respectable) of any judgment at all. And if anyone now contemplates carrying out such a study today, I am sure he or she does not think it will be perfectly easy and straightforward (i.e., it will not be: "just go out and record these responses and we will then calculate rational consensus by inputting the data into our Lehrer and Wagner computer program"). And with the kind of case I propose - viz., (c) for "p" taken to refer to (4) - further requirements beyond mere rational consensus will have to be satisfied, since it is not mere rational consensus that makes a proposition an intuition. Rather, some high degree, or special variety, of rational consensus is required (as mentioned in note 6 above). One result of these conclusions is that no one before (or, say, before 1970, to be very safe about it) has ever known that some proposition is Lehrerishly intuitively true - knowledge which has the form of (c). For the outlines of a method to come to acquire this knowledge (which is all that we have now I think in Lehrer 1981a) did not even exist before (say) 1970.

Now these consequences do not make it logically or mathematically impossible that anyone ever does come to know that some proposition is intuitively true. And be careful to remember what the issue is here. It is not the issue of whether anyone ever does know some proposition to be true, where the proposition is an intuition (Lehrerishly) aside from knowing that further fact. That is, I am not considering the case of having intuitive knowledge, but rather the case of knowing that I have intuitive knowledge. I might know something which by its nature makes the knowledge I have a case of intuitive knowledge without realizing it. What I am considering is the case of realizing that some cognition I have is intuitive knowledge - something that entails the form (d). To approach that knowledge that I know that p is an intuition (rationally consented to), I have to first acquire knowledge of the sort (c)[7]. That is, I have to learn or discover that p is rationally consented to. That project, I suggest, has never ever been carried out by anybody (and if it has recently, it certainly never was before 1970). Since the difficulty of these determinations is so high, I submit that my (or anyone else soon) learning that I (or they) know that (4) is a Lehrerishly intuitive truth is practically impossible. It may be logically or mathematically possible (which I think is all Lehrer has so far been interested in), but as a matter of fact - for ordinary humans (and even extraordinary epistemologists) - it is still practically impossible. (Or, as Descartes might have said, it is morally impossible, even if not metaphysically impossible.)

So, I conclude that Lehrer's theory only allows the merest logical or metaphysical possibility to knowing that one knows that p - when p is what the traditionalist would call an object of *a priori* intuition (something knowable directly, nondemonstrably with absolute certainty). This is not a bonus for Lehrer's theory. Of course, a Lehrer fan can reply that it's an obscure criticism at best. "For one thing," he may continue "the traditional approach to the special sort of knowledge called *a priori* was very mysterious, inherently doubtful, and (at worst) mystery mongering. It can lead to absolutely silly forms of rationalism, like Leibniz' in which there are no genuine contingent truths to be known at all and every cognizer is metaphysically trapped in his own universe forever and is even eternally unchanging (no monad literally changes). So what if determining whether one knows something intuitively turns out to be something absolutely difficult to do. Maybe it ought to be, now that I think of it." "Let's trumpet it (or at least package it) as a new discovery," Lehrer himself might add. "We have now discovered (i) it is very difficult to determine whether what one knows is intuitive knowledge (rationally consented to appropriately by one's fellow speakers), even if it is. Your hunches and knacks for it are about the best you'll practically attain (and some of them will turn out to be simply false, only mere beliefs that something was rationally consented to). In principle, it could be figured out whether some bit of knowledge you have is a so-called intuition. But it is certainly not worth the trouble it would take, and practically speaking (for us today) it may well be impossible!" (This is no worse than Quine trumpeting the demise of the analytic/synthetic distinction.)

If I had nothing more to say about Lehrer's theory, then I would have to admit that these kinds of replies are somewhat persuasive. For who does care about knowledge of the so-called intuitiveness of some other knowledge? Absolutely no one, as a matter of fact, besides a few epistemologists (today or ever). However, the same kind of criticism also applies to Lehrer's general definition of knowledge. So, it is not just knowing that one sort of philosopher's kind of knowledge occurs - viz., whether something you know, you know intuitively - but rather the same thing for all knowledge. This would get Lehrer's attention I think: the claim that it is practically impossible for anyone to know that he knows something. Of course, the challenge is not to violate NON-ITERATION. It is just that sometimes, somehow, somewhere, or somewho, it must - mustn't it? - be possible that someone does know that p and also does know that he knows that p. (This possibility I sometimes think of as a "corollary" to NON-ITERATION.) The denial of NON-ITERATION requires anyone to be a super-epistemologist in order to know anything at all. Fine, don't deny it. But should we at the same time require (or almost require - the matter may be "merely" a practical one) that no one can ever know that he knows that something?

Why do I think Lehrer's theory can lead to that ? If we are careful in reading Lehrer's theory, we will prevent ourselves from mistakenly understanding him to have violated NON-ITERATION. To get to my criticism it is helpful to see how such a mistaken understanding could occur. One might say that the nature of Lehrer's complete justification requirement - in his particular variety of coherence required for justification - involves a cognizer actually determining (discovering, coming to know) for a given proposition whether it does "beat" or "neutralize" all its competitors with respect to inclusion in the system of propositions already accepted (acceptance system A). And this is very difficult to do. For short of the problems of applying some method of making the needed relative-reasonability judgments (supposedly via something "corresponding" to Lehrer's probability model for aggregating weighted judgments), it is very difficult to even become aware of what all the relevant competitors are that need to be considered. It is absolutely implausible that anyone does do it (even unconsciously, and automatically, as Lehrer and Cohen seem to suggest, or meta-mentally as in recent Lehrer). But this would mean that it is absolutely implausible that anyone ever does know anything at all. (For such knowledge would require as part of the achievement specifying all those competitors and making all those reasonability judgments required - even to simply know one proposition.) But Lehrer's reply is obvious. His theory is not that kind of theory (violating NON-ITERATION). You do not have to make all those subsidiary discoveries and judgments. (Similarly, you don't have to discover whether there is a system that is appropriately "verific" for verificness to apply.) Rather, the facts that such a gargantuan task would discover to be true when someone knows something (via complete justification) simply have to be true. They do not have to be known to be true. As a matter of fact, the known proposition (in addition to being true and accepted) must cohere via actually beating or neutralizing all its competitors (in a relative-reasonability cum probabilistic sort of way). But the cognizer does not have to know it coheres. One is simply justified if it does.

Fine. Move on to my question - which is not simply the question of whether Lehrer's theory satisfies or simply does not conflict with one of my general facts (and/or requirements) that specific cognition theories must honor. For what I raised about intuitions above - viz., that it be possible that one knows that one knows for at least some cases - is not a fact or general requirement. Maybe as a result of reading this you may want to propose that. I do not propose it now (or yet). However: look at it. Is Lehrer's general theory such that one could not - either absolutely or just practically - ever know that one knows anything? I think it is.

III

I have just argued that on Lehrer's account it is practically impossible that anyone ever does know that he knows when the case is one of "intuitive" so-called *a priori* knowledge. Now I raise the same issue with regard to any sort of knowledge - common sense perceptual cognition, memories, communicable knowledge, scientific knowledge, etc. Could one actually come to know ("reflectively" as I shall say) that p, where p is the proposition that one knows that q (for q being some distinct proposition such as that it rained today, one is over 20 years in age, the language one speaks is English, Ronald is the first Hollywood movie actor to become U.S. President, etc.). In sum, is the following schema ever satisfied for Lehrer: "Kp & KKp".

It seems to me that I can easily argue that this is practically (at least) impossible for Lehrer's theory. Leave aside for the moment the problem of "verificness" (which I think will similarly doom, as will "ultraness", any easy solution to this problem), and just consider simple justification (something like Lehrer's personal justification without the need to label it that since we are pretending it is the only kind of justification) - where justification is taken as Lehrer describes. One *is* justified with regard to proposition p if and only if it "coheres" with the rest of what one accepts - where it does so if and only if it "beats" or "neutralizes" every competitor. (Again, leave aside neutralizing to make the discussion simpler.) To be justified with respect to p, then, is for p to "beat" its competitors. How would one know this. One would know that by knowing that it is more reasonable to accept p than to accept q for every proposition q which competes with p. In earlier statements of his theory, this reasonability was simply identical to or coincident with a complicated probability relation. More recently (Lehrer 1986a), Lehrer simply holds that there is a close "correspondence" between such probabilistic considerations and reasonability. Consider the earlier alternative first. One is justified in accepting p if and only if it is more probable with regard to other propositions already accepted that p is true than that q is for each proposition q that does compete with p. As a short-hand for Lehrer's more complicated notion of "competing," just think of q-s being any propositions that are one-by-one logically incompatible with p. Some of these other propositions will themselves be probabilistic, so that some separate relative-probability relationships will involve iterated probabilities (at least to the second-level: probabilities of probabilities). Prominent among these will be facts about one's own reliability (e.g., the reliability of the perceptual mode involved when p is "based on" perception - say, that it is now raining on me (visual, tactual)). One can parallel these probability of probability judgments (e.g., weighting my own reliability high under certain circumstances) to the weighting of experts' judgments (which might in turn be probabilistic) in the determination of rational social consensus. And the troubles will be analogous.

I proposed that it would be practically impossible to discover what the rational consensus was for an allegedly "intuitive" belief, due to the difficulty of ever coming to have the required information (about what experts and others sought, not to mention the mere(?) mathematical calculations involved in aggregating probabilities). But the same schematic requirements carry over - the same sorts of information needed about the judgments (or possible judgments) of others, now needed about aspects of oneself. (Indeed, one of Lehrer's achievements has been to make the possibility of calculating such aggregations of probabilities possible - contrary to Hume's claim that iterations of probabilities must eventually produce low, or near-zero, probabilities - cf. Lehrer 1986a and Lehrer and Cohen 1983.) I take it that several judgments about one's own reliability (probabilistically) can be involved in a typical justification - e.g., that it is now raining on me (judged via vision and touch). Now I certainly grant that I can easily make presumptions (assumptions, presuppositions) along this line. I quite easily assume (don't estimate or judge via reflection on past evidence) that my sight and hearing is fairly good - and that it is particularly reliable (99% accurate) in situations just like the present one. I think Lehrer IS on to something in building something like the presumption of my own reliability into his account of justification. But now I am considering the case of knowing that I am justified. So, it is not just a matter of correct or plausible presumption, but of learning (say, for competitor q_i) that p - say, p = that it is raining on me now - is more probable than q_i. This seems easy enough for something like (the philosopher's) q_i to the effect that I am now having a tactual hallucination. (I know something about hallucinations and myself. This is not at all the right sort of situation to expect tactual hallucinations. Or so we might pretend. For me today, this is not true. Due to recent minor surgery on my forehead I now have peculiar sensations and numbness on the top of my head - evidently due to minor nerve damages in the surrounding skin.) However, there are at least several other such reliability questions that I must also discover and make estimates about. In fact, I am quite sure that I cannot by myself discover all of these - even though I am a well-trained and highly-experienced epistemologist. I would probably (*sic*) have to consult Lehrer himself to make any confident judgment about whether I had raised for consideration all the propositions q (or a subset of them, the q_is concerning my own reliability) that I ought to.

In short, I (an epistemologist) will have to undertake something like a research project in order to carry out the analysis (data collection and evaluation) necessary to acquiring knowledge that I am justified in my acceptance of p (that I am being rained on right now). Maybe the case is a little more tractable with respect to mere knowledge that I am justified in believing that I am being rained on now than it was for the case of the rational consensus sort of account of intuitive knowledge (e.g., that the proposition that contradictions are never true *is* a case of intuitive knowledge for me). Two other matters, however, make it fall to the same low level of plausibility as that retained by the rational consensus case. First is Lehrer's recent retreat to a mere "correspondence" between probability and reasonability. Since probability is not exactly what is at the bottom of reasonability (actually, I think it still is for Lehrer and that the retreat is somewhat misleading or insincere) we are left with only an analogical vagueness. I might do something or other roughly analogous to aggregating probability judgments to discover whether p is more reasonable for every competitor q, but it is not clear exactly what this is. That new unclarity does not improve the plausibility of ever coming to know that I am justified.

The second matter produces a death-dealing blow: VERIFICNESS. How could one every know or learn that one's verific acceptance system was actually involved in facts or judgments that p is more reasonable than q (for each competitor q). To be completely justified, one must be verifically justified. The problem here is just a very specific application of the following objection to an undefeated-justified-true-belief theory of knowledge. Granted that if knowledge were simply justified true belief, then it would not seem too difficult to conceive of how it is possible to know that one knows that p. One has to know *inter alia* that one is justified in believing that p. Imagine that one does know that with respect to belief that p. now come the defeaters. To know that one is undefeated in having some justification or other with respect to believing p is to know quite a bit more. If you would doubt this, scan the kind of defeaters raised in Shope's (1983) summary of these discussions. I submit that it would be a very rash person - or a very wise and self-confident epistemologist (i.e., not me) - who would assert with respect to any particular proposition that he does know his justification has no defeaters. But that is what he would have to claim in order to claim to know that he has undefeated justification for it. The same thing applies to Lehrer's complete justification (and, analogously, to ultra justification). To be completely justified he must know enough of his acceptance system is true (not that it simply be true, he must know it is) for the reasonability judgments to stand - containing as they do reference to the verific acceptance system (a sub-system of the personal acceptance system). No simple research project in collusion with Lehrer is going to come up with clear support for my claim to know what my verific system is.

    This may not be news to Lehrer - that knowing that you know something is very difficult. Many philosophers expect it to be difficult. Adopting an iterative-Cartesian position - that one could easily know that one knows that p - is not even advisable for Descartes. He certainly didn't think it was easy to know that he knew things (thus, the *Meditations*). And Lehrer can say that since Descartes, it has never been thought to be easy. The recent insight has been that we should not - on pain of walking into skeptical traps - adopt views or theories about human knowledge which have the effect that one must be able to know that one knows if one can know at all. (I particularly admire Dretske's reformulation of this mistake as one of trying to guarantee "channel conditions" in merely using a channel of information transmission.) However, for some simple cases - say, ones that parallel the one about knowing that one's knowledge is intuitive (involved in knowing that one knows something when the embedded knowledge *is* one of so-called intuitive *a priori* knowledge) - it seems to me that it should sometimes (or for some certain cases) be practically possible that one does know that one knows - involving *inter alia* knowing that one is justified. Recently, Lehrer defends his coherentism via allusions to "meta-knowledge". But for exactly the reasons I have stated above, it seems to me that we can never (at least practically) come to possess any of this meta-knowledge. At least, not reflectively.

IV

    But what does that mean - "reflectively"? This is a closely related matter I will now discuss. One kind of answer Lehrer can make to my charges here is to say that further theorizing about how concretely we ever do achieve any knowledge does produce something akin to knowledge that one is justified. Lehrer (with Cohen 1983, 197ff) fodorizes his theory. He proposes that an appropriate interpretation of Reid's epistemology can be identified with a Fodor-inspired model of cognition in which is contained a two-part sub-system of "Input" component and "Central Processing" component. (Think of Central Processing as something akin to Reid's faculty of reason and/or understanding, a capacity for generating perceptual knowledge out of sensations - or so I suppose; cf. Lehrer 1986b.) Mere sensory-perceptual beliefs are generated in the Input component via sensory-stimulation (as input to the Input component). On the views of Dretske, Goldman, and some others, if such beliefs are appropriately related to the sensory stimulations, and they in turn, to extra-cognizer events and facts - say, via carrying the genuine "information" in Dretske's theory - then they would be (or be candidate for being) themselves cases of knowledge. Lehrer's view is not this sort, but is one which introduces an evaluative procedure. Something evaluative must be done to sensorially generated beliefs (acceptances) before they are candidates for being genuine cognitions. Lehrer proposes what I myself would call a filtering function. There is, in generating inputs for so-called Central Processing (where reasoning and understanding is carried out in a cognizer's mind), an additional bit of processing of outputs of the Input component to turn them into inputs to Central Processing. One might consider this to be achieved through a "cognitive justification" filter. That is, Lehrer proposes as a real component - at some appropriate level of abstraction *vis a vis* neural equipment - a filtering function that carries out in fact what has to be achieved in reducing the set of (say, sensory-perceptual) acceptances to those which are (or are candidates for being) cognitions (i.e., justified acceptances).

> The highly intellectual account offered in terms of personal justification, coherence, and prevailing over competition, is, we suggest, knowledge at the level of Central Processing System. Such knowledge involves acceptance in the interest of obtaining truth and avoiding error, acceptance aimed at intellectual goals, and, though habitual, is not automatic and may be influenced by background information. Such acceptance certifies the belief of the input System and converts them to knowledge. This way of conceiving of the matter should help to alleviate conflict with those who think of knowledge as merely belief appropriately caused or nomologically connected with fact. Such belief is, to be sure, information, but conversion to knowledge requires acceptance in light of background information, a function of the Central Processing System.(1983, 198.)

(I suggested that the "conversion" was via a filter before or at the entry point of Central Processing, rather than in it. It does not appear that anyone proposes that this kind of refined input (or immediate achievement) need be the only input to (or achievement in) Central Processing.)

I concluded above that it was almost (and maybe actually) impossible that anyone would ever know that he knows a proposition to be true on Lehrer's account. Leaving aside the difficulties produced by verificness and by other defeaters, merely knowing that q - when q is some proposition to the effect that p is personally justified - would seem to be virtually impossible. (Knowing that q would certainly be part of what is required to know that one knows that p.) Now, in light of his Fodorish (as vs. Dretskean) information processing model of cognition, Lehrer can reply that in a certain sense (or way), anyone who is personally justified with respect to p (in his theory) does "know" it - viz., his justification filter "knows" it. This achievement is some kind of tacit and/or implicit knowledge, not of a type easily transformed into conscious or reflective knowledge. Yet, it is there nevertheless. It doesn't give a direct solution to my "KK" problem (that somehow some cases of knowledge ought to be capable of being known to be knowledge), but it gives an indirect one. For one to *be* justified (personally) one has to have a (reliable!) filtering function in actual operation. So, being justified with respect to p is in a way tacitly knowing that one is - in that one's filtering capacity "knows" it. Lehrer can even defend the nature and utility of this claim (against the criticism that it is merely a verbal point) by using - rather than abusing - a point of Chomsky's.

Chomsky claims (i) that significant parts of one's genuine knowledge of one's language (what one knows when one is fluent in, say, English as one's first language) is knowledge of rules and principles of the grammar of one's language and (ii) that these rules and principles are not just difficult to introspectively notice, but in important cases are impossible to introspect. They are impossible to introspect (in contrast to the introspectibility of one's use of consciously learned rules for, say, "doing long division") due to their particular combination of abstractness and complexity. (Cf. Chomsky 1968, 43-45, 1975, Chap. 1, 1980, Chaps. 2 and 3.) Now some philosophers have balked at calling such abstract and non-introspectible features of our minds literally knowledge - or genuinely cognitive contents. Thomas Nagel, for example, proposes that any supposed element in such tacit knowledge that cannot in principle be brought to the surface of consciousness (be literally introspected, even if only under very special conditions) should not be thought to be knowledge (Nagel 1969, 176-177). Further, he proposes that any such non-introspectibles which are innate (built-in, biologically determined) should not be called knowledge either - since even if the capacity has to use his language *is* suitable for calling knowledge, still the capacity for merely acquiring such a capacity is not suitable for being called knowledge (it is a mere capacity for knowledge not the actual possession of any, as the first-level capacity (linguistic competence) would be). (Cf. Nagel 1969, 180-181.) This seemingly half-way agreement of Nagel with Chomsky does not reach the Chomskyan point I want to emphasize. For Chomsky would certainly reply to Nagel that there are very good reasons for not taking his (Chomsky's) claims about innate aspects of linguistic knowledge to be merely about a capacity for a capacity (for speech and understanding). Quite simply, the innate elements are the same kinds of elements as the acquired elements. For they are rules and principles too; i.e., some rules and principles (and constraints on rules and principles, taken as further more "abstract" rules and principles) are not learned or acquired at all, but rather are present from the beginning as a basis for explaining how the others are acquired. (The main argument here is the "poverty of the stimulus" analysis - that too little about what is in the end acquired (cognitive competence) is actually extractible from the experimental data supplied to any language learner. Thus, some of the resulting content must have been there all along.)

I see no reason why Lehrer should not adopt Chomsky's approach here. To wit: there are rules and principles of justification that are "internalized" so as to constitute the above-described justification-filter (to supply a subset of true perceptual beliefs, for example, to Central Processing - a subset which is, in fact, "coherent" in Lehrer's sense). Then Lehrer can claim that, like Chomsky, there is a sense to there being tacit elements of knowledge (not just linguistic knowledge) "internalized" in these principles (with no doubt some elements or aspects innate for the same "poverty of the stimulus" sort of reasons). In the application of the cognition-filter in any particular case, the rules and principles of coherence-making (relative to other actual possessed beliefs, system A) actually apply correctly to constitute the mental state of being justified. Being justified (here, personally) is not identical to, nor a sufficient condition for, knowing that one is justified - in the reflective propositional sense of knowledge under discussion. Yet, in another sense of "know", being justified is knowing one is justified - for it is the tacit, automatic (perhaps entirely non-introspectible - as in language use) application of some knowledge (underlying cognitive rules and principles) to "know" (i.e., literally filter out) which belief does appropriately cohere.

In ordinary knowing (as fodorishly sketched), then, we might say that there are elements of tacit knowledge. A person has tacit knowledge that he is justified in believing that p simply because his cognition-filter operates properly to make him in fact justified in believing p. Tacit knowledge here is simply correct operation of the cognitive mechanisms. So, I have produced a kind of image of my "corollary" (that it is possible to know that p and know that one knows that p). For having non-tacit knowledge that p, there is (perhaps! - I am not spelling out all the details) tacit knowledge that p is justified and subsequently known. I believe that non-tacit knowledge is simply what is traditionally called "reflective" knowledge. (I use subscripts "t" and "r" for "tacit" and "reflective" below.) Reflective knowledge is so-called because it can (in principle) be reflected-on - not because it always or easily is reflected on. So, for some proposition p, it is possible (perhaps always required) that if $K_r p$, then $K_t K_r p$. And it's possible that $K_r p$ & $K_t K_r p$ is an image of the "corollary". From this image, we can (I speculate) envision an alternative to the usual approach to knowing (reflectively) that one knows (reflectively) that p. On the usual, traditional approach, that is possible because conscious reflection on what one is thinking (such as in conscious entertainment of one's belief that p) can produce knowledge. That is, first-level knowledge$_r$ that p is called reflective simply because it can easily be noticed - i.e., it is easy to know$_r$ that one knows$_r$ that p by reflection. So, whether a cognition actually *is* reflected-on is not necessary to it's simply being reflective. But with fodorized Lehrer, we have the possibility of another route to reflective knowledge that one reflectively knows that p - viz., the supposedly scientific route (via "cognitive" science) of studying some one particular case of $K_r p$. If what I propose here is viable, then in one of my particular cases of $K_r p$, there is $K_t K_r p$ (since correct operation of my cognitive mechanism is a sort of tacit knowledge). Couldn't (in principle) this operation be scientifically observed (doubtlessly very indirectly), so that non-tacit knowledge of its operations was achieved (even by me)? On the basis of my tacit knowledge that I know$_r$ that p, some scientific knowledge of it could be developed - leading, in the end, to $K_r K_t K_r p$. But this last achievement can be reduced to $K_r K_r p$ (by logical entailment). This result could serve as a Lehrerish substitute for the traditional direct-and-conscious introspective noticing that I know$_r$ that p (merely self-reflecting consciousness producing $K_r K_r p$). That is, it would be possible that one knows that p and knows that one knows it (all reflectively) without reliance on any conscious introspection, but rather via advanced study and observation via "cognitive" science. (Of course, a serious drawback is that no one has yet ever known that he knows something - non-tacitly, reflectively - even though it is, in principle, possible; on the other hand, cf. Peterson 1986.)

In conclusion, a brief word on rivals. Lehrer (1986a and 1988) feels his theory has some aspects of typical externalist theories (e.g., knowledge depending on reliable information processing systems producing knowledge with some resulting connection between internal representation and external fact) and some aspects of typical internalist theories (e.g., epistemic evaluation as central, with justification as normative rather than causal). But consider typical externalisms - e.g., Armstrong's (1976) theory, Dretske's (1981) information-transmission theory, and Alston's (1976) reliabilism.[8] What about the mere possibility of knowing that one knows that p for any of these? Imagine knowing, concerning Dretske's theory, that some item of information within oneself *was* appropriately digitalized, at the second-level of intensionality, and appropriately guiding action (so not only was it appropriately informationally-caused, but it achieves the controlling function needed to make it suitable for being knowledge). There is absolutely no component of Dretske's theory which concerns internal observation of any of these required facts within oneself. That is, there is no direct Prichardian (1957) route to just noticing of, or in, oneself that one knows something. The Kp & KKp possibility seems even worse for Dretske than for Lehrer. For Lehrer we can imagine cognitive science research (social-psychological) to help us acquire some knowledge of something about my own cognitive (internal) state - and, thereby, to acquire some knowledge that I know something. The same sort of project would also seem to be the only route to knowledge of knowledge for Dretske. But the Dretskean research project would be at least as difficult, and perhaps more difficult, to imagine achieving than Lehrer's.

Of course, adding considerations produced by post-verificness defeaters and/or ultra justification makes the matters worse for Lehrer *vis a vis* the possibility of Kp and KKp. Whether Lehrer's current notion of ultra system (a set of corrected background acceptance systems) can be in any way fodorized (as I have sketched it above) - so that the mere possibility of KKp (or some image of it) is retained - is a very good question.[9]

NOTES

1. Actually, in most of his formulations, there is a fourth condition, an anti-defeaters clause to the effect that the justification does not depend on any false proposition. At first glance this condition seems redundant given the strict requirements of verific justification. However, some defeaters slip through verificness as evidenced by Lehrer's more recent proposals about justification via ultra systems (1986c, 1988). Now Lehrer proposes that justification is achieved when it is totally undefeated; i.e., an accepted proposition is undefeatedly justified (I would say for Lehrer here, "ultrajustified") if it is justified on the basis of "every system that is a member of the ultrasystem of S" (Lehrer 1988, p. 344). The ultrasystem is a set of systems such that each member system is "constructed from the acceptance system of a person by making one or more weak [=deleting false belief] or strong [=replacing false belief with denial] corrections in the acceptance system of the person" (1988, p. 343). So, complete justification via personal and verific justification is replaced in Lehrer's theory with ultra justification. Since these refinements (which move Lehrer in the direction of what he calls "meta-knowledge") won't matter much for the type of criticisms I shall make, I will leave my discussion in the terminology of Lehrer 1986a.
2. In (L) and elsewhere below, I use the notation "=df./IFF" to represent the peculiar relationship between so-called definiens and definendum which is not lexical definition (concerning the meaning of terms in a particular natural language, or even across natural languages in universal semantics) and is not merely necessary and sufficient conditions (which can be much too broad and not illuminating at all). Philosophers such as Lehrer are seeking "definitions" of some other type - what I myself think of as philosophically significant analyses of concepts, analyses the understanding of which requires prior understanding of the lexical meaning of the terms. To understand, for example, Plato's very speculative proposal for "defining" (in this philosophical style) justice requires prior understanding of what "justice" already means in English (if you are an English-speaking student in philosophy, say).
3. I shall ignore herein the difference between regarding background system A as a set of propositions rather than a "system", even though I think Lehrer is right to regard it as a proper system (since the way in which it must be a system is the way in which a theory or explanation of some data and facts must be distinguished from the mere set of propositions that are contained in the theory or explanation). Another point: Lehrer's set-up here makes a foundationalist program seem possible - i.e., building up the system A recursively starting with some proposition that beats all competitors when system A is empty, adding that "winner" to the empty A, and then proceeding on to other propositions adding subsequent winners to A to build it into a system of inter-relating propositions believed. Though possible for Lehrer, this is not his theory; e.g., recall his fallibilism (1986a, p. 14). But the mere possibility will help a little to explain why Lehrer's theory seems somewhat like Chisholm's foundationalism (of the Second Edition, *Theory of Knowledge*, 1977). For at the bottom of some of Chisholm's principles are some coherentistic sorts of relationships; cf. Principles G, M, and I.
4. And remember that competitorship is also a matter of reasonableness (and, thus, probability); i.e., p competes with q (for S given A) if and only if accepting p and not-q is more reasonable than accepting p and q (for S given A).
5. I view the task of evaluating knowledge theories as involving specifying phenomena (data) and general facts about cognition against which allegedly explanatory theories (like Lehrer's) can be judged. Data and phenomena for knowledge theories include instances of cognitions classified with respect to basic descriptive categories (such as the five dimensions I mentioned at the outset). The general facts that need explanation in any such theory (and which can't be violated, or must be "honored" at least) were stated in (1) above. For more discussion of this approach to evaluating knowledge theories, see my ms. "How to Evaluate Lehrer's Coherence Theory".
6. In (c), I use "is rationally consented to" to abbreviate a much longer phrase - viz., "is a matter of rational (in Lehrer & Wagner's special sense) social consensus of a particular sub-type - the sub-type corresponding to so-called non-demonstrative *a priori* certainties in traditional epistemologies". Just as it is not mere social consensus (e.g., such tacit agreement in one's group) that makes for genuine intuitions, but rational social consensus, so it is also not just mere rational social consensus that supports supposed intuitions, but a further special sub-type of it. For not every socially consented-to proposition that is genuinely rational for Lehrer would be a candidate for being an intuition. Some would be much too complex and lengthy, for example. As far as I can tell, Lehrer does not tell us how the particular sub-class of rationally consented to propositions that are intuitions would be defined or determined (but merely assumes that there must exist such a sub-class). Another point: Lehrer's fairly brief account of such intuitions (being certain rationally consented beliefs) is supported to some degree by his account of knowledge of one's own language (also dependent on tacit rational consensus). Thus, to criticize fully Lehrer's account of so-called *a priori* intuitions, one should also criticize his account of natural-language knowledge (linguistic competence). I omit this criticism due to space limitations. For details of it, see my above mentioned ms. "How to Evaluate Lehrer's Coherence Theory".

7. Matters concerning iterated epistemic operators (or modalities) can be confusing. I would like to convince the reader that I am not confused (or am relatively unconfused). Notice that (e) is ambiguous between (e1) and (e2):

(e) I know that p intuitively $\Bigg\{$

(e1) (I know that p) & (the style, manner, method or mode of knowing is intuitive)

(e2) I know that q, where q = p is intuitively true

Also, (e1) does not entail (e2), but (e2) does entail (e1) - where, remember, (e2) just is (c) above. It seems (to me) clear that (d) - knowing that you know that p is intuitive - entails simply knowing that you know that p. To simply know that you know that p (KKp for p = (4)) would traditionally be thought to involve (c) - i.e., knowing something about the kind of truth (4) is.
8. I leave Goldman's (1986) view out, as being less than puristically externalist - for a vital part of his theory are apparently internalized epistemic evaluation principles. About these, I recommend Chomskyizing as I just sketched for Lehrer.
9. Lehrer has made one of the best attempts, to my mind, at defending or developing ANTI-MALCOLMISM. (It's not the only attempt. Chisholm's theory (1977, Second edition) can be interpreted so as to also be anti-Malcolmian (cf. Lehrer 1983, p. 203).) One way of stating anti-Malcolmism is simply what Lehrer calls the "truth connection" - viz., that the right kind of very complete justification compels truth. Thus, there won't be any possibility of the only difference between any case of knowledge and a parallel case of belief simply being one of truth and falsity (if true, knowledge, and if false, belief). However, I think the price is much too high - viz., the practical (at least) impossibility of ever knowing that we know. It seems to me we have a dilemma here. We can come very close to (and maybe even achieve) knowledge that we know something if we ignore verificness and further defeaters and stick to personal justification (e.g., via fodorizing). Sometimes, of course, when we think we know that we know we will be wrong - and only believe we know (where, in turn, we may believe we know and the belief be true or we may believe we know and the belief be false). But in the right cases we will have knowledge of knowledge. However, the price will be Malcolmism. (For these cases of knowledge (i.e., KKp cases), the only difference between knowledge (KKP) and belief (BKp) will be truth and falsity.) On the other hand, if we re-consider verificness (i.e., Lehrer's actual theory), then we regain anti-Malcolmism but we lose any possibility of knowing that we know (KKp). In sum, Lehrer can only gain anti-Malcolmism (as he clearly wants to via his truth-connection) on pain of losing the possibility of knowledge that one knows and can only acquire the possibility of knowledge that one knows by losing anti-Malcolmism (the truth-connection).

REFERENCES

Alston, William. "Two Types of Foundationalism." *Journal of Philosophy*, 73 (1976), 165-185.
Armstrong, D. M. *Belief, Truth, and Knowledge.* Cambridge: Cambridge University Press, 1976.
Chisholm, Roderick. *The Theory of Knowledge.* Second Edition, Englewood Cliffs: Prentice Hall, 1977.
Chomsky, Noam. *Language and Mind.* Harcourt, Brace, Jovanovich, 1968.
-----. *Reflections on Language.* Pantheon, 1975.
-----. *Rules and Representations.* Columbia University Press, 1980.
Dretske, Fred. *Knowledge and the Flow of Information.* Cambridge: MIT Press, 1981.
Goldman, Alvin. *Epistemology and Cognition.* Cambridge: Harvard University Press, 1986.
Lehrer, Keith. *Knowledge.* Oxford: Oxford University Press, 1974.
-----, and Wagner, Carl. (1981a) *Rational Consensus in Science and Society* . Dordrecht: D. Reidel.
-----. "A Self-Profile." (1981b) In *Keith Lehrer* R. J. Bogdan, ed., Dordrecht: D. Reidel.
-----. "Knowledge, Truth, and Ontology." In *Language and Ontology.* Dordrecht: D. Reidel, 1982.
-----, and Cohen, Stewart. "Justification, Truth, and Coherence." *Synthese,* 55 (1983), 191-207.
-----. "The Coherence Theory of Knowledge." (1986a). *Philosophical Topics,* 14(1), 5-25.
-----. "Metamind: Belief, Consciousness, and Intentionality." (1986b). In *Belief: Form, Content, and Function* , R. J. Bogdan, ed., Clarendon Press.
-----. Lectures on Knowledge. (1986c). NEH Institute on the Theory of Knowledge, University of Colorado, Boulder, June 16-19, July 10, August 7-8.
-----. "Metaknowledge: Undefeated Justification." *Synthese,* 74, (1988), 329-347.
Malcolm, Norman. "Knowledge and Belief." In Phillips Griffiths 1967.
Nagel, Thomas. "Linguistics and Epistemology." *In Language and Philosophy* , S. Hook, ed.. New York: New York University Press, 1969.
Peterson, P. L. "How to Infer Belief from Knowledge." *Philosophical Studies,* 32 (1977), 203-209.
-----. "On Lehrer's Proof that Knowledge Entails Belief." *Southern Journal of Philosophy,* 21 (1983), 271-79.

-----. "Real Logic in Philosophy." *The Monist,* 69(2) (1986) 236-263.
Phillips Griffiths, A., ed. *Knowledge and Belief.* Oxford University Press, 1967.
Prichard, H. "Knowing and Believing." In Phillips Griffiths, 1967.
Shope, R. K. *The Analysis of Knowing.* Princeton: Princeton University Press, 1983.

When Can What You Don't Know Hurt You?

Bruce Russell
Wayne State University

There seem to be Gettier cases that do not involve any false beliefs that the coherentist must say involve knowledge. In order to avoid this result the coherentist must attribute false *assumptions* to the subject, but that forces him to say that knowledge is lacking in certain cases involving misleading, unpossessed evidence. I will argue that the coherentist cannot escape this dilemma. That is because knowledge requires reliable, non-negligent belief formation where, in addition, the subject does not hold a true belief by sheer luck, and coherentism cannot adequately account for any of these conditions.

I. The Dilemma

Suppose Nogot has a reputation for honesty but decides one day to play a trick on his friend Jones. In the sincerest tones he tells Jones that he owns a Ford and backs up his lie with fake ownership papers. Jones concludes that someone in his office owns a Ford since he believes with justification that Nogot does and that Nogot is in his office. Havit is in Jones' office, too, and he does own a Ford. So Jones is justified in believing that someone in his office owns a Ford, and someone does. But Jones lacks knowledge. This is the stuff of which Gettiers are made, as we all know (or at least are justified in believing).

But how can a coherentist account for the lack of knowledge in cases of this type? Doesn't "Someone in the office owns a Ford" cohere with the rest of Jones' beliefs? More specifically, isn't it undefeated by his other beliefs? But then coherence plus truth is not sufficient for knowledge.

There are two ways that a coherentist might handle Gettier cases. First, he might simply require that for a belief to constitute knowledge it must not depend essentially for its justification on any false beliefs.[1] Jones' belief that someone in his office owns a Ford fails this requirement since it depends essentially for its justification on his false belief that Nogot owns a Ford.

Second, the coherentist might require that a belief cohere with not only the subject's actual beliefs (or acceptances) but also with the set of beliefs consisting of the subject's true beliefs and the beliefs he would have if his false beliefs were replaced by true ones (see Lehrer, 1988, 343-44). In this way one can show that Jones is not completely justified in believing, and so does not know, that someone in his office owns a Ford since that belief is defeated by the true belief that Nogot does not own a Ford, a belief which is in the relevant set. So even a coherentist can hold that what a person doesn't know can hurt him - epistemically.

But imagine a more complicated version of the Nogot-Havit case in which Jones' belief that someone in his office owns a Ford does not seem to depend essentially for its justification on any false beliefs. Suppose Nogot asks his wife to get fake ownership papers on a Ford made up. She happens to be cleaning out the attic and discovers ownership papers on a Ford that Nogot still owns and, as she now remembers, has for years kept parked in his uncle's barn far across the country. She leaves the papers on the kitchen table for Nogot with no note explaining her discovery. Nogot thinks they are faked ownership papers, shows them to Jones and tells Jones he owns an old Ford, all the time thinking he does not.

In this case Jones' justification for thinking that Nogot owns a Ford does not seem to depend on any false beliefs. He believes that Nogot has shown him *bona fide* ownership papers to a Ford, that Nogot is an honest person and that Nogot has not lied to him on this occasion. All of these beliefs are true, the last since Nogot must tell a

J.W. Bender (ed.), The Current State of the Coherence Theory, 94–102.
© *1989 by Kluwer Academic Publishers.*

falsehood if he is to lie and he has told the truth, even though he thinks he hasn't.

How can a coherentist account for Jones' lack of knowledge regarding Nogot's ownership of a Ford? It would seem that Jones' belief that Nogot owns a Ford coheres with both his actual set of beliefs (his acceptance system in Lehrer's terminology) and with the set of beliefs consisting of Jones' true beliefs plus the beliefs he would have if his false beliefs were replaced by true ones (that set being a member of Jones' ultrasystem in Lehrer's recent terminology).

The coherentist must attribute certain false beliefs or assumptions to Jones the denials of which will defeat his justification for his belief that Nogot owns a Ford. What might these be? Well, it might plausibly be said that Jones assumes that Nogot is not trying to deceive him on this occasion, that belief is false and its denial will defeat Jones' justification for "Nogot owns a Ford."

Now a critic might reply that Jones might not assume any such thing because it is possible that no such thought ever entered Jones' mind. (For a similar point see Davis and Bender, 1988.) But this response won't do since we can assume certain things without actually forming any beliefs about them. I assume that the chair I am sitting on will not collapse though up until a moment ago I had formed no belief about the chair's stability.

A critic might grant that a person can assume something without ever having formed the relevant belief, deny that a person can assume something if she is not capable of forming the relevant belief and add that a person might not be capable of forming the belief, say, that the chair she is sitting on will not collapse. A small child, for instance, might lack the concepts to form the relevant belief and yet be said to assume, and know, certain things.

Perhaps all that is required for someone to assume something in believing something else is the following: if he believed the denial of what he assumes then he would not believe that other thing. For instance, even if Jones were not even capable of forming the belief that Nogot is not trying to deceive him, Jones still assumes that he is not because if Jones believed that Nogot was trying to deceive him he would not believe that Nogot owns a Ford.

But this proposal isn't quite right either. Suppose Jones believes that Nogot owns a Ford both on the basis of the evidence Nogot offers and because Nogot's uncle tells Jones that Nogot has had an old Ford parked in his barn for years. Jones assumes that Nogot is not trying to deceive him but, on the basis of the uncle's testimony, he would still believe that Nogot owns a Ford even if he thought that Nogot was trying to deceive him.

The above considerations prompt the following revision: if a person believes something on the basis of something else, then that person makes a certain assumption just in case he would fail to believe what he believes on that basis were he to believe the denial of the assumption and believed what he believes *solely* on the basis in question. In other words: if S believes p on the basis of r, then S assumes q just in case S would fail to believe p if S believed not-q and had no other basis for believing p but r.

Even this revision won't do. Suppose Jones so admires Nogot for his honesty that he would still believe what Nogot told him even if he learned that Nogot was trying to deceive him. Because of his admiration for Nogot and some psychological quirk or defect, on coming to believe that Nogot is trying to deceive him Jones will rationalize, "Nogot probably is self-deceived and really does own a Ford even if he thinks he doesn't." In such a case it could still be true that Jones assumes that Nogot is not trying to deceive him even though he would not cease to believe that Nogot owns a Ford if he believed the assumption were false.

Suppose we require that if S believes p on the basis of r, then S assumes q just in case S would fail to believe p if S believed not-q, had no other basis for believing p but r, and S were epistemically non-defective. With the introduction of epistemic non-defectiveness we get a normative account of what it is to assume something in believing something else, but the account might still be naturalistic since non-defectiveness might be understood naturalistically (e.g., as freedom from certain empirically discoverable defects). On this account it can still be said that Jones assumes that Nogot is not trying to deceive him even if Jones has the psychological defect discussed above and even if Jones believes that Nogot owns a Ford partly on the basis of the uncle's testimony.

Can the critic of coherentism offer a case where someone does not know something even though, on the above account, it can be argued that he holds no false beliefs and makes no false assumptions and so, according to the coherentist, knows? For instance, can some sort of Nogot-Havit case be constructed where according to the above account Jones neither believes nor assumes, say, that Nogot is not trying to deceive him? The coherentist might argue that no such example can be constructed because for there to be such an example it must be possible for there to be a defeater but for the subject to fail to assume the denial of the defeater. Applied to the Nogot case and given the above account of assuming, this means that it must be possible for Nogot to be trying to deceive Jones and for Jones to believe that Nogot owns a Ford, even if Jones were epistemically non-defective, believed Nogot was trying to deceive him and believed that Nogot owns a Ford solely on the basis of the evidence that Nogot presented. For any example proposed the coherentist could maintain that Jones is epistemically defective, and so we are not entitled to conclude that he does not assume the denial of the defeater.

There are two problems the coherentist faces if he takes this approach. To defend against the possibility that no false assumptions are made in cases where knowledge is lacking, it appears that the coherentist must adopt an account of assuming that makes reference to epistemic non-defectiveness. But without an account of epistemic non-defectiveness his account will be seriously incomplete.

Second, without supplementation, the coherentist's account will force him to say that people lack knowledge where intuitively it seems they don't. Consider the Tom Grabit case introduced by Lehrer and Paxson (1978, 150). I see Tom Grabit take a book from the shelf, put it under his coat and walk out of the library. Assuming Tom Grabit took the book, then I know he took it even if his demented mother, who is also a compulsive and pathological liar, falsely said that he was far away at the time and that his identical twin, John (who is only a figment of Mrs. Grabit's imagination), was the person in the library. I will know Tom stole the book provided that I am non-culpably ignorant of what Mrs. Grabit said. According to the account given of assuming, I assume that Tom Grabit's mom did not say that Tom was elsewhere, etc., for if I believed she said that Tom was far away at the time, etc., I would no longer believe that Tom stole the book if I were epistemically non-defective. But then I make a false assumption that will be replaced in a set in my ultrasystem by the true statement that Tom's mom said that Tom was elsewhere at the time, which will defeat my belief that Tom stole the book. So according to the coherentist I don't know that Tom stole the book. The coherentist gets it right in the Nogot cases at the price of getting it wrong in Grabit-type cases.

Can the coherentist argue that I assume not only that Tom's mom did not say that Tom was elsewhere at the time, etc., but also that Tom's mom is not demented? If he can, then the statement that Tom's mom is demented, and a compulsive and pathological liar, will also be in my ultrasystem and will neutralize the claim about what she said. Hence even according to the coherentist I will know that Tom stole the book.

But on the account of assuming developed above it cannot be claimed that in believing that Tom stole the book I assume that Tom's mom is not demented. I would still believe that Tom stole the book even if I were epistemically non-defective, believed that Tom's mom was demented, and believed Tom stole the book on the basis of what I observed in the library.

There is a problem with the account of assuming I've offered. While it follows from that account that in believing Tom stole the book I do not assume that Tom's mom is not demented, it also follows that I assume the conjunction that Tom's mom did not say Tom was far away, etc., and that Tom's mom is not demented. That is so because I would fail to believe Tom stole the book if I did not believe the relevant conjunction because I believed Tom's mom did say Tom was far away, etc. For the same reason it will follow that I assume every possible conjunction that has as one of its conjuncts the statement that Tom's mom did not say Tom was far away, etc..

To avoid this result I will require that in order for S to assume some conjunction it must be true that S assumes each conjunct independently. Thus it will follow that I assume that Mrs. Grabit did not say Tom was far away but don't assume that and that she is not demented since I don't assume the second conjunct independently.

There is a larger problem with the account of assuming I have offered which threatens to undermine the dilemma I have posed for the coherentist. We can certainly imagine cases where we would say that I assume Mrs. Grabit exists and believe that Tom stole the book, but where I am epistemically non-defective, yet would not cease to believe that Tom stole the book if I came to believe that Mrs. Grabit did not exist. But according to my account of assumption, I would have to say that such a case is not possible. So even if the conditions I gave for assuming something in believing something else are sufficient, they are not necessary. Hence I cannot use my account of assuming to argue that I don't assume Mrs. Grabit is not demented. So I can't show that it is possible for me to assume that Mrs. Grabit didn't say that Tom was far away at the time, etc., and at the same time not assume that it is false that she is demented, a pathological liar, etc.

But isn't it obvious that this is possible? Why couldn't I fail to assume anything about Mrs. Grabit's being demented and a liar? In that case I would not assume that she is demented and a pathological liar nor would I assume that it is false that she is demented and a pathological liar. Hence "she is demented and a pathological liar" would be neither in my acceptance system nor in any set in my ultrasystem. Thus it could not neutralize "Mrs. Grabit did say that Tom was far away at the time, etc.." and so according to Lehrer, but contrary to intuition, I would not know that Tom stole the book.

To avoid this result Lehrer must offer an account of assumption from which it will follow that I *must* assume either that Mrs. Grabit is demented, etc., or assume that that is false. In that case a defeater of "Mrs. Grabit said that Tom was far away, etc.." will either be in my acceptance system or in some other set in my ultrasystem. But any account that has that result will probably also have as a result that I must assume either p or not-p, (at least) for every p I can comprehend (for instance, if the test of whether I assume p is whether I would answer "yes" to the question, "Do you believe p?"). Not only does that seem implausible but it has the following untoward result when coupled with Lehrer's theory: I can fail to know something which is true, which I believe is true, which (in any ordinary sense) I am completely justified in believing is true and which involves no Gettier problems.

Consider the following example: it is true that the dusky seaside sparrow is extinct, I believe that it is and my belief is justified because I have read it in all the papers. I falsely assume that no eminent ornithologist thinks otherwise and have good grounds for thinking that. However, some eminent ornithologist on his death bed in a Tibetan monastery thinks wrongly that there are some dusky seaside sparrows left. He is so eminent that his opinion would undercut my justification if I were aware of it, but no one is aware of his opinion and no one is negligent in being ignorant of it. This is not a Gettier case since my false assumption does not form any part of my grounds for thinking there are no more dusky seaside sparrows, and it is not just by luck that I am unaware of the ornithologist's opinion. If anything, I would be lucky to know of it.

Lehrer has to say that I do not know that the dusky seaside sparrow is extinct because my false assumption that no eminent ornithologist thinks otherwise will be replaced by a true belief in my ultrasystem and that belief will defeat the justification I have for believing the little birds are extinct. But intuitively I think we see the relevant ignorance as harmless relative to my knowledge that the birds are extinct.

Lehrer can avoid the difficulties I have raised if he can show that Jones must assume that Nogot is not trying to deceive him and that I must assume that it is false that Mrs. Grabit is demented, etc.. The only way he can do that promises to imply that we assume something about everything we can comprehend and that knowledge is lacking where intuitively it is not.

In the remainder of the paper I will explore some views that promise to account for our intuitions in Nogot-Havit and Grabit-type cases and ultimately offer an account which requires the rejection of coherentism.

II. A Non-Coherentist Solution

What is the difference between the Nogot and Grabit-type cases? Why is knowledge lacking in the one but not in the other? According to earlier Lehrer I know that Tom stole the book because my justification for believing he did does not depend on my being completely justified in believing it to be false that Mrs. Grabit said that Tom was far away at the time, etc.. In contrast, in the original Nogot-Havit case, Jones' justification for thinking someone in his office owns a Ford does depend on Jones' being completely justified in believing it to be false that Nogot does not own a Ford.

But what Lehrer says here seems mistaken. My justification for believing Tom stole the book *does* depend on my being completely justified in believing it to be false that Tom's mom said that Tom was far away, etc., for if I believed Tom's mom said what she did, and were completely justified in believing it, then my justification for thinking Tom stole the book would be undercut (provided I assumed she was sincere and not demented). In the respects Lehrer focuses upon, the Tom Grabit case is like the original Nogot case. In the latter case Jones' justification for believing that someone in his office owns a Ford depends on Jones' being completely justified in believing it to be false that Nogot does not own a Ford because if Jones believed, and were completely justified in believing, that Nogot did not own a Ford then he wouldn't be justified in believing that someone in his office owns a Ford.

Perhaps the difference between the Nogot and the Grabit case in some way has to do with the *relative accessibility* of the potential defeater. Perhaps in some sense the potential defeater in the Grabit case is "farther away," less accessible, than the potential defeater in the Nogot case.

But this difference cannot be the essential difference between Nogot-type and Grabit-type cases, for suppose two of my sisters know what Mrs. Grabit said, do not know she is demented and a liar, and would tell me what they know if I just asked. Then the potential defeater of my belief that Tom stole the book is very accessible, more accessible than the potential defeater is to Jones in the Nogot case. Still, I would know that Tom stole the book.

Nor can the difference between the modified Nogot case and the Grabit case be accounted for by the *relative closeness* of the potential defeater to its potential defeater. One might think that I know that Tom Grabit stole the book because, in some sense, the fact, or my belief that, Mrs. Grabit is a liar and demented is "relatively close to" the fact that, or my belief that, she said that Tom was far away, etc.. So what undercuts Mrs. Grabit's testimony is "in the same neighborhood" as that potential defeater of my knowledge. If I came to learn that Mrs. Grabit said Tom was far away, I would also come to learn that she was demented and a liar. In contrast, in the modified Nogot case, the wife or the uncle's testimony is "relatively far from" the potential defeater, viz., that Nogot is trying to deceive Jones. It is not likely that if Jones came to learn that Nogot is trying to deceive him he would also come to learn of the wife's or uncle's testimony that Nogot does indeed own a Ford.

But the relative closeness of the defeater's defeater to it is not essential to whether or not there is knowledge. Again, imagine that my two sisters know what Mrs. Grabit said and so the potential defeater is fairly close. Imagine, also, that neither my sisters nor many others know that Mrs. Grabit is a liar and demented. I would still know that Tom stole the book, provided the information my sisters possess is not so close as to make me negligent in not being aware of it.

Perhaps the difference between the original Nogot case and the Grabit case is that in the Nogot case part of the actual reasoning that leads Jones to the belief that someone in his office owns a Ford contains the false belief that Nogot owns a Ford while no reasoning in the Grabit case contains a false belief, in particular, not the false belief that Mrs. Grabit did not say that Tom was far away, etc.. But the reasoning in the modified Nogot case does not contain any false beliefs either since it is assumed that no part of Jones' reasoning involves the false belief that Nogot is not trying to deceive him. Still, Jones does not know that Nogot owns a Ford.

My suggestion is that the difference between the modified Nogot case and Grabit-type cases is that in the former case the relevant belief is not based on reliable evidence whereas in the latter type of case it is. For the most part, if a person tells you what he believes is false, and shows you evidence that he thinks is forged, in order to get you to believe something, then what he is trying to get you to believe generally will be false. If it turns out to be true and you believe it, you will luckily believe the truth, in the same way that the person who is, and believes he is, looking at a real barn, in circumstances where there are many indiscernible barn facades about, luckily believes the truth. So in the modified Nogot case, Jones luckily believes the truth when he believes that Nogot owns a Ford. In contrast, since the evidence of the senses is reliable, I do not luckily believe the truth when I believe that Tom Grabit stole the book, regardless of what Tom's mom said, provided I am not culpably ignorant of what she said. Given the other circumstances in the Grabit case I know Tom stole the book, but Jones does not know Nogot owns a Ford.

Of course the cases could be modified so that things are different. If I knew what Tom's mom said, but did not know that she is a liar and demented, then I would have reason to believe that the evidence I had for thinking Tom stole the book was not reliable and so would not know that Tom stole the book. Nor would I know that Tom stole the book if I did not in fact know what she said but should have known. And if Tom had many identical siblings about town, then I would not know that Tom stole the book even if his mom had said nothing. That would make the Grabit case very much like the one involving the barn facades. Further, if Jones knew that Nogot's wife, or uncle, were sure that Nogot did own a Ford, and based his belief, at least in part, on that, then Jones would have a reliable basis for his belief and so would possess knowledge. So it looks as though my belief must not rest solely on unreliable evidence, or be produced solely by an unreliable mechanism, if it is to constitute knowledge. And I must not be justified in believing that the evidence is unreliable, even if it is in fact reliable, as is shown by the case where I know what Mrs. Grabit said but do not know she is a liar and demented. In that case my senses would be a reliable basis for identifying Tom though I would not be justified in believing they were.

While these considerations will enable us to handle many cases correctly, they will not help with others. Suppose Nogot is not trying to deceive Jones but that Jones believes Nogot owns a Ford on the basis of seeing him drive around in one that in fact is borrowed. On the basis of believing that Nogot owns a Ford, Jones then believes that someone in his office owns a Ford. We can assume that Jones' seeing Nogot driving around in a Ford is reliable evidence that Nogot owns a Ford and, given Jones' background knowledge, reliable evidence that someone in his office owns a Ford. Still, contrary to the suggestion above, Nogot does not know that someone in his office owns a Ford. Perhaps knowledge requires that the relevant belief neither be based on *false nor unreliable* evidence, where false evidence is evidence the statement of which is a falsehood. To handle cases involving overdetermination, this could be modified to say that the relevant belief must not be based *solely* on false or unreliable evidence.

But isn't my belief that Tom Grabit stole the book *based on* the false evidence that Mrs. Grabit did not say that Tom was far away? Given what I said about assumptions above, I must grant that I *assume* Mrs. Grabit did not say Tom was far away. And given what I said against Lehrer above, I must grant that my justification for believing that Tom stole the book depends on my not being justified in believing that Mrs. Grabit said Tom was far away. But since the belief that Mrs. Grabit did not say that Tom was far away does not constitute part of my *evidence* for believing Tom stole the book, my belief that Tom stole the book is not based on any false evidence. On the other hand, part of Jones' evidence that someone in his office owns a Ford is the false belief that Nogot owns a Ford. Jones' reasoning that leads him to hold that someone in his office owns a Ford implicitly rests on his belief that Nogot owns a Ford while no reasoning (if there is any) that leads me to believe that Tom stole the book rests on a belief that Tom's mom did not say certain things.

The above considerations support the following account of knowledge:

> S knows that p if and only if:
>
> (1) p
> (2) S believes p
> (3) S justifiably believes p
> (4) S's belief that p is not luckily true
> (5) S's belief that p is not based solely on (a) unreliable or (b) false evidence.

(3) will imply that S is not negligent in failing to be aware of potential defeaters of p. It will also imply that I do not justifiedly believe either that my evidence, or the mechanism that produced my belief, is unreliable, regardless of whether or not it is.

Let's apply the above analysis to a case offered by John Bender (1988). Johnny's mother believes truly that Johnny is not taking drugs, and she believes this on the grounds that if he were she would know it and know of any evidence supporting the claim that he is taking drugs. She is justified in all her beliefs and they are true. But she doesn't realize that Johnny is hiding drugs at home. That fact is a potential defeater of Mom's belief but it would in turn be defeated by the fact that Johnny is hiding the drugs for a friend. Johnny's snoopy sisters know that Johnny is hiding the drugs and they are worried that they are his, not a friend's. Bender says that in these circumstances Mother does *not* know that Johnny is not taking drugs and asks, "How can she know, when, in one sense, she knows less than her daughters?".

Bender distinguishes the above case from the Tom Grabit case by pointing out that the potential defeater in the Grabit case is "not in the public domain" (Bender, 1988a, note 29). But, again, it is possible for me to know that Tom stole the book even if two of my sisters knew that Mrs. Grabit said that Tom was far away and his identical twin was in the library at the time, but did not know she was demented and a liar. It all depends on whether I was just lucky in not knowing what my sisters knew. If I was, then I will not know that Tom stole the book. However, if I was not just lucky, say, because my sisters never tell me secrets, then I would know even if there was a potential defeater "in the public domain." Many times I will be lucky not to know of a potential defeater "in the public domain," but not always. So whether the potential defeater is in the public domain or not cannot account for Bender's claim that Mother does not know that Johnny is not taking drugs.

Since this case *is* relevantly similar to the Tom Grabit cases, I think Johnny's mother does know that Johnny is not taking drugs. And the same result will follow on the account I have given. The evidence Johnny's mom has that he is not taking drugs is reliable since in this example any evidence there is that he is taking drugs will be misleading when Johnny is not in fact taking drugs. Given that Mom will know if Johnny is taking drugs, and know of any evidence that he is taking drugs when he is, any evidence which Mom lacks that he is not taking drugs when he is not will not undercut or override the grounds Mom has for thinking Johnny is not taking drugs. By hypothesis Mom cannot believe falsely that Johnny is not taking drugs (though she can believe falsely that he is). Thus Mom is completely reliable concerning the belief that her son is not taking drugs. And her belief that Johnny is not taking drugs is not based on false evidence since it is assumed that no part of her evidence or grounds for thinking Johnny is not taking drugs is based on a belief that Johnny is not hiding any drugs at home. Assuming Mom is not negligent in failing to realize that Johnny is hiding drugs at home, she is justified in believing that he is not taking drugs. Further, it does not seem that Mom holds a true belief by sheer luck of the type involved in the barn facade cases. Hence according to the account I offered above, Mom knows that Johnny is not taking drugs.

If your intuitions are that Mom does not know that Johnny is not taking drugs, perhaps it is because you think she holds a true belief only through sheer luck or because she is negligent in not knowing of the hidden drugs. If so, then our conflicting intuitions will be over how to draw the line with my thinking she is not negligent or lucky in holding the beliefs she does and your thinking she is. But both of us should be agreed that the coherentist cannot account for the relevance of luck or negligence to the presence or absence of knowledge. A belief might cohere with everything I believe and assume and yet I might be lucky or negligent in failing to be aware of a defeater of that belief. That will be possible even if I am generally a trustworthy evaluator of evidence and of my own evaluative powers. Or you might be thinking that this case is relevantly similar to one where Johnny's mom grounds her belief that Johnny is not taking drugs on the false belief that if he were she would be aware of the evidence, overlooking the fact that this subjunctive is true in the original example.

Even if I do not agree with Bender's intuition in his example, I think he was on the right track in his implied objection to coherentism. It appears that knowledge can be defeated even when the subject holds no false background beliefs - as in the modified Nogot case. To account for the lack of knowledge in such cases the coherentist will have to argue that, perhaps contrary to first appearances, false *assumptions* are involved. The danger then is that he will also be forced to say that false assumptions are made that defeat knowledge in cases where there is misleading, unpossessed evidence and where intuitively knowledge is present - as in the Tom Grabit cases.

I have tried to distinguish the modified Nogot case from the Tom Grabit case on the grounds that in the former case, but not in the latter, the relevant belief is based on unreliable evidence. For the most part, when a person is trying to deceive someone what that person is trying to get the other person to believe will be false. I have tried to distinguish the Tom Grabit case from one where Jones comes to believe that someone in his office owns a Ford, on seeing Nogot driving around in one, on the grounds that Jones' reasoning implicitly relies on the false belief that Nogot owns a Ford, whereas in the Grabit case the observer's reasoning (if there is any) to his belief that Tom stole the book from the library does not in any way rely on a false belief. It does not because the observer's assumption that Mrs. Grabit did not say that Tom was far away at the time does not constitute any part of the observer's grounds or support for believing Tom stole the book.

The general idea behind my account is that knowledge is justified true belief where the believer is not just lucky in holding such a belief and not just lucky in being ignorant of potential defeaters. But there are many ways a believer might be lucky in holding a true belief. It may be out of sheer luck, as when he is in a situation where he could easily have held a false belief and not been able to tell the difference. Or it may be because he was negligent and just lucky to have believed the truth. Or it might be because his belief was formed by an unreliable belief forming mechanism or process so it was unlikely that his belief would be true. Or his reasoning might contain a false belief so that the conclusion he reaches is only accidentally related to his premises.

The coherentist cannot account for the difference between a coherent set of true beliefs, where the believer is lucky that he holds true beliefs, and where he is not. That is because whether a belief is luckily true or not depends on the believer's culpability or on some factor external to the believer and his beliefs, neither of which can be accounted for by the coherentist.[2]

The moral of this story is that what you don't know can, but need not, hurt you. The Nogot cases show that what you don't know can undermine what you otherwise would know; the Grabit case shows that it need not. Coherentism cannot properly account for when what you don't know hurts you and when it doesn't.[3]

NOTES

1. It is possible to hold that a belief can be justified if it is based on, that is causally sustained by, a false belief, and that it cannot be justified if it depends essentially for its justification on a false belief. For instance, a belief might be justified if a person is aware of incontrovertible evidence in its favor, and aware that it is strong evidence, even if his belief is based on prejudice and the associated false beliefs (Lehrer, 1988, 339-40). On the other hand, a belief might fail to be justified if what the person takes to be provide grounds for the belief contains false beliefs, even if it is causally sustained by true beliefs.
2. A coherentist could claim that he is merely offering an account of epistemic justification, agree with Gettier that justified true belief is not sufficient for knowledge and hold that the problems I have focused on are Gettier problems that must be solved by some supplementary, non-coherentist requirement. This might be true, though for reasons given by Davis and Bender (1988), Plantinga (1986), and others I do not think the coherentist can offer even an adequate account of justification. If it is true, then Lehrer's recent attempts to include within the conditions of complete justification requirements needed to solve Gettier problems will either be inadequate or go behond anything that could properly be called coherentism.
3. I want to thank my colleagues at Wayne State University for their comments on a much earlier (and rougher) draft of this paper. My special and heartfelt thanks are to Jack Bender whose tireless probing and questioning of points in earlier drafts have made this paper much better than it otherwise would have been.

REFERENCES

Bender, John W. "Knowledge, Justification, and Lehrer's Theory of Coherence." *Philosophical Studies* (1988), (forthcoming).
Davis, Wayne A., and John W. Bender. "Fundamental Troubles With The Coherence Theory," this volume.
Lehrer, Keith, "Metaknowledge: Undefeated Justification." *Synthese* 74 (1988), 329-47.
-----. "The Coherence Theory of Knowledge." *Philosophical Topics* 14 (1986), 5-25.
-----, and Paxson, Thomas. "Knowledge: Undefeated Justified True Belief." *Journal of Philosophy* 66 (1968) 225-37. Reprinted in *Esasys on Knowledge and Justification*, George S. Pappas and Marshall Swain, eds., Cornell University Press, 1978, 146-54.
Plantinga, Alvin. "Coherentism and the Evidentialist Objection to Belief in God," in *Rationality, Religious Belief, & Moral Commitment*, Robert Audi and William J. Wainwright, eds., Ithaca: Cornell University Press, 1986: 109-38.

iii. focus: laurence bonjour's

THE STRUCTURE OF
EMPIRICAL KNOWLEDGE

BonJour's *The Structure of Empirical Knowledge*

Alvin I. Goldman
University of Arizona

The Structure of Empirical Knowledge (BonJour, 1985) is a detailed and subtle defense of a coherentist account of epistemic justification. It can plausibly be claimed that it is unsurpassed, in thoroughness and sophistication, by any other sympathetic treatment of coherentism. Nonetheless, there are in my view serious problems with some of the book's central theses. This discussion will concentrate on several of the problem areas that I take to be crucial to BonJour's position.

The book begins with a discussion of the concept of epistemic justification. BonJour writes:

> The basic role of justification is that of a *means* to truth... We cannot...bring it about directly that our beliefs are true, but we can presumably bring it about directly ... that they are epistemically justified. And, *if our standards of epistemic justification are appropriately chosen,* bringing it about that our beliefs are epistemically justified will also tend to bring it about ... that they are true. If epistemic justification were not conducive to truth in this way ... then epistemic justification would be irrelevant to our main cognitive goal and of dubious worth. ...Epistemic justification is therefore in the final analysis only an instrumental value, not an intrinsic one...Any degree of epistemic justification, however small, must increase to a commensurate degree the chances that the belief in question is true ... for otherwise it cannot qualify as epistemic justification at all. (7-8)

To a reliabilist like me, these remarks are very congenial, since they place an appropriate emphasis on the role of truth conduciveness in the concept of epistemic justification. However, BonJour imposes additional constraints on justification and subsequently makes it perfectly clear (as he has done in previous writings) that he rejects reliabilism, or any other version of externalism. Let us see how he arrives at those additional constraints.

Soon after the just-quoted material, BonJour writes:

> Part of the task of (a theory of empirical knowledge) is evident: to provide an appropriately detailed account of the standards of criteria for the epistemic justification of empirical beliefs, of the conditions under which empirical beliefs qualify as epistemically justified. (9)

He here introduces a critical notion: a notion of a standard, or criterion, of epistemic justification. Surprisingly, BonJour says rather little about the nature of epistemic standards. But he does say this much: a standard is something that specifies the "conditions under which empirical beliefs qualify as epistemically justified." This characterization, however, is not wholly clear. The most natural reading of it is that a standard of justification is a set of conditions that purports to be necessary and sufficient for a belief's being justified. A belief that meets a standard, at least a *correct* standard, thereby qualifies as justified.

Unfortunately, this straightforward understanding of a standard of justification is not compatible with what BonJour goes on to say about justification. In light of a further constraint he introduces, it may be impossible for anything whatever to count as a correct standard of justification. The notion may simply be inconsistent, at least relative to this further requirement. I have in mind his requirement of a *metajustification*.

> (O)n the present conception, the main task of a theory of empirical knowledge divides into two parts... . The first part is to give an account of the standards of

105

J.W. Bender (ed.), The Current State of the Coherence Theory, 105–114.
© *1989 by Kluwer Academic Publishers.*

> epistemic justification: and the second is to provide what I will call a
> *metajustification* for the proposed account by showing the proposed standards to
> be adequately truth-conducive. (9)

BonJour does not mean merely that there should be a metajustification that can be given by epistemologists. He means that each believer himself should be in possession of the metajustification.

> If a given putative knower is himself to be epistemically responsible in accepting
> beliefs in virtue of their meeting the standards of a given epistemological account,
> then it seems to follow that an appropriate metajustification of those standards
> must, in principle at least, be available *to him*. For how can the fact that a belief
> meets those standards give that believer a reason for thinking that it is likely to
> be true ... unless he himself knows that beliefs satisfying those standards are
> likely to be true? Why should the fact that a metajustification can be supplied
> from the outside by an epistemologist, or is available in some other way which is
> beyond the believer's own cognitive grasp, mean that his belief (as opposed to an
> analogous belief held by the outside observer) is justified? Of course, his grasp of
> such a metajustification may be more or less tacit or implicit, and this provides
> some room for maneuver. (10)

What BonJour seems to be saying, then, is that S's belief B is justified only if B not only meets a correct standard of epistemic justification, but also S possesses a metajustification for the correctness of that standard, i.e., a justification for the thesis that that standard is truth conducive. But if this requirement is imposed, nothing can constitute a correct standard of justification understood as a (necessary and) *sufficient* condition for justifiedness. For any standard D you choose, meeting that standard cannot suffice for justifiedness, because justifiedness requires, in addition, possession of a metajustification of D's truth-conduciveness.

Perhaps this just shows that a standard of justification cannot be understood as a set of necessary and sufficient conditions of justifiedness. But how, then, should it be understood? Merely as a set of necessary conditions? That is surely a very weak reading, and unlikely to be the one intended. In any case, BonJour owes us a fuller explanation of what he means by a standard of justification, and a demonstration that what is intended by this term is compatible with his metajustification requirement. He also owes us an account of what it is for a standard of justification to be *correct*. Is truth conduciveness of a standard sufficient for correctness, or are there other constraints as well?

A further problem with BonJour's metajustification requirement is that it seems to introduce a circularity into his account of justified belief. The theory he ostensibly endorses says: "S's belief B is justified if and only if there is a correct standard D that B meets and S is justified in believing that D is truth conducive." This theory, however, itself employs the term "justified," and thereby suffers from circularity. The situation is not improved if one says (as BonJour sometimes does) that S must have "good reasons" for believing that the standard in question is truth conducive. "Good reasons" is an epistemic phrase on a par with "justified," and is equally inappropriate in an account of justification. (I have elsewhere argued that epistemologists should provide a factual, nonepistemic set of conditions for justifiedness, just as normative ethics should provide factual conditions for rightness. See Goldman (1979) and Goldman (1986).)

BonJour is at least somewhat sensitive to this problem. On page 10 he worries whether a metajustificational argument can appeal to the same standard of empirical justification as a normal empirical belief, and rejects this possibility on grounds of circularity. This is not the very same problem of circularity I have in mind, but his response may suggest how he wishes to reply to my problem as well as to his own. BonJour says that an argument that provides a metajustification for a standard's truth conduciveness must be purely *a priori* in character: it should not appeal to any empirical premise. This suggests a possible response to my circularity worry as well. BonJour might say that the core of his book is not an account of justification in general but of *empirical* justification. If, moreover, the metajustification requirement is rendered expressly in terms of *a priori* justification, then the apparent circularity is removed. The new theory would read: "S's belief B is *empirically justified* if and only if there is a correct standard D that B meets and S is *a priori justified* in believing that D is truth conducive."

This response, however, gives rise to several worries. First, *a priori* justification is itself a species of epistemic status. If a theory of epistemic status should get outside the nexus of epistemic categories altogether, appeal to this variety of justification will still be unsatisfactory. Second, it might seem that BonJour's move to *a priori* justification only postpones the difficulty: for won't there have to be an *a priori* metajustification of every *a priori* justified belief? And won't we now have the kind of cirularity I was worried about in the first place? BonJour has a straightforward reply to this concern. He rejects any need for a metajustificatory argument in the realm of *a priori* beliefs. However, this reply is itself problematic. BonJour's main defense of the need for a metajustificational requirement is an appeal to what he calls "epistemic responsibility." A person is epistemically responsible in his cognitive endeavors only if he accepts beliefs which he has good reason to think are true. And this, according to BonJour, leads to the metajustification requirement. But epistemic responsibility is called for as much in the realm of the *a priori* as the realm of the empirical. So BonJour's fundamentally different treatment of *a priori* justification is unsatisfying. I shall return to this point at the end of the paper.

Let us now turn to more careful scrutiny of BonJour's argument for the metajustification requirement (in the realm of empirical knowledge). He writes:

> If the account of epistemic justification just set forth is correct, then it seems to follow as an unavoidable corollary that one can finally know that a given set of standards for epistemic justification is correct or reasonable only by knowing that the standards in question are genuinely conducive to the cognitive goal of truth. And this in turn apparently means that it is incumbent on the proponent of such an epistemological theory to provide an argument or rationale of some sort to *show* that his proposed standards of justification are indeed truth-conducive, that accepting beliefs in accordance with them would indeed be likely in the long run to lead to truth. (9).

The first sentence of this passage says that one can *know* a set of standards to be correct only by *knowing* that they are truth conducive. This seems unexceptionable, granted that correctness of standards (logically) implies truth conduciveness. But how would this get BonJour what he needs? What BonJour needs to establish is that if any empirical belief B of S is justified, then not only does B meet some standard, or set of standards, D that is correct, but S knows or justifiably believes that D is correct. But this hardly follows from the first sentence of the passage. In the second sentence of the passage, BonJour concludes that it is incumbent on the proponent of a given set of standards to *show* that they are truth conducive. Here we must ask: incumbent on him if he is to achieve what? If he is to *know* that his standards are correct? Or if he is to have a (first-level) justified belief? The first we have already granted, but it is irrelevant to the issue at hand. Only the second is at issue, but it is not established by anything said here. Perhaps BonJour is trying to show that a necessary condition of a standard *being* correct is that a proponent *knows*, or *is justified in believing*, that it is truth conducive. But this does not follow from the first sentence of the passage. The latter only says that *knowledge of correctness* implies knowledge of truth conduciveness. It does not follow that *correctness* implies knowledge of truth conduciveness. To conflate these two implications would be a commission of what William Alston has aptly called a "level confusion" (see Alston, 1980). Although the matter is somewhat clouded, there is some ground for suspecting that BonJour is guilty of such a confusion.

Another revealing passage is one we quoted earlier:

> If a given putative knower is himself to be epistemically responsible in accepting beliefs in virtue of their meeting the standards of a given epistemological account, then it seems to follow that an appropriate metajustification of those standards must, in principle at least, be available *to him*. (10).

The thorny phrase here is "accepting a belief in virtue of its meeting the standards of a given epistemological account." This phrase admits of two interpretations: (l) accepting a belief which *in fact* meets standards of epistemic justification, and (2) accepting a belief as a result of an inference from the *premise* that having that belief would meet standards of epistemic justification. Under the first interpretation, there is no clear reason why the knower must possess a metajustification of the standards. If all that is necessary for epistemic responsibility is *meeting* (correct) standards, then he does not need to possess a metajustification of them. On the second interpretation, on the other hand, such a metajustification would seem to be needed. An inferential belief based on the indicated premise could not be justified unless the premise belief is justified. Apparently, then, BonJour intends the second interpretation. But this just raises the question: Does justification of (first-level) beliefs really require epistemic responsibility in the sense specified? In order to have (first-level) justified beliefs, do people always have to make an *inference* from a (higher-level) belief concerning an epistemic standard and its truth-conducive property?

It should be clear on reflection that this is a severely unrealistic demand. It is most implausible to suppose that garden-variety perceptual beliefs and memory beliefs are based on inferences from premises of the indicated sort. Yet we commonly impute knowledge and justification in these cases. Not only are very few beliefs actually based on such inferences, it seems likely that the only people who possess the relevant premise beliefs (or even possess the constituent concepts) are people with epistemological training and sophistication. It would therefore follow on BonJour's view that only these people are deserving subjects of the terms "knower" and "justified believer." But is it plausible to suggest that philosophical sophisticates are the only people with knowledge or justified belief?

BonJour is not oblivious to this line-of criticism. He grants (52-53) that his approach imposes standards for justification "that many commonsensical cases of knowledge will fail to meet in any full and explicit way. And thus on such a view, such beliefs will not *strictly speaking* be instances of adequate justification and of knowledge." He accepts this consequence on the grounds that judgments of common sense as to which of our beliefs qualify as knowledge are not sacrosanct. While I agree that commonsense judgments should not be sacrosanct, wholesale abandonment of commonsense constraints on theory would leave it unclear how epistemological theories can be tested. We need to keep commonsense judgments in our bag of instruments for testing these theories. As judged by such tests, however, BonJour's theory does not fare well.

How has BonJour been led to his counterintuitive theory? As I have been intimating, he may have gone astray by confusing the concept of justified belief with that of an *iterated* epistemic concept, viz., being justifed in believing that one has a justified belief. The metajustification requirement makes sense in an analysis of the iterated concept; but it is a level-confusion to insert it into an analysis of the *un*iterated concept. As I shall argue next, BonJour's criticism of foundationalism also shows signs of level-confusion.

BonJour's main objection to foundationalism is the incoherence, as he sees it, of the idea of basic beliefs. His objection goes as follows (see 31). Let F represent the feature or characteristic which allegedly distinguishes basic empirical beliefs from other empirical beliefs. Then empirical belief B could qualify as basic only if the believer is *justified* in believing that B has feature F and in believing that beliefs having feature F are highly likely to be true. But if this is correct, B cannot be basic after all, since its justification will depend on that of at least one other empirical belief: either "B has feature F" or "Beliefs having feature F are highly likely to be true."

This argument confuses (A) what is required for a belief to *be* basic (that is, basically justified) with (B) what is required for a person to be *justified in believing* that his belief is basic. Let B* be a higher-order belief by person S, the belief that a first-order belief of his, viz. B, is basic. Then we may grant that B* does not get to be justified simply because the first-order belief B has feature F, and F is truth-associated. The justifiedness of B* depends on S's justifiably believing (i) that B has F, and (ii) that F is truth-associated. But it does not follow from this that the first-order belief B is not justified, or basic, unless the person is justified in believing these things.

In the text of his discussion, the tell-tale sign of level-confusion occurs in the following passage.

> If B is to actually *be* basic, then presumably premise (1) would have to be true as well, but I am concerned here only with what would have to be so for it to be reasonable to *accept* B as basic and use it to justify other beliefs. (31)

Why, we may ask, is BonJour concerned only with the conditions of its being *reasonable for S to accept B as basic* ? The phrase "accept B as basic" strongly suggests that the belief in question is the second-order belief, B*, whose content is: "B is basic." BonJour seems to be saying that the primary question is: when does a person have a justified higher-order belief B* that a given first-order belief B is basic? But that isn't the primary question. The primary question is what it is for the first-order belief to *be* basic. I do not see that BonJour has shown that *being basic* requires more than possession of a suitable property F where perhaps F must be truth associated. He has merely clouded the issue by making a level switch at a crucial juncture. In a footnote, BonJour addresses the suggestion of an anonymous reviewer that he might be involved in a level-confusion (235, note 18), and denies it. But, his denial notwithstanding, I believe he is involved in one.

Of course, BonJour would reply that what I am defending here is the possibility of "externalist" foundationalism, and he takes himself to have shown the futility of such a position. In place of externalist foundationalism, BonJour advances his own theory of internalist coherentism. According to this theory, it is not enough for a belief to be justified that it belong to a system of beliefs that are in fact highly coherent. It is further required (A) that the believer S be justified in believing that it belongs to a highly coherent system, and (B) that S be justified in believing that this membership makes it likely that the belief is true. Is this internalist form of coherentism a defensible doctrine? Anthony Brueckner (1988) has given a cogent critique of this position, showing among other things that BonJour is driven to a view which closely resembles the externalist foundationalism that he decries. Brueckner's critique is worth reviewing.

BonJour himself introduces the need for internalist coherentism by indicating that his own arguments against externalist versions of foundationalism apply to coherentism as well. To get justified beliefs, the fact of coherence must be "accessible," he says, to the believer; and this means that he must have beliefs about the coherence of his system and these beliefs must be justified. In short, the believer must have empirical metabeliefs, to the effect that he has such and such specific beliefs, and these metabeliefs must themselves be justified. Can these metabeliefs be justified by virtue of their coherence with the rest of his system of beliefs? BonJour says no.

It is beyond any doubt viciously circular to claim that the

> metabeliefs which constitute the believer's grasp of his system of beliefs are themselves justified by virtue of their coherence with that system... . How can my metabelief B' that I have a certain other belief B be justified for me by appeal to the fact that B' coheres with my total system of beliefs when I have no justification apart from the appeal to B' and similar beliefs for thinking that I even have that system of beliefs? ... It is quite clear, therefore, that this grasp, upon which any nonexternalist appeal to coherence must depend, cannot itself be justified by appeal to coherence. And thus the very idea of a coherence theory of empirical justification threatens to collapse. (102. I have slightly changed the notation.)

Although BonJour himself is aware of difficulties in this area, Brueckner shows convincingly that the difficulties are even more serious than BonJour realizes. For one thing, he shows that BonJour's internalist coherentism threatens to generate an infinite regress of beliefs about beliefs ... a regress that BonJour cannot countenance since he acknowledges the finitude of human mental capacity (23-24). BonJour's introduction of what he calls the "Doxastic Presumption" can short-circuit this regress (although the regress is not BonJour's avowed reason for introducing the Doxastic Presumption). But Brueckner shows that the Doxastic Presumption commits BonJour to a dialectically untenable position *vis-a-vis* foundationalism.

The Doxastic Presumption says that a believer's representation of his overall system of beliefs is approximately correct. In other words, it guarantees that the metabeliefs are largely true. BonJour calls it a "presumption" because he takes it to be presupposed in our very cognitive or epistemic practice. As Brueckner indicates, it is in fact rather mysterious how the Doxastic Presumption is supposed to solve the problem of how the metabeliefs are *justified*. But, at any rate, their justification does not arise from the usual combination of (a) their being likely to be true due to their coherence with the rest of one's beliefs and (b) a justified belief as to (a)'s being the case. Nor is their justification made possible by the availability of the Presumption as a justifying premise in a justificatory argument. The upshot of the Doxastic Presumption, then, is a highly significant qualification in the internalist position that BonJour otherwise has endorsed.

Brueckner formulates BonJour's internalism with what he calls the "Internalist Principle":

> (IP) For all S and P (where P is an empirical proposition), if S is epistemically justified in believing that P, then there are propositions which make S's belief that P likely to be true and which S justifiably believes.

Brueckner shows how BonJour relies on (IP) in arguing against externalist foundationalism. However, introduction of the Doxastic Presumption constitutes a crucial abandonment, or qualification, of (IP). It has the consequence that it is not the case that for every justified belief that P, the believer must justifiably believe some propositions which make his belief that P likely to be true. In particular, any one of the metabeliefs we have been discussing violates this general rule. It turns out, then, that (IP) is false. Indeed, on BonJour's view, metabeliefs satisfy the characterization of *basic empirical beliefs,* a class of beliefs which BonJour has claimed to be empty!

As Brueckner notes, BonJour might simply qualify (IP) by saying that there are no (empirically) justified beliefs meeting the description in question *except for metabeliefs.* But this would be an unsatisfying reply. Since BonJour admits that there are cases of justified empirical belief in which the believer has no justified beliefs as to why his belief is likely to be true, how can he still charge that a believer who satisfies an externalist condition for having a more familiar kind of basic belief really lacks justification *because* he fails to satisfy (IP), (that is, because he is unaware of any reason why his belief is likely to be true)? Thus, by restricting (IP) for the case of metabeliefs, BonJour loses any principled reason he had for rejecting externalism.

In fact, the dialectical situation is doubly bad for BonJour. Not only does he, in effect, admit that the indicated metabeliefs don't need the usual metajustification, he also acknowledges, as we have seen, that *a priori* beliefs need no such metajustification in order to be justified. Since there seem to be several types of *admitted* exceptions to the internalist constraint, how credible can BonJour's insistence be that externalism is untenable for all other cases of belief? I shall return to this point later.

I want to turn now to other features of BonJour's coherentism. Like most coherentists, BonJour rejects the claim that justification must be "linear". In trying to explain what a "nonlinear" conception of justification might be like, he distinguishes local and global levels. The local level concerns the justification of a single empirical belief within the context of a system of beliefs whose overall justification is (more or less) taken for granted. Justification at the global level concerns the justification of an entire system of empirical beliefs. A bit later BonJour says that the justification of a particular belief finally depends, not on other particular beliefs, but instead on the overall system (92). I don't really understand what BonJour is claiming here. How can the justification of particular (inferential) beliefs fail to depend on other particular beliefs? What are we to make of the contrast between justification depending on other particular beliefs and its depending on the system? Isn't the system itself a set of particular beliefs?

Perhaps BonJour means merely to be saying that a particular empirical belief is justified (given the Doxastic Presumption) if and only if it belongs to a system of actual beliefs that is sufficiently coherent. What is crucial, then, is the degree of coherence of the entire system, not the target belief's relationship to other particular beliefs. If this *is* what he is saying, it is surely inadequate. This theory would imply that a doxastic system either contains all justified beliefs or all unjustified beliefs: justified in case the system is sufficiently coherent and unjustified otherwise. That is unacceptable. Coherentism would thereby exclude the plausible and presumably common scenario in which some of a person's beliefs are justified and some unjustified. (Admittedly, BonJour's clearest statement of when a belief is justified - the summary on 153-55 - reminds us that there are further restrictions on a system's adequacy beyond its being highly coherent. However, even with these additional restrictions, the same objectionable consequence appears to follow.) To put my complaint another way, in focusing so heavily on the properties of empirical belief *systems,* BonJour pays too little attention to the justificational requirements for individual beliefs.

Although it is unfortunate that BonJour says so little about the justificational status of individual beliefs, one cannot minimize the importance to coherentism of an account of what makes a system coherent. So let us see what BonJour says on this score. BonJour's initial account is sensible, though self-confessedly sketchy. He formulates five principles of coherence (95-101):

(1) Logical consistency is necessary for coherence.
(2) A system is coherent in proportion to its degree of probabilistic consistency.
(3) Coherence is increased by the number and strength of inferential connections between its component beliefs.
(4) Coherence is diminished by the number of inferentially unconnected subsystems.
(5) Coherence is decreased by unexplained anomalies in the system.

One principle to which I take exception is (1). Logical consistency is not necessary for coherence, at least if coherence is necessary for justified beliefs. Anyone who believes that at least one of his beliefs is false has an inconsistent belief set: but surely it is wrong to decree that *none* of the beliefs in this set can be justified. This paradox-of-the-preface difficulty is acknowledged by BonJour in a single footnote sentence (240, note 7), but unfortunately he just sets it aside.

A different sort of difficulty with BonJour's coherentism (and most other forms of coherentism) is its inattention to questions of psychological realism. This crops up especially in his Doxastic Presumption. The Doxastic Presumption asserts that a believer has a cognitive "grasp" of his whole system of beliefs. BonJour grants that no actual believer possesses an explicit grasp of his overall belief system, but says that believers must have a tacit or implicit grasp of their systems. But is this psychologically plausible? Most of a person's beliefs are stored in long-term memory, and it is doubtful that one has, even implicitly, anything like a complete grasp of *all* of them. Indeed, many stored beliefs are quite difficult to access: and certainly it is impossible to retrieve them all simultaneously. (For some discussion, see Goldman (1986) chapter 10.) The Doxastic Presumption also seems to imply that a believer usually has a correct belief about *how* coherent his set of beliefs is. But is this psychologically plausible for unsophisticated cognizers, e.g., children or philosophically uneducated adults? These people may not even possess the relevant notion of coherence (which, especially as BonJour articulates it, is quite complex).

In my final remarks, I want to comment on BonJour's treatment of *a priori* justification. BonJour relegates this topic to an appendix, which I suppose is defensible since the book's main target is empirical justification. On the other hand, this appendix lets important skeletons out of the closet. Since it is crucial for an understanding and appraisal of the central issues in BonJour's theory of justification, it is unfortunate that it appears in an appendix.

BonJour's account of *a priori* justification is the traditional rationalist account. It says that such justification arises from an intuitive "grasp" or "apprehension" of necessity (194, 207). This is intended to accord with the standard distinction between the *a priori* and *a posteriori,* where the latter is explicated in terms of *experience* -based justification. BonJour's explication of "sense-experience" is different from most, since he elsewhere introduces a special sense of "observational". An experiential belief, for BonJour, is any sort of cognitively spontaneous, or input, belief, and this can include not only sense experience in the narrow sense, but also introspection, memory, and nonsensory forms of input like clairvoyance and telepathy (if these should exist). The crucial difference, then, is that empirical beliefs concern the specific character of the actual world as opposed to other possible worlds. The form of insight essential for *a priori* justification is an intuition or apprehension of some sort of necessity, of truth in all possible worlds.

There is a technical problem here. Suppose there is some mental operation or belief-forming process that can generate beliefs in *both* contingent and necessary propositions. By BonJour's stipulation, this is not eligible for producing *apriori* justification. But surely it should be. Belief in a mathematical proposition may be epistemically licensed precisely because of the deployment of this operation.

I want to concentrate, however, on other issues. There are two features of BonJour's theory of the *a priori* that merit emphasis. First, he offers an explicitly *noncoherentist* account of *a priori* justification. Second, this account explicitly omits the metajustification requirement. The reason he gives for the former is this:

> A *priori* knowledge is essential to provide the very ingredients of the concept of coherence (one of which is logical consistency) and thus could not without vicious circularity be itself based on coherence. Accordingly some other sort of account is needed for *a priori* knowledge, if such knowledge - and arguably any knowledge - is to exist at all. (193).

It turns out, then, that BonJour's theory of epistemic justification is fundamentally bifurcated. Coherence is not an essential feature of all justification, only *a posteriori* justification. This bifurcation is reinforced by the rejection of a metajustification requirement for *a priori* justification. Unlike the case of empirical belief, the cognizer does not need to be able to show that intuitive apprehension is truth-conducive (210).

This thoroughgoing bifurcation in BonJour's theory is troubling. Epistemic justification, one would have thought, is a unitary concept. There must be some property (or family of properties) that all justified beliefs have in common: and this common feature or features is what a theory, or analysis, of epistemic justification should provide. But it now emerges that BonJour's theory has no unitary account. Coherence is not essential for justified belief: nor is possession of a metajustification. Indeed, it is no longer clear to me just what *is* supposed to be going on when one has a justified belief, according to BonJour. If BonJour provided a general *criterion* of rightness for belief-forming processes - analogous to the reliabilist criterion I have offered, for example - then I would have some handle on his general view of justification. But he rejects coherence as such a *general* criterion. Metajustification could not serve as a criterion, since it is supposed to show the truth-conduciveness of some *other* criterion: and it is anyway rejected for the general case. So what *is* the general criterion BonJour offers? Perhaps he would like to say that there is no general criterion, only one for each separate brand of justification. But, actually, he denies that there is *any* criterion or standard for *a priori* justification (210-211). This makes me wonder if I understand what he means by a criterion or standard (a worry I expressed earlier), or if he really means what he says in originally introducing a criterion as what "qualifies a...belief as...justified". How could there *fail* to be a criterion of *apriori* justification, so understood? Doesn't there have to be *something* in virtue of which a belief in a mathematical or logical proposition qualifies as justified (or unjustified)?

A process reliabilist like myself has a ready answer, part of a *unified* account of justified belief. Mathematical and logical beliefs get to be justified in the same way that other beliefs do: by getting formed (or sustained) by reliable cognitive processes. BonJour has this sort of account available to him indeed, one might even suppose he has it in mind, since he says throughout that justification must be truth-conducive. True, he rejects the traditional idea that intuitive apprehension need be infallible or certain (208). But this is compatible with its having a *high* truth ratio.

It would be a welcome clarification for BonJour to assert explicitly that acts of intuition, to confer justification, must be reliable. It would also, in my opinion, make the theory more satisfactory. After all, there could be types of intuition that regularly generate false beliefs in possible-world propositions. Beliefs so produced would not qualify as justified, surely not as knowledge. But if BonJour accepted this account of *a priori* justification - an account that features reliability without metajustification - he would certainly be left with an oddly mixed theory. Why, one would want to ask, can reliability without metajustification confer justification in the *a priori* realm if it cannot confer it in the empirical realm? Of course I have claimed that BonJour gives no convincing arguments for saying that it *cannot* confer justification in the empirical realm. The putative arguments to this effect involve level-confusions. And we have also seen that he is forced to allow (empirical) metabeliefs to be justified even without a metajustification. From a dialectical point of view, however, it is very revealing to see BonJour explicitly acknowledge that justification in one entire domain does not require metajustification. That is why the appendix on *a priori* justification is so important. Once the radical disunity in his overall theory is noted, one should feel a strong impulse to critically re-examine the arguments for metajustification in the empirical realm, even if one found them initially appealing. As I argued earlier, a close examination of those arguments does not warrant the conclusion that metajustification is required even for first-order empirical propositions. Thus, despite much valuable discussion in the book as a whole, BonJour's defense of internalist coherentism is open to numerous serious objections.

REFERENCES

Alston, William . "Level-Confusions in Epistemology," in Peter French, Theodore Uehling, Jr., and
    Howard Wettstein, eds., *Midwest Studies in Philosophy*, vol. 5. Minneapolis: University of Minesota
    Press, 1980.
BonJour, Laurence. *The Structure of Empirical Knowledge*. Cambridge, Mass: Harvard University Press, 1985.
Brueckner, Anthony. "Problems with Internalist Coherentism." *Philosophical Studies* 54: 1 (1988), 153-160.
Goldman, Alvin. "What Is Justified Belief?", in George Pappas, ed., *Justification and Knowledge*
    Dordrecht: D. Reidel, 1979.
-----. *Epistemology and Cognition*. Cambridge, Mass.: Harvard University Press, 1986.

BonJour's Coherence Theory of Justification[*]

Marshall Swain
Ohio State University

Laurence BonJour's book, *The Structure of Empirical Knowledge,* is among the most detailed and resourceful efforts to present a coherence theory of empirical justification produced thus far. Although my own account of justification is different in kind from BonJour's, there is much that I admire in his work. Some of what I admire is solidly substantive, including specific examples, arguments, and instances of philosophical theorizing. I also find admirable the refreshing candor with which BonJour approaches epistemology. There is no pretense here of having found all the answers, nor even all the questions for which answers may be required. There is instead a healthy sense of speculation and a willingness to admit that the solutions to certain problems are out of reach at the present time.

Throughout his book, BonJour adheres to a number of broad assumptions. For example, he assumes the traditional account of empirical knowledge as epistemically justified true belief, a correspondence theory of truth, and a robustly realistic view of the external world. He assumes, as well, that the notion of epistemic justification (that kind of justification which is necessary for knowledge) is distinguished from others by virtue of its essential relation to the cognitive goal of truth. These, and other assumptions, will simply be granted in this commentary.

Within the framework of the traditional account of knowledge, BonJour confines his attention to the concept of justification. It is clear from the outset of the book that he is primarily concerned with broad structural and theoretical considerations, not with the construction of precise definitions or close conceptual analysis. The discussion of justification is framed against a backdrop of skepticism, particularly the kind of skepticism about justification which results from the regress argument. The regress argument is given a very traditional formulation (see 17-25), and the traditional responses to it set the framework for the main divisions of the book. One can respond to the regress argument by embracing skepticism, embracing the regress, adopting some form of foundational view (which blocks the regress), or by adopting a non-linear, or holistic, view of justification which avoids the regress by rejecting the fundamental (i.e., linear) view of the structure of justification upon which it is based.

If there is a traditional non-skeptical response to the regress argument, it is the adoption and defense of some form of foundational theory. BonJour devotes the first of two main sections of his book to a taxonomy of the main kinds of foundationalist view, arguing at some length against all such theories. The arguments cover both internalist and externalist versions of foundationalism. His conclusion (given that he is not a skeptic) is that only some form of holistic view has any hope of being correct. The main task of the book is to lay out the large features of such a view.

A holistic view is one which characterizes justification of a belief in terms of the doxastic system, D, of which that belief is a member. Only if the doxastic system has a specified property, or set of properties, J, can the beliefs which are members of it be justified. The usual candidate for the property J is the property of coherence, and this is the key property for BonJour . It is not, however, the only property of a doxastic system which is relevant on BonJour's view to holistic justification. Also relevant are "stability over the long run," (153, 170) "satisfaction of (what BonJour calls) the Observation Requirement," (153, 170, and Chapter 6) and "accessibility to the believer of the members and justification-making properties (including coherence) of the belief set D." (154) Before turning detailed discussion of BonJour's view, I will discuss each of these properties of doxastic systems as they play a role in his theory.

115

J.W. Bender (ed.), The Current State of the Coherence Theory, 115–124.
© *1989 by Kluwer Academic Publishers.*

1. Coherence. One of the most disappointing features of BonJour's book is the lack of detail provided in connection with the central notion of coherence. No effort is made at defining this concept. Instead, we are given several rather vaguely formulated conditions which loosely characterize coherence. These are:

> (1) A system of beliefs is coherent only if it is logically consistent.
>
> (2) A system of beliefs is coherent in proportion to its degree of probabilistic consistency.
>
> (3) The coherence of a system of beliefs is increased by the presence of inferential connections between its component beliefs and increased in proportion to the number and strength of such connections.
>
> (4) The coherence of a system of beliefs is diminished to the extent to which it is divided into subsystems of beliefs which are relatively unconnected to each other by inferential connections.
>
> (5) The coherence of a system of beliefs is decreased in proportion to the presence of unexplained anomalies in the believed content of the system. (95-101)

Each of these conditions is open to considerable discussion. It is not clear, for instance, that logical consistency [condition (1)] of a belief set is a necessary condition for justification, and so it is not clear that it is necessary for coherence. While inferential connections [condition (3)] are clearly important to coherence and justification, it is not clear that the *number* of them matters. It is even less clear that in all cases a system of beliefs which divides into unrelated subsets [condition (4)] is, thereby, rendered less coherent than others. I shall not pursue any of these possible problems in this commentary.

One important question about coherence should be raised at this point, for it leads to a central aspect of BonJour's work. Let us grant that coherence can be understood along the lines BonJour has vaguely characterized. Then, we can ask, what reason is there for thinking that a set of beliefs which is coherent under this description is also such that its members are epistemically justified? Belief sets can have any number of holistic properties, such as the property of being held in the 20th Century, none of which would lead us to conclude that these beliefs are justified. What is so special about coherence? Answering this question is one of the main concerns of BonJour's book. Later on, I will return to consider his answer in some detail.

2. Stability. One of the important and innovative features of BonJour's coherence theory is the recognition that there is a distinction between static and dynamic coherence. A system of beliefs might be coherent at a given moment in time, or during a brief interval of time, but be highly incoherent over a longer stretch of time. We might imagine, for instance, that this is the case in some forms of insanity. On BonJour's view, the justification of a belief at a given time is a function of the coherence of the subject's belief system over "the long run." To say that a belief system is a *stable* one is to say that it "converges on and eventually presents a relatively stable long-run picture of the world." (170) It is obvious that a great deal needs to be said about this notion of stability, certainly more than is found in BonJour 's book. The notion of stability plays an important role in BonJour's metajustificatory argument to show that coherence leads to truth, and thus to justification, so we will have further occasion to consider it later.

3. Observation. One of the standard objections to traditional forms of coherence theory is that such theories are insensitive to input from the external world. If coherence is the *only* condition for justification, then a coherent set of beliefs which is entirely apocryphal will be as well justified as any other, for coherence (alone) does not require

observational input. To meet this objection, BonJour constructs an account of observational input which (he suggests) is distinctly coherentist in nature. In my opinion, BonJour's effort on this topic is the greatest accomplishment of his book, and one of the more interesting recent developments in justification theory.

On many foundational accounts of the justification of observational beliefs, such beliefs are noninferentially justified. This usually means that such beliefs are neither arrived at by inference nor justified inferentially by other beliefs. Such a view is anathema for the pure coherentist. However, the coherentist can accept the idea that some beliefs are *arrived at* noninferentially (that is, literally, they come about, or are caused, in some way other than by inference). For the coherentist, it is the suggestion that some beliefs are *justified* noninferentially which is taboo. So, a possible view for a coherentist (and the actual one for BonJour) is that there is a class of beliefs which arise in a belief system without being inferred from other beliefs, but which are justified within that system only by appropriate relations to (coherence with) other beliefs in the system. BonJour calls these beliefs "cognitively spontaneous." (117) These are beliefs which simply occur to one, in a manner which is "involuntary and quite coercive." (117) As examples he refers to the belief that there is a red book on the desk and the introspective belief that I seem to see something red.

Given this notion of a cognitively spontaneous belief, BonJour then formulates what he calls the Observation Requirement. This is a requirement to be satisfied by a set of beliefs, D, if the members of D are to be justified. BonJour does not precisely express this requirement anywhere, but I believe it can be pieced together as follows:

A system of beliefs, D, is epistemically justified only if (a) it contains a reasonable variety of cognitively spontaneous beliefs and (b) it also contains believed laws attributing to those cognitively spontaneous beliefs a high degree of reliability, and (c) the user of the system has made a reasonable effort to seek out relevant beliefs of the cognitively spontaneous variety. (see section 7.1, and 153-4)

BonJour's idea is that if a belief system satisfies this requirement, then it will have at least *apparent* observational input. As we will see, arguing to best explanations provides a way of moving from what is thus apparent to what is true. In this way, BonJour hopes to distinguish belief systems which are arbitrarily constructed from those that are observationally grounded, thereby avoiding the "lack of input" objection.

4. The accessibility requirement. In addition to his rejection of foundationalism and subsequent adoption of a coherence view, BonJour rejects externalism in favor of internalism. One primary distinguishing feature of an internalist view is the requirement that one's beliefs and justifications be accessible, either explicitly or implicitly. A coherentist need not be an internalist. If one were to hold that justification is a matter of coherence but that the subject need not (or could not) be aware of this property, then one would (to that degree) be an externalistic coherentist. BonJour is an internalistic coherentist, for he believes that coherentism without accessibility leads to a variety of problems.

The accessibility requirement comes out most explicitly in what BonJour calls the "Doxastic Presumption." His most focused discussion of this is in section 5.4 of the book, but even here I find his remarks to be extremely hard to unravel. He says that a necessary condition of a belief set being justified is that the believer have a "grasp" of the contents and coherence of the belief set. In other words, if you are to be justified in believing that I am now talking to you, then you must have a grasp of your entire set of beliefs, of which that one is a member, and of the coherence of that set. Two things cry out for clarification: what does it mean to have a grasp of your beliefs and their coherence? How explicit or complete must this grasp be? Concerning the second question ("how explicit must the grasp be?"), BonJour says only that it cannot be entirely explicit, but only somewhat so. (102)

The other question is in some respects more important ("what does it mean to have a grasp of your beliefs and their coherence?"). The most obvious answer to this question would be that the grasping is a form of *belief*. BonJour himself sometimes speaks this way, referring to a "metabelief" about one's own belief system. But, as BonJour recognizes, (102), speaking in this way is fraught with danger for a coherentist. First, if this grasping of your belief system is just another belief, then it is also in your doxastic system and must be grasped, which suggests a potential regress. Second, if the grasping is a belief in the system, then it, like other beliefs, must be justified. But, for a coherentist, every justified belief is justified only by its relations to other beliefs. So, we would have to ask, what beliefs are involved in the justification of this metabelief? Since it is required within BonJour's theory, for the justification of all other beliefs in the doxastic system, the answer should be that there are no other beliefs which justify it. But, this makes it look as though there is a belief which is required for the justification of others without itself being justified, and that sort of claim looks very much like foundationalism.

Faced with these problems, BonJour gives a largely negative characterization of the Doxastic Presumption. The metabelief about, or "grasp" of one's belief system and its coherence is presumed as one of the conditions for raising the question of justification, and in this sense it is necessary for justification. But, this metabelief does not play a role as a premise, it does not need to be (indeed, cannot be) justified. It is one of the features which defines the justification game (104-5).

Although BonJour is concerned to deny it, the Doxastic Presumption looks to me to be foundationalist. I am not, however, sure that I can provide any very convincing arguments for that, given that the Doxastic Presumption requirement, and the discussion of it, are both so vague. Of greater interest to me is the more manageable part of BonJour's internalist accessibility requirement, that which pertains to specific beliefs and justifications other than the very general metabelief required by the Doxastic Presumption. BonJour holds that each justified belief and its justification must be accessible to the believer. His views on this are intertwined with his arguments against externalism, to which I now turn.

BonJour's counterexamples to externalism. As part of his strategy to establish an internalistic coherentist position, BonJour argues against both foundationalism and externalism. The arguments against these two general positions are intertwined, and are found in Chapters 2 and 3. Although I am highly sympathetic to BonJour's arguments against foundationalist views (but will not discuss them here), I find his attack on externalism to be considerably less convincing.

The argument against externalism primarily consists of a group of counterexamples, all of which are variations on a single theme. The theme is the supposition of completely reliable clairvoyant power in an individual, with the variations expressing differing degrees and respects in which the individual in question possesses or lacks information concerning the clairvoyant ability. In the course of this discussion, BonJour considers and rejects the externalist views of Armstrong (1973) (who is a reliabilist), and considers ways in which Armstrong might respond to some of the examples (see especially Chapter 3). I will not be concerned here with this specific theory. Rather, I want to consider whether BonJour's examples provide reason for wholesale rejection of externalism. I do not think that they do, and if this is right then there is less of a reason than BonJour thinks for embracing the radical internalism reflected in his views.

The most challenging example BonJour gives involves Norman, and is described by BonJour as follows:

> CASE 4. Norman, under conditions which usually obtain, is a completely reliable clairvoyant with respect to certain kinds of subject matter. He possesses no evidence or reasons of any kind for or against the thesis that he possesses it. One day Norman comes to believe that the President is in New York City, though

he has no evidence either for or against this belief. In fact, the belief is true, and results from his clairvoyant power under circumstances in which it is completely reliable. (41)

BonJour claims, and I think most of us would agree, that Norman is irrational in his belief, that his belief is completely unjustified. However, on the kind of externalist view propounded by Armstrong, in which justification is defined in terms of reliability, it follows that Norman's belief is justified. BonJour generalizes on this result to conclude that there is a fundamental problem for externalism: no externalist condition can be sufficient for justification if the satisfaction of that condition is beyond the ken of the believer. BonJour would grant justification to this belief of Norman's only if Norman knows about his clairvoyant ability, and this is an internalist move. Not only must the belief be accessible, so must that which justifies it (in this instance, the reliability of the process which produced the belief). BonJour summarizes the situation as follows:

We are now face-to-face with the fundamental - and obvious - intuitive problem with externalism: *why* should the mere fact that such an external relation obtains mean that Norman's belief is epistemically justified when the relation in question is entirely outside his ken? (42)

In defending externalism against BonJour's attack, I will develop two points. First, it is possible to have an externalist view on which the external relation between belief and fact is "beyond the ken" of the believer which does not give the result that Norman is justified. Second, the direct answer to BonJour's question about why this should be sufficient for justification results partly from the unacceptable of imposing a strict accessibility constraint on justification (a point which BonJour himself seems to grant later in the book).

The account of justification with which I am most familiar is the one that I developed in my book *Reasons and Knowledge* (Swain 1981). On this view, epistemic justification is defined in terms of reliable indication. Although this view is not a "pure" externalist one, for it requires that one's reasons for belief be in principle accessible, it is externalistic in the sense that BonJour is concerned about. The external facts having to do with reliability of the believer need not be known to the believer in cases of justification. A belief is justified provided that it is more likely to be true, given the reasons upon which the belief is based and relevant characteristics of the believer, than any competitor of the belief. The likelihood in question is objective, or external, and the characteristics of the believer which condition it need not be known to the believer.

On this account, Norman's belief that the President is in New York City, when it occurs under the circumstances described by BonJour, is unjustified. Why so? Because of relevant characteristics of the believer, and the effect of these characteristics on the relevant probabilities. In the case of Norman, we have a person who suddenly comes to have a belief about the whereabouts of the President. This belief has not been inferred from other beliefs, nor does it have any obvious relation to the rest of Norman's doxastic domain. Although not an observational belief, it has many of the characteristics of what BonJour calls "cognitively spontaneous beliefs." Unlike the cognitively spontaneous beliefs of observation, however, there is no cogent argument that Norman can construct, implicit or explicit, in favor of acceptance. Norman, in other words, is entirely irresponsible in the maintenance of this belief, which fails entirely to cohere with his other accepted beliefs. From an objective point of view, these facts about Norman and his belief constitute significant negative evidence with respect to the likelihood that the President is in New York City.

Norman does, however, have one characteristic which is strongly positive, namely that he is a clairvoyant with respect to the President's whereabouts. Given this characteristic, it is likely that his belief is correct. So, you might ask, isn't Norman justified after all? As I have constructed this theory, the answer is negative. When listing relevant characteristics, those which guarantee the probabilistic facts all by themselves must be excluded from the list. So, we do not list the clairvoyant ability in determining the probabilities for Norman's belief. By analogy, in a straight case of perception, we would not include the characteristic of being an infallible perceptual discriminator of x's in the determination of the probability of one's belief that an x is being perceived - it can be argued that allowing such characteristics leads to clear counterexamples, of the kind BonJour is urging.

This is not the place to argue for my own theory of justification. The point of the above is that one *can* have an externalist view which gives the desired result in the case of Norman, from which it should be concluded that BonJour has failed to refute generic externalism. If that is right, then we are still left with the question, raised above in the quote from BonJour, of why an external relation between belief and fact, when beyond the ken of the believer, should be sufficient for justification? Even more generally, why should *any* set of conditions for justification (externalist or otherwise) be sufficient for justification if their satisfaction is (wholly or partially) beyond the ken of the believer?

Part of the answer is: Consider the alternative! The alternative is to require for justified belief the accessibility of virtually everything relevant to one's justification, the view which BonJour seems to accept in his book.

It is not entirely clear to me why BonJour embraces such a robust and all-encompassing internalism, unless it is because he thinks his arguments against externalism leave no choice. If that is the reason, then what I have suggested above could lead to a softening of this view. Perhaps there are other reasons (I cannot find any clearly expressed in the book). It is clear, however, that BonJour is *worried* about the excessiveness of this requirement. He notes, for example, that the various presumptions and requirements of his view make it unrealistic and inapplicable to most human beings (151). We do not, as a matter of empirical fact, have the grasp of our belief systems, implicit or explicit, required by the Doxastic Presumption. People do not, generally, formulate inferences, nor would most people even recognize them, particularly the complex inferences involved in observation. BonJour in fact seems to grant the main points of this objection, and suggests that his view be considered an idealization, to which actual cases of justification and knowledge are only loose approximations. (152)

If BonJour were to ease up on the scope of his accessibility requirements, this would go a long way toward reducing the gap (which I take to be undesirable) between what will satisfy the theory and how things are with actual cognizers. This can be done, moreover, without abandoning the good reasons for imposing accessibility constraints on a theory of justification. There has been a tendency, I find, for justification theorists to take a "black or white" position with respect to internalist versus externalist constraints. If you are going to be an externalist, perhaps a reliabilist, then you cannot allow any internalist constraints, particularly having to do with the accessibility of reasons. On the other hand, if you are going to be an internalist, then you must wholly reject all externalist conditions for justification, particularly those which cannot be accessed by the cognizer. This is, however, a false dichotomy, and I think that philosophers are beginning to see that it is.

In "An Internalist Externalism," (1988) for example, William Alston proposes a hybrid view, combining reliabilist conditions with a minimal version of an accessibility requirement. According to this kind of accessibility requirement, the subject's reasons for believing that p must be of a type which is accessible to normal human beings under some circumstances, even if they are not accessible to the subject at the time. This applies, however, only to those beliefs (or other psychological states) of the subject which actually produce the belief that It need not hold for all the various background beliefs that one may have, nor for unbelieved facts about one's reliability. This kind of proposal has great appeal, in my opinion (and, is similar in many ways to my own). The accessibility requirement, even though minimal, accomplishes what such requirements are designed to accomplish, namely, to provide for a certain degree of epistemic responsibility on the part of the agent. On the other hand, this view has all the benefits of a reliability account, including the emphasis on actual psychological processing in the formation of belief.

A hybrid view could be formed out of BonJour's in much the same way. Such a view could include a minimal accessibility requirement, similar to Alston's. Instead of reliabilist conditions, or criteria for justification, however, it would have coherence conditions of the kind BonJour discusses, including perhaps some version of the Observation Requirement. The accessibility requirement, being minimal, would not extend to these facts of coherence, so they could be entirely outside the ken of the cognizer. But the cognizer would be required to be responsible at least to the point of being able (implicitly) to provide the reasons upon which a belief is based. This latter requirement might rule out the clairvoyant objections (since, I take it, Norman is completely incapable of providing any reason for believing that the President is in New York City), but will not be so strong as to rule out ordinary people.

Getting even bolder, one could form a hybrid view out of BonJour's, Alston's, and the reliability view. On the theory that I have in mind, there would be a minimal accessibility requirement, a set of coherentist conditions for the corpus of one's beliefs, and a reliable indication and/or processing requirement to establish input from the external world. Such a view could be either foundationalist or nonfoundationalist (BonJour, I assume, would opt for nonfoundationalism). It would cut across the boundaries of traditionally drawn battle lines among epistemologists, but I see no reason why such a view is not possible. Indeed, as with Alston's recent work, it seems to me that such a view is quite attractive.

This is all very speculative, of course, and probably not very clear. The point is, in part, that it is a mistake to think of externalism and internalism as views which are wholly inconsistent with one another. Specific versions of these kinds of views are inconsistent with one another, but at the generic level there is plenty of room for compromise. BonJour has, I believe, been too hasty in his rejection of externalism, and too extreme in his endorsement of the internalist requirements.

The Metajustificatory Argument. In constructing his theory of justification, BonJour considers two related tasks to be essential. The first is the presentation of a set of criteria, or standards, for epistemic justification. This results in the coherence theory in all its various details. The second task, already referred to above, is to provide a justification for thinking that beliefs which satisfy these standards of justification are likely to achieve the desired epistemic goal of being true. Only if the second task is successful can we be confident that our standards are standards for epistemic justification (since truth-conduciveness is the defining characteristic of such standards). Providing such a metajustification for one's epistemic standards is a desideratum for any epistemology, not just a coherence theory.

In developing his metajustification, BonJour is concerned with belief systems that are held over significantly long periods of time. In any given instance, however, we will be concerned with whether a belief held at a particular time is epistemically justified. For BonJour, the long-term history of the belief system in which the momentary fragment is being judged is relevant to justification. It is also relevant to his metajustificatory argument. He wants to show that long-run adherence to his principles of coherence, coupled with the stability of the belief system during that time, is likely to produce true beliefs. The kind of argument he gives is a version of the inference to best explanation strategy. Let us have a look at the ingredients of this argument.

First, BonJour is concerned to prove the following claim:

(MJ) A system of beliefs which (a) remains coherent (and stable) over the long run and (b) continues to satisfy the Observation Requirement is likely, to a degree which is proportional to the degree of coherence (and stability) and the longness of the run, to correspond closely to independent reality.

His argument for this involves two steps, as follows:

(P1) If a system of beliefs remains coherent (and stable) over the long run while continuing to satisfy the Observation Requirement, then it is highly likely that there is some explanation (other than mere chance) for this fact, with the degree of likelihood being proportional to the degree of coherence (and stability) and the longness of the run. [This, he claims, is virtually self-evident]

(P2) The best explanation, the likeliest to be true, for a system of beliefs remaining coherent (and stable) over the long run while continuing to satisfy the Observation Requirement is that (a) the cognitively spontaneous beliefs which are claimed, within the system, to be reliable are systematically caused by the sorts of situations which are depicted by their content, and (b) the entire system of beliefs corresponds, within a reasonable degree of approximation, to the independent reality which it purports to describe; and the preferability of this explanation increases in proportion to the degree of coherence (and stability) and the longness of the run. (171)

He admits that this is all very vague, and indicates that he is hoping only to make a *prima facie* plausible case. Even granting the vagueness, I am not convinced that BonJour's metajustification establishes even a *prima facie* case for the conclusion (MJ).

BonJour anticipates the kind of objection that I have in mind, but I do not find his response to be convincing. In a normal, full-blown belief system, there are a number of types of beliefs. Some will be of the variety that BonJour calls "cognitively spontaneous." These are the observational beliefs about things around you at the time, beliefs about your present aches and pains, and so forth. Others will be relatively straightforward inferential beliefs, based largely on your present observations. For example, if I hear a siren, I may inferentially believe that a fire-truck is passing by. If attention is restricted to beliefs such as these, then I am inclined to agree with BonJour that long-run consistency, predictability, and coherence are best explained by the hypothesis that such beliefs correspond closely to the way the world is. There are, of course, competing explanations of why we have such beliefs, including radical skeptical hypotheses, but these seem less likely to be true than the normal hypothesis. Or, at least, I am willing to grant this part of BonJour 's claim for now.

It is the other beliefs found in normal full-blown belief systems which concern me - and, are of concern to BonJour as well. These are beliefs which are more theoretical in nature, farther removed from the arena of direct observational confirmation and disconfirmation. These are the beliefs which we tend to add to those which arise through the compelling stream of observation, and they are often 'designed' specifically to be both explanatory and coherent. Such beliefs could be false while still occupying a central place in a system of beliefs which satisfies all of BonJour's criteria.

In his book *Thought*, (1973, 133) Gilbert Harman presents a case which he thinks is troublesome for the view that only true lemmas can be involved in justifying inferences. Embellishing on this case, and adapting it to the present circumstances, let us imagine a fisherman who is pragmatically wise in the ways of the weather, barometers, and the like, but who is nevertheless very unsophisticated when it comes to the theoretical justification of his practical inferences. Through experience, he has learned that certain movements of the needle on his barometer are almost invariably accompanied by rain within twenty-four hours. He has become a highly discriminating weather predictor. Given just this much, we would normally grant that the fisherman is justified in his expectations, even if he is wrong some of the time. Now we add to the story by supposing that the fisherman has held for some time a misguided meteorological theory ('theory' may be too strong a term here). He believes that there are periodic increases in the force of gravity. When this happens, the increased gravitational force results in the needle on the barometer being pulled out of position, and then also results later in rain being pulled out of the clouds.

Even with this addition, we would still grant that the fisherman is justified in believing that it will rain - he is just wrong about the underlying causes of the phenomena.

The relevance of this case to BonJour's argument is straightforward, I think. We can suppose that the fisherman's belief system, even though unsophisticated in part, is very coherent in all the respects required by BonJour. It is consistent, both logically and probabilistically, it has a significant number of inferential connections among its members, it is not subdivided into disconnected subsets of beliefs, it does not contain unexplained anomalies (it does contain some pretty bad explanations, but that is another matter), and it has as much stability in its world view as one can reasonably expect. And yet, in whatever way we are going to measure likelihood (BonJour does not tell us about this), it is only unlikely that all the members of the fisherman's belief system are true.

As I mentioned above, BonJour anticipates this kind of objection, and has a response to it. His discussion of this falls under the category of alternative explanatory hypotheses which are "normal" (173-178). These are hypotheses which entail that the world is different from the way we think it is, but still causally responsible for our observational beliefs. From the fisherman's point of view, the correct explanation of meteorological phenomena in terms of barometric pressure would be a normal alternative explanation of the correlation between needle-pointings and rainfall. Our fisherman, of course, will never have thought of this explanation; he is, after all, an unsophisticated theorizer.

As I understand what BonJour says about this, it is unlikely, on apriori grounds, that our fisherman's belief system could remain coherent and stable over the long run while continuing to be so far off theoretically. BonJour says the following sort of thing about such cases:

> "...if it is conceded...that the cognitively spontaneous beliefs which satisfy the Observation Requirement are indeed objectively reliable, it becomes unlikely, on purely *apriori* grounds, that a system of beliefs will remain coherent (and stable) in the long run while continuing to satisfy the Observation Requirement and still fail to depict the unobservable aspects of the world in an at least approximately accurate way." (176)

But, it seems to me, this is exactly what is happening in the case of the fisherman. His world view is seriously off when it comes to the unobservable aspects, but his observations and inferences are impeccable. There is nothing apriori unlikely about such a scenario, nor about its indefinite continuation. Indeed, I suspect, it happens all the time, especially with theoretical beliefs that are not so radically misguided as the one we have imagined.

As another illustration of the problem involved here, consider religious beliefs. They are wide-spread, and they have a strong apparent explanatory role to play in the belief systems of many people. Moreover, these beliefs can cohere beautifully with observation, and with other theoretical beliefs. Such beliefs can even provide an increase in the coherence of a belief system by reducing the number of apparently unexplained anomalies (one of the chief virtues of religion is its ability to provide apparent explanations of things which are otherwise a mystery). Even when other explanations of phenomena are developed, and labeled 'scientific', those who hold religious beliefs can continue to maintain them by making relatively minor modifications in other parts of their belief systems. Now whatever one might think of the merits of religious belief, the apparent conflict between such beliefs and those of science, the lack of verifiability or falsifiability of such beliefs, and so on, it must be granted that systems which contain them can be highly coherent over the long run. Shall we conclude that it is apriori likely that such beliefs are true? I can find nothing in what BonJour says to prevent this conclusion, which I take to be unacceptable.

Perhaps BonJour can answer such objections, but I am dubious. It is interesting to note, in conclusion, that if one were to adopt some version of a reliability view, either of the reliable processor or reliable indicator variety, then the provision of a metajustificatory argument looks more promising. If a belief set is the result of reliable processing, or if the believer is a reliable indicator, then it *is* more likely that the beliefs in question are true than false, for that is what 'reliable' means.

I will close by noting that although I have raised a number of concerns and objections to BonJour's view, and find that there are some serious disagreements between us, I remain in great admiration of this book. It is, I would suggest, one of those books that must be read by any serious contemporary epistemologist.

NOTES

*. This paper was originally written for a special symposium on Laurence BonJour 's *The Structure of Empirical Knowledge*, at the annual meeting of the Central Division of the American Philosophical Association, Chicago, Illinois, April 1987. The other symposiasts were Alvin Goldman and BonJour . BonJour 's role in the symposium was to respond to the comments provided by Goldman and me. His response was quite illuminating, and worthy of further discussion. However, I have left my paper substantially unchanged, except for minor stylistic revisions.

REFERENCES

Alston, William. "An Internalist Externalism," in a special issure of *Synthese*, edited by Stephen Luper-Foy, 1988.

Armstrong, David. *Belief, Truth, and Knowledge*. London, Cambridge University Press, 1981.

BonJour , Laurence. *The Structure of Empirical Knowledge*. Cambridge, Mass., Harvard University Press, 1985.

Harman, Gilbert. *Thought*. Princeton, Princeton University Press, 1973.

Swain, Marshall. *Reasons and Knowledge*. Ithaca, Cornell University Press, 1981.

BonJour's Coherentism

Alan H. Goldman
University of Miami

In *The Structure of Empirical Knowledge,* Laurence BonJour defends a coherence theory of justification as part of a standard analysis of knowledge as justified true belief. Justification attaches first to systems of beliefs, in so far as they are internally coherent, as viewed from the perspective of the subject whose beliefs they are. Particular beliefs are justified if and only if they are part of a coherent system of beliefs (and to the degree to which the system of which they are a part is coherent). Coherence is measured not simply in terms of consistency, but in terms of inductive, probabilistic, and explanatory connections among members of the set.

I shall argue here that such justification of true beliefs is neither necessary nor sufficient for knowledge. I shall defend a concept of foundational beliefs against BonJour's argument that such beliefs are impossible and shall show why the demonstration of knowledge requires a perspective beyond the subject's internal system of beliefs. Epistemologists begin this demonstration with their own foundational beliefs, but infer to an external relation (in addition to truth) as the source of knowledge. In order to defend their belief that this external relation obtains and is a source of knowledge, they must adopt an interpersonal perspective beyond that of their individual belief systems. Awareness of the internal coherence of an individual's belief system is both too much to ask of an ordinary knowing subject and insufficient to transform true belief into knowledge.

I.

I begin with the claim that coherence is insufficient when added to true belief to generate knowledge, that BonJour's analysis is too weak. One standard problem facing coherence theories is that there can be incompatible but fully coherent systems of belief. If these sets of beliefs are incompatible, then for realists, only one such set can correspond or connect to the world so as to make all its member beliefs true. But if these sets are equally coherent, then, according to coherentist theories, beliefs within them must be equally justified. Epistemic justification must conduce to truth, since our epistemic goal is to have many true and few false beliefs of the types we seek. Our problematic scenario shows, however, that when beliefs are members of sets as described above, they can be fully coherent without being probably true. If only one such set can contain all true beliefs, and if they can diverge widely with no coherentist grounds for choosing among them, then coherence does not indicate probable truth. It cannot, therefore, constitute justification either.

The moderate foundationalist's response to this problem is to require a set of foundational beliefs that are justified independently of their relations to other beliefs in a coherent system. Once a sufficient set of such beliefs is in place, it is much less likely that there will be incompatible doxastic systems all equally coherent with it on inductive grounds (in terms of explanatory simplicity, depth, and so on). If foundations are required only to solve this problem, then foundationalism can remain moderate, since it need claim neither that basic beliefs must be infallible nor that all other beliefs trace their justification directly back to the basic ones. It can allow coherence to continue to function as a mark of justification, once a set of beliefs as a whole is anchored to reality and truth by means of foundations. Epistemic principles themselves, for example, can be justified in terms of the coherence of sets of beliefs formed by using them, without being justified ultimately by appeal to foundational beliefs alone.

BonJour defends coherentism by proposing a solution to the standard problem along the lines of the moderate foundationalist, but without requiring foundational beliefs.

J.W. Bender (ed.), The Current State of the Coherence Theory, 125–133.
© *1989 by Kluwer Academic Publishers.*

The trick is to require observational input while arguing that observational beliefs themselves are justified only in relation to higher order beliefs about their reliability in certain conditions in which they are acquired. Observational beliefs are acquired noninferentially but justified by their coherence within broader doxastic systems. Such coherence consists in agreements between perceptual beliefs acquired at different times and by different senses, as well as causal explanations for these beliefs that endorse them as accurate. Since justification in BonJour's view depends only on a subject's fulfilling his epistemic responsibilities, it is reliability from the subject's point of view, not the actual reliability of perceptual beliefs, that counts. The subject must be able to recognize certain noninferential beliefs as observational, and he must have sufficient meta-beliefs about their reliability in normal conditions of perception. (BonJour, 122)

The requirement for perceptual input substitutes for the requirement for foundations by anchoring coherent belief systems to the real world. Unconnected coherent systems no longer qualify as justified, and so the fact that they will not be true no longer constitutes a problem for coherentist justification. BonJour holds that only long run coherence in the face of continuous observational input indicates truth. (BonJour, 144) I shall consider his argument to that conclusion later. Here we must evaluate the test of observational input as it eliminates many incompatible coherent systems of belief. If BonJour's requirement, which maintains a thoroughly coherentist criterion of justification, blocks as many incompatible sets of beliefs as do foundations, then the standard objection to coherentism is not particularly an objection to his version.

But now consider the following example. A madman, whenever he looks out over a crowd, believes it to be the Napoleonic army that he is about to lead into battle. He also has meta-beliefs about the reliability of such perceptions, at least to the extent that normal perceivers have such beliefs. Madmen, like others, typically believe their perceptual beliefs to be true, since to have beliefs is to believe them to be true. If they reflect on these beliefs, as they might, they are likely, if they are mad enough, to consider their sources to be reliable. They need not be less reflective or internally coherent than others: often there is a certain coherence to mad reasoning and beliefs, albeit a coherence out of touch with reality. The madman in our example might even integrate his Napoleonic delusion into the full set of his other beliefs, say by means of a bridge set of beliefs about time travel, containing a primitive theory of how such travel is accomplished (no more primitive than most persons' understandings of how airplanes travel).

If our madman suffers only from this delusion, then he may well survive and even achieve long run coherence with continuous observational input. (In any case, what must matter from the internal perspective that BonJour endorses is only what appears to be long run coherence.) Of course his theoretical beliefs regarding the acquisition of at least his delusional beliefs may not be as coherent as a scientific theory of perception, but neither will the average person's theory of perception. The madman's delusional beliefs will be members of a coherent set and so justified according to this theory, at least if average perceivers have perceptual knowledge and are therefore justified in their beliefs.

BonJour admits that it is possible to construct such fanciful systems of belief that meet his criterion of justification. (BonJour, 149) He holds that a subject who has such a system of beliefs, if she could not help acquiring it, has not violated any epistemic responsibility and so is in fact justified, as his theory implies. (BonJour, 150) The mad subject who is nevertheless coherent and blameless is on this view like the victim of a Cartesian demon, who is justified in her beliefs but lacks knowledge because of their falsity. We can picture ourselves as such victims and as nevertheless continuing to be justified in our ordinary beliefs, although ignorant. If the blameless madman is similar, then he too is justified, and we have no counterexample to BonJour's account of justification.

For what it's worth, however, (I don't think that it's crucial to a proper account of knowledge) my intuition persists that the madman is unjustified in his delusional perceptual beliefs, while the demon victim, if she is otherwise just like us, is justified in her perceptual beliefs. The latter must be so if the distinction between justified and unjustified is to mark a difference between cognizers as they take account of the evidence available to them. But the madman is more like a person who forms beliefs about the colors of objects while completely ignoring abnormal lighting conditions. Such a person would not be justified in her ascriptions of colors, even if she ascribes them compulsively and so cannot be blamed for her odd practice, and even if she persists in ascriptions once having made them, thus maintaining coherence. (She might also have false but coherent beliefs about lighting conditions.) Epistemic justification, even if it has to do with believing what in some sense one ought to believe, seems not to presuppose that one must have a genuine choice in forming beliefs. (If the application of the concept of justification did depend on that presupposition, then it would probably be an empty notion.) In short, the difference between our madman and the demon victim is that the latter forms beliefs as we do based on the evidence available to anyone in similar conditions, while the former does not.

If the madman is not justified in his deviant perceptual beliefs even though these are members of a coherent doxastic set, then we have a counterexample to BonJour's account of justification. If such beliefs were justified, then any beliefs could be justified if combined with sufficiently mad but coherent meta-beliefs. As remarked above, I take these points to be less than crucial to a proper account of knowledge because, as I shall argue below, justification, coherentist or otherwise, seems not to be necessary for knowledge. The more important point for the present thesis is that the perceptual beliefs of the madman that are part of his Napoleonic delusion but happen to be true (for example, that the third man from the left in a crowd before him has a brown horse) do not count as knowledge. What prevents the madman's coherent beliefs from counting as knowledge is not simply their lack of truth. Instead it is clear from such examples that BonJour's coherence is not sufficient when added to true belief to generate knowledge. He mentions Gettier cases but then ignores them. But this cavalier attitude will not do if cases such as this one indicate that a very different sort of account of knowledge is required. Even if his account of justification captured some intuitive notion (if there is such a notion divorced from that of knowledge), it would surely be of less interest if not part of an analysis of knowledge.

If the coherence of an entire belief system conferred justification on each of its members, and if justification were what had to be added to true belief to get knowledge, then, once a subject achieved a coherent set of beliefs, all his true beliefs would count as knowledge. But in fact some true beliefs within a coherent set will count as knowledge and others may not, depending on the sensitivity of the subject in question to changes in the facts and in the way that changes in his belief system are occasioned by changes in the facts. Continuous coherence in the face of such changes is not enough, since the madman may achieve that by continually revising his meta-beliefs to endorse his deluded perceptual beliefs.

Before seeing whether such examples plague foundational accounts as well, I turn to the question of whether internal coherence is necessary for knowledge, whether the coherentist account is too strong. BonJour argues convincingly that justification must be an internal affair; it must depend only on what is in some sense accessible to the subject. If some external relation between a subject and a state of affairs were sufficient to justify her belief about that state of affairs, then she might be justified even though she was totally irrational, irresponsible, or superstitious and had the best of reasons for thinking the belief false, for thinking the relation in question did not hold. (BonJour, 38-43) The reasonableness of the subject and the justification of her beliefs must depend on her grasp of the situation. This is a convincing reductio of the externalist concept of justification, if that concept is to retain its roots in the realm of ethics and action.

We noted one disanalogy above: a subject's being epistemically (as opposed to morally) responsible or irresponsible does not seem to presuppose genuine choice in the formation of belief (as opposed to action). But surely the notions of responsibility and obligation must remain relevant to epistemic as to moral justification, at least in so far as a subject who is irresponsible and fails in his obligations cannot be justified in either realm. Some epistemologists continue after Gettier to speak of justification as whatever must be added to true belief to obtain knowledge. But if Gettier's examples and others show that internal justification is not that third condition, I nevertheless side with BonJour that we cannot divorce the notion of justification from that of subjective responsibility and obligation.

BonJour's internalist account is too strong, however, as can be seen first by the fact that it generates a regress. It is not sufficient for this account that a subject's true belief cohere, for that fact once more might be external to his reason for holding the belief, and therefore it seems that he might once more hold a coherent belief irresponsibly. The relation on which justification depends must not only indicate probable truth; the subject must also be aware of this relation and of the fact that it is an indication of probable truth. Thus, for a belief to be justified, its holder must believe that it coheres with his doxastic system and hold it at least in part for that reason. But even this requirement seems insufficient from the thoroughly internalist perspective that BonJour appears to endorse. The subject might still believe that this relation of coherence obtains as a matter of pure whim or wishful thinking. The same reasoning that requires awareness of coherence leads to the conclusion that a subject must justifiably believe that the justifying relation holds for any belief that is justified. Hence the regress.

BonJour tries to avoid a regress of this sort by beginning his reconstruction with a basic presumption. We assume that a subject has a given system of beliefs and that he has an implicit grasp of this system, and then we ask whether this system (and hence its members) is justified. He calls this the Doxastic Presumption. (BonJour, 102-3) Unfortunately, it does not block the particular regress that was developed above. According to that line of reasoning, which is motivated by the internalist demand to be a fully responsible epistemic subject and meet all obligations, it is not enough that a subject grasp his system of beliefs. He must also justifiably believe that this system with which his present belief coheres is itself as a whole coherent. *This* clearly we cannot presume, for that would be to assume justification, which is the very thing we are trying to show.

It is obvious aside from this problem of regress that the requirement of justification as a grasp of the coherence of one's belief system is too strong to be part of an analysis of knowledge. The Doxastic Presumption is first of all probably false, with the qualification needed only because it is not clear from BonJour's statements of it how implicit an implicit grasp of one's belief system can be. More important, even if normal subjects have some grasp of their entire belief systems, they will not grasp all the coherence relations within them and, clearer still, will not hold many of the beliefs that qualify as knowledge, for example simple perceptual beliefs, because they fit the totality of these relations.

Naive subjects acquire much knowledge without grasping or appraising for coherence their entire belief systems and certainly without an inkling of the complex and controversial epistemologist's argument that overall coherence is linked to truth. Their actual belief systems contain all sorts of anomalies and outright inconsistencies, many of which may not be irrational to maintain. (It may be rational for me to believe each sentence of this paper, but not their conjunction.) These inconsistencies render belief systems incoherent but in no way affect simple items of perceptual knowledge acquired in isolation from them. The coherence of a belief system as a whole seems simply irrelevant to the epistemic status of many of its members.

I have suggested a simpler criterion for justification. If a subject acquires a belief in a normal way in relation to the evidence available to her, then we consider her to be justified in holding the belief (if the question ever arises). But even this weak (and weakly internalist) conception of justification is too strong to enter an account of knowledge. If there were clairvoyance, for example, then true clairvoyants would know the future, although they would not acquire beliefs in the normal way in relation to the evidence. One might hold that the clairvoyant only gains knowledge when she acquires meta-beliefs in the usual inductive way by reflecting on the reliability of her beliefs about the future. But our ascriptions of knowledge, at least by hindsight, would not await the ascription of such meta-beliefs, which, we have noted, naive knowers ordinarily lack. My intuition even in BonJour's cases of abnormal but perfectly reliable cognizers who have inductive reasons for believing their beliefs false is that their cognitions, connected in lawlike ways to the facts to which they refer, produce knowledge, although not justified beliefs.

On a more mundane level, if we consider the fact that ordinary, unreflective and naive subjects nevertheless acquire, and must acquire, much knowledge about their environments, together with the arguments for (somewhat) internalist conceptions of justification, then we arrive at the conclusion that knowledge does not require justification. This general conclusion only reinforces the point that BonJour's strongly internalist and holistic conception of justified belief must be too strong for an account of knowledge true to our ordinary concept. His concept is too strong if any but the most reflective and skillful epistemologists are to be granted knowledge, as I believe they must be. BonJour allows that the ordinary garden variety of knowledge may be only an approximation to his ideal, (BonJour, 152) but he offers no convincing reasons for seeking to replace the former concept with the latter. Knowledge in the ordinary sense, the right relation of belief to fact, is what ordinary agents aim at, and ordinarily all they need to aim at. The epistemologist's task is different, but he too needs more (and less) than internal coherence with observational input.

II.

The epistemologist, unlike the ordinary knower, must demonstrate that we have the various kinds of knowledge that we claim to have. To do so, he cannot simply show that his own belief system is internally coherent and contains noninferential members. The madman, after all, can truly make the same claim. As we have seen, BonJour admits the possibility of incompatible, justified (coherent) belief systems, even after his test of observational input is added. He nevertheless continues to view internal coherence as the only criterion of justification and truth available to epistemologists, in part because he believes that he provides a decisive general argument against all forms of foundational epistemologies.

This argument attempts to show that there cannot be a justified belief that does not depend for its justification on other beliefs. Foundations must be either cognitive states with propositional content, presumably beliefs, or nonpropositional states. States without propositional content, BonJour assumes, cannot justify beliefs with such content. Consider now a belief alleged to be foundational. Each justified belief or genuinely cognitive state, whether purportedly foundational or not, must have some feature that confers its justification, some feature that indicates its probable truth and makes it a plausible candidate for the status of knowledge. From the internalist perspective that is the cornerstone of the view defended throughout BonJour's book, this feature must be believed to be present by the subject, so that she does not hold the purportedly foundational belief irresponsibly. The internalist demand, however, makes it clear that the alleged foundation cannot really be foundational, since the subject's justification in holding it now depends on at least one other belief, the belief that the justifying feature is present. (BonJour, 31-2) In short, if a cognitive state has no epistemic content, then it cannot justify other cognitive states, that is beliefs, that do; but if it has such content, then it must be justified by appeal to other beliefs. (BonJour, 69)

We have seen that the sort of internalist demand that supports the argument against foundational beliefs leads to a regress. The answer to this problem of regress for the ordinary knower is that she need not believe anything, justifiably or otherwise, about the relation that gives some of her beliefs the status of knowledge. What about the epistemologist? He can first of all show, despite BonJour's argument to the contrary, that there are foundations that do not depend on other beliefs to indicate their truth. I shall ignore here the possibility that nonepistemic states might serve as foundations, that an object's appearing blue might in itself (without my believing that it appears blue) justify my belief that it is blue (if I am sufficiently sensitive to lighting conditions). Aside from this possibility, there are beliefs which indicate their own truth apart from their relations to the other beliefs of those who hold them. Such beliefs are self-justified, indicative of their own truth to a subject who reflects on them in the right way. BonJour assumes that if a belief stands in need of justification, then it cannot be foundational, (BonJour, 72, 78) ignoring the possibility that it may be self-justifying. Self-justification of beliefs, in a sense to be briefly explained, need not depend on subjects' believing them to be self-justified, although of course we will not realize that they indicate their own truth, that they are self-justified, unless we reflect on them.

For the externalist on knowledge, a belief counts as knowledge if and only if it stands in the proper lawlike relation to the fact (or type of fact) to which it refers. I have argued at length elsewhere that this relation consists in the fact's entering prominently into the best explanation for the belief's being held. (Goldman, Part I) For most beliefs, the facts referred to are only parts, and more or less indirect parts, of those explanations. My belief that there is a fire engine passing on the street outside my window is explained not simply by the fact that there is, but by the additional fact, for example, that I see it. As an epistemologist seeking to demonstrate my knowledge of the fire engine or justifying my belief about it, I would then have to justify my claim to see it, or my belief that I do. The former belief is justified only if the latter is and only in relation to it. The explanation for my belief that I see the fire engine is that I am looking in a certain direction and that there appears to me to be a fire engine there, that is, that I am appeared to in certain ways. As an epistemologist, I once more have to justify those claims.

At this stage in demonstrating my perceptual knowledge, I arrive at beliefs about the ways I am appeared to. The explanation for my belief that I am appeared to redly, for example, is simply that I am so appeared to. Here we arrive at a belief whose explanation lies in its truth alone. (Goldman, Ch. 7) This, I claim, is a self-justified belief and can therefore be counted a foundation. The epistemologist, of course, appeals to other beliefs in demonstrating the truth of such a claim, for example the belief that it is self-justifying. But the indication of its truth does not lie in other beliefs, but is instead self-contained for one who asks the proper question.

The madman too, to return to the main line of our criticism of BonJour, could truly claim (if he were an epistemologist) that the best explanation for his beliefs about the ways he is appeared to is that he is appeared to in those ways. There does appear to him to a be a Napoleonic army before him, for example. The more significant, although less obvious, break with BonJour occurs in the next step of the epistemologist's demonstration. Here he argues that the best explanation for various patterns of appearances, especially given (apparent) interpersonal agreements, is a physical world (containing other subjects and) structured in various ways. If the madman were a sufficiently skilled epistemologist to argue in the same way to the truth of his deluded perceptual beliefs, he would be wrong.

Given this false conclusion on the part of the mad epistemologist, we cannot argue directly from the coherence of a single belief system, given only the requirement of observational input, that the member beliefs of the system are probably true. This is precisely the "meta-justification" for his internalist criterion of justification that BonJour offers. He argues that the best explanation for the long run coherence of a belief system with continuous observational input is approximate truth. (BonJour, 171) But the tendency to fabricate coherence where the observational input might otherwise upset it weakens this short argument. If there is a natural drive toward coherence, given whatever input in the form of stimulation occurs, even among madmen, then internal coherence in itself does not indicate truth. We have some empirical evidence that perceptual consciousness does indeed operate to integrate perceptual data into prior expectations or belief sets.

BonJour assumes as a premise required for his argument that if a coherent system does not correspond to reality, then further observational input will tend to upset its coherence or prompt revision in the direction of correspondence. (BonJour, 172) But the power of the mind, especially in madness, to alter its natural data and at the same time adjust its higher order beliefs so that the two levels concur calls this assumption into question. This power can replace the appeal to truth in the explanation for the coherence of a given single belief set.

If the sane epistemologist (Is there such a creature?) is to show that he is not in the position of the madman, he requires a longer and more complex argument than BonJour provides. His emphasis must first of all lie on interpersonal agreement, not an explicit requirement for an internally coherent belief system in BonJour's epistemology. While a madman might ignore or even adjust observational reports of others, he would be unlikely to place great weight on them in constructing an explanatory scheme into which to incorporate his own perceptual beliefs. The epistemologist must reverse this emphasis in his reconstruction, acknowledging the social aspect of legitimating knowledge claims.

We can see that the actual best explanations for the mad beliefs of madmen do not appeal at all, even indirectly, to the truth of those beliefs. It is perhaps somewhat more difficult to see how we know that we are not mad, or at least in the same position when it comes to knowing the truth about physical reality. If we are speaking of real madmen, however, then we know that we can place emphasis on our interpersonal agreements and on the social aspects of our claims to knowledge, whereas they do not. The skeptical challenge posed by madmen and our initial response to it are similar to the Cartesian problem of dreams: we know that real dreams differ from waking experiences in marked ways, but it is possible to imagine dreams that would be indistinguishable.

Given such imaginary alternatives to appeal to the real world in explanations for our perceptual experiences, we must argue, along with BonJour, that the alternative explanations are not as good on ordinary inductive grounds. The same argument is not convincing, I have pointed out, if we remain solely on the level of a single belief system viewed internally. While individual madmen can survive and even achieve and maintain internally coherent belief systems, it is less likely that we would have survived as a species and as technological cultures if our interpersonal belief systems had been as out of touch with reality as those of madmen. Thus we can show that we are probably not in the position of madmen to the extent that we can confirm our beliefs as members of knowledge seeking or using subcultures within such broader groups.

The adoption of this interpersonal and partly external viewpoint still depends on inferences to the best explanations for data within our belief systems on several levels. Any realist epistemology, BonJour's included, must eventually defend the claim that the principle of inference to the best explanation itself tends to preserve truth, at least in certain contexts. (BonJour does not explicitly provide what he might call this meta-meta-justificatory argument.) Here again it will be necessary to adopt both an interpersonal and a naturalistic point of view. From that viewpoint, it can be argued, beginning on the perceptual level, where an analogue of explanatory inference generates perceptual beliefs from stimulation, that this form of inference has evolved in the species to provide information about the environment accurate enough to allow survival and reproduction. The latter require at least information about the locations and properties of middle sized objects that might pose threats, constitute sources of food, and so on. Thus, it is unlikely that quasi-inferential perceptual mechanisms that generate perceptual beliefs (that explain the data of raw stimulation in terms of certain properties of middle sized objects) lead to thoroughly false explanations.

This sort of justification of explanatory induction is in part circular, or at least self-supporting, but at this level of generality and depth only such arguments could be available. Such justifications of fundamental epistemic principles are neither trivial nor vacuous, since there are, for example, many conceivable rules of induction that could not be so justified. An additional problem for the particular naturalist argument being suggested here lies in the attempt to extend it beyond the level of perception and beliefs about observable objects.

The use of the explanatory form of induction to develop scientific theories about unobservables takes us far from its primitive use in perception. Between lies inference to unobserved but observable states of affairs (also necessary for survival), where confirmation can follow and establish coherence between genuine explanatory inference and direct observation. Even on the deepest levels, it can be argued that explanatory theories correct for systematic errors of perception, as in the naive ascription of color properties. Scientific theories do so under control by the environment in the form of experimental testing, which might be viewed as an analogue, albeit inexact, of the natural selection of the form of inference itself as it operates at less sophisticated levels. If these arguments can be provided, then the sort of justification I am suggesting can be extended from the use of the principle when inferring to observables to its use in theory formation.

Clearly defense of such basic epistemic principles requires complex and difficult arguments, and this is not the place to flesh them out. (see Goldman, Ch. 13) It is more fashionable nowadays to dismiss all appeals to environmental selection, natural or otherwise, as justificatory. But I believe that this sort of answer to fundamental skeptical challenges has a better chance of success than BonJour's narrowly internalist meta-justification, which remains constricted to an appeal to the coherence of a single belief system, and which presupposes without defending the epistemic principle in question. My purpose in this section has been only to suggest an alternative to the narrower coherentism. The latter continues to be defeated by the problem of incompatible coherent belief systems. The only other alternative is skepticism, once we accept a realist view of truth for our beliefs about the physical world, a view that BonJour and I take to be more coherent than anti-realisms.

The skeptic leans heavily on the problem of underdetermination of theory by input, which just is the problem of incompatible but equally coherent or inductively tied belief systems. However, while this problem continues to be insuperable if we limit our view to single belief systems (even with continuous observational input), it is not so clearly overwhelming when we consider instead theories developed and accepted by whole scientific communities, at least those theories that admit of clear physical interpretations. It is not as easy to develop genuinely competitive theories, tied an all inductive or explanatory grounds, as it is to maintain coherence within the explanatorily much poorer belief systems of single individuals.

BonJour's meta-justification of his requirement for internal coherence fails to show that such coherence in itself indicates truth, just as he failed to show that this requirement is necessary or sufficient for knowledge when added to true belief. The criterion of coherence fails to indicate truth for the same reason that it is not sufficient for knowledge when added to true belief, namely that it can be met by incompatible belief systems. BonJour's additional requirement of observational input attempts to overcome that problem, but does not succeed in doing so. The problem of justifying broader, interpersonal belief systems is both similar and different. It is different in that the central problem becomes that of justifying those interpersonal, inductive principles of reasoning that generate such systems. It is similar in that the problem of underdetermination remains the main challenge. But here the skeptic cannot so readily produce concrete examples of incompatible systems that equally satisfy our epistemic criteria (beyond internal coherence) in the longer interpersonal run. In any case, the deepest skeptical challenge to epistemic principles themselves is one that BonJour too would have to meet, as a realist, once he broadened his narrowly internalist perspective.

BonJour does broaden the perspective of earlier coherentists by adding the requirement of observational input. In doing so he narrows the gap between internalist and externalist, and between coherentist and foundationalist, epistemologies. Such interpersonal convergence is arguably an indication of an approach toward a fully defensible position, for epistemological theories as for others. Further convergence could be achieved by further explicitly broadening the perspective from which we might be expected to meeting the skeptic's challenge.

REFERENCES

BonJour, Laurence. *The Structure of Empirical Knowledge*. Cambridge: Harvard University Press, 1985.
Goldman, Alan. *Empirical Knowledge*. Berkeley: University of California Press, 1988.

Circularity, Non-Linear Justification and Holistic Coherentism

Timothy Joseph Day
Indiana University

Laurence BonJour defends the coherence theory against the charge of circularity.[1] Part of his defense seems to rely on a non-linear theory of inferential justification. In this paper I will examine this response to the charge of circularity. I hope to show that BonJour (and other amenable coherentists) can and do respond to the circularity problem but that the response does not rely on any non-linear theory of inferential justification. The response instead relies on some more fundamental features of the coherentist view.

I

We can understand the coherence theory as a response to the epistemic regress problem. The regress comes about as a result of trying to understand inferential justification. The most ordinary way to understand inferential justification is on the model of logical inference. If belief B implies belief A (according to some acceptable logical rules) then A is justified if B is. To justify B we appeal to some further belief, C, and we are off on the regress. To avoid the infinite regress of justification a theory must accept basic beliefs of some sort or allow circular justification. The coherentist allows the latter possibility.

However, in order to respond to the problem raised by the regress a theory must explain how a belief can be justified unconditionally.[2] Simply allowing circles does not seem to accomplish this. If the inferential justification chain circles back on itself then we get the result that A is justified if A is justified. This is true, but not very helpful. It appears, then, that circular justification will not provide any useful response to the regress problem.

BonJour responds to this objection to circular justification by claiming that it assumes that inferential is linear. The objection assumes that inferential justification "...involves a one-dimensional sequence of beliefs, ordered by the relation of epistemic priority, along which epistemic justification is passed from the earlier to the later beliefs in the sequence via connections of inference"(90). The holistic coherentist claims that there is no such linear ordering relation among beliefs. We should note that the defender of linear inferential justification relations need not claim that there is any a priori ordering among beliefs imposed by a relation of epistemic priority. It is enough that on any given occasion of inferential justification there are some beliefs that must be justified prior to being used in any justifying inference. The inferences used will impose a linear ordering in that case, whether or not there is any antecedent relation of epistemic priority among the beliefs.

At any rate, the crucial feature of the linear theory is not that it assumes a relation of epistemic priority. According to the linear theory, appropriate inferential relations pass justification from one belief to another. If we accept this, then we will have reason to reject circles that purportedly justify beliefs. Each belief in the circle will ultimately justify itself. It is true that this conclusion relies on the transitivity of the inference relation. This transitivity is part of what a non-linear theory would reject. If, however, we deny that justification is a property of beliefs that is passed from one to another, then it will not matter that certain inference relations are transitive. I think that a coherence theory, as developed by BonJour, denies exactly this. Because they deny the transmission of justification, coherence theorists need not claim that inference is non-linear. A coherence theory cannot hold that justification is passed along a chain of inferences.

J.W. Bender (ed.), The Current State of the Coherence Theory, 134–141.
© 1989 by Kluwer Academic Publishers.

In denying that justification is transmitted across inferential connections we do not need to give up BonJour's central antifoundational arguments in which he objects to basic beliefs. The question for foundationalism, as BonJour states it is as follows: "Where does the noninferential justification for basic empirical beliefs come from?" (30).

For BonJour, as for many of us, justification has a truth directed aspect. For a theory of justification to make sense there must be reasons for thinking that following the standards offered by that theory will most likely lead to truth. BonJour concludes, ". . . if basic beliefs are to provide a secure foundation for empirical knowledge, if inference from them is to be the sole basis upon which other empirical beliefs are justified, then that feature, whatever it may be, by virtue of which a particular belief qualifies as basic must also constitute a good reason for thinking that the belief is true." (30-31)

At this point BonJour is offering an *ad hominem* argument against the foundationalist. The point is that if we are to accept any particular belief as basic then we must also accept that the belief has a feature that makes it highly likely to be true.

BonJour's argument here is not entirely without problems. I mention it only because it might be thought that in order to raise this argument against the foundationalist, BonJour must appeal to a justification transmission condition. I do not think this is so. The basic beliefs are supposed to be noninferentially justified. BonJour argues that they cannot be. If they are likely to be true, and they are held in an epistemically responsible way, then they must be inferentially justified, in the sense of inferentially justified accepted by the foundationalist. The coherentist need not accept the same account of how inference functions in justification in order to make this objection against the foundationalist.

Inference, whether linear or not, serves a different purpose in a coherence theory. Justification arises out of or perhaps supervenes on inference relations. The circles that the coherentist allows are not circular paths along which justification travels. I hope to show that this is the key coherentist insight in responding to the regress problem. Furthermore it is not an insight that depends on the non-linearity of inferential relations.

II

BonJour suggests that ". . . inferential justification, despite its linear appearance, is essentially systematic or holistic in character: beliefs are justified by being inferentially related to other beliefs in the overall context of a coherent system" (90). Justification, on such a model is holistic. This does not mean that the inferences involved must also be holistic. Nevertheless, BonJour, and other coherentists sometimes talk as if the inferences involved were holistic. We might refer to reciprocal or mutual support between beliefs. Such connections will be involved in holistic justification. This mutual support among beliefs does not necessarily require non-linear relations. There may be different linear relations imposing different orders. We can use entailment relations, but also explanation, confirmation and probability connections between beliefs. These relations may order the beliefs, but in different ways. This seems to be involved in a holistic theory that allows inference type relations to play any role at all in justification.

More important for a holistic theory than non-linear relations is that we understand what is being justified. A holistic theory is holistic because it treats justification as a property of systems of beliefs. When he is being careful, BonJour admits that single beliefs are said to be justified only in the sense of belonging to a coherent system. Justification is a holistic property of systems of beliefs. "According to a holistic view, it is such a system of beliefs which is the primary unit of justification; particular beliefs are justified only derivatively, by virtue of membership in such a system . . ."(24). Beliefs gain membership in such sets by virtue of being inferentially related to other beliefs already present. This is not to say that justification is a property that is passed from one belief to another.

In discussing justification we can distinguish between generative and transmission devices. In a foundational theory this distinction makes perfect sense. Justification is generated by perception or memory which give rise to a distinguished subset of beliefs (foundations). Inferences then transmit the justification to other beliefs. A coherence view rejects the foundational beliefs and generates justification by means of the inferential connections themselves. Justification is generated only in an appropriate set of beliefs. It is in this sense that systems of beliefs are the primary units of justification and single beliefs are justified only derivatively.

My belief that there is a yellow piece of paper in front of me is justified. It acquires its justification only within the larger context of my entire set of beliefs (or enough of a subset). According to a foundational theory it might be possible that my belief about the yellow page is justified in virtue of some relation it has to some non-belief mental state that results in the justification of that single belief. On the coherentist approach there is only one way for beliefs to be justified, membership in the coherent system.

In an effort to clarify the role of linear inference in justification BonJour draws a distinction between two different levels of empirical justification. There is the local level of justification. This is the level at which justification can appear to be linear. We justify a particular belief in the context of an established system of beliefs by seeing if the former is derivable (in a linear fashion) from the system. At the same time there is the issue of how this system is justified. BonJour thinks that it is at this global level that the issues of coherence and holistic justification are crucial.

So BonJour is not denying that we sometimes justify a belief in a linear fashion on the basis of other beliefs. At the local level justification can proceed in a manner that is familiar even to a foundationalist. At the local level, justification appears linear and it is. But that is because we are essentially operating within a contextualist framework in the local level. We accept certain aspects of the underlying system as given and then use these "contextually basic beliefs," as BonJour suggests they might be called, to justify other beliefs. At this level inference is used not just to generate coherence. Inference seems to be actually transmitting justification in just the way that it does according to the linear theory.

This local level, however, is not operating in the same way as do basic beliefs and inferences for a foundationalist theory. It is perhaps better to think of the local level as the accessed subset of one's entire coherent system of beliefs. For very many justificatory purposes we need to access only a portion of our doxastic system. The assumption is that this portion, which may be only one belief, is coherent with the entire system. By showing that the target belief is coherent with this accessed part, we show, through transitivity of the coherence relations, that it coheres with the entire system. At the local level, then, we do not have any new or different sort of justification. The entire coherent set of beliefs is justified. The individual belief can be accepted as part of that set.

This local level can also make sense of the notion of epistemic responsibility. An agent is epistemically responsible in holding a belief if he has good reasons to think that the belief is true. To meet one's epistemic obligations should require no more than being able to show that the target belief coheres. BonJour has given us a way to do this that does not require us to go through our entire doxastic system every time we accept a belief. The justificatory starting points that BonJour calls upon here are not basic beliefs. There is no reason to think of them as even contextually basic beliefs. They are beliefs that are accepted as elements of a coherent system. When I justify my belief that there is a yellow paper before me I need only connect it inferentially to some small subset of my doxastic system.

In seeking justification we cannot remain at the local level. This level does not explain how justification enters the system. When we ask the global question concerning the justification of this system of beliefs, then we are asking about a holistic system of justification. If we challenge the system of beliefs long enough we eventually circle back. This circle is bad if we continue to think in terms of a linear model. However an attack on the entire system is not to be answered on the basis of the linear model. When we answer questions about non-derivative justification, we need to use a non-linear approach. At the global level ". . . the relation between the various particular beliefs is correctly to be conceived, not as one of linear dependence, but rather as one of mutual or reciprocal support"(91).

It is at this global level that justification is actually generated. Local linear justification is better thought of as a way to show that a belief is a member of the set. The local level is the level at which we show that a belief is justified. Justification is generated at the global level. According to BonJour a fully explicit justification of an empirical belief consists of four steps.

(1) The inferability of that particular belief from other particular beliefs and further relations among particular empirical beliefs.
(2) The coherence of the overall system of empirical beliefs.
(3) The justification of the overall system of empirical beliefs.
(4) The justification of the particular belief in question, by virtue of its membership in the system. (92)

He then says that it is the neglecting of steps (2) and (3) that ". . . lends plausibility to the linear conception of justification and thus generates the regress problem"(92). The neglecting of steps 2 and 3 amounts to neglecting the possibility that justification might arise from relations between beliefs other than the sort of inferential relations used in constructing the regress.

We need to realize that there is an important difference between coherence and the inferential relations that generate the regress. The key issue seems fairly straightforward. When we approach problems of justification by way of the regress it is easy to think that the regressive relation (that linear ordering relation) is the only one that is relevant for justification. This is clearly not the case and the holistic coherentist recognizes that it is not. It is crucial for the coherentist that there be more relations that can hold between beliefs in ways that are relevant to justification. Many different proposals have been made as to what these relations might be. BonJour thinks that inference relations are among the relations that can serve this role. To do so an inference relation must ". . . be to some extent truth-preserving; any sort of relation which meets this requirement will serve as an appropriate positive connection between beliefs, and no other sort of connection seems relevant here."(96) These systematic, truth-preserving relations generate justification. However it is ultimately worked out, there will be many different relations involved in producing the coherence needed for justification. There is no reason to think that these relations must be non-linear.

Regardless of the linearity of the relations, the holistic coherentist has an important and interesting point here. If we approach the regress problem with more or less foundationalist preconceptions then we are not likely to pay much attention to the particular relation that is ordering the beliefs. Any inference relation that meets certain conditions will transmit justification. This approach overlooks the fact that there may well be several sorts of relation relevant to justification. This is certainly true, even for the foundationalist who ultimately locates justification in some set of distinguished beliefs (the self-warranted ones perhaps). But for the foundationalist it would not make much difference if there were just one relation that transmitted justification from foundational to nonfoundational beliefs.

It is not clear to me whether there are coherence producing relations between beliefs that are non-inferential. Even if it is possible to construe all the various relations as inferences it still seems desirable to recognize differences between, for example, explanation and logical implication in general. These sorts of differences are blurred when we construct the regress in terms of a single "justifies" relation. On the coherentist model it is important that we have positive connections between beliefs that can generate justification for the set. It is not enough to have generic inferences that will pass along justification from belief to belief. This is why it is an important part of a coherentist view to actually say what coherence is, while it is not so, for a foundational theory. We can see here, though, that the issue separating the coherentist and foundationalist at this point is not that one has a linear theory and the other does not. The dispute here involves something more fundamental. The real issue concerns the object of justification. The original regress problem is a problem for justifying a belief. The coherentist turns this into a problem about justifying systems of beliefs. In talking about systems of beliefs it is natural and perhaps necessary to consider more than one sort of relation. In fact, it is necessary to consider any sort of relation that might contribute in any way to the overall coherence of a system. This is especially important since a coherence theory uses inferences and other relations between beliefs in a different way than does the foundationalist or the regress defender.[4] The latter two think of justification as a property of beliefs that is passed along through inferences. In this case we need only one such relation (though there may be others).

III

Coherence is taken to be a holistic property of sets of beliefs. Put shortly and somewhat metaphorically, it is the property of the beliefs in the set hanging together. Coherence is the property, the possession of which transforms a set of beliefs into ". . . an organized, tightly structured system of beliefs, rather than either a helter-skelter collection or a set of conflicting subsystems"(93).

We have already seen that BonJour thinks that any truth preserving relation between propositions is relevant to justification generating coherence. Many of these sorts of relations will also induce a linear ordering on the set of beliefs. What little BonJour tells us about coherence reinforces this impression that his fundamental disagreement with the regress defender is not over the difference between linear and non-linear justification. The real disagreement is over what is being justified and how.

BonJour gives us some conditions for coherence. First a coherent set of beliefs is both logically and probabilistically consistent. But more than this the beliefs in the set have certain positive connections between them. As we saw, some positive connections are inference relations. The inference relations are ". . . any sort of relation of content which would allow one belief or set of beliefs, if justified, to serve as the premise(s) of a cogent epistemic-justificatory argument for a further belief"(96). These seem to be the sort of relations that generate the regress. Coherence is also increased by explanatory connections between beliefs.

All this seems correct and acceptable. What is not so clear is just what it is that is being said to be non-linear. We can understand that ". . . the justification of a particular empirical belief finally depends, not on other particular beliefs as the linear conception of justification would have it, but instead on the overall system and its coherence"(92). We can also accept coherence as a holistic property of sets of beliefs. If nothing else, it is a property of the whole set. Moreover, this is a property that is important and desirable for a system of beliefs regardless of where justification ultimately comes from. Still, the relations called upon to provide the coherence all seem quite linear in nature.

John Pollock in his book, *Contemporary Theories of Knowledge* contrasts linear and holistic coherence theories. A linear theory is one in which "a reason for a belief is either another individual belief or a small set of beliefs . . ." (73). This seems to treat linearity in terms of a geometric metaphor. Two points (beliefs) determine a line (a justificatory structure). The holistic theory, on the other hand, holds that ". . . in order for S to have reason for believing P, there must be a relationship holding between P and the set of all of his beliefs . . ." (73). Pollock makes it sound as though the distinction of interest is between linear and holistic theories. I do not think that this is quite right.

BonJour used 'linear' to refer to a kind of inference relation. On the other hand, 'holistic' was what coherence was said to be. Coherence was holistic because it could not be predicated of anything except the entire set of beliefs. Then we try to make sense of coherence (which according to the theory is the same as justification) in terms of non-linear relations holding between beliefs. Pollock says that ". . . even linear theories can be more holistic that one might initially suppose" (74). This should not surprise us if we realize that linearity and holism are properties of two different kinds of things. There is no reason that we cannot have a holistic theory of coherence built on linear relations.

IV

The crucial part of the coherentist response to the regress is not that inference relations are non-linear. The coherentist does not need non-linearity. The important revision that the coherentist makes is to deny that justification works in the way the regress assumes it does. Justification, according to the coherentist is not passed along from one belief to another. Justification is a property of systems of beliefs that supervenes on certain relations that hold between beliefs. There seems no reasons to require that these relations be non-linear. I find it still unclear just what such a non-linear relation would be.

BonJour says that justification is a property of systems of beliefs. This is the key move that resolves the circularity problem. The epistemically desirable property of beliefs is membership in a justified set. The vicious circle is a circle of beliefs in which each belief is justified by earlier beliefs. This model quickly (or eventually) leads to a belief that justifies itself. The problem with that story is not that it relies on a linear theory of justification. Rather the problem is that it relies on a theory according to which beliefs are justified and can (somehow) transfer this justification to other beliefs. There is no problem with accepting a linear theory. It seems very useful to have such linear relations to establish the positive sorts of connections that BonJour wants. But it is only a linear theory of relations between beliefs. And that is not going to generate justification of a belief.

So, BonJour is right, but he is, at times, too easy on the foundationalist and the regress defender. He ought to rule out the sort of justification relied on to generate the regress. Instead he makes it justification at one level. This is a mistake and leads him to a defense of a non-linear theory of justification that is simply not forthcoming. The claim of non-linearity is a bit of a confusion on the part of the coherentist. The demand for a non-linear theory of inferential justification has never been worked out in any detail, and I suspect this is because it is not a workable hypothesis. The coherentist turns to a non-linear theory in order to respond to the problem of circularity. We can now see how another response to circularity is more appropriate.

The coherentist does not think that justification moves in a circle. Justification does not move at all. It is better to say, as Plantinga does, that "A pure coherentist rejects warrant transmission altogether; for here all propositions that enjoy warrant in a noetic structure are properly basic in that structure." [5] Linearity is a problem so long as we think of the inferences as transmitting justification. There is no danger of circular justification on the coherentist view of things. The only circles here involve the inferential connections between beliefs. If we begin with belief A and work through the system we eventually can get back to A. But the conclusion from all this is not that A is justified if A is justified. The conclusion is, rather, that A is a member of a coherent system. This is shown by our being able to move from A through the other beliefs and back to A using whatever acceptable coherence producing relations we have. Moreover, these relations may be linear, in the sense of imposing a linear order on the beliefs that they relate.

The coherentist response to the threat of circularity relies on a more fundamental feature of the coherentist position. The circularity problem is answered by denying the picture of justification according to which justification is primarily of beliefs instead of belief systems. But the idea of a linear inferential relation between beliefs is one that the coherentist can certainly use. The web of beliefs that make up the coherent system is held together by many such linear relations. There is simply no reason for the coherentist to deny this. Linear inference relations are quite acceptable so long as they are not used to do more than they are meant to do. They do not pass justification from one belief to another.

This last remark should not be taken to imply that we do not come to believe some things on the basis of inferences. Of course we do. I believe that whales are mammals because I believe that someone told me that and that the person who did is trustworthy about such things. Hence they are correct about this and so, whales are mammals. But these are not justification transmitting inferences. These are coherence producing inferences. They can show that the belief that whales are mammals fits in with my finite and coherent system of beliefs. Hence, that belief is justified, for me, in the derivative sense of fitting in to a coherent system.

It might also be thought that what I am saying here conflicts with a fundamental tenet of coherence theories of justification. The most well known of coherence conditions, namely, that only a belief can justify a belief. This condition is not so central as it appears. Understanding justification in the way I am suggesting allows us to remain with a doxastic theory. Justification of beliefs requires more than just a relation to some other belief. The raw material of justification is still other beliefs and the relations that hold between these beliefs.

The charge of circularity has been answered. The answer does not depend on any non-linear theory of inference, much less of inferential justification. The answer to the charge of circularity depends on being clear about what is being justified and how it is justified. The key elements in the coherentist response are the denial that particular beliefs are the primary objects of justification and the denial that inference relations can transmit justification.

The emphasis on non-linearity has blurred some crucial distinctions between the coherentist and the non-coherentist attitudes towards justification. The set of beliefs that go to make up the coherent set that is justified are related by many different relationships. Among these are inference relations, explanatory connections and others that are yet to be specified and studied in any great detail. I do not think that there is any problem in thinking that at least some of these relations are "linear". Where "linear" here means transitive and asymmetric. Allowing some of these relations to be linear would not rule out the sort of mutual or reciprocal support that the coherentist wants. There are, after all, many different relations to consider.

NOTES

1. BonJour (1985). References to this work will be parenthetical in the text.
2. For more complete discussions of the problem raised by the regress see BonJour (1986), 17-20. A nice survey of the kinds of problems that the regress has been thought to raise is given by Haker (1984). Clark (forthcoming) also argues that the problem with the regress is that it provides at best conditional justification.
3. On this distinction see Audi (1988), 71f., and Plantinga (1987).
4. By 'regress defender' here I mean anyone who thinks that the regress poses a real threat to a theory of

justification.
5. Plantinga (1986), 125. Plantinga says "pure coherentist" to distinguish this view from one that would allow transmission at perhaps a higher level. I have tried to show that such transmission principles serve no purpose in a coherence theory.

REFERENCES

Audi, Robert. *Belief, Justification, and Knowledge* . Belmont, CA: Wadsworth, 1988.
BonJour, Laurence. *The Structure of Empirical Knowledge.* Cambridge: Harvard University Press, 1985.
Clark, Romane. "Vicious Infinite Regress Arguments." Forthcoming in J. Tomberlin, ed. *Philosophical Perspectives* Vol. VI.
Harker, Jay. "Can There be an Infinite Regress of Justified Beliefs." *Australasian Journal of Philosophy* 62, (1984) , 255-264.
Plantinga, Alvin. "Coherentism and the Evidentialist Objection to Belief in God." in R. Audi and W. Wainwright, eds. *Rationality, Religious Belief, & Moral Commitment.* Ithaca: Cornell University Press, 1986, 109-138.
Pollock, John. *Contemporary Theories of Knowledge.* Totowa: Rowman & Littlefield, 1986.

Coherentist Theories of Knowledge Don't Apply to Enough Outside of Science and Don't Give the Right Results When Applied to Science [1]

James Bogen
Pitzer College

I.

This paper argues for its title by considering and generalizing from difficulties in BonJour's program for a coherentist account of what it is to have good reason to think one's beliefs are true.[2] I chose BonJour as a representative of coherentism because his is by far the most candid, well worked out, and fruitful advocacy of the coherentist position of which I am aware. As he would be the first to admit, what BonJour offers is a program and an apology for coherentism rather than a detailed theory; to expect more at this point would be quite unreasonable. I can't rule out the possibility that if there were a fully worked out coherentist theory of justification, its details would answer the complaints this paper develops. But I will argue that my objections should apply not only to theories which fit specifications peculiar to BonJour's program, but also to coherentist theories which depart from it in some respects.

II.

BonJour wants to show what a coherentist characterization of ideal epistemic responsibility should look like, what difficulties it would have to overcome, and what its advantages would be. His program includes somewhat more refined and detailed versions of the following conditions for epistemically responsible belief.
A person, a, is ideally epistemically responsible only if

> (1) a 'accepts all and only those beliefs which [a] has good reason to believe are true' (8).

In order for (1) to be satisfied,there must be standards determining the epistemic goodness of putative reasons for believing, and

> (2) a must, in principle at least, be able to tell whether the reasons available to him for holding any given belief meet the standards. (8).

Call these (whatever they turn out to be) 'epistemic standards'. Furthermore,

> (3) The epistemic standards should be *truth conducive* - the standards should be such that beliefs supported by reasons which conform to them tend to be true, and have a significantly better chance of being true than beliefs which are not so supported. (8).

A peculiar (and, to me, attractive) feature of BonJour's program is that it construes the truth of a belief as requiring some sort of correspondence between its content and the way the world is. In particular, BonJour rejects accounts which equate truth with warranted assertibility or justified belief. (157-169) However, the main claims in this paper do not depend upon this. The problems which beset BonJour's coherentism should arise in pretty much the same form in connection with coherentist theories which do not treat truth as depending on correspondence.
Conditions (1)-(3) - spelled out in more detail and supplemented by an account of the relevant epistemic standards, an explanation of what it is to "have" reasons, etc.- would constitute what I'll call 'a theory of justification'. The theory of justification would provide

142

J.W. Bender (ed.), The Current State of the Coherence Theory, 142–159.
© *1989 by Kluwer Academic Publishers.*

necessary conditions for epistemically responsible belief. But even if a cognizer held all and only beliefs which meet the conditions set by a theory of justification this would not be sufficient for epistemic responsibility. A further requirement is that

> (4) ...an appropriate metajustification of...[the epistemic] standards must in principle at least be available to *him* [the cognizer]...

For how can the fact that a belief meets those standards give that believer a reason for thinking that it is likely to be true (and thus an epistemically appropriate reason for accepting it), unless he himself knows that beliefs satisfying those standards are likely to be true? (10)

Condition (4) requires (a) good reasons to think beliefs whose justifications meet the relevant epistemic standards are likely to be true (and more likely than beliefs that do not). It also requires (b) that a metajustification of those reasons is 'in principle at least available to...' the cognizer. A leading idea in what follows is that central features of coherentist theories of the kind BonJour envisages make it impossible to show that the weaker of these conditions, (4a) can be met for large classes of beliefs to which an epistemological theory should apply. I will have little to say about the stronger condition (4b) that a metajustification should be available in principle to the cognizer.

III.

Conditions (1)-(4) above are not peculiar to coherentist theories of epistemic responsibility. They could be embraced by foundationalists, probabilists, reliabilists, and epistemologists of other non-coherentist persuasions as well. The peculiarly coherentist features of BonJour's program come from his response to the following kind of argument.

Suppose I believe a number of things (propositions, belief contents, or what have you): $p_1, p_2,......p_n$. For any p_i and p_j (where $j \geq 2$ and $\leq n$) suppose that p_j is my reason for believing p_i If epistemic responsibility requires me to believe only what I have good reason to believe, and if I should not base any belief on any p_j I have no good reason to believe, then it would seem to follow that if I don't have good reason to believe p_j it would be epistemically irresponsible for me to believe p_i. But then it would seem that for every p_k which figures in my reasons for believing p_j, there must be yet another proposition which I have good reason to believe, and so on. Unless we allow circular chains of reasons (such that one and the same belief is both justified by, and figures indispensably in the justification for one of the p_js), we seem to have the beginning of an infinite regress. It's at least psychologically unrealistic to think that at any one time a person could be justified in believing any p_i as well as an infinite number of other beliefs. Therefore the regress is psychologically vicious, and there is no p_i which it would be epistemically responsible for me to believe.(10)

BonJour considers and rejects a number of responses to this sort of argument. In particular, he rejects foundationalist views according to which the regress ends with self-justifying beliefs. (chs.2,3) His solution is to require that p_i and its justifications belong to a "system of beliefs" (held by the cognizer who believes p_i) which is coherent to an acceptable degree, and to propose that an acceptably high degree of coherence (together with additional features to be mentioned presently) confers epistemically responsible credibility on members of the system. Furthermore, coherence is a crucial feature in the assessment of the *adequacy* of a theory of justification. A theory of justification (as I am using that phrase) specifies conditions which reasons for believing must meet to be considered by the believer to be good reasons. The theory will be adequate if reasons meeting its conditions are truth conducive. And BonJour thinks the coherence of a belief system argues for the truth conduciveness of the conditions for goodness of reasons which the believer's reasons for accepting beliefs satisfy. The features just noted are what make BonJour's a coherentist program [3]

Coherence is a complex feature depending upon a number of factors, the following of which will be relevant to the present discussion. Where S is a system of beliefs, the coherence of S

> (C1) *requires* that S is logically consistent[4] (95),
>
> (C2) is *proportional* to its degree of probabilistic consistency (95), and
>
> (C3) is *increased* by 'the presence of inferential connections between its component parts and increased in proportion to the number and strength of such connections' (98), where the inferential relations may be of many different sorts including (but not limited to) deductive entailment and probabilistic connections. (96-98).

Under the heading of 'inferential connections' BonJour means to include any relation in virtue of which one belief provides an epistemic reason to believe another. Furthermore, the coherence of **S**

> (C4) is *decreased* 'to the extent to which it is divided into subsystems of beliefs which are relatively unconnected to each other by inferential connections' (98) and
>
> (C5) is *decreased* ' in proportion to the presence of unexplained anomalies in the believed content of the system'(99).

(An unexplained anomaly is some sort of regularity or recurring pattern of events, facts, features of things, etc. believed (for good reason) to obtain, but not explained by other beliefs in S.)

Conditions (C1)-(C5) are intended to indicate what factors would be relevant to the measurement of coherence and to provide something like a contextual explanation or definition of that term.

But a cognizer might have a very small system of beliefs which meets all the conditions just given for coherence, and contains justifications for its members, but whose beliefs are quite unlikely to be true. For example, suppose S includes a small, consistent collection of mutually supporting contingent beliefs about what the world is like together with a principle (e.g., that the senses are not to be trusted) which rules out all empirical evidence which might cast doubt on or justify the denial any of the rest of the system. In response to such possibilities BonJour imposes an observationality requirement:

> (O): '...in order for the beliefs of a cognitive system [a system of beliefs] to be even candidates for empirical justification, that system must contain laws attributing a high degree of reliability to a reasonable variety of cognitively spontaneous beliefs (including...introspective beliefs...required for the recognition of other cognitively spontaneous beliefs)...[A]ny claim in the system which is not justified *a priori* should in principle be capable of being observationally checked, either directly or indirectly, and thereby either confirmed or refuted.(141)

(BonJour uses the term 'cognitively spontaneous' to mark a distinction between beliefs arrived at through inference, calculation, etc., and beliefs acquired more directly from sensory and introspective experience. For example, if the visual appearance of the thermometer you look at is your reason for believing it reads about 98° F, your belief is cognitively spontaneous. If you don't look at the thermometer and acquire your belief by inference from the belief that the thermometer is in good working order, that it has just come from the mouth of a normal, healthy adult, etc., the belief that the thermometer reads approximately 98° F is not cognitively spontaneous). The function of (O) is to require beliefs which ought to be checked against sensory or introspective evidence to be so checked so that systems (like the one described above) whose coherence depends mainly on the exclusion of empirical beliefs can be ruled out.

IV.

Suppose a reasonably extensive, highly coherent system of beliefs meeting the observationality requirement includes a belief, p, along with reasons to believe it which get high marks according to a reasonable theory of justification. Is that any reason to believe p is true, or likely to be true? BonJour's answer is an inference to the best explanation argument- the truth of a substantial number of well justified members of a highly coherent system which meets the observationality condition is the best explanation for its high degree of coherence; therefore, it is reasonable to expect p to be true. But BonJour thinks this needs qualification because a system of beliefs could both meet (O) and be highly and equally coherent at two different times even though many beliefs belonging to it at one time were logically incompatible with beliefs it contained at the other time. Incompatible beliefs can't all be true. Therefore, contrary to the inference to the best explanation argument, the system could be largely false at one of the two times at which it nevertheless accorded with (O) and was highly coherent.[5] To rule this out, BonJour imposes the last of the conditions I will consider-the stability requirement: A belief system, S, should

> (S) '...gradually converge [over time] on some definite view of the world and thereafter remain relatively stable, reflecting only those changes (such as the passage of time and the changes associated with it) which are allowed or even required by the general picture of the world thus presented.' (170)

BonJour's metajustificatory argument is intended to show that because the best explanation for a system's remaining highly coherent while satisfying (O) and exhibiting stability (S) over the long run is that it "corresponds...to independent reality...to a degree which is proportional to the degree of coherence (and stability) and the longness of the run..." (171).

V.

To recapitulate, the leading ideas of BonJour's coherentist program are as follows. To be epistemically responsible, a cognizer must follow a strategy which gives him the best chance of accepting beliefs when and only when they are likely to be true, and rejecting beliefs when and only when they are likely to be false. To this end then, one is to accept beliefs only when one has, and is able to tell one has, reasons for acceptance which meet some epistemic standard. The cognizer must also have good reason to believe that his strategy is truth conducive. The best reason he can have for this is an inference to the best explanation argument, according to which beliefs are likely to be true if they are supported by good reasons and belong to a reasonably coherent system which meets the observationality condition and is stable over the long run. A cognizer who accepts all and only beliefs he has good reason to accept, whose belief system meets the conditions of reasonably high coherence, etc., and who has access (in principle at least) to the inference to the best explanation argument is epistemically responsible.

Although BonJour doesn't say so explicitly, I assume epistemic responsibility, so characterized is an ideal which real life cognizers should be required only to approximate. Thus I don't read BonJour as holding that all cognizers who are unable to grasp completely the details, and appreciate the power of a fully developed version metajustificatory argument are therefore epistemically irresponsible. [6] Instead, I read him as holding that a cognizer is epistemically responsible if and only if he approximates reasonably well to the ideal. I think BonJour's coherentism leads to highly implausible conclusions about science, but as I read him, it is no objection that a flesh and blood scientist could not completely attain ideal epistemic responsibility. Instead, I will object that what I take to be epistemically responsible scientific practice cannot approximate to any significant degree to BonJour's ideal. Similarly, I don't think it's an objection that BonJour's standards for epistemic responsibility are set too high to be fully attained by any flesh and blood non-scientist. Instead I will argue that in many cases, there is no way to tell whether a non-scientific belief comes close enough to meeting BonJour's ideal because we typically lack access to what we'd have to know to apply BonJour's standards for epistemic responsibility.

VI.

On BonJour's account, a first condition for the assessment of epistemic responsibility with regard to a given belief is access to the beliefs (if any) which constitute the cognizer's reasons for holding the belief of interest. I submit that this condition is not typically satisfied for everyday, non-scientific beliefs. Right now I confidently believe (and think I am epistemically responsible in believing) that Thelonius Monk composed 'I Mean You' after 1935. I could find you good reasons to believe it too-if you'd give me enough time to look it up or ask an expert. But that neither means nor provides any evidence to show that I presently have access to good reasons for holding that belief. Right now I haven't the faintest idea who or what first told me about that tune, what, if anything lead me to trust whatever convinced me Monk wrote it after 1935, etc.. Right now I simply can't retrieve any good reasons for presently believing Monk wrote 'I Mean You' after 1935 - let alone any reasons for accepting the reasons a coherentist requires me to have. And I don't think anyone else has kept careful enough records of my cognitive affairs to have any more access to my reasons than I do.[7] Perhaps I'm wrong about this. Perhaps under hypnosis I could recall reasons I'm not now aware of possessing. But I have no reason to think so. The burden of proof is on the coherentist who thinks BonJour's tests can be applied to everyday beliefs to show that I do have access to my reasons.

A coherentist might reply that if I don't have access to my reasons it is epistemically irresponsible of me to believe Monk wrote the tune after 1935. But right now I am no more able to retrieve good reasons for believing my last name is 'Bogen' and it seems quite unreasonable to say that I am not epistemically responsible in believing that it is.[8] The difficulties in applying BonJour's coherentism multiply when we consider coherence and stability. The last time I cooked a dinner with Peter Machamer, he told me before beginning to make a pasta sauce that because of the way his stock tasted he believed the sauce would need more Gorgonzola than usual.[9] A BonJourian assessment of Peter's epistemic responsibility in this case would require access to Peter's entire belief system. His reasons, along with the rest of the system would have to be capable of being represented in a form allowing for the application of whatever mathematical and logical operations are required to determine which probabilistic, logical, explanatory, and other relations hold between which of its members. For example, if (as (C1) requires) the system must be checked for logical consistency, Peter's beliefs and reasons must be representable as propositions in a suitable logical notation. Furthermore, the metajustificatory argument required by (4a) is impossible without access to the history of the system as it developed over a long enough time to allow us to assess its stability (S). Neither this nor the application of BonJour's standards would be easy. What justified Peter in his belief about the sauce was largely a matter of culinary skills, sensibility, and experience without which the taste of the stock would have told him nothing. To set this out in the form required by condition (C1) would be no easier than producing a propositional representation of the skills, sensibilities, and experience which enable a good bicycle rider to lean the right way as he executes a turn.

I assume that on any plausible interpretation of 'probabilistic consistency' an assessment of the belief system by (C2) would require a non-arbitrary assignment of probabilities to Peter's culinary beliefs relative to many other beliefs (on very different topics) belonging to the system. Imagine seriously trying to determine, e.g., the prior probabilities of the sauce needing more cheese, of the stock tasting as it does, and of the many things Peter takes to be the case about such extraneous matters as current research on Galileo. Next, try imagining what it would be to calculate the probabilities of any one of these beliefs relative the others. I don't see how any such calculations could be made. At the same time, I can't see how (C2) could measure the coherence of the system without such calculations.

Suppose (what I claim is psychologically impossible) that we or Peter had access to all or even most of his belief system as it was at the time he was making the sauce. Suppose we could (as I claim we could not) apply (C1)-(C5) to it. This would be less than half the battle, for by (4a) and (S) we would then have to retrieve and apply the same tests to enough earlier stages of Peter's belief system to make projections of long run stability

As before, the coherentist could say that if the belief about the sauce cannot be accessed according to BonJour's conditions, then it was not epistemically responsible of Peter to hold it. But this is unfair to good cooks-and to a great many other cognizers, the assessment of whose beliefs by BonJour's conditions would involve analogous difficulties of application. If BonJour's conditions cannot be applied to the beliefs of such cognizers, I think the most plausible conclusion to draw is that coherentist theories of the kind he advocates can't provide an account of epistemic responsibility for typical sorts of non-scientific belief.

VII.

BonJour's coherentism accounts for epistemic responsibility only where beliefs and their justifications are clearly accessible and can be realistically represented as propositions belonging to systems whose probabilistic, logical, and explanatory structures can be clearly discerned. Furthermore, the coherentist needs cognizers whose epistemic standards and practices can be ascertained and accurately described. For example, the observationality requirement assumes a clear view of the way a cognizer uses empirical evidence to decide which of his beliefs are justified. The argument of section VI was that we can't realistically expect these conditions for the application of BonJour's coherentism to be met for many of the beliefs of non-scientific cognizers. The prospects seem better for beliefs involved in well developed sciences. Here we find beliefs (hypotheses, laws, etc.) which actually do belong to well articulated systems of propositions (theories). Furthermore, scientists tend to be both highly aware of, and quite willing to investigate and carefully evaluate reasons for and against accepting theories and their components. They (and we) can therefore have much greater access to (what the coherentist takes to be) epistemically relevant factors than could be expected for many non-scientific beliefs. And because the well developed sciences are generally and correctly thought to involve clear cases of responsibility, an epistemological theory certainly ought to be able to provide an adequate account of them. For these reasons, I think the sciences provide critical test cases for coherentism. Let's look at one.[10]

VIII.

In order to confirm the law of gravitation, Newton had to establish its generality. One of the issues involved in this was:

> (a) the question whether the same force, operating according to the same laws could be at work in the production of effects as apparently different as the rotation of a planet around the sun or a moon around a planet, the acceleration of a body in free fall, the acceleration of a body rolling down an inclined plane and the motion of a pendulum at the surface of the earth. Another issue was:
>
> (b) the question whether the same forces operated on both sublunary and superlunary bodies.

(This is one of the chief questions which separates 17th century from ancient physics. Where the 17th century physicist looks for forces whose magnitudes depend on features common to bodies of all kinds in all places (eg., mass and distance between two or more bodies) the ancient physicist holds that neither bodies composed of different stuffs nor bodies of the same stuff in different places are subject to the same forces. On this picture the 17th century goal of discovering perfectly general, quantitative laws of motion is unattainable in principle.) [11]

The hypothesis Newton wants to confirm is

> H] All bodies are attracted to one another by one and the same gravitational force whose strength is inversely proportional to the squares of the distances between them.

In textbooks, the equation for the strength of the gravitational force is written for two bodies as:

$$H'] \quad G = g\left(\frac{mm'}{r^2}\right)$$

where G is the force of gravity, g is a constant, r is the distance between the two bodies, and m and m' are their masses. An instance of H] would be that the gravitational force between any two bodies accords with H'].

Newton's strategy in confirming H] was to consider several cases of motion in which the acceleration of one body is due to the attraction of the other, and to argue that an inverse square force is at work in each case. Newton's cases include the motions of planets around the sun, the motions of the moons of Jupiter around Jupiter, the motions of the moon around the earth, the motion of an object in free fall near the surface of the earth, and the oscillation of a simple pendulum.[12] If forces which obey the same inverse square law are identical, and if Newton's examples include enough different sorts of sublunar and superlunary phenomena to qualify as a representative and unbiased sample, his results should count as good reasons to believe H], especially as responses to doubts involving questions (a) and (b) [13].

Consider Newton's use of evidence concerning the orbit of the moon. His argument supposes

> (1) that in traveling around the earth, the moon obeys Kepler's law of equal areas[14], and
>
> (2) that the path of the moon around the earth is a circle lying in a plane. [15]

Newton claims these suppositions are empirically confirmed. In addition, he supposes

> (3) All bodies moving in a circular or elliptical orbit in a plane around a point which is either stationary, or moving without acceleration, and which conform in their motions to Kepler's law of equal areas are attracted toward the point around which they move by a centripetal force.' [16]

Then, if

> (4) the earth does not accelerate as the moon travels around it [17]

he says it follows straightaway from (1) and (3), that

> (5) The force which keeps the moon in orbit (preventing its inertial motion from carrying it off in a straight line) is directed toward the earth. [18]

Next Newton argues that

> (6) the magnitude of this force is inversely proportional to the square of the distance from the center of the earth to the moon. [19]

The argument for this requires two simplifications. First, the only general principle available for the deduction of (6) from (1)-(5) [20] doesn't apply unless the moon reaches its apogee at the same place (relative to fixed stars) every time it completes a revolution. As Newton himself acknowledges, this is not the case. On observations he accepts, the apogee moves forwards 3°, 3' in each revolution.[21] To argue for (6), Newton must ignore this and assume

> (7) that the apogee of the moon is stationary.

The second simplification is to treat the system as though

> (8) only the earth exerts an attractive force on the moon.

This is required by (2), the claim that the moon's orbit is circular, and Kepler's law of equal areas, both of which are needed to argue for (6). If Newton had had to calculate and argue from the actual path of the moon, taking into account deviations from a circular orbit due to the pull of the sun, the proof would turn into a computational nightmare. His justification for ignoring the force exerted by the sun on the moon is that its effects are so small that the resulting error should not be intolerably large. [22]

From (6), together with (1), the claim that

> (9) the radius of the moon's orbit is 60 times the radius of the earth, [23]

and an estimate of the mean of the observed period of the moon's rotation around the earth, Newton calculates that

> (10) if the moon's motion had no rectilinear component, it would fall toward the earth, traversing $15\frac{1}{2}$ Paris feet during the first minute of its fall. [24]

Using (6) again, he calculates that if the moon continued to fall,

> (11) at the surface of the earth, it would traverse 15 Paris feet, 1 inch, 1 line, 4/9 in one second. [25]

Newton claims that

> (12) This is the same speed calculated for the downward component of the motions of pendulums and for bodies in free fall at the surface of the earth, [26]

and therefore,

> (13) the force of attraction which keeps the moon in orbit obeys the same inverse square law as the force which attracts the pendulum and the falling body.[27]

From this he concludes that the force of gravity which operates at the surface of the earth is identical to the force exerted by the earth on the moon.[28] If so, we have three instances (the pendulum, the body in free fall at the surface of the earth, and the moon) for which H] holds.[29]

IX.

We certainly don't have access to Newton's entire belief system, but this example provides something far closer to the access required by BonJour than did the non-scientific examples of §vii]. Newton is explicit (if hard to follow) about many of the claims, principles of argument, bits of evidence, etc., which figure in the argument. Where he is not explicit, his presentation-supplemented by the rest of *Principia* and his other writings-often allows the recovery of unstated assumptions and steps. Furthermore, Newton provides arguments for many of the propositions of his physics, including principles and empirical claims used in the argument we looked at. We thus have access to a substantial portion of the belief system to which H] belongs[30] - the portion which is most relevant to its justification of H] and to Newton's employment of it elsewhere in his natural philosophy. Call this fragment of Newton's belief system 'N.' N includes enough beliefs and has a well enough articulated structure to give us some idea of how a real scientist would fare on BonJour's tests for epistemic responsibility. I submit that he would fare so badly that only a highly skeptical attitude toward science could ward off the suspicion that something is wrong with the BonJour's coherentism. The following are only some of the reasons Newton would test poorly.

The application of Kepler's law of equal areas to the moon (1) assumes that the moon's orbit is a Euclidean (two dimensional) circle. Not only is this false, but according to the very theory Newton is trying to confirm, every body exerts an attractive (gravitational) force on every other body, and therefore the moon (along with every planet, and the moons of every planet) must be pulled out of a circular path in different directions as it changes its position relative to the sun and other heavenly bodies.[31] And it is obvious that (8) (according to which only the earth exerts an attractive force) flatly contradicts the theory of universal gravitation;   Incredible as it seems, at least four of the claims (i.e., that the moon travels over a circular path, that it obeys the law of equal areas, the law of equal areas itself, and the claim that only the earth attracts the moon) which are crucial to Newton's to justification of the belief that H] are *logically inconsistent* with the theory they are used to confirm![32]   A breathtaking inconsistency is involved in Newton's use of (4). If, as (4) supposes, the earth did not accelerate, it could not move in a circle (or follow any but a rectilinear path). This would make the earth a counter example to Kepler's laws which are required by all of Newton's arguments for the universality of the gravitational force.

Thus (4) is incompatible with what Newton needs to justify H] in this as well as the other arguments (eg., from the motions of the planets)[33]. Now, if N includes Kepler's laws, etc., along with the theory of gravity, and what we know Newton believed about the planets, the moons, and their motions (just the belief that there are a number of planets and moons whose distances from one another change as they move through the heavens will do), then N is logically inconsistent. This violates BonJour's (C1) according to which logical consistency is a necessary condition for coherence of any degree[34]. Furthermore, if N is logically inconsistent, it presumably runs afoul of (C2) which measures coherence according to degrees of probabilistic consistency. On the other hand, if we make N consistent by excluding the likes of (1), (2), (3), (4) and (8) then the system contains no good reasons to believe H] or anything else whose justification depends upon it. Therefore what it takes to make N pass tests (C1) and (C2) guarantees poor performance on (C3), the condition which measures coherence by the number and strength of inferential connections between beliefs in a belief system.

(7), like (1), is inconsistent with Newton's own theory. But quite apart from that, Newton had enough empirical evidence to convince him that both are false[35]. Thus Newton's reasons for believing H] include items which would be refuted by empirical evidence even if they were logically consistent with the theory of universal gravitation. This is only one of several cases in which Newton has empirical evidence *against* claims he uses (and needs) to confirm H]. For example, contrary to (9) the distance between the earth and the moon is *not* 60 times the radius of the earth. Newton was aware of estimates ranging from $56\frac{1}{2}$ earth radii to $60\frac{1}{2}$ some of which are more plausible than (9).[36] Contrary to (12), the rate of fall at the surface of the earth calculated at Newton's time differs beyond the range of experimental error from the rate predicted by Newton's argument [37]

These last examples generate failures in coherence when taken together with the observationality requirement. (O) requires Newton to admit into N reliable empirical evidence against (7), (9), (12) as well as other empirical claims required by his confirmation of H]. Because Newton admitted such discrepancies as those between (7) and (12) and values calculated from empirical evidence, N seems to accord with (O) But the empirical beliefs admitted in accordance with (O) stand in strong inferential relations to the denials of claims used by Newton to justify H]. To remedy this by excluding the troublesome empirical evidence would make the system violate (O).[38]

Finally, consider (C5) according to which the coherence of N is diminished by the presence of unexplained anomalies. In many cases, what Newton can explain are not facts about the motions of the planets and moons. Instead the theory explains highly idealized and simplified (and therefore, false) descriptions of facts. For example, N contains principles which explain in effect why Kepler's law of equal areas, *would* hold *if* the orbits of the moons and planets *were* closed curves in planes.[39] But we saw the orbits do not (and on Newton's theory cannot) have such shapes and that equal areas are not actually swept out in equal intervals of time. On the one hand we have idealizations (like Kepler's equal areas law) which are not facts. On the other hand, we have facts (e.g., that the areas swept out by a moon or planet during two equal periods of time differ by empirically discernible quantities). It is striking that Newton can explain only the former. For each idealization explained in N, there will be at least one genuine (non-idealized) fact which cannot be explained and which will qualify as an anomaly.[40] In general, wherever N lacks the computational resources to explain a fact and can therefore be applied only to an idealized or simplified version of the fact, it loses coherence according to (C5). Thus for almost every explanation Newton can produce, we are guaranteed an unexplained anomaly and a loss in coherence.

X

Here is our story so far. Newton's strategy for confirming H] and the explanatory resources of his theory are such that N cannot be adequately coherent on BonJour's standards. But BonJour's idea was that the justification of a belief makes it reasonable to expect that belief to be true only if the belief and the cognizer's reasons for holding it belong to a highly coherent belief system. On BonJour's account, then, Newton had no good reason to believe that H] is true, or likely to be true. Therefore, in accepting H], he (along with countless others who accepted it for the same sorts of reasons) was epistemically irresponsible. BonJour's account of epistemic responsibility did not apply at all to the non-scientific beliefs of §vi]. Hence the first part of my title. If the beliefs I looked at were representative, BonJour's theory doesn't apply to enough outside of science. BonJour's tests for coherence had a much better chance of applying to H] but according to them, Newton's belief that H] is epistemically irresponsible. There are many suggestions a coherentist might make to take the sting out of this result. Perhaps Newton was not epistemically responsible. Perhaps, for all he knew, the law of universal gravitation was not likely to be true. Perhaps Newton's confirmation of H] is not typical of good scientific practice. Perhaps it is typical, and therefore, the best evidence scientists have to offer for their theories doesn't make it epistemically responsible to accept their best confirmed hypotheses. Perhaps an account of epistemic responsibility need not tell us anything about the sciences. But if these suggestions are incorrect-as I think they are - BonJour's theory gives us the wrong results for an important class of beliefs to which it does apply. Hence the second part of my title.

XI.

This paper has no space to canvass all of the alternatives just listed. I won't consider the skeptical idea that it is in general epistemically irresponsible to believe scientific principles as well confirmed, successfully applied, and deeply entrenched as was the law of universal gravitation. I won't try to prove that a theory of knowledge should cover scientific as well as non-scientific belief, except to repeat that the success and the widespread, informed acceptance of science certainly seems to warrant the presumption that the sciences provide examples of epistemic responsibility and well justified belief.[41] But I do want to briefly consider the suggestion that the Newtonian case is not typical of good scientific practice for, if this seems plausible, the Newtonian example can't have much force against BonJour's account, let alone against coherentism in general.

Some of the problematic claims of §viii], are idealizations describing unreal or imaginary systems which bear some resemblance to the real system of interest (i.e., the solar system), while others are simplifications of real, empirically determined quantities. In some cases of simplification, approximately correct (hence somewhat incorrect) values are assigned to quantities which haven't or can't be more precisely determined. In other cases, an empirically determined value is replaced to facilitate computation. In extreme cases simplifications are indispensable because the available mathematics can't deal with more accurate values. I don't think Newton was trying to deceive anyone. He resorted to idealizations and simplifications because Newtonian physics doesn't know how to deal with anything that cannot be calculated from a very few quantities (such as mass, time, and distance). Nor can it deal with any but relatively simple objects in Euclidean geometrical configurations (e.g., idealized versions of the paths traveled by the planets and moons). Even if (as is far from being the case) Newton could have made precise calculations of all quantities involved in all initial and background conditions of the motions of bodies in a real system, his laws would not apply to them. Factors to which the theory doesn't apply would have to be ignored.   And factors to which the theory does apply must be represented as quantities which the mathematics at Newton's disposal can compute.

Although some of the simplifications we looked at were required only to make calculations easier, idealizations are needed to make calculation possible. Newton's problematic evidential claims reflect the use of simplifications and idealizations, most of which were unavoidable given the limitations imposed by the very nature of Newton's physics and mathematics.[42]

An indication of how widespread are the use and the need for idealizations and simplifications in science is Nancy Cartwright's remark that "...the distinction between the tidy and simple mathematical equations of abstract theory, and the intricate and messy descriptions in either words or formulae, which express our knowledge of what happens in real systems made of real materials...," once led her to believe that, "...there were no quantities in nature-no attributes with exact numerical values of which it could be said that they were either precisely equal or unequal to each other."[43]

She no longer thinks there are no genuine quantities in nature. But she continues to think the laws of physics can be applied only to idealized models and simplified representations of phenomena.[44] If idealization and simplification are widespread and unavoidable for confirmation, prediction, explanation, and for practical applications of the exact sciences[45], then the BonJourian incoherence illustrated by the confirmation of H] will be the rule rather than the exception in good science.

Furthermore, neither the failure of application to non-scientific beliefs nor the low assessment of coherence resulting from the application of BonJour's tests to the Newtonian example result from accidental or dispensable features of BonJour's version of coherentism. One peculiarity of BonJour's program is its insistence on a realistic (correspondence) conception of truth. If we replaced this with any of the most popular non-correspondence accounts, we would get exactly the same results. Suppose for example that truth were equated with warranted assertibility.[46] This would have no effect whatever on the problems of accessibility which prevented the application of BonJour's tests to the non-scientific examples in §vi]. Nor would it make N look any better. For if we eliminated from N everything whose assertion would conflict with the assertion of H], the system would contain no warrant for the assertion of at least some of its crucial hypotheses. On the other hand, if we left N intact, the system would including beliefs warranting the denials of Newton's reasons for believing the law of universal gravitation, or beliefs which defeat his justifications. Similar results remain on any conception of truth compatible with standard logics.

We could try eliminating some of BonJour's tests-(C5) perhaps, or even (C2) or (C3). But as long as we require logical consistency and retain some acceptably strong version of (O), either N, will turn out to be seriously incoherent, or H] will have to be judged unjustified. And there are no coherence tests whose elimination would solve the access problem for non-scientific beliefs.

We could eliminate the requirement that the cognizer have access to his own belief system. But this still wouldn't help with the Newtonian example, and it would leave the question of whether non-scientific beliefs are justified unanswerable wherever we don't have enough access to the system to test for coherence. Thus if the results of §vi] and §ix] are difficulties for BonJour's own account, they present problems to other coherentist accounts as well.

XII.

The coherentist proposes that the more coherent a belief system is, the more reasonable it is to think that its well supported members are likely to be true. But there is a much weaker coherentist proposal which I think is too plausible to reject.

Suppose that with regard to a particular question, the evidence and the background knowledge possessed by a cognizer argue for incompatible beliefs. Suppose the acceptance of any one of them would make it impossible for the cognizer to explain a significant number of what he takes to be facts. If he cannot find a way to resolve the conflicts and reduce the confusion, it would certainly be more epistemically responsible for the cognizer to follow the skeptic's advice and suspend judgment than to accept one of the competing beliefs[47]. The cognizer would be far better off epistemically if he could find a principled way to introduce order into his belief system, e.g., by finding a new belief which the evidence supports in a less confusing and more consistent way, or by showing that some of the evidence can be discounted, or by telling a plausible story to account for the ways in which his evidence and bits of background knowledge seem to conflict. In view of this, it's quite plausible that there is a *kind,* or that there are *kinds* of incoherence which must be alleviated if the acceptance of a belief is to be epistemically responsible. By the same token, it's entirely plausible that the reduction or elimination of such incoherence or kinds of incoherence improves the cognizer's epistemic position. I don't see how it could be a mistake to accept this. It does not require that all justified beliefs belong to belief systems which can be represented propositionally and assessed according to BonJourian tests. It does not require entire belief systems or even substantial subsystems to be accessible. It does not commit us to any particular set of tests for coherence, to BonJour's metajustification. It does not even claim that any particular sort of coherence is truth conducive. Furthermore, the watered down coherentism I propose has to do with local rather than global coherence and incoherence. It does not involve anything like the requirement that every one of the cognizers beliefs be collected together into a system to be judged for global consistency, etc. Nor does it involve anything like the large claim that epistemic responsibility, justification, knowledge, and the like can be completely or even largely characterized and accounted for in terms of coherence. All that watered down coherentism claims is that in certain kinds of cases, incoherence of some kind, or kinds is an obstacle to epistemically responsible belief, and that reducing the incoherence can improve the cognizer's epistemic position.

That can't be wrong, but to make it worth considering, a modest coherentist would have to descend from the level of abstraction, and generality at which I sketched the proposal. He would have to show us-among other things-just what sorts of incoherence are epistemically damaging, how they differ from epistemically benign varieties of which I take the BonJourian incoherence of N to be a cardinal example. We'd want to know what sorts of remedies are effective against the damaging varieties, and how the remedies improve the cognizer's epistemic position. For example, just what was it about Newton's use of idealizations and simplifications which kept the incoherence of N from vitiating his confirmation of H]? And why was the incoherence of the evidence mentioned in footnote 40 epistemically vicious in ways that Newton's was not? These are the sorts of things a modest coherentist should tell us. I have no positive suggestions to make about this. Instead, I want to conclude with a methodological recommendation.

XIII.

For decades, the most influential British and American epistemologists have relied on a peculiar sort of *a priori* argumentation closely identified with what is called 'analytic philosophy'. The procedure is to suggest necessary or sufficient conditions e.g., for knowledge or justification, and test them against bizarre and vehemently counterfactual hypothetical cases. The hypothetical cases are sparsely described. And they are considered pretty much in isolation from the sorts of historical, sociological, and cultural features of local context which typically influence the course of real world debates about whether a belief is justified, or whether a knowledge claim should be accepted. You know those stories. Suppose Smith's reason for believing a proposition of the form 'p v q' is strong evidence for 'p' together with the knowledge that 'p' entails 'p v q'. If the disjunction turns out to be true because 'q' is true while 'p' is false, and Smith had no reason to believe that q, should we say that he knew that (p v q)?[48]   Suppose a pyromaniac believes a match will light because he is aware that he is striking it, that the match is dry, that there is plenty of oxygen, and so on, but unbeknownst to him, the match is defective, and striking it cannot raise it to its abnormally high combustion point. If the match lit because '...an extremely rare burst of Q-radiation happened to arrive...' just in time to ignite it, should we say the pyromaniac knew it would light?[49]   Suppose Cecil, who has a great deal of evidence for an answer to some historical question, possesses what, unbeknownst to him, is a highly reliable crystal ball which would have led him to a different answer if he'd consulted it and accepted what it told him. Suppose the crystal ball's answer would have been wrong. If Cecil didn't consult the crystal ball anyway, should we say he was justified in accepting the answer supported by his evidence?[50]   Suppose I believe Tom is stealing a book from the library because I'm watching him take the book before my very eyes and I know exactly what he looks like. Suppose that unbeknownst to me, his mother will later defend him by claiming falsely that he was miles away but has an identical twin brother who went to the library. If I had no way to know she would be lying (even if I knew what she would say), should we say I now know Tom is stealing a book?[51]   Proposals are rejected or modified if they lead to results which conflict with what philosophers' intuitions tell them we should say about such cases. New or modified proposals are then tested against new and equally unworldly hypothetical cases.

If we wanted to pursue the modest coherentist suggestion of §xii] (to try, for example, to find out what kinds of incoherence are epistemically harmful and what kinds are tolerable) I don't think it would be a good idea to employ the method just illustrated. For one thing, there is a distinct possibility that philosophers' intuitions about what to say of the bizarre cases are artifacts of professional training and socialization. We have very little real experience with cases like these. There is seldom any practical need to answer questions like those the philosophers ask about them. The descriptions of the hypothetical cases don't begin to provide the sorts of details and information about context we rely on in real life epistemic situations. Because of this it's possible that our feelings about whether to say S knew that p aren't indicative of much besides the way our training in seminars and other professional philosophical settings leads us to respond to sparsely described, bizarre hypothetical cases. If this is so, philosophers' intuitions needn't reveal much about how beliefs are assessed by real life cognizers in real situations where epistemic responsibility is a serious issue. On the other hand, suppose philosophers' intuitions about the hypothetical cases were not artifacts of philosophical training and the constraints of professional settings. Even so, the cases are too otherworldly for it to be at all obvious whether and how intuitions about them bear on the mundane epistemic situations for which an epistemological theory should account.[52]

Austin once said that a philosopher who speculates briefly in his armchair is unlikely to come up with distinctions as useful as those developed in real situations, culled, and modified as required to meet practical needs over long periods of time.[53] For much the same reasons, I think the study of scientific case histories and of the what the best literature in the philosophy, history, and sociology of science can tell us about them is bound to be more helpful to an epistemologist than the method of considering what we think we might say about the Q-ray that lit the match, the crystal ball Cecil didn't consult, and so on. In particular, as I hope the Newtonian example suggests, the study of well documented scientific practice can reveal interesting problems and uncover important facts about epistemic responsibility that would not be likely to occur to anyone who had not looked at the details of case histories in the sciences.

I advocate the development of a watered down, rather than a grand coherentism. And for the reasons just given, I think the history, philosophy, and sociology of science are far more fruitful guides to its development than the hypothetical examples usually considered in the recent philosophical literature on the theory of knowledge.

NOTES

1. A good deal of this paper developed from discussions with Marshall Swain, George Pappas, Brad Armendt, and students who attended a seminar in the theory of knowledge I taught at Ohio State University during the 1987 winter term. I have borrowed extensively from Ronald Laymon's publications on confirmation theory and the history of science. I am heavily indebted to him for his generosity and patience in explaining his work on Newton to me and to Ted McGuire and James Woodward for convincing me of the extent to which epistemology needs to take account of the philosophy, history, and sociology of science. These people are responsible only for the true statements in this paper.
2. L.BonJour, *The Structure of Empirical Knowledge*, Cambridge: Harvard University Press, 1985. Unless otherwise noted, page and chapter references in parenthesis cite this book.
3. It's not clear to me exactly which point of the infinite regress argument this proposal attacks. It is compatible with at least the following different responses to the argument: (a) the cognizer's belief that p_i is epistemically responsible if it and every reason the cognizer has to believe it belong to a closed circle which in turn belongs to a highly coherent belief system, or (b) even though some of the cognizer's reasons for believing p_i are themselves unsupported by reasons for which additional justifications are included in the system, the system may still be coherent enough to make the cognizer's belief epistemically responsible. According to (b) the chain of justifications can end somewhere; according to (a) it is a continuous circle. BonJour characterizes his response to the argument as holistic (e.g., 24). As far as I can tell, his remarks about holism are compatible with, but don't specify (a), (b) or any other specific version of the response.
4. Marshall Swain observed (in conversation) that BonJour doesn't say whether this is a necessary condition whose violation reduces the coherence of a system to zero, or whether it just reduces incoherence to an unacceptably low level. I will treat (C1) as necessary for any degree of coherence, but my arguments are compatible with the weaker interpretation.
5. To imagine such a case, consider a system which includes first one and then another batch of theoretical beliefs (inconsistent with the first) confirmed by and used to explain beliefs derived from observation and experiment, eg., the belief system of an astronomer who begins with a geocentric theory and later converts to heliocentrism, or a physicist who begins as a Newtonian and becomes a follower of Einstein. The theories could be equally well justified by the evidence available to the science at each stage of the development of his belief system. They could provide as many explanations for the phenomena the cognizer can detect at each stage, and in general, the belief system could be as coherent at one stage as at another. I don't see why the Newtonian stage of the belief system shouldn't include considerably more false beliefs than the Einsteinian, and why the geocentric system shouldn't include considerably more falsehoods than the heliocentric system. It follows that equally coherent systems can include significantly different percentages of false beliefs. Although most people's beliefs about physics and astronomy probably do not take up a large portion of their total belief systems, these cases confer at least some plausibility on the scenario which worries BonJour.
6. There are many reasons to doubt the cogency of philosophical appeals to inference to the best explanation arguments, not the least of which is that no one has so far come up with a satisfactory account of explanation. Instead of questioning BonJour on this point, I will ask whether metajustifications are available even if inference to the best explanation arguments are legitimate. But my neglect of the question of their legitimacy should not be taken to be an endorsement of these arguments.
7. George Pappas and Richard Feldman have a variety of examples to question whether there is a plausible interpretation of the claim that cognizers must have reasons for their justified beliefs. See, for example, Pappas (1987).
8. Examples of this sort are discussed by Wittgenstein in *On Certainty* : §7, 10, 84, 92, 111,125,126,234,250,282,etc.
9. A magnificent sauce: For 4-6 people, dice 4 oz. pancetta and sautee gently (with a few cloves of garlic finely sliced, if desired). Add 2 cups rich turkey stock,bring to a boil, and reduce by half. Lower flame to a gentle simmer. Add thick cream and stir constantly. When mixture begins to simmer, reduce flame and stir in 4 oz. crumbled *Gorgonzola dulce*. Stir until cheese is melted and the sauce is well mixed. If too thick, more stock may be added. Add one-quarter cup chopped martini olives (stuffed with pimento), salt (if needed) and ground black pepper to taste. Serve over freshly made basil fettucini.
10. The case to be considered has been discussed in detail by Clark Glymour (1980), 203-226 and Ronald Laymon (1983), 179-200.

11. For an excellent discussion of this difference between 17th century and ancient Greek Physics, see Dijksterhuis (1986), 309-314, 495-501. Some details of Aristotelian 5-element physics are discussed in Bogen and McGuire (1987), 387-448.

12. I. Newton, *Principia, vol. II* , 406-409.

13.The fact that Newton's theory of gravitation isn't quite right, and that there are empirically determinable phenomena which are better handled by relativity theories is no objection to its use as an example here. Epistemic responsibility does not require *true* belief. It requires instead that the cognizer accepts beliefs only when he has, and is able to tell that the has good reasons to think those beliefs are true. H] - supported by Newton's argument, and versions of the argument employing similar sorts of idealization and simplification - met this condition not only for Newton, but for generations of excellent physicists before Einstein. Thus even though H] belongs to an imperfect theory, it is at the very least a *prima facie* example of an epistemically responsible belief. Furthermore, the use of simplifications and idealization which for my purposes are the most striking features of Newton's evidence and his application of it to H] are by no means peculiar to this example. They are quite widespread in the natural and the social sciences. (See Laymon (1983), (1984), and (forthcoming).

14. Newton, *op . cit* . Phenomenon VI, Book III, 405 Draw a straight lines at two different times from the center of the earth to the circle around which Newton supposes the moon travels. Let t be the interval between the two times. If we connect the points where the lines intersect the circle we have a triangle of a definite area. By Kepler's law of equal areas, the areas of all triangles similarly produced for intervals of t will be identical. The law is supposed to hold for all elliptical orbits in a plane, circular orbits comprising a special case.

15. This must be assumed by Newton in order for him to use Propositions II and III, Book I in the argument. cp. Laymon, 'Newton's Demonstration of Universal Gravitation and Philosophical Theories of Confirmation', 188 ff.

16. Newton, *Principia,* vol.I, Prop II Book I, 42.

17. Newton says he could give an alternative argument assuming that the earth accelerates, and using Prop III, Book I in place of (5). According to proposition III, the acceleration of the moon would be due to a force compounded from an inverse square force pulling the moon toward the center of the earth and 'all the acelerative force by which [the earth] is impelled'. But he does not develop the alternative in arguing from the motion of the moon to H].

18. Newton, *Principia* vol. II, Prop III Book III, 406.

19. *ibid*.

20. Newton, *Principia* , vol. I, Cor i, Prop XLV, 145.

21. Newton, *Principia,* vol.II, 406.

22. Newton, *op. cit.* Prop III Book III, 406 Cp. Laymon, 'Newton's Demonstration", 192 ff.

23. Newton, *op. cit.,* vol II 407-408.

24. Newton, *op. cit.,* Prop IV Book III, 408.

25. *ibid*.

26. *ibid*.

27. *ibid*.

28. *ibid*. The inference depends upon two rules: a rule of parsimony (Rule 1) and a rule according to which, all things being equal, similar effects should be accounted for by similar causes (Rule 2). Newton, *op. cit.,* 398.

29. For an anachronistic, but clear account of this, and Newton's argument from the accelerations of planets orbiting the sun, see Born (1962), 58-64. Born's account is helpful on most of the points which are relevant to this paper. Glymour's and Laymon's accounts are both more detailed, and more historically accurate.

30. Because Newton deliberately refrained from using the calculus he had just invented we know that these arguments for universal gravitation don't represent all of his relevant beliefs, and we can assume that there are further departures from his actual belief system elsewhere in *Principia*. But Newton's actual belief system did not contain the computational resources needed to confirm H] without recourse to idealizations and simplifications of the kinds I've mentioned. And in any case, we can realistically imagine a cognizer whose belief system is like the one I've described. Many of Newton's readers would have had such belief systems.

31. Newton was aware of this, for he asked Flamsteed, the royal astronomer, to calculate the perturbations for him. But in spite of this, an instance of the equal area law is used not only in connection with the orbit of the moon, but also, in connection with arguments from the orbits of other heavenly bodies. See Laymon, *op. cit.,* 188.

32. In fact, the arguments from the moons of Jupiter, and the orbits of the planets as well as the present argument from the motion of the moon require three Keplerian laws which are incompatible with Newton's theory of universal gravitation. In addition to the law of equal areas, and the law that orbits are plane ellipses, Newton employs the law that the ratios of the cubes of the radii of the orbits to the squares of the periods of rotations for all planets. (Born, 58-64.) This, like the equal areas law presupposes Euclidean

elliptical orbits which are ruled out by the principle that all bodies attract each other and the fact that the real system includes enough bodies to cause peturbations.

33. An alternative argument for H] allowing, e.g., for the acceleration of the earth would still require idealized, simplified, and therefore false representations of the phenomena, some of which would be as inconsistent with Newton's theory as these.

34. If (C1) is read instead as saying that logical inconsistency greatly reduces coherence, we can still conclude that the inclusion of Kepler's laws and the rest argues against a satisfactorily high degree of coherence for N.

35. Indeed we saw above that Newton acknowledges observational evidence against (7) and accepts a calculation of the movement of the moon's apogee.

36. Newton, *op. cit.*, 407-8.

37. Laymon *op. cit.*, 189. Newton himself mentions Huygens' calculations for pendulums, according to which his own prediction is off by 3/9 of a line.(408) (a line is approximately 2 1/4 mm.)

38. This is an especially bad result, because BonJour's metajustificatory argument applies only to systems which accord with the observationality requirement. BonJour, 170.

39. Laymon (*op. cit.* , 190) suggests treating Newton as explaining a counterfactual.

40. Someone will object that Newton says such things as that the rotation of the apogee, the perturbations, etc. are due to the influence of the sun, etc., and therefore, contrary to my claim that they are anomalies, they are explained in N. The answer to this objection is twofold. First, merely saying that such and such is due to so and so is not to offer a systematic explanation for it. (See Bogen and Woodward (1988). Secondly, in order to provide a systematic explanation of the perturbations, Newton would have to take into account the mutual attraction of all of the bodies of the system. Even if he used all of the mathematics at his disposal, (a) the explanation would be computationally impossible, and (b) it would involve principles which contradict idealizations and simplifications required for the confirmation of H]. Thus even if explanations of the perturbations were possible (as they are not), they would cost Newton further contradictions.

41. However if I was right to say that BonJour's account does not apply to much outside of science (because of lack of accessibility), there isn't much left for it to tell us about if it doesn't apply to science either.

42. A familiar example of this is Newton's inability to calculate the forces and accelerations involved in a system of two or more bodies without ignoring some of the forces they exert on one another.

43. Cartwright (1983), 128.

44. See for example, Cartwright, 128-162. The moral Cartwright is mainly concerned to draw - that the basic laws of physics are false, and that true laws are not required for adequate explanation - does not bear on the concerns of this paper. What is relevant is Cartwright's thesis that science cannot get along without idealizations, simplifications and approximations, all of which provide false descriptions of the systems with which the scientist deals.

45. Dramatic examples are provided in engineering.

46. E.g., after the manner of Carnap (1947), 205-221, or Dummett, 'Truth', 1-24 and 'Realism', 145-165.

47. A fascinating example of this is the 19th and early 20th century debate over locationism, the doctrine that specific basic psychological functions are seated in or carried out by specific parts of the brain. The classical experiments and observations used to test this thesis included lesioning or ablating parts of the brain to see if the same psychological deficits were caused by damage to the same anatomical regions (e.g., Flourens, Goltz, Lashley), *post mortem* examinations of the brains of humans and animals who had exhibited deficits when alive (e.g., Broca, Gall), experiments in which specific brain regions are stimulated with weak electrical charges to try to cause specific physiological and psychological effects (eg., Fritsch and Hitzig, Sherrington, and later, Penfield) and comparative anatomical studies of animals belonging to different species whose members exhibited different sorts of natural behaviors, abilities, etc. (e.g., Gall). The evidence from comparative anatomy, typically argued for locationism, while lesioning and ablation typically argued against it. *Post mortem* examinations produced highly controversial evidence for both sides. Until the speculations of Hughlings Jackson promised ways to resolve the complications and confusions which marked the evidence, it is hard to see how an epistemically responsible neuro-scientist could have done more than suspend belief (even though few neuro-scientists of the period followed this policy). For a highly suggestive and fruitful historical sketch of this, see Luria (1980); Head (1926). Part I is an extraordinary history of debates over locationism with regard to speech functions, and includes a reliable and clear account of Hughlings Jackson's contributions.

48. Gettier (1970), 38.

49. B. Skyrms, (1967), 103.

50. BonJour, 49

51. Discussed by Harman (1973), 142-44, and devised by Lehrer and Paxson, 150-152.

52. Deborah Bogen tells me that if hypothetical questions asked in legal proceedings are not sufficiently detailed, or if their relevance cannot be established, a counsel may object and the client may be instructed not to answer. I speculate that this is at least partly because it is thought that answers to hypothetical questions wit either of these defects cannot be counted on to shed light on the real situation of interest. My

view is that a similar policy should be adopted with regard to hypothetical questions about what we'd say in hypothetical cases like those I've been complaining about.
53. J. Austin (1970),182.

REFERENCES

Austin, John Langshaw. "A Plea for Excuses" in Austin, J. L., *Philosophical Papers,* 2nd ed. London: Oxford University Press, 1970, 175-204.

Bogen, James and McGuire, James Edward. "Aristotle's Great Clock: Necessity, Possibility and the Motion of the Cosmos in De Caelo 1/12," *Philosophy Research Archives,* XII (1986-87), 387-448.

Bogen, James and Woodward, James. "Saving the Phenomena," *The Philosophical Review,* (July,1988).

BonJour, Laurence. *The Structure of Empirical Knowledge.* Cambridge: Harvard University Press, 1985.

Born, Max. *Einstein's Theory of Relativity.* New York: Dover, 1962.

Carnap, Rudolf. "Empiricism, Semantics and Ontology," in Carnap, Rudolf, *Meaning and Necessity.* Chicago: Chicago University Press, 1947.

Cartwright, Nancy. *How the Laws of Physics Lie,* Oxford: Clarendon Press, 1983.

Dijksterhuis, Eduard Jan. *The Mechanization of the World Picture, Pythagoras to Newton,* trans., Dikshoorn, C. Princeton: Princeton University Press, 1986.

Dummett, Michael. "Realism," in Dummett, Michael, *Truth and Other Enigmas,* Cambridge: Harvard University Press, 1978, 145-165.

-----. "Truth" in Dummett, Michael, *Truth and Other Enigmas,* Cambridge: Harvard University Press, 1978, 1-24.

Gettier, Edmund. "Is Justified True Belief Knowledge?" in Roth, M., and Galis, L. eds., *Knowing,* New York: Random House, 1970.

Glymour, Clark. *Theory and Evidence,* Princeton: Princeton University Press, 1980.

Harman, Gilbert. *Thought,* Princeton: Princeton University Press, 1973.

Head, Henry. *Aphasia and Kindred Disorders of Speech,* vol. I, London: Cambridge University Press, 1926.

Laymon, Ronald. "Applying Idealized Scientific Theories to Engineering," forthcoming in *Synthese.*

-----. "Newton's Demonstration of Universal Gravitation and Philosophical Theories of Confirmation," in Earman, John, ed., *Testing Scientific Theories (Minnesota Studies in the Philosophy of Science,* vol.X).

-----. "The Path from Data to Phenomena," in Lepplin, J., ed., *Scientific Realism,* Berkeley: University of California Press, 1984.

Lehrer, Keith and Paxson, Thomas. "Knowledge: Undefeated Justified True Belief," in Pappas, G. and Swain, M., *Essays on Knowledge and Justification,* Ithaca: Cornell University Press, 1978.

Luria, Aleksandr Romanovich. *Higher Cortical Functions in Man,* 2nd ed., trans., Haigh, B., New York: Basic Books, 1980.

Newton, Isaac. *Principia,* vols. I and II, trans. Motte, Andrew, Cajori, Florian, Berkeley: University of California Press, 1962.

Pappas, George. "Suddenly He Knows," in Luper-Foy, Stephen, ed., *The Possibility of Knowledge,* Totawa: Littlefield, 1987.

Skyrms, Brian. "The Explication of 'X Knows Y'," (1967) in Roth, M., and Galis, L., *Knowing,* Lanham, MD: University Press of America, 1984, 89-111.

Wittgenstein, Ludwig. *On Certainty,* Anscombe, G.E.M, and von Wright, G.H., eds., New York: Harper, 1969.

The St. Elizabethan World

Joseph Thomas Tolliver
University of Arizona

I take the following to be a platitude about knowledge: there would be no problem of knowledge if everything always had been, were, and always would be just as we believe it to be. In one way or another the problem of knowledge is motivated by of our familiarity with the gap between appearance and reality. So it is an intuition that survives our reflections on knowledge that what we might call "an incorrigible world," any world ω where for all propositions p, if S believes that p at ω, then p at ω, is a world where one knows to be true everything one believes to be true. One might hope that our best account of the nature of knowledge might explain why this platitude is platitudinous. If not, one would at least hope for the preferred account to be compatible with it. Unfortunately, coherence accounts of knowledge do not fulfill this hope, for they imply that there are some incorrigible worlds that are epistemically inaccessible. I will consider the coherence analysis offered in *The Structure of Empirical Knowledge*, by Laurence BonJour as a representative case, showing why that analysis is inconsistent with the above platitude, and suggest why this is general problem for coherence theories. I end by suggesting that a solution to the problem is to abandon the presupposition present in many coherence theories that coherence properties are world-invariant.

Briefly put, according to BonJour, S's belief that p is justified just in case it is inferable from a justified system of beliefs. A system of beliefs is justified just in case it is coherent and stable and has remained so for some time and has been in conformity with the observation requirement during that time. The coherence of a set of beliefs is determined by (i) the degree of deductive systemization of the set, (ii) the degree of positive probabilistic relevance among the members of the set, (iii) the extent to which it is free from explanatory anomalies, unexplained facts or unexplained explainers of facts, (iv) the degree to which its members stand in relations of inferability to each other, and (v) the degree to which the set consists of isolated subsystems of beliefs unconnected by inferability relations.

Presumably there is some minimum or threshold degree of coherence required for a system of beliefs to be justified, but BonJour does not specify one and does not think such specification is necessary in practice. He claims that it is sufficient to specify that "the system of beliefs in question be coherent to a *high* degree and more coherent than any alternative which would also satisfy the...(Observation Requirement)" (154, italics added) The Observation Requirement is that:

> ... a coherence theory of empirical justification must require that in order for the beliefs of a cognitive system to be even candidates for empirical justification, that system must contain laws attributing a high degree of reliability to a reasonable variety of cognitively spontaneous beliefs (including in particular those kinds of introspective beliefs which are required for the recognition of other cognitively spontaneous beliefs). (141)

Cognitively spontaneous beliefs are those that are, in the circumstance of their acceptance, noninferential, involuntary, and "coercive" (117). They are beliefs that seem to be forced upon me by something external. BonJour thinks that the Observation Requirement flows from the requirement on any adequate theory of epistemic justification that it explain why justification is truth-conducive - why justified beliefs are more likely to be true than unjustified ones. (140-141 and Chapter 8)

The details, and there are many, of BonJour's account of, and defense of, cognitive spontaneity, the Observation Requirement, or the concept of coherence will not concern me

J.W. Bender (ed.), The Current State of the Coherence Theory, 160–167.
© *1989 by Kluwer Academic Publishers.*

here. The problem I will point out will arises however these notions are understood. What will concern me is the requirement that a justified system of beliefs be highly coherent and stable, and more coherent than any alternative system of beliefs available to a person that satisfies the Observation Requirement. It implies that it is possible to have knowledge only in a world that is minimally coherent. This just seems plainly false.

Consider the following case. John H. is a patient in St. Elizabeth's Hospital. It is a hospital for the insane, deranged, deluded, and demented. Mr. H. has a very incoherent and unstable belief system. His beliefs change wildly from one moment to the next. A doctor walks in. John believes that the doctor is Napoleon. A few moments later John sees him as a talking coyote claiming that he can factor numbers in his head. The next moment he believes he is standing on some alien world shivering in a cave of methane ice. And so it goes. John has a large number of false beliefs. He also has a system of unjustified beliefs, according to BonJour's analysis, for his world view is just too incoherent and unstable. We might even suppose that John satisfies the observation requirement, for all we need to do is to suppose that John is very gullible. There are large classes of beliefs, many and various, that he takes to be cognitively spontaneous and which he regards as reliable. This fact about John does not save him, his system is still unjustified no matter how much it is driven by apparent input from something beyond him.

Now let us suppose that there is a possible world, call it "the St. Elizabethan world," where all of John's beliefs are, have been, and always will be true. Although incoherent in all other ways, his world view is at least consistent, so the St. Elizabethan world is among the logically possible worlds. Does John H. have knowledge at such a world? BonJour's account implies that he does not. A justified system of beliefs must be highly coherent, and an important element of this coherence is explanatory coherence.

> Explanatory connections are not just additional connections among the beliefs of a system, however; they are inferential connections of a particularly pervasive kind... . What Hempel calls "systematic unification" is extremely close to the concept of coherence.
>
> One helpful way to elaborate this point is to focus on the concept of *anomaly*. For my purposes, an anomaly is a fact or event, especially one involving some sort of recurring pattern, which is claimed to obtain by one or more of the beliefs in the system of beliefs, but which is incapable of being explained (or would have been incapable of being predicted) by appeal to the other beliefs in the system. (Obviously such a status is a matter of degree.) The presence of such anomalies detracts from the coherence of the system to an extent which cannot be accounted for merely by appeal to the fact that the belief in an anomalous fact or event has fewer inferential connections to the rest of the system than would be the case if an explanation were available... . The distinctive significance of anomalies lies...in the fact that they undermine the claim of the allegedly basic explanatory principles to be genuinely basic, and thus threaten the overall coherence of the system in a much more serious way. (99)

John's world view has no explanatory coherence, and mere logical and probabilistic consistency confers upon the system that has these properties "only a very low degree of coherence." (96) So, John's beliefs are not justified because they form a system that possesses only a minimal degree of coherence. He fails to have knowledge in a world made-to-order for him.

But surely if anyone has knowledge at the St. Elizabethan world John H. does. His belief system is as coherent as it can be and still be as correct as it is. Any explanatory principles or laws that he might introduce into his world view are not going to correspond to the way the world is; so, John can hardly be faulted as epistemically irresponsible in not adding, or seeking to add, such principles to his belief system. He has no reason to believe that such laws exist, and, indeed, they do not. Of course if he were to add them, his doxastic system would look better by coherentist standards. The lover of coherence would especially like to see explanatory theories of the events in John's world as well as various "metaprinciples" of his own reliability. We can envision John's doxastic system as a subpart of a much larger, much more comprehensive and coherent world view. A world view that contains very little more truth and, because the instruments of its greater coherence do not reflect reality, much more falsehood. The coherentist's suggestion is that this more comprehensive and coherent world view is a proper means to knowledge in the St. Elizabethan World, but not John's world view. This strikes me as an implausible suggestion. Since his beliefs are true, and since his beliefs form a system that is as coherent as it ever can be and still contain as much truth as it does, it would seem that John has the strongest claim to knowledge at the St. Elizabethan world that could possibly be made.[1] After all his beliefs are maximally coherent relative to his world and incorrigible at his world. Therefore, I submit that it is a minimal adequacy condition on any coherence account of empirical justification that it imply that John has justified beliefs, and therefore knowledge, at the St. Elizabethan world. As we have seen BonJour's account does not meet the condition. Note that this failure is not due to the beliefs being the beliefs of a madman. BonJour considers such cases and claims that a madman could have justified beliefs if his madness produces a system of beliefs that is sufficiently systematic. (150)

It should be evident that any coherence theory of empirical justification that requires any form or degree of coherence beyond mere consistency will also fail to meet this requirement. For any threshold of minimal coherence greater than consistency there is a St. Elizabethan world less coherent than that and a corresponding belief system which, at that world, constitutes a knowledge system. Of course defenders of coherence theories agree that more is required than consistency. Two influential reasons for this are: (i) to rule out the possibility of an indefinitely large number of equally coherent yet incompatible belief systems, and (ii) to make plausible that suggestion that there is some connection between coherence and truth.[2] Unfortunately, these theoretical goals drive a coherence theory to require too much systemization for the resulting account to square with the platitude that we have knowledge in any incorrigible world, including the St. Elizabethan world, if our beliefs are incorrigible in it.

There are several lines of response open to the coherence theorist: (1) deny that there could be cognizers such as John that occupy a St. Elizabethan world, or (2) make a case for a synthetic *a priori* principle that some minimum degree of coherence in the world is necessary for it to be an object of knowledge, i.e., try to carry out Kant's program in the *Critique of Pure Reason*, (3) deny that our alleged platitude is really platitudinous, (4) construe coherence in such a way that a person's belief system is maximally coherent at an incorrigible world regardless of the content of the beliefs in the system.

I regard the second alternative as a nonstarter and certainly a dialectically imprudent response, for it requires the coherence theorist to make out a case frighteningly more difficult than a case for a mere coherence theory of justification ever could be. The first is more interesting. The defender of coherence theories could claim that evolutionary theory implies that living systems could not originate nor sustain themselves in a chaotic world. So he might claim that John's circumstances, while logically possible, are not physically possible, because evolutionary forces control the development of living and cognitive systems at every physically possible world and those forces cannot produce a living cognitive system such as John at a world as chaotic as the St. Elizabethan world. This response rests upon an empirical claim for which there is no evidence, but apart from this the response is beside the point. Nothing in the case requires that John H. be a living system. Let John be some nonliving individual with a psychology and personal history exactly like John's. John need not have evolved in the St. Elizabethan world for the world to conform to his beliefs. Although BonJour explicitly states that he intends his theory to be an account of human justification, nothing in it limits its applicability to members of a particular biological species. Surely this is as it should be. The boundaries of our theories are fixed by relevant differences among domains of phenomena, not by stipulation. If there are no epistemically relevant differences between human John and his nonhuman counterpart we want any adequate theory of empirical justification to account for the epistemic status of each. So I take it that the first line of response is inadequate also.

The third possibility was that maybe it is simply not true that at an incorrigible world all one's beliefs are knowledge. I characterized an incorrigible world as a world ω where for all propositions p, if S believes that p at ω, then p at ω. We should notice that so understood a world is incorrigible relative to a person, so what we have defined is "ω is incorrigible for person S." But suppose that at his incorrigible world S has only one belief (or a very small number of beliefs), such as "The White House is white." Suppose this belief (and any beliefs he has to have to have this one) is true. Surely this single true belief does not look like a instance of knowledge; it is just an isolated true belief. But if S has one and only one belief at ω, and it is true, then ω is incorrigible for S. The initial informal statement of the platitude, "There would be no problem about knowledge if everything always had been, were, and always would be just as we believe it to be," invites one to consider the normal situation: that a person much like yourself is fortunate enough to live in a world were there is no appearance/reality distinction - a world where there is never any rude awakening. The definition of an incorrigible world does not yet quite capture this picture.

There are several ways to improve things. We could require that a person has an incorrigible world only if the person has a reasonably large number of beliefs on a wide variety of topics. This would be a form of complexity requirement. The other way would be to interpret the conditional in the definition, "if S believes that p at ω, then p at ω," as implying that if it had not been the case that p at ω, then S would not have believed that p at ω. This would be a form of reliability requirement. Of course we could also combine the complexity and reliability requirements. I propose we do just that. So we can say that a world ω is incorrigible for a person S if, and only if, ω is a world where S has a reasonably large number of beliefs on a wide variety of topics at ω and, for all propositions p, if S believes that p at ω, then p at ω, and if it had not been the case that p at ω, then S would not have believed that p at ω. We can make clear that only a weak reliability requirement is involved here by specifying that the quantifier over propositions introduced in the definition is a substitutional quantifier ranging over the belief contents of S at ω, i.e., we are saying of all the propositions S believes at ω that if they had not been true, he would not have believed them. So understood it seems that we do express an obvious truth when we say that whatever S believes at an incorrigible world he knows to be true. After all it is no accident that all of his beliefs are true. All his beliefs are true because he occupies an incorrigible world and it is no accident that he occupies an incorrigible world. It is no more an accident that S occupies an incorrigible world than it is that anyone occupies the world that he does.[3] So our platitude is indeed a platitude.

There is of course another way out for the coherence theorist. He can alter his view by making coherence world-relative. He can then grant that relative to the St. Elizabethan world the coherence of John's beliefs is very great. In fact any alternative belief system that is more coherent than John's (for example, by containing, for some unrelated p and q in

John's belief system, "p explains q") will be less accurate (because, for example, at the St. Elizabethan world p does not explain q). Therefore, he might suggest that we should understand the coherence of a belief system in such a way that if, at a world ω, every alternative belief system that contains more systematic connections has fewer truths and/or more falsehoods than S's belief system at ω, then S's belief system is maximally coherent at ω. He can then happily accept the implication that John has a justified belief system at the St. Elizabethan world by coherence standards. Of course in doing so he renders the degree of coherence of a system of beliefs relative to the proportion of truths and falsehoods that system contains, and this, of course, depends on the way the world is. This amounts to embracing a notion of coherence according to which systematic connections enhance coherence if, only if, they enhance the likelihood of truth. Thus understood the coherence properties, and thereby the justificatory status, of a system of beliefs is world-relative. This is known as biting the bullet, but it seems a far more savory alternative than any of the others available.

A case for the world-relativity of coherence could be pressed by means of Quine's arguments for regarding all truths about implicative facts as empirical truths. World-relativity seems itself a platitude with respect to explanatory coherence. The explanatory coherence of a person's beliefs seems to be dependent on what explains what at the world of the believer. Take the world view of the believer in astrology. To the nonbeliever the astrologer's beliefs are incoherent because they are based on such astoundingly bad reasons. For example, if S is an astrologer he might believe that the fact that Einstein was a Pisces (e) explains his discovery of spacetime relativity (d). Of course, e does not explain d; e is no reason to believe d. If S is a good astrologer, then he will have some reason r (expressing various principles of astrological explanation applied to Einstein's case) for believing in a rational connection between e and d. But, of course, r is a bad reason to believe that e is a good reason to believe d. Likewise, all of S's reasons for believing r might also be based on a set of systematic yet false beliefs about the relationships between patterns in the lives of humans and patterns in the positions of heavenly bodies at the moment of the human's birth. If *all* of S's explanatory principles are false, the collection of them does not provide good reason to believe that e explains d. Everyone (even the astrologer) will grant this, for surely everyone will grant that it does not enhance the explanatory coherence of a world view to connect entirely unrelated events. Thus the astrologer's world view has its coherence enhanced by the inclusion of the belief that e explains d only if *some* of the beliefs that form the basis of this belief are true. Surely what explains what depends on the way the world is and the character of our relation to it. So the explanatory coherence of the astrologer's world view depends on the way the astrologer's world is.

Perhaps what this case best illustrates is a need to distinguish between the systematicity of a world view and its coherence. Let us say that the *systemization* of a world view is just the sum of the relations of deducibility, probability, and explanation that exist among the elements of a world view, *from the standpoint of the believer*. One might undertake to generate a psychological theory T of these relations for the believer in question. T would entail, for example, a theory of deducibility for the believer - entail all sentences of the form "A is deducible from B" that the believer accepts either explicitly or tacitly. T would entail similar theories of probability and explanation for the believer and, thereby, for his world view. T might be true (i.e., entail that "A is deducible from B" if, and only if, A is deducible from B), or it might be false while yet being true to the believer (i.e., entail that "A is deducible from B" if, and only if, the believer accepts that A is deducible from B)[4]. The believer's world view might be quite systematic even if the theory T that captures its systemization is mostly false, i.e., each of the person's beliefs might be involved in many of the entailments of T while most of the entailments of T are false. The case of the astrologer suggests however that if T is completely false, then the world view whose systemization is well represented by T is incoherent. So one can have systemization without coherence. Contrariwise, poor deluded John has a world view that is quite unsystematic, yet, at the St. Elizabethan World, where all of his beliefs are true, his world view is, as I suggested above, maximally coherent because any increase in its systemization would detract from its reliability. So one can (and sometimes must) have coherence without systemization.

So, one alternative is biting the bullet; swallowing a world-relative notion of coherence. If a coherence theorist finds this unpalatable it might be because he has internalist leanings. An internalist views the epistemic merit of a doxastic system as dependent upon properties of the doxastic system that are internal to the mind of the believer, properties that the believer could acquire knowledge of by meditation on the matter. To the coherence theorist of internalist tastes the coherence properties of a belief system seem to be world-invariant properties of the system. To him coherence properties seem to be properties a doxastic system has in virtue of the propositional content and the logical form of the beliefs in that system. For example, "Everyone in Paris is French" coheres with "Someone in Paris is French" in virtue of the logical form of the two propositions. This is a necessary property of these propositions; their possessing the property is not dependent on what the world is like. On the other hand, "The King died" and "The Queen died of grief" cohere, if they do at all, only because of their content (presumably, because the pair together have a content that explains the death of the Queen).

But here too their coherence, if they cohere, does not depend on the way the world is. If the King's death gives one good reason to believe that the Queen died of grief, then it does so regardless of whether either fact really obtains. Or suppose that both are true, but that the King's death does not explain the Queen's death (she was grieving the death of her lover Cassio), still the one belief has a systematic relation with the other for any believer who believes that the one *does* explain the other.

But it was suggested above that: (i) believing that the King's death explains the Queen's death enhances the coherence of one's world view only if one has good reason to believe that the one event explains the other; and that (ii) some part of the basis of this belief must be true for the reasons to be good ones. On what does the goodness of one's reasons depend? The coherence theorist of an internalist stripe will insist the it depends on the content of what one believes (or, perhaps, what one believes and experiences), i.e., on the content of one's evidence beliefs and on what deductive, probabilistic, and explanatory relations exist between one's beliefs and their evidential bases.[5] The point here is that it appears to such an internalist that once one fixes the propositional content and logical form of the elements of a doxastic system, one has fixed the coherence properties of that system. In other words the coherence properties of a belief system appear to supervene on the propositional content and logical form of the elements of that system; *no difference in coherence without a difference in content or form.*

So, on the one hand, the world-relativity of coherence is suggested by the fact that a systematic but completely false world view - false in its apparent observations, false in its deductive and inductive principles, false in its explanatory principles - can only, perhaps, *appear* coherent from the inside; it cannot *really be* coherent. Surely if coherence is a property a world view can appear to have but lack, then the systematic but totally false world view is the paradigm example. No matter how intricate the systemization of a set of beliefs is, if it is *totally* false it will make no sense to anyone who is not similarly deluded. So, when a world view is so false that there is but a distinction of the reason between it and gibberish, what is to be made of the claim that its systematicity renders it coherent? Not much, I fear. So the systematic complete delusion is a clear example of a doxastic system whose coherence is world-relative.

On the other hand, accepting a world-relative notion of coherence involves accepting an externalist element in the coherence account of justification. It involves accepting the externalist's contention that the epistemic merit of a person's beliefs can be influenced by factors external to the mind of the believer. Internalist scruples aside, there should be no problem for the coherentist in accepting this. I see no reason for accepting the world-invariance of coherence other than an alleged supervenience of coherence on content and no reason for accepting the supervenience doctrine other than a commitment to internalism.

Therefore, there is a solution to the St. Elizabethan World problem available to any coherentist who is willing to reject internalism. The solution is to accept that the coherence properties of a system of beliefs are contingent properties of that system, i.e., properties that can vary depending upon the way the world of the believer is. This of course requires the rejection of any doctrine that implies that coherence properties are necessary properties of belief systems. One such doctrine is the supervenience of coherence on content. Since content properties are necessary properties of the beliefs that have them, they are necessary properties of the doxastic system that consists of those beliefs. Thus, if coherence supervenes on content, the coherence properties of a doxastic system will be necessary properties of the system. This means that contingent world-variant coherence properties can only be accommodated by rejecting the supervenience doctrine and the internalism that motivates it.

Conclusion.

The coherence theorist appears to advance a principle of empirical justification that implies that if a person has justified beliefs, then he has a system of beliefs that has some minimal degree of order. His principle implies that knowledge is impossible for some cognizer whose world view is less orderly than this standard requires. But this is surely false, for in an incorrigible world, one has knowledge regardless of how chaotic that world may be. The coherence theorist must deny this. He must claim that even if one's beliefs are as coherent as the world is and all true, one's failure to meet a standard of coherence higher than mere consistency degrades one's epistemic status. I have argued that this is a serious mistake. It runs counter to what is a central intuition about knowledge: the problem of knowledge arises from the possibility of getting things wrong. When this possibility does not exist, as in the case of John in the St. Elizabethan World, whatever one believes one knows.

I suggested that there is a solution available to the St. Elizabethan World problem. One has merely to accept the world-relativity of coherence. This is a natural enough move once one accepts the possibility that one's world view might possess an elaborate systematicity and thus appear very coherent from the inside and nevertheless be very incoherent because the principles and laws that form the basis of that system are all false. Of course this same world view would be very coherent indeed were the deductive, inductive, and explanatory bases of its systematization to reflect the way the world actually is, i.e., if the theory T that well represents the systemization of that world view were to be true. Since the truth of T is contingent, the coherence of a world view with T as its systemization is contingent. Accepting this contingency of coherence allows the coherence theorist to maintain the principle that if a person has a justified system of beliefs, then he has a world view that has some minimum degree of coherence without having to confront the St. Elizabethan World problem.[6]

NOTES

[1] Ernest Sosa expresses much the same sentiment about just this kind of case in Sosa (1985): "How plausible is it to insist even for such a world (*e.g. a St. Elizabethan World*) that knowledge even of the mind/world interface is aided by the most elaborate possible webs both worldward and mindward? Surely it is very little plausible to suppose that such artificial and wholly false webs add anything at all to one's knowledge of what is there knowable."

[2] I find these reasons to be particularly bad ones. I know of no compelling reasons why we should not admit that there are many equally justified systems of empirical beliefs. The suggestion that we would then have no grounds for preferring our own system of beliefs over those of someone else who has an equally coherent but incompatible set is implausible. I find sufficient epistemic reason to prefer my own system in the fact that it is my own. I also find the suggestion that there is some connection between justification and truth unmotivated. This, in part, is why I think that justification is not necessary for knowledge.

[3] I assume that it is no accident that I occupy this world and not some other. It is indeed a contingent fact that I occupy this world, for I might have occupied a world different in some respects from this one. But though I stand in a contingent relation to this world, it is a nonaccidental one.

[4] One problem here is deciding what is to count as accepting that A is deducible from B. Is it assenting to the proposition, "A is deducible from B," or is more required, perhaps having a cognitive system that tends to infer A from B? I think that some condition like the latter, i.e., a functional role criterion, is both necessary and sufficient for accepting the proposition in question.

[5] Note here that a coherence theorist cannot, on pain of circularity, make use of a notion of coherence in explaining what counts as good reasons. Having good reasons is just having (prima facie) justifying reasons. We cannot make use of some notion of justifying reasons to explicate coherence, and then use this notion of coherence to explicate empirical justification and, thereby, what makes reasons justifying reasons. Of course if we can give an account of justifying reasons without making use of any coherence notions one wonders what we need a coherence account of empirical justification for.

[6] I extend thanks to Keith Lehrer and Vann McGee for comments on an earlier draft of this paper. This paper was written during the tenure of a Ford Foundation Fellowship for Minorities during the academic year 1987–88.

REFERENCES

Armstrong, D. M.. *Belief, Truth, and Knowledge.* London: Cambridge University Press, 1973.
Bonjour, Laurence. *The Structure of Empirical Knowledge.* Cambridge: Harvard University Press, 1985.
Sosa, Ernest. "The Coherence of Virtue and the Virtue of Coherence," *Synthese* 64 (1985), 3–28.
Tolliver, J. T.. "Basing Beliefs on Reasons," *Grazer Philosophische Studien* 15 (1982), 149–161.

Coherence, Observation, and the Justification
of Empirical Belief*

Stuart Silvers
Tilburg University, The Netherlands

Introduction

Coherence theories of empirical knowledge would seem to arise out of the ashes of burned-out foundationalism. As Lehrer (1974) suggests, the weakness of foundationalism, i.e., its inability to detach the justification of any particular belief from the system of beliefs of which it is a constituent, is the strength of coherence. For on the coherence view, specific beliefs are justified only in terms of their relation to other beliefs. Perhaps this amounts to making a virtue of necessity but the point is just how virtuous the notion of coherence can be made to be. Given that the task is to construct an acceptable theory of empirical belief justification on the basis of a coherence relation among beliefs (none of which enjoys any epistemic priority), the virtues of coherence are required to be very considerable.

Internalist theories of (empirical) knowledge are constructed only from resources that are specified wholly within the theories. The distinction between internalism and externalism as predicates of epistemological theories is not without its difficulties. "Theories that invoke solely psychological conditions of the cognizer are naturally called 'subjective', or 'internal' theories." (Goldman, 1986, 24) According to internalist theories of epistemic justification, in order for a belief to be justified it is necessary that the believer (or cognizer) have access to or in some way be aware of that which justifies his having the belief in question. In this paper I shall be concerned with BonJour's internalist coherence theory of empirical belief justification, in particular, his arguments for the connection between the properties in virtue of which a doxastic system is coherent and the properties of a coherent doxastic system in virtue of which it is empirical.

I.

BonJour distinguishes his version of the coherence among beliefs as follows: "...the main idea is that inferential justification, despite its linear appearance, is essentially systematic or holistic: beliefs are justified by being inferentially related to other beliefs in the overall context of a coherent system." (90)

For the purposes at hand I take the notion of inference quite liberally, i.e., the inferences may be as loose as simple associations, so that the doxastic system may be viewed as an associative network. The key property of the system is its being holistic. Belief-fixation, on this view, is determined by the relations it bears to other beliefs that are relevant to it. There are then what we might call saliency relations among beliefs in a doxastic system that serve as conditions of justification for the target belief. But even more than being conditions of justification, the saliency relations also figure crucially in marking out a relevance domain or epistemic field, as Lehrer (1974) calls it. For BonJour, "...the relation between the various particular beliefs is correctly to be conceived...as mutual or reciprocal support." (91)[1]

Since the thesis is that epistemic justification is properly a matter of coherence within a doxastic system, and coherence is a holistic property of such systems then in order to understand the mechanism of epistemic justification we will need to have an account of holism. But even without attempting to unravel the hoary knots inherent in holistic views, there are some consequences of holism with regard to belief justification that are of immediate concern. In particular I want to look at the idea of holistic belief-fixation for it is arguably one of the fundamental (normative) tasks of the epistemological enterprise to investigate the conditions of rational belief-fixation.

J.W. Bender (ed.), The Current State of the Coherence Theory, 168–177.
© 1989 by Kluwer Academic Publishers.

The connection between belief and (semantic) meaning is particularly tight in virtue of the fact that belief-fixation on the holistic approach is a function of the way a target belief is related to others of the system to which it belongs. However one conceives of belief or belief-states (or propositional attitude states in general), they are the paradigmatic bearers of meaning. The further justificatory requirement of the right kind of relations, i.e., relations that satisfy the norms of internal coherence, issues in the arguments about just what the norms should be.[2] The appeal that holism holds for coherence theorists lies in the explanatory contribution holism makes to the phenomenon of rational or epistemic belief justification. Hence, one is epistemically justified in believing that P if, *ceteris paribus,* that P stands in the appropriate relations to (enough) other beliefs that S has. What makes this kind of justification via coherence an internalist theory of belief justification is the additional requirement that S must also have cognitive access to the relations that his belief that P maintains to his other beliefs. That is,

> ... the person must have a reflective grasp of the fact that his system of beliefs satisfies the third condition (to wit, the system of beliefs in question must be coherent to a high degree and more coherent than any alternative...), and this reflective grasp must be, ultimately but perhaps only very implicitly, the reason why he continues to accept the belief whose justification is in question."
> (BonJour, 1985, 154, his emphasis; the parenthetical insertion cites a portion of the preceding paragraph on the same page.)

Since I am not here taking issue with any arguments for or against the various suggestions that have been made concerning what kinds of relations subserve the concept of coherence, my discussion of epistemically justified belief-fixation is neutral with regard to the adequacy of any of the competitors. I shall, however, moralize a bit in the sequel on the need for precision rather than vagueness in the assessment of coherence-making properties of doxastic systems. My point here is rather to illuminate the notion of holism presupposed by coherence theories of belief justification. In fact, it matters little, if at all, that coherence theories are frequently associated with an internalist perspective in epistemology. The reason is that the primary distinction (as vague as it is) between internalist and externalist theories of justification relates to the cognitive status of the person whose belief is in question. Consequently, one can, as BonJour notes, embrace both coherentism and externalism as well as coherentism and internalism.

Although it is an intuitively motivated assumption of coherence theories that the degree of systematic coherence and the degree of belief justification covary, Thieu Kuys has noticed that it is a separate but crucial question of whether epistemic justification supervenes on holistically defined coherence in the way required. The mere fact that S's belief that p increases the coherence of S's belief system does not entail an increase in justificatory strength, at least not without independent argument. In short, there is no obvious positive relation between increased coherence and increased justification. (For example, as Kuys suggests, my belief that the rest of my beliefs are true adds coherence to my belief set without adding a greater degree of justification to any member of the set.) Another revealing case is this: the Pope, it is said by those who maintain the doctrine of papal infallibility, is infallible. For those so believing, it follows that the belief that the Pope is infallible obviously upgrades the coherence of the Pope's beliefs (i.e., his pronouncements) but this is an increase in coherence that leaves the question of increased justification completely untouched. As obvious as this point turns out to be, it is no less critical for a coherence theory of justification. It establishes what is required of any serious coherence theory of justification, viz., that there is no escaping the task of analyzing the specific properties of holistic systems that contribute to epistemic belief justification.

II.

Where the person is aware not only of the coherence of his belief system but also aware that his belief that his doxastic system is the right kind coheres appropriately with that system, then in addition to the holistic character of the justification, the person also satisfies the requirement of internalism. The problem with requiring that beliefs be justified from within is how to avoid the threat of cognitive relativism inherent in such a seemingly circular structure of justification. Under these conditions a belief system, in effect, predicates of itself that it possesses the properties required for epistemically justifying beliefs of that same system. The question then becomes, what is there about the justificational system that endows it with the properties needed for belief justification, on the one hand, and blocks the route to relativism, on the other. BonJour formulates the problem of relativism for coherence theories of knowledge:

> According to a coherence theory of empirical justification, at least as so far characterized, the system of beliefs which constitutes empirical knowledge is epistemically justified solely by virtue of its internal coherence. But such an appeal to coherence will never even begin to pick out one uniquely justified system of beliefs, since on any plausible conception of coherence, there will always be many, probably infinitely many, different and incompatible systems of belief which are equally coherent. (107)

While acknowledging this standard objection as a "obviously very forceful", BonJour thinks he can defuse it by answering another objection that he considers to be even more pervasive, viz., the problem of input.[3] "Coherence is purely a matter of the internal relations between components of the system of belief; it depends in no way on any sort of relation between the system of beliefs and anything external to that system." (108) If a coherence theory is to yield a notion of epistemic justification for empirical knowledge then it is obvious that some provision needs to be made to account for the empirical content of the beliefs that the theory operates on. The coherent system is going to have to be connected to the 'external' world if it's to make good its claim to justify beliefs about the external world, which is patently what coherence theories of knowledge purport to do. It is for this reason that BonJour argues for his 'Observation Requirement'. Whether satisfying the conditions that constitute the Observation Requirement resolves the 'input problem' depends on the adequacy of those conditions.

It is, of course, the bane of any coherence theory that is should adopt a position *vis-a-vis* empirical content that collapses the theory into foundationalism. The idea is to come up with a concept of a belief that is noninferential in origin and justified not merely in virtue of its coherence within the system but "...whose coherentist justification depended in some way on the manner of its noninferential origin." (BonJour, 1985, 113) Any belief such that "...it simply occurs to me, 'strikes me', in a manner which is both involuntary and coercive; such a belief is, I will say, cognitively spontaneous." (117, BonJour's emphasis) For a cognitively spontaneous (C.S.) belief to count as observational and hence contribute empirical content, it must satisfy three conditions. (i) An C.S. belief must be of a certain kind, i.e., classified in terms of "...the intrinsic character or content of the belief, however it may in fact have been caused."(118)[4]   (ii) Observational conditions must be (functionally) normal or standard. Given that (ii) is satisfied, (iii) C.S. beliefs must be reliable, i.e., likely to be true.

A detailed analysis of the conditions will not be attempted here. Instead, I'll try to paint a picture, using admittedly broad brush strokes, to illustrate why BonJour's conditions, if necessary, rule out the possibility of a coherence theoretical justification of empirical belief and if sufficient rule out the possibility of a unique coherence theoretical justification of empirical belief. On the one hand, if the conditions are necessary for C.S.

beliefs to qualify as having empirical content there are reasons to believe that no C.S. belief, as characterized by BonJour, has empirical content. On the other, if a C.S. belief does satisfy the conditions then there are also reasons to believe that such a C.S. belief will not be distinguishable from other such beliefs with which it is intuitively incompatible, thus admitting an unresolvable relativism.(Cf. Goldman, 1980, 37)

Condition (i) refers to kinds of belief defined, not by causal connections to truth-conditions, but to content in another sense.[5] But empirical belief content must ultimately bear some relation to the conditions responsible for it having the content it has, and sooner or later, it surely must be some sort of causal responsibility. For even if the content of a belief, i.e., what the belief is about, is not what caused it, as in an hallucination or other less spectacular kind of perceptual error, the falsity of the belief would seem to be dependent upon most of the others of its kind being true.[6] So much seems intuitively acceptable. There is, however, an ambiguity in BonJour's specification of belief-kind. One which I think turns in part upon the conflation of two different aspects of belief-content, the phenomenological and the intentional. (Cf. Burge, 1986) There are kinds of belief such as visual, auditory, etc. (BonJour deals only with visual beliefs.) It is, in his view, 'misleading' to talk of visual beliefs as being

> ...about the color and general classification of a 'medium-sized object' [since] ...the term 'visual' suggests a classification in terms of causal etiology, whereas what is intended here is a classification concerned only with the intrinsic character or content of the belief, however it may have been caused. (118)

There are two components involved in the specification of belief content. One is that the believer has the specific belief in question: this is, according BonJour, guaranteed by his Doxastic Assumption, viz., the believer is presumed to have a (cognitive) grasp of his overall system of beliefs and that his grasp is accurate. Despite its essential character for BonJour's enterprise, it is not at all obvious how the application of such a Doxastic Presumption, i.e., in virtue of what resources, such a presumption determines the content of one belief as distinct from another. Of the other component BonJour remarks

> The obvious supplement to classification in terms of content, given that classification in terms of causal etiology is not in general available in an unproblematic way (though it would be available in cases where much other empirical knowledge could be presupposed), is classification of the belief by reference to introspectively accessible concurrent events. Thus there is some plausibility to the view that part of what is involved in classifying a belief as, for example, visual is its being accompanied by certain distinctive sorts of events, roughly what have been called 'sense impressions' or 'sensa'. (129)

Causal talk is, of course, externalist and hence not part of the internalist's view. Yet the classification of a belief kind in terms of its being, e.g., a visual belief, by alluding to concurrent 'sense impressions' and other internal co-occurrences, is merely to distinguish the belief-kind vis-a-vis something like sensory modality. In this sense of belief-kind the classification provides grounds for answers to epistemological questions like "How do you know it was a horse in the kitchen?", viz., "I saw it there." The response identifies the way in which the belief was acquired, viz., visually. If, however, the classification of belief-kind is to serve to distinguish beliefs from one another in virtue of their content, so that a (visually acquired) horse-belief is distinct from a (visually acquired) mule-belief, something else will be required in addition to the usual concomitant sensa. The reason is, obviously, that we need to distinguish the kind of events concurrent with horse-beliefs from the kinds of events concurrent with mule-beliefs. For if the concurrent events determine that a belief is a visual belief there still needs to be an account of belief classification in terms of content. As long as we remain within the internalist purview and refuse to admit the sorts of external (truth) conditions that distinguish tokens of horse from tokens of mule, the system is deprived of the means to distinguish belief-kinds in terms of content.

The content of a belief is its meaning, i.e., it's the content of my horse-belief that is the effect of my standing in the right sort of relationship to tokens of things that in normal circumstances cause me to token (visually acquired) horse-beliefs, that explains my believing it's a horse rather than a mule. If the content (i.e., meaning) of a belief were determined by "...its being accompanied by certain distinctive sorts of events, roughly what have been called 'sense impressions' or 'sensa'" (BonJour, 129) the sensa would also need to be sorted in order for the belief to be of this or that specific kind. Without some mechanism for external input that distinguishes between tokens of sensa of kind A (e.g., horse) and tokens of sensa of kind B (mule) it does not seem that an internalist system can account for the required distinctions to classify belief kinds according to content. If usual or normal visual belief kinds are just those that are typically accompanied by the concurrent events that individuate them, then an internalist conception of belief-kind classification can yield at best a classification of sensory modality. So anything that can boot the system into the appropriate set of internal events that is identified with visual experience can be a possible perceptual object for the system. This characterization seems to be at considerable odds with the intuitive causal concept of a visual belief kind, viz., the one that marks out belief kinds in terms of a determinate content that is causally responsible for the (perceptual) belief.[7]

Condition (ii) is designed to ensure that most beliefs of the kind that satisfy (i) are true in virtue of the normalcy of the conditions in which they cognitively spontaneously occur. That is, a C.S. belief of kind K would occur if the observational conditions were normal and the normalcy of the observational conditions is evidenced by the occurrence of belief kind K. BonJour refers to the circularity of his definition of normal condition as harmless, preferring to treat it as a species of the element of coherence that characterizes his system. Intuitions on points like this tend to conflict rather fundamentally. Resolution requires developing substantial theory. Still, it does seem that in the quest for a theory of justification of empirical belief provision needs to be made for the epistemic independence of empirical hypothesis and evidential base. If the desired concept of coherence can blur the independence of evidence and hypothesis, the empirical dimension of the thesis is threatened. The circularity is blatant; it needs to be shown to be benign. (Cf. Silvers, 1985)

Condition (iii) requires that the C.S. beliefs are highly reliable, which, of course, given enough normalcy as in condition (ii) they are, tautologically, likely to be. But notice that (i), according to the objection above, does involve causal etiology, for how else might we conceive of false C.S. beliefs. Condition (ii), as BonJour alludes to it, glosses the significant problems of specifying the relations between 'standard conditions' and 'normal functioning'. While condition (iii) simply assumes, without discussion, that high reliability is truth likelihood. Such assumption neglects the obvious cases of reliability of prediction based upon false hypotheses. And to demand of such reliability that "...it is a true law of nature concerning me and a large, though indefinite class of relevantly similar observers ...that our cognitively spontaneous beliefs of that kind are highly reliable, that is, likely to be true" requires a specification of just what sorts of natural laws are involved.

Consider that only nomic properties can figure in the laws that are true of me and my conspecifics. The relations that instantiate natural laws are nomic relations. Hence the laws holding among conspecifics are true of them in virtue of their nomic properties, where such properties, *vis-a-vis* observation, are ones that enter into,e.g.,psychophysical relations. The psychophysical properties that figure, e.g., in visual processes include distribution of light intensity values, reflectance, spatial position and orientation, etc.. In general, psychophysical relations pertain to the quantitative magnitudes of properties of stimulus objects and sensory activation. Observation, in the relevant epistemic sense, involves perceptual objects. The properties of perceptual objects are characteristically nonnomic, e.g., being a dented fender or being a pair of bifocals, etc.. There are then, strictly speaking, no natural laws into which properties of typically perceptual objects may enter, *a fortiori* no "true law true of nature concerning me and a large, though indefinite class of relevantly similar observers..." *vis-a-vis* observed perceptual objects. (Cf. Silvers, forthcoming) Less than strictly speaking, there are relativized domains or contexts in which causally sufficient 'lawlike' generalizations involving nonnomic properties do obtain for me and a large enough number of contextually similar observers. Of these, the ones true of me and my contextually or culturally defined conspecifics will advert to cognitively spontaneous beliefs about perceptual objects in terms of properties that, as it were, locally instantiate nomic (psychophysical) relations.

The reliability of these 'lawlike' generalizations is a function of the causal sufficiency of the nonnomically instantiated property triggering the C.S. observational belief. The reliability and the concomitant causal sufficiency fail, however, when the defining contextual boundaries are transgressed. A tennis ball, for instance, has psychophysical (i.e., nomic) properties which account for it figuring in sensory activation in dogs as well as in communities of observers where tennis is a radically alien phenomenon. But the nonnomic properties in virtue of which the stimulus object is (seen as) a perceptual object, i.e., a tennis ball, are circumscribed in terms of contextual relativity. This is an obviously much weaker kind of generalization. If it is this kind of generalization that suffices for C.S. observational beliefs it would seem to open the way for one of the standard objections to internalism in epistemology, viz., the relativity of epistemic justification.

A reply to this line might be that as an objection to a theory of knowledge it isn't very interesting since it is hardly the job of a coherence theory to make pronouncements about the objects of knowledge. The reply seems, however, not well taken. If the coherentist is serious about the content of the empirical beliefs his system is designed to justify and he does not fall prey to the idea of content as being fully specified by reference to the activation of sensory modalities and is, furthermore, unwilling to settle for phenomenalism, then there would seem to be no option but to parse 'belief content' realistically. And BonJour does just that. Under these conditions, it is not unreasonable to expect of a coherence theory that it specify the objects that figure in the beliefs it justifies even if, in epistemological tradition, one denies that it need not say anything about belief acquisition.

None of the objections I have suggested in connection with BonJour's three conditions on observational belief totally undermines his thesis but collectively I think they provide a basis for finding them less than convincing. The significance of the sorts of conditions one imposes on observation extends, on the one hand, quite obviously, to the issue of empirical content of belief systems. But on the other, it is equally important to understand what the conditions on observation presuppose about the mechanisms implicated in the acquisition of empirical belief. This is, of course, a particularly disputed point on which the disputants (viz., externalists and internalists) regularly beg the question of belief justification against one another. So it must suffice here to say only that even if, *mirabile dictu*, a case could be made for determining belief kind in terms of content without causal input, as condition (i) prescribes, the distinction relevant to condition (iii) between local causal sufficiency and global nomic necessity is crucial to any serious theory of human knowledge. For if observational beliefs are to be cognitively spontaneous they are also to be appropriately selective psychological states. If the states are lawfully selective responses in the global sense of instantiating a nomic relation, then such states are not the cognitive kinds of contentful belief states required for epistemic analysis. As I have suggested, the belief states in question should be defined, consistent with our intuitions about cognition, in terms of selective sensitivity to nonnomic (and epistemically relativized) properties of perceptual objects. Only then are such beliefs the proper subjects of the further reflection and deliberation characteristic of epistemic evaluation.

III.

There is, furthermore, something ambiguous in the idea of cognitive spontaneity. This is important because the ambiguity that underlies the claim is systematically involved in the internalist program. The distinctive feature of the justification of cognitively spontaneous beliefs is the appeal to introspective accessibility. To say that a belief is cognitively spontaneous is to say,

> that its occurrence at the moment in question is not the result of a discursive process of reasoning or inference, where this claim must be understood to exclude not only fully explicit discursive processes but also those which are only tacit or implicit. (BonJour, 129) [8]

The ambiguity in question concerns the notion of discursive processes that are only tacit or implicit. The point is, how far the internalist is willing to go in acknowledging an implicit discursive process as susceptible to introspective reflection. On BonJour's view a belief is cognitively spontaneous in an overall system in virtue of "...the absence from that system of any beliefs which could serve as plausible premises or intermediate steps for a discursive derivation of the belief in question...". (130)

It seems at least plausible that the demand of (almost) simultaneous reflection is too severe, since the amount of time required for the needed reflection varies quite substantially among individual (witness students in elementary logic!) but also within the workings of a single system, depending upon the character of the C.S. belief. So there is an important sense in which it may be questioned whether an individual holds a certain belief in the sense that upon reflection it might occur to him that he does hold it, or at least the disposition to acknowledge it when prodded. But that is an important element in the decision to treat a belief as not only being part of the system because of its 'objective' inferential connections with other beliefs, were it to be held, but as being held, upon reflection. The grounds upon which one distinguishes between dispositional beliefs that are introspectively accessible and inferential processes that are not is obviously crucial for internalism.[9] If implicit states are admitted it becomes ambiguous as to whether the role such states play in belief justification is genuinely open to an internalist conception. To say, as BonJour does, that it is a question of idealization is equally available to the externalist with respect to some class of objective conditions which if internalized would count as good reasons for holding a given belief.[10]

Having argued that the conditions on observation do not solve BonJour's 'input problem' and moreover, implicitly suggesting that no such set of conditions can, it is hard to resist asking why one ought to bother to pursue the quest. If the intuition that the right kind of coherence is truth-conducive is blunted by the simple consideration that even the greatest thinkable degree of coherence (and reliability for that matter) is compatible with mutually incompatible truth claims then why not simply bite the coherentist's bullet and jettison the demand for unique empirical content? If, that is, it's coherence that's your epistemological game, then it seems to be a worthy policy to play it rather than your opponent's. Of course, if you can beat your opponent at his own game, so much sweeter the victory but the risk is very great indeed; you lose control over your own game.

IV.

A theory, it is often said, stands or falls on the basis of the accuracy of its predictions. Perhaps this is a bit too much instrumentalism for this kind of criticism to be really good, especially if it is taken to be decisive, but it does convey the import of the role of testing as a disideratum. For it does seem too that theories may be judged on the basis of the plausibility of their presuppositions. Coherence theories of knowledge, like BonJour's, try to use the conceptual resources available intra-systematically to determine and justify belief about the world external to the system. That such systems acknowledge an external world of a determinate kind commits them to a realist perspective, which, as I have tried to suggest, has the coherentist pulling in different and incompatible directions at the same time. Hardly an advertisement for coherentism. But the arguments offered for both belief state individuation and justification are less than convincing as regards how the external world can have the role it is ascribed in the theories.

Internalist epistemology draws support from the plausibility of the intuition that for a belief to be justified the believer must have cognitive access to the justifying grounds for the belief. The intuition is motivated by the view that coincidence and luck are not epistemically valuable. One effect of internalism in epistemology is to make the belief condition on knowledge quintessentially necessary. The tradition of this approach has been to pursue the analysis of justified belief independently of (empirical) investigation into the nature of mental phenomena. It does seem, however, that if epistemology is going to be a proper part of the cognitive enterprise then it cannot ignore analyses of phenomena that are taken to be one of its necessary conditions. It is at least defensible that a theory of belief justification not be incompatible with (empirical) constraints on the nature of belief as a mental phenomenon. I think that Descartes' analysis of the mind as transparent and independent of an external world is crucial to his internalist (although foundationalist) theory of knowledge. If, as in the case of Descartes, the epistemological concerns are prior to and determinate of the concept of mind, then good methodology prescribes that, *ceteris paribus*, independently-obtained results about the nature of the mind be taken as relevant evidence of the adequacy of the theory of knowledge. It does not, however, follow automatically from such a prescription that there is no autonomous domain for epistemology as a critical constraint on cognitive practice.[11]

NOTES

*   I wish to thank Thieu Kuys for his comments on earlier versions of this paper.
1. Although I shall not offer any detailed analysis of the nature of the inference sanctioned by traditional theories of epistemic justification, it is important to note that it is precisely the question of the inferential norms that is the crux of the dispute between epistemologists and experimental cognitive psychologists. The inferences generally sanctioned by epistemological theory as the norms that are to be respected in determining epistemic justification are those governed by the rules of deductive logic and the rules of the probability calculus. For critique see Wason and Johnson-Laird (1972), Tversky and Kahneman (1982), Evans (1983) and for defense see Cohen, (1980).
2. For revisionist views on the psychological reality of the traditional norms of epistemic evaluation see, Harman, (1986), Cherniak (1986), and Stich (forthcoming) and note 1.
3. According to Dancy (1985) who calls it the plurality objection "Nothing in the notion of coherence, as defined, gives us any right to say that there is a unique most coherent set." (113) He cites Blanchard's indignant reply to the objection that is a straw man, which does nothing to defuse its charge. Dancy's own preference for some form of coherence does not blind him to the relevance of the objection. If fitting the facts is the goal of a coherence theory there is nothing to rule out the possibility of more than one coherent set of propositions fitting the facts equally well. "So the coherentist cannot really give a good sense to the notion that the different theories compete or are incompatible, it seems." (115) It is, as Dancy points out, in the coherentist's favor that ". . .there is no such thing as a theory-free, external, point of view." (115)
4. Heil (1988) argues that the epistemology of belief-state content determination can be explained independently of externalism. His argument is not, however, concerned with specifically observational beliefs nor with the notion of cognitive spontaneity.
5. According to Chisholm's (1958) version of internalism "[t]he meaning (i.e., content) of thoughts is to be

analyzed in terms of the meaning of lanuage, and not conversely." (529)   See also Rosenthal (1986) for a discussion of the intrinsic intentionality of thought.

6.   There is an ancient tradition, one which Fodor (1987) tries to exploit, that maintains that truth is necessary truth and falsity (i.e., error) is accident.   It is supposed to follow from this view that truth is ontologically prior to falsity in the sense that if a belief is false it is so in virtue of its having to be a truth which it gets wrong.   "In consequence, you can have false beliefs about what you can have true beliefs about (whereas you can have true beliefs about anything that you can have beliefs about at all.)" (107)

7.   Burge (1986) makes a similar point in his discusison of the Cartesian concept of mind.   He criticizes the inference from what he calls the 'Cartesian thought experiments' (that he, Descartes, is radically mistaken about the nature of the empirical world) to the conclusion that the nature (content) of belief states is determined independently of the believer's environment: "It begins by noting that we could have the same perceptual experiences, same perceptual representations, whether these were verdical perceptions, misperceptions, or hallucinations.   Similar points can be made for other intentional phenomena.   The argument concludes from these observations that perceptual experiences are independent for their intentional natures from the perceiver or thinker's environment.   This inference has no force.   Questions of veridicality are judged with respect to given mental states.   It is a further question how those states are determined to be what they are.   The natures of such states are determined partly by normal relations between the person or organism and the environment.   Error is determined against a background of normal interaction." (125)

8.   BonJour discusses two objections to his characterization of introspection.   The account leads to a regress if introspection counts as observation, since the introspective beliefs would also be cognitively spontaneous requiring introspective justification.   And, C.S. beliefs can occur without "introspective monitoring of mental processes leading up to them. . ."(130)   His reply is that "cognitive spontaneity is often justifiable simply by appeal to my grasp of my overall system of beliefs. . . ."   This grasp, in its turn, is grounded in what BonJour calls the Doxastic Presumption.   That presumption is that enquiring into the conditions of empirical belief justification presupposes "that I do indeed hold approximately the system of beliefs which I believe myself to hold. . . ."(103)   The contribution of the Doxastic Presumption to the justification of empirical belief is, however, unclear.   It seems that in order to stop the regress, the internalist must embrace circularity and then claim that it's non-vicious.   But it's dubious at best.   If my grasp of my overall system of beliefs is part and parcel of the presumption that I do (in fact?) hold the system of beliefs I hold then my grasping my overall system of beliefs, under the presumption, amounts to my (in fact?) grasping it.   This, I submit, does little to tell us what the grasping comes to and how it differs from failing to grasp.

9.   Stich (1978) provides a detailed discussion of just these points.   The focus of his analysis is the relationship between beliefs and subdoxastic states in terms of what he takes to be two pre-theoretic criteria for a state to be a belief, access to consciousness and inferential integration.

10.   A distinction that has appealed to a number of philosophers (Dennett, Field, Fodor, Lycan, and Cummins) is the one between core beliefs and derived or generated beliefs.   Of course it is far from clear if core beliefs are implicit in BonJour's sense for they may well count as derived as a result of being generated by reflection.   The point is, however, that the question of whether a belief is actually held has no unambiguous answer.   There is no reason to think that the kind of reflective practices that internalism sanctions, viz., introspective, can be the exclusive source of epistemic justification.   The notion of epistemic justification is allied to epistemic power.   Our empirical beliefs obtain their justification in terms of the epistemic access they provide to the world through which we are obliged to manoeuvre ourselves.   Epistemic power, which is like the proof of justification, derives from successful reflection on cognitive practice.   Such cognitive practices are not adequately characterized in purely internalist-coherentist terms.   The reason why they are not is to be found in the insistence that whether or not a belief is justified by the system to which it purportedly belongs is a question of the long-run coherence of the system.   For we have already seen that even long-run coherence is compatible with the world (as truth condition) being other than the way it is represented in the belief system.

The point of the coherentist's enterprise is to use some acceptable notion of coherence to justify empirical beliefs.   In order to ensure that the beliefs acknowledged by the system are empirical in the sense that they are about external world in the way that we normally take observational beliefs to be, the system requires some means of accessing the outside world.   A belief that is merely cognitively spontaneous may have all the marks of the right kind of obsrevational belief and still fail to be about the external world.   For if belief state content is independent of the conditions causally responsible for its tokening then it is either an empirically false belief (a misrepresentation of that which normally causes beliefs of that kind) or it fails to be an empirical belief.

11.   In his celebrated "Minds, Brains, and Programs," Searle (1980) remarks that psychofunctionalism, because of its insistence on the irrelevance of the medium of mental state realization, entails dualism.   Psychofunctionalists generally emphasize the ontic neutrality of their views, preferring instead to point the compatibility of functionalism in psychology with physicalism.   The point here is that if Searle's charge is cogent and entailing dualism is tantamount to a reductio of psychofunctionalism, then it holds *a fortiori* of epistemological theories of justification that are neutral *vis-a-vis* the contexts of belief state realization.

REFERENCES

BonJour, Laurence. *The Structure of Empirical Knowledge.* Cambridge, Mass.: Harvard University Press, 1985.
-----. "Cartesian Error and the Objectivity of Content," in Pettit, P. and McDowell, J., eds., *Subject, T Thought, and Context.* Oxford: The Clarendon Press, 1986.
Cherniak, Christopher. *Minimal Rationality.* Cambridge, Mass.: Bradford Books/M.I.T. Press, 1986.
Chisholm, R. M. "Intentionality and the Mental," in Feigl, H., Scriven, M., and Maxwell, G., eds., *Concepts, Theories, and the Mind-Body Problem:* Minnesota Studies in the Philosophy of Science, Vol. II, Minneapolis: The University of Minnesota Press, 1958.
Cohen, L.J. "Can Human Irrationality Be Experimentally Demonstrated?," *Behavioral and Brain Sciences* 4 (1981), 317-331.
Dancy, Jonathan. *An Introduction to Contemporary Epistemology.* Oxford: Basil Blackwell, 1985.
Fodor, Jerry A. *Psychosemantics.* Cambridge, Mass.: Bradford Books/M.I.T. Press, 1987.
Goldman, Alvin I. "The Internalist Conception of Justification," in French, P.A. et. al., eds., *Midwest Studies in Philosophy V: Studies in Epistemology.* Minneapolis: University of Minnesota Press, 1980.
-----. *Epistemology and Cognition.* Cambridge, Mass.: Harvard University Press, 1986.
Harman, Gilbert. *Change in View.* Cambridge, Mass.: Bradford Books/M.I.T. Press, 1986.
Heil, John. "Intentionality Speaks for Itself," in S. Silvers, ed., *Representation: Readings in the Philosophy of Mental Representation.* Dordrecht: D. Reidel (Kluwer Academic Press), 1988.
Kahneman, D., Slovic, P., and Tversky, A. *Judgment Under Uncertainty: Heuristics and Biases.* Cambridge: Cambridge University Press, 1982.
Lehrer, Keith. *Knowledge.* Oxford: Oxford University Press, 1974.
Rosenthal, David "Intentionality," in French, P. et al, eds., *Studies in the Philosophy of Mind: Midwest Studies in Philosophy,* Vol. 10. Minneapolis: University of Minnesota Press, 1976.
Searle, John R. "Minds, Brains, and Programs." *Behavioral and Brain Sciences* 3 (1980), 417 - 457.
-----. *Intentionality.* Cambridge: Cambridge University Press, 1983.
Silvers, Stuart. "Natural Teleology." Presented to the 12th Annual Conference of the Society of Philosophy and Psychology, held at the University of Toronto, Toronto, Canada, 1985.
-----. "Representational Capacity, Intentional Ascription and the Slippery Slope." *Philosophy of Science,* forthcoming.
Stitch, Stephen. "Beliefs and Subdoxastic States." *Philosophy of Science* 45 (1978), 499-518.
-----. "Could Man be an Irrational Animal," In Kornblith, H., ed., *Naturalizing Epistemology.* Cambridge, Mass.: Bradford Books/M.I.T. Press, 1985.
-----. *The Fragmentation of Reason.* Cambridge, Mass.: Bradford Books/M.I.T. Press, forthcoming.
-----, and Nisbett, R.E. "Justification and the Psychology of Human Reasoning." *Philosophy of Science* 47 (1980), 188-202.
Wason, P.C. and Johnson-Laird, P.N. *The Psychology of Reasoning: Structure and Content.* London: Batsford, 1972.

Epistemic Priority and Coherence

Noah M. Lemos
The University of Texas at Austin

There are two related topics considered in this paper. The first topic concerns the status of basic beliefs and the thesis of epistemic priority, and the second concerns the justification of observational and introspective beliefs within a coherentist approach to justification. These issues are related since the proponents of coherence theories typically deny the thesis of epistemic priority and the existence of basic beliefs, and since those sympathetic to the thesis typically maintain that our introspective beliefs are among the clearest examples of basic beliefs. In the first section I shall consider an argument by Laurence BonJour against the existence of basic beliefs and the thesis of epistemic priority. Though I believe that the argument is unsuccessful, it provides an important challenge to foundationalist views of justification. Still, this argument presupposes a certain view of what is required for justification, and in the second section I argue that this view of justification presents problems for BonJour's positive account of the warrant of observational and introspective beliefs. In addition to BonJour's views, I shall also consider a brief proposal by Roderick Firth in response to the objection that coherence theories cut off justification from the world.

I

In "Coherence, Certainty, and Epistemic Priority," Roderick Firth states what he believes C. I. Lewis took to be the central thesis of the coherence theory of justification. Lewis put the thesis thus:

> *ultimately* every statement that has some degree of warrant for me has that degree of warrant, because and only because, it is related by various principles of inference to (that is to say "coheres with") certain other statements. (549)

Lewis, of course, rejected this view of justification, embracing instead the apparent alternative to the coherence theory which Firth calls "the thesis of epistemic priority". According to Firth, this thesis maintains that,

> some statements have some degree of warrant which is independent of (and in this sense "prior to") the warrant (if any) that they derive from their coherence with other statements. (553)

A commitment to the thesis of epistemic priority may take many forms. Lewis, for example, seems to have held that such non-inferentially warranted statements are those which characterize the content of one's present sense experience. He also held that such statements were certain, i.e., that no other statement at that time is more warranted for that person. Firth appears to have accepted the view that the non-inferentially warranted statements are about one's present experience, but he observed that the thesis of epistemic priority does not commit one to the view that these statements are certain. There are degrees of epistemic warrant weaker than certainty which one may attribute to the class of independently warranted statements without abandoning the thesis of epistemic priority.

In addition to there being a variety of views on the degree of warrant enjoyed by the class of independently warranted beliefs, there are also a variety of views on what makes the independently warranted beliefs warranted. The thesis of epistemic priority does not, of course, deny that *something* makes these independently warranted beliefs justified. I will simply mention three possibilities, of which the first two are considered by Firth. The

178

J.W. Bender (ed.), The Current State of the Coherence Theory, 178–187.
© *1989 by Kluwer Academic Publishers.*

first view considered by Firth holds that "the statement...'It looks as if I am seeing something red' is warranted (or given some warrant) for me simply by the fact that it *does* look as if I am seeing something red."(553) On this view, the independently warranted statement or belief is warranted by the fact that one is having a certain sort of experience. What makes that particular belief warranted is not another belief, but simply the fact that it does look as if one is seeing something red.

The second view is roughly that the statement, "It looks as if I am seeing something red," is warranted for me because it is (a) "a statement (whether true or false) that *purports* to characterize (and only to characterize) the content of my present experience"(553), and (b) it is such that "I either now believe to be true or should now believe to be true if I had just now decided whether it is true or false."(554) This view maintains, roughly, that the independently warranted statements are warranted for a person at a particular time because they purport to characterize the content of one's experience and one accepts them. It is this fact rather than the fact that one is having a certain sort of experience which makes the belief warranted.

Finally, one might hold that the acceptance of some statements is warranted because the acceptance of those statements is the product of, or sustained by, a process of belief formation which is highly reliable from the standpoint of producing true beliefs. On this view, it is the origin or sustenance of a belief by such a process which makes the belief warranted independently of any inferential relations it bears to other beliefs.

While there are clearly a variety of forms which a commitment to the thesis of epistemic priority may take, the thesis is one of the main tenets of foundationalism, and it is also one of the main targets of anti-foundationalist arguments. One such argument has been presented by BonJour. In *The Structure of Empirical Knowledge*, he puts the argument this way:

> (1) Suppose that there are basic empirical beliefs, that is, empirical beliefs (a) which are empirically justified, and (b) whose justification does not depend on that of any further empirical belief.

> (2) For a belief to be epistemically justified requires that there be a reason why it is likely to be true.

> (3) For a belief to be epistemically justified for a particular person requires that this person be himself in cognitive possession of such a reason.

> (4) The only way to be in cognitive possession of such a reason is to believe *with justification* the premises of an argument from which it follows that the belief is likely to be true.

> (5) The premises of such a justifying argument cannot be entirely *priori*; at least one such premise must be empirical.

> (6) Therefore, the justification of a supposed basic belief must depend on the justification of at least one other empirical belief, contradicting (1); it follows that there can be no basic empirical beliefs. (32)

It is important to note that BonJour's argument does not simply involve the claim that a belief is justified for a person only if there are other things which he is justified in believing. Rather, his view is about what makes something justified or about that upon which epistemic justification depends. His view is that a belief, B, is justified for a person,

S, in virtue of S's having certain other beliefs from which it follows that B is likely to be true; that any belief which is justified for S is justified only in virtue of S's having certain other justified beliefs.

Defenders of the thesis of epistemic priority have at least two sorts of responses to this argument which merit consideration. The first sort of response has been suggested by Ernest Sosa. According to Sosa, epistemic justification or warrant is best thought of as an evaluative feature of a person's belief, for when we say that someone is justified in believing something it seems clear that we are evaluating his belief in a certain (positive) way. Moreover, we should think of epistemic warrant, like other evaluative features, as supervening or depending upon the non-evaluative. In other words, just as we take the goodness of an apple to supervene upon its being sweet and juicy and the rightness of an act (on one view of the matter) to depend upon its producing as much pleasure and as little pain as any possible alternative, so too we should view the warrant of a belief as depending upon the non-epistemically evaluative features of that belief. Sosa argues that BonJour's view leads to a denial of the highly plausible view that epistemic warrant is an evaluative characteristic and like other evaluative features it depends ultimately upon the non-evaluative. He argues that if, as the argument claims, a necessary source for the justification of any belief is other justified beliefs, then there is no possibility of there being a wholly non-epistemic source of justification for any belief. In other words, if every belief has as its only source of justification other justified beliefs, then there will never be anything which is a non-epistemic fact in virtue of which a belief is justified. Thus, Sosa argues that BonJour's view "would preclude the possibility of supervenience, since it would entail that the source of justification *always* includes an *epistemic* component." (Sosa, 18)

It is worth noting that the thesis that epistemic justification supervenes upon the non-epistemic may also be accepted by proponents of the coherence theory who reject the thesis of epistemic priority. One could maintain, for example, that a belief is warranted in virtue of the fact that it is a member of a coherent body of beliefs or in virtue of the fact that it bears certain inferential relations to a coherent body of beliefs. But Sosa observes that if BonJour's argument were successful against traditional forms of foundationalism, then it would be equally damaging to these forms of coherentism insofar as they take epistemic warrant to supervene upon the fact of coherence.

The second sort of response to BonJour's argument is simply to deny that the only reason for thinking that a belief is likely to be true consists of one's other justified beliefs. Consider, for example, the view mentioned above according to which the proposition that it looks as if I am seeing something red is justified for me because it does look as if I am seeing something red. On this view, one's belief is justified, not in virtue of another belief, warranted or not, but in virtue of the fact that one is having a certain sort of experience. To the question, "What reason do you have to think that your belief that it looks as if you are seeing something red is likely to be true?", the proponent of this view takes it to be a perfectly good answer to say that it is because it does look as if he is seeing something red. Similarly, to the question, "What reason do you have to think that your belief that you have a headache is likely to be true?", he takes it to be a perfectly good answer to say that it is because he does have a headache. The proponent of this view holds that reasons for believing need not be themselves beliefs or doxastic states. BonJour, of course, rejects this view. He writes,

> the proponent of the given is caught in a fundamental and inescapable dilemma: if his intuitions or direct awarenesses or immediate apprehensions are construed as cognitive, at least quasi-judgmental (as seems clearly the more natural interpretation), then they will be both capable of providing justification for other cognitive states and in need of it themselves; but if they are construed as

noncognitive, nonjudgmental, then while they will not themselves need justification they will also be incapable of giving it. (69)

But it is far from clear why the second horn of this dilemma is true. It is not clear why one's having a headache cannot be a source of justification for one's belief that one has a headache, in the sense that the belief's being justified supervenes upon the fact that one has a headache. Of course, the headache is not itself a belief or a doxastic state, but why should we think that only beliefs can be the source of warrant or justification? For consider such things as morally right or morally justified decisions or choices. In some cases it seems that what makes these decisions and choices right are not other decisions and choices, but rather the consequences of those decisions in terms of pleasure and pain or happiness and unhappiness. In such cases the "rightness" of the decision supervenes not upon another decision but upon its consequences. But if the source or supervenient basis of the evaluative property of being morally right need not be other decisions, it is not clear why we must think that the source or supervenient basis of the evaluative property of being warranted must be other warranted beliefs. (cf. Sosa, 7-8 and Van Cleve, 97-99)

II

In light of the sorts of responses considered above, BonJour's argument against the existence of basic beliefs is at best inconclusive. At this point, however, I wish to consider BonJour's positive account of the justification of observational and introspective beliefs. BonJour recognizes that there are several problems which confront the coherence theory in the justification of observational beliefs such as the belief that there is a red book on the desk. I shall argue that one serious problem for his account arises from his view about what is required for justified belief, a view which is presupposed by the anti-foundationalist argument considered above.

As we have seen in his argument against the thesis of epistemic priority, BonJour maintains that an empirical belief is justified for a person only if he is justified in believing other propositions from which it follows that the belief is likely to be true. The following, he suggests, is the justification for the belief that there is a red book on the desk.

(7) I have a cognitively spontaneous belief of kind K that there is a red book on the desk.

(8) Conditions C obtain.

(9) Cognitively spontaneous beliefs of kind K in conditions C are very likely to be true.

(10) Therefore, my belief that there is a red book on the desk is very likely to be true.

(11) Therefore, (probably) there is a red book on the desk.

BonJour says, "if my belief is to be justified by appeal to this argument, the premises of the argument must themselves be justified; and if the resulting account is to be genuinely coherentist, these further justifications must make no appeal to basic beliefs." (118) The problem upon which I wish to focus concerns the justification of the first premise, specifically how, in virtue of what, is it justified? Such beliefs are the product of introspection and we may wonder along with BonJour how we are to understand introspective knowledge of justification within the coherence theory.

One simple view, of course, would be that introspective beliefs are justified in virtue of belonging to a coherent body of beliefs. This sort of view seems to be compatible with the account suggested by Firth, an account which we shall consider below. But we must note that BonJour requires something stronger for the justification of belief than mere membership in a coherent body of beliefs. He holds that a belief is justified only if the subject believes with justification premises from which it follows that the belief in question is likely to be true. This is a stronger requirement because it seems possible for one's introspective belief to be a member of a coherent body of beliefs even if one is not justified in believing premises from which it follows that the belief is likely to be true.

This view of what justification requires naturally suggests that (7) is justified in virtue of the following sort of argument:

> (12) I have a spontaneous introspective belief that I have a spontaneous visual belief that there is a red book on the desk.
> (13) Introspective beliefs (of certain sorts) are very likely to be true.
> (14) The conditions specified in (13) obtain.
> (15) Therefore, my belief that I have a spontaneous belief that there is a red book on the desk is likely to be true.

But it seems that we are justified in believing the first premise of *this* argument, (12), only if we are justified in believing yet a further introspective belief about our introspective belief about our visual belief. This approach apparently involves us in the implausible view that the justification of our introspective beliefs depends upon our having an infinite number of very complex introspective beliefs. BonJour recognizes the failure of this approach to the justification of introspective belief and rejects this sort of solution as implausible.

But if the preceding solution is implausible, then how does BonJour think that (7) is justified? His approach to this problem is puzzling and I shall explain why I think it is unsatisfactory. BonJour holds that the justification of (7) involves an appeal to what he calls "the Doxastic Presumption", but it is not clear what this presumption is or how it justifies belief. We are told, "the Doxastic Presumption is only that my representation of my overall system of beliefs is approximately correct."(104) Now, one might think that the Doxastic Presumption functions as a premise in a justificatory argument for (7), but BonJour denies that the presumption works in this way. And clearly it cannot work in this way, for the proposition that my representation of my beliefs is approximately correct does not entail (7). If the Doxastic Presumption were to function as a premise in such an argument, then as BonJour observes, "I would need further premises to the effect that I do in fact believe myself to have such and such specific beliefs, and the justification of these further premises would obviously be as problematic as before."(104)

But if the Doxastic Presumption does not justify (7) by functioning as a premise in an argument, then how does it do its justificatory work? Let us consider instead of (7), (7') I believe that there is a red book on the desk. BonJour suggests that if someone questions whether I am justified in believing that there is a red book on the desk he must be presupposing or taking it for granted that I *do* believe that there is a red book on the desk. He suggests that the existence of this belief is presupposed by raising the question of justification in the first place. He writes:

> the essential starting point for epistemological investigation is the *presumption* that the believer has a certain specific belief, the issue being whether or not the belief thus presumed to exist is justified, but the very existence of the belief being taken for granted in the context of the epistemological inquiry. And the further suggestion is that this presumption - that the believer in question does indeed accept the belief in question - though clearly empirical in content, is for these reasons available as a premise, or at least can function as a premise, in this context without itself requiring justification.(81)

And he later says, "it is plausible to hold that the existence of the justificandum belief is presupposed, in something like the Strawsonian sense, by the very raising of the issue of justification, so that it does not need to be even included as a premise."(128)

I am not quite sure what to make of BonJour's remarks. It is suggested in these latter remarks that (7') need not function as a premise in an argument for (11). But it is not clear that BonJour really believes this, for he says that "a justificatory argument for positive observational knowledge involves in effect three distinct subpremises: first, that I have the belief whose justification is at issue; second, that it is a belief of a specified kind; and third, that it is cognitively spontaneous."(128) These remarks suggest that (7') is a premise, at least a "sub-premise", in the argument for (11). Indeed, these remarks suggest that (7) can be construed as a conjunction of propositions of which (7') is one of the conjuncts. If so, then it seems that we ought to think of (7') as a premise in the argument. In any case, however, it seems clear that I am justified in believing (7) only if I am justified in believing (7'). It seems clear that I am justified in believing that I have a cognitively spontaneous belief of kind K that there is a red book on the desk only if I am justified in believing that I believe that there is a red book on the desk. Thus, it seems that if I am justified in believing (11) on the basis of an argument of the sort BonJour suggests, my justification for believing (11) depends upon my being justified in believing (7').

But if I must be justified in believing (7') in order to be justified in believing (11), then we may wonder how (7') is justified. It will not do simply to say that one is presupposing the truth of (7') by raising the question of justification. For the fact that I am presupposing that I do believe that there is a red book on the desk when I raise the issue of justification does not clearly obviate the need that this presupposition be justified. Presuppostions, after all, can be warranted or unwarranted. Granting, then, that I am presupposing (7'), if (11) is to be justified *via* an argument from (7), then this presupposition must be justified. But if it must be justified, then it is not clear how the Doxastic Presumption justifies it or how BonJour thinks it is justified. Surely we need more clarification from BonJour on this point.

Yet however BonJour describes the justification of (7'), and ultimately (11), it appears that his view faces the following sort of problem. In his argument against basic beliefs and the thesis of epistemic priority, BonJour claims that the only way for any belief to be justified for a person is for that person to believe with justification the premises of an argument from which it follows that the belief is likely to be true. But if we take this requirement seriously, then it seems that we will face a vicious regress of the sort that BonJour wants to avoid. For, following BonJour, such an argument would have the following form:

> (16) I have an introspective belief that I believe that there is a red book on the desk.
>
> (17) Introspective beliefs (of certain sorts) are very likely to be true.
>
> (18) The conditions specified in (17) obtain.
>
> (19) Therefore, my introspective belief that I believe that there is a red book on the desk is likely to be true.

But if the first premise of this argument is something that we believe with justification, then it seems we must also believe with justification the premises of an another argument for (16) and so on and so on. This regress can be avoided if one abandons the view that an emprical belief is justified for a person only if he is justified in believing premises from which it follows that it is likely to be true. But to abandon this view to give up one of the key premises in BonJour's argument against basic beliefs and the thesis of epistemic priority. It seems to me, therefore, that either BonJour must abandon his argument against the thesis of epistemic priority or accept a view of justification which leads him to a highly implausible account of the warrant of introspective and observational beliefs.

To avoid this problem it will not do merely to suggest that (7) or (7') are justified by an appeal to the Doxastic Presumption. For an appeal to the Doxastic Presumption either (i) involves an appeal to premises which one is justified in believing and which imply that (7) or (7') are very likely to be true or (ii) such an appeal is not involved. If an appeal to the Doxastic Presumption involves (i), then one confronts the regress. If, on the other hand, the Doxastic Presumption involves no such appeal, then it is not necessary for justified belief in (7) or (7') that one be justified in believing premises from which it follows that they are likely to be true. But, again, this is to admit that one of the premises in the argument against basic beliefs is false. This latter option seems to be more promising, in part because the sorts of responses considered in the first section have already thrown doubt on the strength of the argument. Yet if one does take this option the problem of clarifying the nature and justificatory role of the Doxastic Presumption remains. In particular, one may wonder whether a belief which is justified by the Presumption is justified, as Lewis says, "because and only because, it is related by various principles of inference to certain other statements." If the answer is no, then such a theory would seem as committed to the thesis of epistemic priority as any traditional foundationalist account.

III

At this point, I wish to consider briefly Firth's attempt to describe a coherence theory which can meet the often-made objection to coherence theories that they do not allow justification to be "tied down to the world." What precisely is meant by this objection? Firth tells us that Lewis held "that the coherence theory provides no way of distinguishing the actual world from other 'possible worlds', since statements describing any of these worlds will form equally coherent systems."(555) On the understanding of the coherence theory with which Lewis was working one might be as well justified in believing that he is reading this essay as he would be in believing some consistent fairy story. Surely, Lewis would say, this notion of justification cannot be correct if it leads to this consequence.

Perhaps the objection can be more fully understood if we consider an example provided by Sosa. Consider a man who has a splitting headache and whose belief that he has a headache coheres with the rest of his beliefs. Let us assume that this poor fellow's belief is justified for him. But now suppose that this man's belief is altered so that he does *not* believe that he has a headache and let his other beliefs be altered where necessary to cohere with this belief. Thus, he now believes that he has no pain, that he has not recently desired aspirin, etc. In this case, the belief that he has no headache would not be, I think, a justified belief. The problem is that the basis upon which justification supervenes has been too narrowly construed by the coherence theory. Perhaps this point can be made clear if we consider two men in "mirror" worlds who have all the same experiences. In our example let one man be suffering a painful headache and believe that he has a headache and let this belief cohere with all his other beliefs. Imagine, however, that our man in the other world suffers from a headache which is equally painful and let him have almost the same body of beliefs, a body of beliefs which differs only in that he believes that he has no headache, is not in pain, has not recently desired aspirin, etc. Are we to conclude that each man is equally justified in his belief about his headache? I do not think so.

I think one might hold that the first man is justified and the second is not or that the each man is justified to some degree, but not equally justified. But if we hold merely that the first man is *more* justified in his belief about his headache, then it would seem that he is more justified in virtue of something other than the coherence of his beliefs, and one plausible candidate for the source of this greater justification is the fact that he does have a headache. If this is right, then perhaps we can see somewhat more clearly what is involved in the charge that the coherence theory cuts justification off from the world. If the coherence theory holds that our two men are equally justified, then justification is cut off from the world insofar as the theory recognizes no basis or source of justification beyond the circle of one's beliefs. It recognizes no basis or source of justification in such things as one's having a headache or one's being in pain.

Firth recognizes that there is a problem of the sort raised by Lewis, a problem of tying justification to the world, but Firth suggests that this is a problem only for a naive coherence theory. According to Firth, the coherence theory faces this problem only if coherence is taken to be no more than mere consistency. But Firth observes that a coherent system is more than a consistent set of propositions and if a basic set of warrant-conferring beliefs can be identified, then the coherence theory can overcome the problem of separartion from the world. This set of basic statements need not include all warranted statements and it might include many statements which are not warranted. Yet if this set of basic statements can be identified by something other than mere coherence, one could "tie the entire set of warranted statements to the world in which we actually live."(555) If this approach were to succeed Firth believes it would allow us to accept the coherence theory and yet also to agree that no inferential relationship *by itself* can ever be sufficient to establish the warrant of any statement.

Firth's proposal, it is hoped, can avoid the sort of objection to the coherence theory raised by Lewis and Sosa, but the solution is not entirely clear. It is not clear, for example, that one can accept both the coherence theory *and* the claim that no inferential relationship by itself can ever be sufficient to establish the warrant of a statement. The two claims seem incompatible. But let us consider the proposal more closely. Suppose that we call the basic set of statements "B". Firth says that B may contain statements which are warranted as well as statements which are not warranted. Statements outside of B are derivatively warranted in virtue of the fact that they cohere with the members of B. But, we may ask, how are the members of B warranted? If some of the members of B are warranted, then are they warranted in virtue of their coherence with other members of B or are they warranted in virtue of something other than coherence? If they are warranted by something other than coherence, then this is not compatible with the claim that ultimately all warranted statements are warranted in virtue of coherence. For if they are warranted even to some degree by something other than coherence, then it is false that every warranted statement is warranted ultimately by coherence.

On the other hand, if the members of B are warranted simply in virtue of their coherence with one another, then it is not clear that Lewis's problem has been avoided. For it seems that there might be many consistent sets which could comprise the members of B. And, of course, depending on the set which is taken as basic, the beliefs outside of B which are taken as justified will vary with the basic set involved. At this point our friends with the headaches again enter the picture. Suppose that as before each has a headache, but one man has basic set B and the other has basic set B'. Are they equally justified if the first man believes he has a headache and the other does not ? Again, I do not think so. I do not see how the introduction of the notion of a basic set has gotten us any farther in tying our beliefs to the world. Perhaps the problem with Firth's proposal becomes clearer if we imagine a slightly different example. Suppose that our two men in mirror worlds share precisely the same body of beliefs and almost identical experiences. Imagine now that each man believes that he has a splitting headache, desires aspirin, etc., but only one of them has the headache. If we think merely that the man with the headache is more justified in believing that he has a headache than the man without the headache, then his greater justification must depend upon something other than the coherence of his beliefs, for his body of beliefs is as coherent as the other man's. Since each man has the same body of beliefs, it seems that each would share the same set of basic beliefs. If so, it is not clear how the introduction of a basic set of beliefs brings us any closer to meeting the objection.

Now, one might urge that there is a class of beliefs, including beliefs about appearances and about such things as headaches, which are justified if they are "cognitively spontaneous" and there is no "defeater" of such beliefs of which one is aware. Furthermore, one might urge that if each man has the cognitively spontaneous belief that he has a headache and if this belief coheres with all of his other beliefs, then there is no defeater for his belief that he has a headache, and thus his belief that he has a headache is justified. Yet this view assumes that the fact that the man has no headache is *not* a defeater for his belief. It assumes that the fact that the man has no headache is not a reason for him to believe that he has no headache. But it is not clear that this assumption is true.

It is not clear that the only things which can defeat the justification for such beliefs are one's other beliefs. Suppose that a man has a cognitively spontaneous belief at one moment that he has a headache and assume that this belief coheres with his other beliefs. But let us also suppose that a few minutes later he has no headache. At this latter time it seems that it would not be reasonable for him to continue to believe that he has a headache and that he ought to give up his belief that he has a headache. Of course, his believing that he has a headache at this latter time might be as coherent with his other beliefs as it was when it was first formed, but the fact that he now has no headache seems to be a reason for him to believe that he has none and thus a reason for him to modify his body of beliefs. To persist in believing that he has a headache would be unreasonable. If this is correct, then it would also appear that if at the time the cognitively spontaneous belief was first formed, the subject had no headache, then the belief that he had a headache was not justified at that time. For if the fact that he had no headache at the latter time was a reason for him not believe that he had a headache, then surely the fact that he had no headache when the belief was formed was just as good a reason for him not to believe at that time that he had a headache.

Still, the proponent of the coherence theory might insist that in the example of mirror worlds each man's belief about his headache is justified to the same degree, and thus there is no need to appeal to anything beyond coherence as a source of justification. It is, I think, hard to see what further arguments one might advance to reconcile the conflicting judgments about this case. But in considering the sorts of examples mentioned thus far we can imagine a succession of gradually varying cases in which the beliefs of our two men remain the same, while the non-doxastic states, such as the desires and sensations, of one of them changes from case to case. We might imagine that the first man in addition to having a headache, desires aspirin, is hungry, and seems to see something blue. And we may suppose that he *believes* that he desires aspirin, is hungry, and seems to see something blue.

But now suppose that our man has all the same beliefs, but in this example he lacks both the headache and the desire for aspirin. In the next example, he has the same beliefs as before but lacks the headache, the desire for aspirin, and the property of seeming to see something blue. As we go through the series of such cases one might urge that each man's beliefs are equally justified whatever non-doxastic states they have, but one can also, I believe, feel that justification has been cut off from the world and is gradually drifting away. I do not know how to reconcile different judgments about such cases. But perhaps we can agree, at least, that if one does find that the two men are not equally justified in their beliefs, Firth's proposal brings us no closer in tying justification to the world. And if one does think the two men are not equally justified, there is no way to account for the difference in their justification in terms of the coherence of their beliefs alone.

REFERENCES

BonJour, Laurence. *The Structure of Empirical Knowledge*. Cambridge, Mass.: The Harvard University Press, 1985.

Firth, Roderick. "Coherence, Certainty, and Epistemic Priority." *The Journal of Philosophy* LXI (1964), 545-557.

Sosa, Ernest. "The Raft and the Pyramid: Coherence versus Foundations in the Theory of Knowledge," in *Midwest Studies in Philosophy* V, Peter French, Theodore Uehling Jr., and Howard Wettstein., eds.. Minneapolis: The University of Minnesota Press, 1980, 3 - 25.

Van Cleve, James. "Epistemic Supervenience and The Circle of Belief." *The Monist* 68 (1985), 90-104.

BonJour's Anti-Foundationalist Argument

Matthias Steup
The University of Wyoming

Philosophers who reject foundationalism affirm either that there is not, or that there cannot be, a foundation of knowledge. A typical argument in support of the former claim runs as follows. For there to be a foundation of knowledge, there would have to be a sufficient number of beliefs that enjoy an evidential privilege such as infallibility, indubitability, or incorrigibility. For only by virtue of possessing such an evidential privilege could a belief be an instance of *direct* knowledge and then serve as a foundation for*indirect* knowledge. However, as a matter of psychological fact, far too few beliefs meet this condition for there to be a sufficient number of foundational beliefs. Hence indirect knowledge does not rest on any foundation.[1]

There are two ways of replying to this argument. First, one might weaken the ;evidential privilege a belief must enjoy for it to be an instance of direct knowledge. Secondly, one might simply deny that a belief can be an instance of foundational knowledge only if it enjoys an evidential privilege. A version of the argument that there cannot be a foundation of knowledge has been set forth by Laurence BonJour in his book, *The Structure of Empirical Knowledge*. According to BonJour, it is possible for a belief to be justified without owing its justification at least in part to other beliefs. Hence there cannot be a foundation of knowledge. In this paper, I shall examine BonJour's argument. I shall argue that it rests on a number of questionable presuppositions and therefore fails to succeed.

1. Minimal Foundationalism

Before I begin to examine BonJour's argument, I shall try to identify what is minimally required for a theory of justification to be foundationalist. Foundationalism is the view that any *nonbasic* belief - any belief which has its justification conferred on it by one or more other beliefs - ultimately depends for its justification on one or more *basic* beliefs - beliefs which are justified without having their justification conferred on them by other beliefs. This view involves two claims: first, that a person's total set of beliefs contains, at any given time, a subset comprised of basic beliefs; secondly, that justification has, at least in part, a vertical structure: it is, ultimately, transmitted from basic beliefs, the foundation, upward to nonbasic beliefs, the superstructure. Foundationalism, then, is the view that justified beliefs belonging to the superstructure ultimately receive their justification from beliefs belonging to the foundation.

Stronger and weaker versions of foundationalism result, first, from different accounts of exactly how justification is transmitted from the foundation to the superstructure. They result, secondly, from different accounts of what conditions a belief must meet for it to be basic. Since the failure of phenomenalism has made it clear that perceptual data don't allow us to deduce knowledge of the physical world, no one defends any longer a version of foundationalism according to which the evidential link between the foundation and the superstructure is deductive. Rather, it is now assumed that the transmission of justification from the foundation to the superstructure is nonconclusive, or defeasible. In other words, it is now assumed that beliefs belonging to the foundation provide *prima facie* evidence for beliefs belonging to the superstructure.[2]

Furthermore, foundationalism has been weakened in a second respect. Typically, it has been thought that, for a belief to be basic, it must enjoy an evidential privilege such as infallibility, indubitability, incorrigibility, or self-justification. However, an analysis of the

J.W. Bender (ed.), The Current State of the Coherence Theory, 188–199.
© *1989 by Kluwer Academic Publishers.*

function foundationalism assigns to basic beliefs reveals that a belief can be basic without enjoying an evidential privilege. The function a basic belief is supposed to fulfill is that of terminating a regress of reasons. If a first belief has its justification conferred on it by a second belief, the first belief will be justified only if the second belief is justified as well. But unless the second belief is basic, its justification will be conferred on it by a third belief. Clearly, unless the regress of justifying beliefs terminates in a basic belief it will continue *ad infinitum*.

What is necessary for the termination of a chain of justifying beliefs? What is necessary is precisely this: the regress must eventually arrive at a belief that is justified without having its justification conferred on it by another belief. It is not necessary that there not be anything that confers justification on the terminating belief. As long as whatever justifies the last link in a chain of reasons is something *other than* a belief, the regress is terminated.

Let us call a belief that is justified by something which is not another belief *nondoxastically* justified. We may now say that a belief can function as a regress terminator only if it is nondoxastically justified. Can a belief function as a regress terminator without possessing an evidential privilege? The answer to this question depends on whether a belief can be nondoxastically justified without possessing an evidential privilege. Let us, then, focus on the concept of non-doxastic justification.

A belief that is justified by something else than another belief is justified by a *nondoxastic psychological state*. Here are two examples. My perceptual belief that the color of the pen on my desk is red is justified by my perceptual state of being appeared to redly by the pen. My belief that I had quail for yesterday's dinner is (at least in part) justified by my psychological state of clearly remembering that I had quail for dinner yesterday. The two psychological states, 'being appeared to redly by the pen' and 'clearly remembering that I had quail for dinner,' are nondoxastic because they simply aren't states of believing. Being appeared to redly by the pen is different from both believing that the pen is red and believing oneself to be appeared to by the pen. For it is possible for me to be appeared to redly by the pen without believing anything about the pen. Likewise, believing that I had quail for dinner is different from the psychological state of clearly remembering that I had quail for dinner. It is possible for me to be in this state without believing what I clearly remember, and without believing that I clearly remember what I clearly remember.

For a psychological state to justify a belief, there must be the right kind of evidential connection between the two. The evidence arising from the psychological state must be undefeated. For example, if it is evident to me that red light is shining on my desk and I believe nevertheless that the pen on my desk is red, then (provided I don't have any independent reasons for taking the pen to be red), my perceptual state of being appeared to redly does not justify my belief that the pen is red.

Let us now consider again the question of whether a belief can be nondoxastically justified without enjoying an evidential privilege. A belief is *nondoxastically* justified if, and only if, it bears an appropriate evidential relation to a nondoxastic psychological state, just as a belief is *doxastically* justified if and only if it bears an appropriate evidential relation to one or more other beliefs. Nothing in the concept of nondoxastic justification requires that, for a belief to be justified by something which is not another belief, it must be infallible, indubitable, or incorrigible. This is, of course, not an argument establishing the possibility of nondoxastic justification. However, if a critic of foundationalism were to argue that, for a belief to be nondoxastically justified, it must enjoy an evidential privilege, the burden of proof would clearly be his.

I conclude: (i) the function assigned to basic beliefs is that of regress termination; (ii) for a belief to terminate a regress of reasons, it must be nondoxastically justified; (iii) a belief can be nondoxastically justified without enjoying an evidential privilege.

2. Foundationalism and the Paradox of Self-Justification

BonJour apparently thinks that foundationalism is committed to the claim that basic beliefs are self-justified. He says:

> ...the very idea of an epistemically basic empirical belief is more than a little paradoxical. On what basis is such a belief supposed to be justified, once any appeal to further empirical premises is ruled out? Chisholm's theological analogy ...is most appropriate: a basic belief is in effect an epistemological unmoved (or self-moved) mover. It is able to confer justification on other beliefs, but, in spite of being empirical and thus contingent, apparently has no need to have justification conferred on it. But is such a status any easier to understand in epistemology than it is in theology? (30)

However, as I argued in the first section, foundationalism need not affirm that a basic belief "is able to confer justification on other beliefs...but has no need to have justification conferred on it." Basic beliefs do have the need to have justification conferred on them. They do not, however, receive their justification from other beliefs but rather from nondoxastic psychological states.

At this point, BonJour might say two things in reply. First, he might argue that nondoxastic justification is impossible. Indeed, his anti-foundationalist argument, if successful, would establish this point. Second, BonJour might argue that nondoxastic foundationalism is a version of *externalism*, which is, from BonJour's *internalistic* point of view, unacceptable. However, endorsing the concept of nondoxastic justification is not at all endorsing externalism. After all, nondoxastic psychological states are not, by any means, external to a person's cognitive perspective. Rather, they are *cognitively transparent*. One can, just by directing one's attention to one's perceptual experiences, see what they are like and consider which beliefs would be justified by them. The disagreement between the coherentist and the nondoxastic foundationalist just isn't a disagreement between the internalist and the externalist. It is a disagreement within the internalist camp.

3. BonJour's Argument

BonJour's anti-foundationalist argument is supposed to prove that it is impossible for empirical beliefs to be nondoxastically justified. If it were sound, it would show that even minimal foundationalism is untenable. In what follows, I shall, step by step, examine his argument.

BonJour begins his refutation of foundationalism by considering what would have to be the case for an epistemologist to be justified in accepting an account of the standards of justification. He says:

> I argued...that the fundamental role which the requirement of epistemic justification serves in the overall rationale of the concept of knowledge is that of a means to truth; and accordingly that a basic constraint on any *account of the standards of justification* for empirical knowledge is that there be good reasons for thinking that following those standards is at least likely to lead to truth. (30, Italics added.)

But surely, we ought to distinguish between (i) a constraint on the justification of empirical beliefs and (ii) a constraint on an account of the standards of the justification of empirical beliefs. In the passage just quoted, BonJour is concerned with (ii). I take it that he wants to assert the following. An epistemologist has good reasons to accept a theory of empirical justification, T, only if he has good reasons to think that a belief that is justified according to a standard endorsed by T is likely to be true. This might very well be true. It remains to be seen, however, whether anything follows from it as far as basic beliefs are concerned.

Next, BonJour considers the conditions that must be satisfied for an epistemologist to be justified in accepting a foundationalist account of empirical justification. According to foundationalism, some empirical beliefs are basic and, by virtue of their being basic, justified. Thus, for an epistemologist to have good reasons to accept foundationalism, he must have good reasons for believing that basic beliefs are likely to be true. BonJour says:

> ... if basic beliefs are to provide a secure foundation for empirical knowledge, ... then that feature, whatever it may be, by virtue of which a particular belief qualifies as basic must also constitute a good reason for thinking that the belief is true. If this were not so, ... foundationalism would be unacceptable as an account of epistemic justification. If we let f represent the feature or characteristic, whatever it may be, which distinguishes basic empirical beliefs from other empirical beliefs, then in an *acceptable foundationalist account a particular empirical belief B could qualify as basic* only if the premises of the following justificatory argument were adequately justified.
>
> (1) B has feature f.
> (2) Beliefs having feature f are highly likely to be true.
> Therefore, B is highly likely to be true.
>
> If B is actually to be basic, then presumably premise (1) would have to be true as well, but I am concerned here only with what would have to be so for it to *be reasonable to accept B as basic* and use it to justify other beliefs.[3] (Italics added.)

BonJour's reasoning has reached a high level of complexity here. It will be helpful to consider a step-by-step reconstruction of it.

> (I) An epistemologist is justified in accepting a standard of justification only if he has good reasons to believe that beliefs that qualify as justified according to this standard are highly likely to be true.
> (II) According to foundationalism, if a belief meets the standard of being basic, it is justified. Thus:
> (III) An epistemologist is justified in accepting foundationalism only if he has good reasons for believing that basic beliefs are highly likely to be true. Hence:
> (IV) An epistemologist is justified *in accepting a particular belief B as basic* only if he has good reasons to believe that B is highly likely to be true - which he does only if he has good reasons to believe that (i) B has feature f, and (ii) beliefs having feature f are highly likely to be true.

So far so good. Let us momentarily grant everything BonJour subscribes to in the above line of reasoning. What, however, is the conclusion that can be drawn from it? It is the following. For an epistemologist to be justified *in accepting a particular belief B as basic,* he must be justified in believing two other things, namely (i) and (ii) of step (IV). Hence, an epistemological belief such as 'B is basic' cannot be basic.

A foundationalist, though, will not be dismayed by this result. He will simply reply that the two propositions, (A) There are basic beliefs, and (B) Beliefs of the form 'Belief B is basic' are not basic are compatible.

Let us suppose that BonJour is right in arguing that a belief of the form 'B is basic' cannot be basic. This would show that there are no basic beliefs only if the following principle were true.

> For a person A to have a basic belief B, it must be the case that A has a justified
> belief to the effect that B is basic.

If this principle were true, it would follow that only epistemologists are eligible candidates for having basic beliefs. I don't think that this is what BonJour wants to establish. Rather, I believe his argument involves a confusion of (i) being justified in having a particular basic belief B and (ii) being justified in accepting a particular belief B as basic. As a result, at certain places in his argument, BonJour is concerned with (ii) when he actually ought to be concerned with (i). The argument he ought to give differs from the one he actually gives. The first sentence of the passage I shall now quote shows that BonJour wants to establish a conclusion with regard to (i), not with regard to (ii). And clearly, this is how it ought to be, for if he wants to show that there cannot be any basic beliefs, he must show that the constraints on *being justified in having a particular empirical belief* are such that there can't be any basic beliefs. BonJour says:

> The other issue to be considered is whether, in order *for B to be justified* for a
> particular person A (at a particular time), it is necessary, not merely that a
> justification along the above lines exist in the abstract, but also that A himself be
> in cognitive possession of that justification, that is, that he believe the
> appropriate premises of forms (1) and (2) and that these beliefs be justified for
> him. (31). (Italics added.)

Here, BonJour isn't concerned with what is required for an epistemologist to be justified in accepting a particular belief B as basic, but rather with what is required for a particular belief B to be justified for a particular person A. With regard to this point, the conditions that must be satisfied for an epistemologist to be justified in accepting foundationalism are irrelevant. What is relevant are the conditions that must be satisfied for any person, epistemologist or not, to be justified in having an empirical belief. So the crucial part of BonJour's argument reduces to the following modification of step (IV).

(IV*) A particular empirical belief B is justified for a person A only if A is justified in believing that (i) B has feature f; and (ii) beliefs having feature f are highly likely to be true.

(IV*) is not supported by premises (I) through (III), which are about what justifies an epistemological theory, not about what justifies an ordinary empirical belief. While (IV) specifies a constraint on the kind of justification an epistemologist needs to be justified in accepting a belief B as basic, (IV*) specifies a constraint on empirical justification simpliciter. And from this constraint it follows immediately that there cannot be any basic empirical beliefs, for, if (IV*) is true, then any empirical belief whatever depends for its justification on at least two other beliefs. Of these, at least one would be empirical, namely (i). Consequently, BonJour says:

> But if all this is correct, we get the disturbing result that B is not basic is not
> basic after all, since its justification depends on that of at least one other
> empirical belief. It would follow that foundationalism is untenable as a solution
> to the regress problem. (32f.)

However, the soundness of BonJour's argument depends on whether there are good reasons to accept step (IV*).

4. The Requirement of Metajustification

Principle (IV*) is not self-evident. BonJour needs to give a sound argument in support of it. Alas, he does not do so. But my main complaint about (IV*) is not that it is hard to see what could be said on behalf of it. Rather, as I shall argue, (IV*) ought to be rejected because the standard of empirical justification specified by it is too strong.[4] According to BonJour, an empirical belief B is justified for a person A only if A holds two further beliefs, namely: (i) B has feature f, and (ii) beliefs having feature f are highly likely to be true.

(i) and (ii) logically imply that B is likely to be true. This means that forming the beliefs (i) and (ii) amounts, in effect, to an evaluation of B's evidential status.[5] Obviously, BonJour holds that an epistemic evaluation of B is a necessary element of B's justification. In other words, BonJour holds that *metajustification*, or higher level justification, is a necessary condition of first level justification. He advocates what I shall call the *requirement of metajustification*.[6]

The requirement of metajustification, however, poses a serious problem. According to BonJour, a particular empirical belief B is justified for a person A only if A forms a belief B* about B, namely that B has feature f. However, B*, being an empirical belief itself, is in turn subject to the requirement of metajustification. It follows that B* is justified for A only if A forms a belief B** to the effect that B* has a feature f by virtue of which it is likely to be true. And, since B** will be an empirical belief again, A must as well form a belief B*** about B**, and so forth.

In this way, the requirement of metajustification generates an infinite regress of doxastic and epistemic levels. It makes doxastic as well as epistemic level ascent a necessary condition of empirical justification. First, for a particular belief B to be justified for a person A, A must form beliefs to the effect that B is likely to be true, which generates an epistemic level ascent. Second, A must form beliefs to the effect that B is liekly to be true, which generates an epistemic level ascent.

Unless the regress of metajustification can be terminated at a very early stage, the requirement of metajustification makes empirical justification, and thus empirical knowledge, impossible. First of all, having an infinite number of beliefs is, at least for human beings, psychologically impossible. Second, an infinite chain of doxastic and epistemic metabeliefs quickly reaches a level of complexity which goes beyond the powers of the human mind.[7] Third, if the ascent to higher and higher justificatory levels never comes to an end, the belief that is located at the first level will ultimately remain unjustified.

Endorsing the requirement of metajustification is tantamount to generating a level regress that cannot be terminated. For the justification of each justificatory metabelief B* would involve attributing a feature f to B*, which, being an empirical matter, would in turn have to be justified by a further metabelief B**. It might be objected that the regress does not get started because justificatory metabeliefs themselves do not need higher level justification. But this would amount to an arbitrary exemption from the requirement of metajustification, inviting the reply that, if the coherentist may exempt justificatory metabeliefs, then the foundationalist may exempt basic beliefs.

BonJour's main anti-foundationalist argument thus turns out to be less formidable than it might appear at first sight. It owes its initial plausibility to the requirement of metajustification, which, if accepted, makes the rejection of foundationalism an easy feat. However, as the requirement of metajustification makes skepticism inevitable, it would be a feat BonJour should find difficult to enjoy.

5. BonJour's Internalistic Externalism

Let us again consider BonJour's constraint on empirical justification.

> (IV*)A particular empirical belief B is justified for a person A only if A is justified in believing that (i) B has feature f and (ii) beliefs having feature f are highly likely to be true.

I assume BonJour wants the phrase 'highly likely to be true' to be understood in the *statistical* sense of probability, as opposed to the epistemic sense of probability.[8] Indeed, if we were to understand 'likely to be true' in the epistemic sense of probability, (IV*) would affirm no more than that metajustification is necessary for first level justification. I take it, however, that BonJour's principle is supposed to be a substantive principle telling us exactly what a subject has to do in order to provide the metajustification that is necessary for first level justification. If so, we must take 'likely to be true' to denote the statistical sense of probability. On this understanding, a belief that has feature f is an instance of a belief type most tokens of which are true. This interpretation of (IV*) is confirmed by the following passage.

> And, if our standards of epistemic justification are appropriately chosen, bringing it about that our beliefs are epistemically justified will also tend to bring it about ... that they are true. If epistemic justification were not conducive to truth in this way, if finding epistemically justified beliefs did not substantially increase the likelihood of finding true ones, then epistemic justification would be irrelevant to our main cognitive goal and of dubious worth. (8).

BonJour argues in effect that a belief is justified only if it is an instance of a kind such that most beliefs of this kind are true. This is quite revealing as far as BonJour's internalistic point of view is concerned. Before I go on to examine the problem that arises for BonJour's principle from its appeal to statistical probability, I shall briefly discuss how BonJour's claim - truth conduciveness is a necessary condition of epistemic justification - relates to the internalism-externalism issue.[9]

Suppose all and only beliefs that have feature f are likely to be true. *Pure externalism* is the view that, if A's belief b has feature f, it is justified for A no matter whether or not A has, among the things that are cognitively accessible to A, a reason for B. A hybrid form of externalism, weaker than the pure one, is an *internalistic externalism* (or an externalistic internalism, for that matter): the view that B is justified for A only if (i) A has a (sufficiently strong and undefeated) reason for B and (ii) B in fact has feature f. *Pure internalism* is the view that a belief's being justified does not in any relevant sense depend on its having feature f. Rather, if a person A has a (sufficiently strong and undefeated) reason for B, then B is justified, no matter whether or not B is in fact likely to be true.

Though BonJour is a proponent of internalism and one of the chief critics of reliabilism, the passage quoted above suggests that BonJour is not a pure internalist but actually holds a view which incorporates a good deal of externalism. BonJour's internalism clearly manifests itself in (IV*), according to which, for an empirical belief B to be justified for A, it is a necessary condition that A have a reason to believe that B has a feature f by virtue of which it is likely to be true. What makes his internalism externalistic is his view that for B to be actually justified, it must have feature f: most tokens of the belief type of which B is an instance must be true. This is an externalistic condition because whether or not it is met might not be cognitively accessible to the agent.

It turns out, then, that BonJour's theory involves a twofold - internalistic and externalistic - appeal to statistical probability and, therefore, is afflicted with a problem I shall discuss in the next section.

6. Internalistic Reliabilism

According to reliabilism, whether a particular belief is justified must be assessed in terms of the reliability of the cognitive process that produced it. This idea underlies a variety of theories of epistemic justification. According to a *purely externalistic* version of reliabilism, for a belief B to be justified, it is sufficient that the cognitive process that produced it is in fact reliable. The agent need not have a belief to the effect that B was reliably produced. Nor need he have any reasons for B. According to a *purely internalistic* version of reliabilism, for a belief to be justified, it is a necessary (or perhaps even sufficient) condition that the agent form a metabelief to the effect that B was produced by a reliable cognitive process.[10]

Furthermore, there are versions of reliabilism that are both internalistic and externalistic. They agree in affirming that, for a belief to be justified, it is not a sufficient but only a necessary condition that it was reliably produced, while they differ in specifying the internalistic constraint in different ways. The internalistic constraint might be that, for a belief B to be justified, it must be based on adequate grounds, where these grounds need not include a metabelief to the effect that B was reliably produced.[11] Alternatively, it might be that, for B to be justified, the agent must form a metabelief to the effect that B has a feature f such that most beliefs having this feature are true. This is the view held by BonJour.

All these theories share a common feature. Each of them is committed to the concept of the reliability of belief producing processes. As a result, each of them is afflicted with what has been called the generality problem, which is most conspicuous in the case of purely externalistic reliabilism.[12] Let P stand for a cognitive process and B for a particular belief that is produced by P and whose justification is to be assessed in terms of the reliability of P. Assume we say that B is justified just in case it is produced by a cognitive process P that is reliable. However, this won't do, for the same cognitive process is reliable under certain conditions and unreliable under other conditions. Color vision, for example, is reliable when the conditions of observation are adequate and unreliable when they are less than adequate. Thus we need to add to the analysis a reference to the specific conditions, C, under which B is formed. But how are we to specify these conditions?

Suppose *everything* is relevant for specifying C. If so, then B's truth value will be relevant. But if a correct specification of C requires that B be true, then the cognitive process P will be perfectly reliable, which means that B will then be justified just in case it is true. Now suppose not everything is relevant for the specification of C. But how are we to determine exactly what is and what is not relevant? We might as well include in C that B be formed at a certain time, a certain place, be held by an agent born on such-and-such a date, of such-and-such a weight, etc., thereby fixing C in such a way that one, and only one, belief meets the conditions specified by C. Again, we get the result that, if B is true, the process P under conditions C is perfectly reliable. In other words, we get the result that B is justified just in case it is true. The generality problem is the problem of avoiding either of these extremes. Its force is that, as long as no adequate solution is offered, purely externalistic reliabilism may justly be charged with being unable to distinguish between a belief's being true and a belief's being justified.

BonJour's principle (IV*) states only a necessary condition of empirical justification. Therefore, it does not have the result that all true beliefs are justified. It is, however, BonJour's aim to state a complete analysis of justification. He ought to tell us, then, which other condition an empirical belief must meet for it to be justified. Alas, he does not do so, but actually seems to think that meeting conditions (i) and (ii) is sufficient for empirical justification. Indeed, as a complete justification of the belief 'There is a red book on my desk,' he offers the following argument:

> (1) I have a cognitively spontaneous belief of kind K1 that there is a red book on the desk.
>
> (2) Conditions C1 obtain.
>
> (3) Cognitively spontaneous visual beliefs of kind K1 in conditions C1 are very likely to be true.
>
> Therefore, my belief that there is a red book on the desk is very likely to be true.

Therefore, (probably) there is a red book on the desk. (118).

But how are we to specify a belief of kind K1? And how are we to specify conditions C1? If our specification of the conditions C1 requires the belief that needs justification to be true, the belief 'There is a red book on the desk' is justified just in case it is true. And if we specify kind K1 in such a way that there is one, and only one, belief of this kind, namely the belief 'There is a red book on the table,' then BonJour's argument has, again, the effect that 'There is a red book on the table' is justified just in case it is true.

BonJour might reply that justifying a belief in such a way would be unjustified, or unreasonable. But why? Does BonJour have an additional account of justification, or reasonableness, that does not appeal to statistical probability? If he does, it is unclear why the appeal to statistical probability is necessary in the first place. And if he does not, he would have to appeal again to statistical probability to justify a certain specification of K1 and C1, as opposed to other, unjustified, specifications. The problem of distinguishing between justified and unjustified specification of the relevant kinds of belief and conditions of observation would then only be shifted to a higher level.

Suppose BonJour's notion of 'very likely to be true' was intended to denote the epistemic sense of probability. Premise (3) would then affirm:

> (3*) Cognitively spontaneous visual beliefs of kind K1 in conditions C1 are reasonable (or probable, or evident).

If K1 and C1 are spelled out, (3*) turns into a material epistemic principle. If such a principle is knowable at all, it is presumably knowable directly and a priori, thereby acquiring foundational status. Although a coherentist obviously would not want to appeal to such a principle, it is questionable whether he can avoid it if he appeals to epistemic probability and makes epistemic level ascent a necessary and sufficient condition of empirical justification.

We can now draw the following conclusion. Should BonJour succeed in solving the generality problem, he can both appeal to statistical probability and stick to his conception of metajustification as a necessary and sufficient condition for first level justification. However, should a solution to the generality problem not be forthcoming, he would have to face the following two options: insistence on his conception of metajustification as both necessary and sufficient for first level justification, which would force acknowledgement of epistemic principles of foundational status, or avoidance of this by accepting the challenge of spelling out his theory in terms of coherence relations that are restricted to the first level.

7. Nondoxastic Justification

I argued that BonJour's anti-foundationalist argument fails to succeed because it rests on the unacceptable presupposition that first level justification requires metajustification. But perhaps coherentism could be defended by an argument to the effect that, whenever an empirical belief is justified, it has its justification conferred on it by other beliefs, where these other beliefs need not be metabeliefs. Such a claim could be supported directly or indirectly. It is doubtful, however, that there is a way of directly and conclusively showing that all justified empirical beliefs are justified by other beliefs. It seems more promising to proceed indirectly. It could be argued that a justified empirical belief always depends for its justification on other beliefs because nondoxastic justification is impossible.

Indeed, BonJour rejects the possibility of nondoxastic justification. He thinks that, if a belief is justified without having its justification conferred on it by other beliefs, it must be justified by virtue of what has been called the 'given'. But the 'given' cannot function as a justifier, for the following reason.

> The proponent of the given is caught in a fundamental and inescapable dilemma: if his intuitions or direct awarenesses or immediate apprehensions are construed as cognitive, or quasi-judgmental ..., then they will be both capable of providing justification for other cognitive states and in need of it themselves; but if they are construed as noncognitive, nonjudgmental, then while they will not themselves need justification, they will also be incapable of giving it. In either case, such states will be incapable of serving as an adequate foundation for knowledge. This, at bottom, is why empirical givenness is a myth. (69).

BonJour's argument, in a nutshell, affirms the following. Either a psychological state is doxastic (a judgmental or quasi-judgmental state) and then needs justification, or a psychological state is nondoxastic (nonjudgmental) and then is incapable of giving justification. If so, nondoxastic justification is impossible. But why is a nondoxastic psychological state incapable of conferring justification on a belief? Because, according to BonJour,

> it is clear on reflection that it is one and the same feature of a cognitive state, namely, its assertive or at least representational content, which both enables it to confer justification on other states and also creates the need for it to be itself justified - thus making it impossible in principle to separate these two aspects. (78).

So, either nondoxastic psychological states don't have representational content and then can't give justification, or they do have representational content and are then in need of justification themselves.

I do not think that this argument is particularly forceful. First of all, we could point to some plausible examples of nondoxastic justification and then turn the argument on its head. Suppose some beliefs are justified solely by nondoxastic psychological states. If nondoxastic psychological states have representational content, then not everything that has representational content is in need of justification. And if nondoxastic psychological states don't have representational content, then not everything that gives justification has representational content. Furthermore, we can reply that BonJour's presupposition that only what has representational content can function as a justifier is by no means self-evident. This presupposition just isn't something that is "clear on reflection."

Let us see, then, whether there are some plausible cases of nondoxastic justification. I now see a red pen on my desk. I form the belief that the pen I am looking at is red. What is it that justifies my belief? Is it justified because it is a member of a coherent set of beliefs? It would be difficult to show this because, since I have also a number of blue pens, believing that the pen is blue would as much cohere with the other things I believe as does believing that it is red. It might be objected that the belief 'This pen is blue' does not cohere with my overall belief system, for it conflicts with my belief that the pen looks red to me. But, first of all, I need not automatically have this belief. Secondly, I might believe both that the pen is blue and that it looks blue to me when in fact it is red and looks red to me, and both of these beliefs would then perfectly cohere with the other things I believe. I conclude, then, that my belief 'This pen is red' is justified not by virtue of coherence with other beliefs, but rather because I am in the perceptual state of being appeared to redly by the pen.

Generalizing, it seems to me that many attributions of simple sensible characteristics, such as 'red,' 'round,' 'square,' 'smooth,' 'sweet,' etc., as long as they are based on one's own perceptual experiences, are, or at least can be, nondoxastically justified. Furthermore, there is another class of beliefs that are prime candidates for nondoxastic justification, namely beliefs about one's own psychological states. What justifies my belief, say, that I have a headache simply is my psychological state of having a headache. What else is there that might play a justificatory role here?[13]

Let us summarize. BonJour's anti-foundationalist argument rests on a principle according to which first level justification requires metajustification. But, first, BonJour does not tell us why we ought to accept this principle.[14] Secondly, his principle makes a rather extreme form of skepticism inevitable. Third, BonJour appears to affirm that, for a belief B to be justified, it is sufficient that it is believed to be a token of a belief type most tokens of which are true. If this is indeed BonJour's view, then it is doubtful that his account of empirical justification allows us to distinguish between true beliefs and justified beliefs - unless, of course, he is prepared to supplement his coherentist theory with epistemic principles of foundational status. Finally, if BonJour were to abandon the requirement of metajustification, his anti-foundationalist argument would collapse. His advocacy of coherentism would then rest entirely on his rejection of nondoxastic justification, which relies on the premise that psychological states with representational content need, and those without can't give, justification. This premise, however, needs argumentation in support of it and should not simply be taken for granted.[15]

NOTES

1. Cf. Pollock (1986), chapter 2.
2. 30f. Notice that the last sentence in the quoted passage suggests that BonJour is concerned with the activity of justifying a belief and not with the property of a belief's being justified. Apparently, BonJour is concerned with the conditions that must be met for successfully using a basic belief to justify nonbasic beliefs. However, foundationalism need not be a theory about the activity of justifying a belief. Hence, if BonJour's argument is indeed intended to be about justification as an activity, it would not be relevant with regard to versions of foundationalism that are concerned with the property of a belief's being justified. Cf. Alston (1983).
4. Cf. Alston (1983). In this paper, Alston discusses BonJour's earlier statement of his main anti-foundationalist argument, to be found in BonJour (1978). He points out that BonJour's principle would have to be argued for. BonJour does not provide a direct argument for his principle, but from what he says about epistemic responsibility, it can be inferred that he thinks that one cannot fulfill one's epistemic obligations without meeting the conditions specified by the requirement of metajustification. Cf. BonJour (1985), 31f. Alston rejects this argument because he rejects epistemic deontologism (see Alston (1985) and (1988)), while I accept epistemic deontologism; cf. Steup (1987). However, epistemic deontologism does not involve a commitment to the requirement of metajustification. Since BonJour does not spell out in detail why he thinks that one fulfills one's epistemic obligations only if one meets the conditions specified by (IV*), there is no need to discuss this issue in this paper.
5. It might be objected that saying of a belief that it is highly likely to be true is not an epistemic evaluation of it. However, according to BonJour, an epistemic evaluation of a belief B is an evaluation of the likelihood of B's being true. BonJour (1985), 8. BonJour's account of the nature of epistemic evaluation is, though, a problematic one. See section 6 of this paper for a critical discussion of it.
6. In the remainder of this section, I give an argument that is developed further in my paper 'The Regress of Metajustification,' forthcoming in Philosophical Studies. In (1989), Alston, too, rejects the requirement of metajustification. Cf. also Pollock (1986), p. 127.
7. For a discussion of this point, see Robert Audi (1982).
8. For a discussion of various kinds of probability, see Pollock (1986), chapter 4, and BonJour (1985), 8.
9. For a discussion of the internalism-externalism issue, see William Alston (1986) and (1989), BonJour (1985), chp. 3, Chisholm (1986) and Pollock (1986), 118ff.
10. This appears to be the view defended by Sellars in (1963); see 169.
11. This, it seems to me, is the view Alston argues for in (1989).
12. For a defense of reliabilism, see Goldman (1978) and (1986). For discussions of the 'generality' problem, see Feldman (1985), Chisholm (1986), and Pollock (1986), 118ff.
13. Of course, for my reply to BonJour's rejection of the given to have full force, it would have to be

supplemented with a plausible theory of nondoxastic justification.

14. BonJour appears to think that considerations of epistemic responsibility provide support for the requirement of metajustification. Cf. footnote 4.

15. A first version of this paper was read at the 1987 NEH Summer Seminar on Reasons, Justification and Rationality, directed by Robert Audi. I wish to thank the participants in this seminar for a helpful discussion of it. For valuable criticisms and comments, I am especially indebted to Robert Audi, Jack Bender, Bruce Russell, William Tollhurst, and Arthur Walker.

REFERENCES

Audi, Robert. "Believing and Affirming." *Mind* 91 (1982), 115-20.
Alston, William. "What's Wrong with Immediate Knowlege." *Synthese* 55 (1983),73-95.
-----. "Concepts of Epistemic Justification." *Monist* 68 (1985) 57-89.
-----. "Internalism and Externalism in Epistemology." *Philosophical Topics* 14 (1986), 27-65.
-----. "The Deontological Conception of Epistemic Justification." *Philosophical Perspectives* (1988) forthcoming.
-----. "An Externalist Internalism." *Synthese*, (1989) forthcoming.
BonJour, Laurence. "Can Empirical Knowledge Have a Foundation?" *American Philosophical Quarterly* 15 (1978), 1-13.
-----. *The Structure of Empirical Knowledge.* Cambridge: Harvard University Press, 1985.
Chisholm, Roderick. *Theory of Knowledge.* Englewood Cliffs: Prentice Hall, 1977.
-----. "The Place of Epistemic Justification." *Philosophical Topics* 14 (1986), 85-92.
Goldman, Alvin. "What is Justified Belief?," in *Justification and Knowledge*, George Pappas, ed., Dordrecht: Reidel, 1979.
-----. *Epistemology and Cognition.* Cambridge: Harvard University Press, 1986.
Feldman, Richard. "Reliability and Justification." *Monist* 68 (1985), 159-74.
Pollock, John. *Contemporary Theories of Knowledge.* Totowa: Rowman & Littlefield, 1986.
Sellars, Wilfrid. "Empiricism and the Philosophy of Mind." Reprinted in *Science, Perception, and Reality.* New York: Humanitites Press; London: Routlege & Kegan Paul, 1963.
Steup, Matthias. "The Deontic Conception of Epistemic Justification." *Philosophical Studies* 53, (1988), 65-84.
-----. "The Regress of Metajustification." *Philosophical Studies*, forthcoming.

Foundations

Carolyn Black
San Jose State University

If the true is what is grounded, then
the ground is not true, nor yet false.
-Wittgenstein, On Certainty 205

In his recent book, *The Structure of Empirical Knowledge,* Laurence BonJour advocates a coherentist view of knowledge and justification, arguing that there is a fatal problem with the purportedly basic beliefs of the foundationalist.[1] Barring skepticism, BonJour contends, coherentism is the only even potentially adequate account of empirical knowledge. Keith Lehrer, a long-time committed coherentist, also finds the basic beliefs of the foundationalist wanting: "The problem with the foundation theory is that it does not provide us with any explanation of why we should accept the postulates, when, in fact, it is perfectly clear why we accept those postulates. The reason is that we think that the beliefs in question are very probably true..."[2]

In the present paper I should like to argue that the case for foundations is not as bad as BonJour and Lehrer make it out to be. There is a way to construe the basic elements of a foundationalism as perfectly acceptable for reasons other than their truth and yet as not in need of outside justification. My point of departure is a certain picture of empirical justification, in particular of basic elements, in the later philosophy of Wittgenstein. I shall then modify this view so as to show, I hope, how one might initiate a sound foundationalism. Coherentists often embrace their view not because of its intrinsic merit but because they perceive serious problems with foundationalism and because they wish to avoid skepticism. Given the following picture of foundations, coherentists might find one fewer reason to adopt their view.

1. Purported Problems

Let us examine BonJour's account of the central difficulties of foundationalist basic elements which is relatively recent, clear and detailed. He claims that "the most fundamental and far-reaching objection to foundationalism...[is that] there is no way for an empirical belief to have *any* degree of warrant which does not depend on the justification of other empirical beliefs..." (SEK 29). The basic empirical beliefs to which foundationalists appeal to justify non-basic beliefs are themselves in need of justification, yet their status as basic needs to be retained (SEK 58). Suppose that, for example, the basic beliefs depend on some kind of direct apprehension or awareness of what is experientially given, say the sensing of sense data. BonJour asks why we should stop here. Can what is thus given skirt the potential problem of an infinite regress of justification? In order to do so the requisite apprehension must be interpreted so as to avoid an (other) act of judgment which in turn would need to be justified while at the same time the apprehension must be able to justify a basic belief. This cannot be done, BonJour claims. The two demands conflict (SEK 64-65). According to him an advocate of the given is caught in a "fundamental and inescapable dilemma": If her apprehension is construed as cognitive or quasi-judgmental, it will be both capable of providing justification for other cognitions and wanting it itself. But if it is construed as noncognitive, then while it will not need justification, it will also be incapable of giving it. In either case such states will be useless for grounding knowledge (SEK 69).

Suppose a foundationalist argues, as does Anthony Quinton, that there is a rudimentary kind of direct awareness of the world the content of which is statementally inexpressible. Foundationalists, he claims, need a notion to capture this, such as "an

J.W. Bender (ed.), The Current State of the Coherence Theory, 200–204.
© *1989 by Kluwer Academic Publishers.*

intuition or apprehension of an external state of affairs."³ From there Quinton moves to the idea of an intuitive belief which is one which, he claims, need not be its own justification, but what justifies it cannot be another belief (FK 545, mentioned by BonJour, 65). What justifies it is "...the occurrence of an experience or awareness of some observable situation" (FK 552, cf. SEK 66). One is directly aware, has direct knowledge of an observable situation. BonJour suggests the example of a belief that there is a red book on the desk. This belief, he conjectures, in an appropriate context might be an intuitive belief justified experientially, but he questions the epistemic nature of the direct awareness. Suppose that the awareness is cognitive, but more primitive than a belief. If so, the awareness, if independently credible, can justify the belief because they have about the same cognitive content. But why doesn't the awareness require justification? It cannot be justified by the book's being on the desk, for first the observer must apprehend that. But, BonJour argues, now we seem to need a second apprehension to justify the original one: "...it is hard to see how one and the same cognitive state can be both the original cognitive apprehension...and at the same time a justification of that apprehension...thus pulling itself up by its own cognitive bootstraps" (SEK 67). Suppose instead, BonJour suggests, that the awareness is noncognitive. This would avoid the need for justification, but it doesn't explain how the awareness is supposed to justify the original intuitive belief: "If the person has no cognitive grasp that the external state of affairs is of any particular sort by virtue of having such an intuition, how then does the intuition give him a *reason* ...for thinking that the belief is true...? [Any answer] tacitly slip[s] back into treating the intuition as a cognitive, judgmental state - and hence as itself in need of justification." (SEK 68).

On the matter of the truth of basic beliefs, Quinton holds that when true they correspond with features of the world (NT 139). But, BonJour claims, on this account we can never know whether any of them are true, since we have no perspective outside our total system of beliefs to see whether they correspond (SEK 68). We shall return to this point later.

These are some of the highlights of the main problems BonJour finds with foundations of knowledge and justification. He rejects all possibility of self justification and claims that the only possible justification of empirical belief is other empirical belief. Let us now examine accounts of foundations which, I shall argue, avoid these criticisms. I shall not be concerned, as BonJour is, with one's purported system of all of one's empirical knowledge, that very abstract and ambitious subject, but rather with knowing in the ordinary course of life.

2. Wittgenstein's Account

In criticizing G.E. Moore's famous purported proof of the external world in which Moore holds up one of his hands, then the other, and then claims to know that he has hands, Wittgenstein argues that a knowledge claim is the wrong one to make here.⁴ The use of "I know," according to Wittgenstein, is very specialized: "We just do not see how very specialized the use of 'I know' is" (OC 11). "One says 'I know' when one is ready to give compelling grounds. 'I know' relates to a possibility of demonstrating the truth" (OC 243). There is no chance of demonstration in the case of having hands, Wittgenstein claims, making the interesting original point that ordinarily "my having hands is not less certain before I have looked at them than afterwards" (OC 245). I might just as well question my vision, or my touching of my hands or the testimony of others that I have hands as question that I have them. "I could say," according to Wittgenstein, "'That I have two hands is an irreversible belief.' That would express the fact that I am not ready to let anything count as a disproof of this proposition" (OC 245).

Other items that we cannot ground, and which, therefore, we cannot know, according to Wittgenstein, include that the earth has existed for many years and that we have ancestors (OC 234; 411). Such items help to constitute an epistemic foundation, Wittgenstein suggests, against which we test other items as knowledge. In practice these *prima facie* empirical matters collectively considered play a not entirely contingent role in justifying knowledge claims. They play what Wittgenstein calls a grammatical role, one having to do with conventions and general practices. They form a framework within which we live and act. Wittgenstein quotes Goethe in *Faust:* "In the beginning was the deed" (OC 402). Wittgenstein says, alluding to such items: "Can't an assertoric sentence, which was capable of functioning as an hypothesis, also be used as a foundation for research and action? I.e. can't it simply be isolated from doubt, though not according to any explicit rule? It simply gets assumed as a truism, never called into question, perhaps not even ever formulated. It may be for example that *all inquiry on our part* is set so as to exempt certain propositions from doubt ...They lie apart from the route travelled by enquiry" (OC 87-88). We exempt certain propositions from doubt and from establishing as true. The basic items are not given once and for all; the items which form the foundation may shift and change. Nevertheless the idea that there are at any given time quasi empirical bases reflects common practice. Generally we can and do, when pressed, cite evidence or reasons for our claims and then if asked to justify the evidence or the reasons we move on to the grounds. But the justification does come to an end. There is no infinite regress. We may simply act.

A central feature of Wittgenstein's account is that the basic elements are not items of knowledge. They are not even true. How could they be, when many of them hark back to actions and practices and thus fall into a different category of items incapable of truth or falsity? They do nevertheless ground knowledge and truth and without them knowledge would not exist. Wittgenstein is succinct: "If the true is what is grounded, then the ground is not *true*, nor yet false" (OC 205). In Wittgenstein's metaphor, the foundations form a river-bed and the items of knowledge form the water. The river-bed may shift; it may disappear altogether. Skepticism may be right after all. But one can usually "...distinguish between the movement of the waters on the river-bed and the shift of the bed itself; though there is not a sharp division of the one from the other" (OC 97 cf. 112, 151). Making another comparison Wittgenstein says that we cannot say that the standard metre in Paris is or is not one metre long because of its "...peculiar role in the language-game [practice] of measuring with a metre-rule."[5] Grounds for knowledge then, according to Wittgenstein, can be neither known nor unknown because of their role in establishing knowledge. Something has to stand fast in order to do this, even if it is a mythology (OC 97).

What happens if one questions the grounding elements? If one tries to doubt or question whether, say, it is epistemically all right to irreversibly believe that one has hands it would be odd at best to look at them or touch them so as to tell. Again, one might as well question one's eyes or one's sense of touch as question one's possession of hands. Furthermore, according to Wittgenstein, doubt requires grounds too. Genuine doubt arises within a context. One's doubting one's hands is hard to place in an ordinary setting. The somewhat unusual circumstances of the medical or the military notwithstanding, why would such doubts arise? In the normal course of life such doubts would be idle or maybe crazy or they might show misunderstanding (OC 217, 220, 231).

Such are some of the central features of Wittgenstein's account of the bases of empirical knowledge. If anything like this view is correct, what BonJour calls the basic anti-foundationlist argument fails to show that empirical knowledge lacks foundations. The argument is as follows: Suppose that there are basic empirical beliefs, viz. empirical beliefs which are epistemically justified and whose justification does not depend on that of any other empirical beliefs. There must be a reason for an epistemically justified belief to be likely. For one's belief to be justified one must have such a reason. The only way to have such a reason is to believe with justification the premises from which it follows that the belief is likely. The premises of such an argument cannot be entirely *a priori*. Therefore, the justification of a supposedly basic empirical belief depends on the justification of at least one other empirical belief, which contradicts the first sentence of the argument. Thus there cannot be any basic empirical beliefs (SEK 32).

A way around this argument is to notice that basic beliefs need not be simply empirical. If some items are accepted, acted upon, perhaps not explicitly formulated, used to ground truths and knowledge, virtually impossible to doubt when individually considered and only quasi empirical there is a sense in which they are justified and basic. Consider for example what seems to be for Wittgenstein a basic belief, that we all have ancestors. While it is related to other empirical beliefs, to see it as basic, as part of the ground, is to see it as not entirely empirical and as not needing a basis or justification of other beliefs. To doubt it or question it would be odd.

In what follows I preserve and endorse central elements of Wittgenstein's account while suggesting an alternative to one feature of it.

3. Another Account

I agree with Wittgenstein that the bases of knowledge are neither known nor unknown. We cannot measure by the ruler and test it at the same time. But I do not think that it is quite right to treat the bases as what Wittgenstein calls irreversible beliefs. Normally we do not have any beliefs at all, irreversible, dispositional or otherwise about, say, the existence of our own hands. We do not believe it and we do not disbelieve it either. If I were asked if I irreversibly believe that I have hands I would not know what to say. The question would be odd.

What then is the nature of the foundations if they are not irreversible beliefs? One might suggest that genuine grounds are often obvious and that where this is the case we need not make inferences or have further bases in order to accept them. I have examined epistemic obviousness elsewhere and do not wish to utilize this notion here.[6] One might make a case that what is obvious can be known whereas here I wish to draw attention to a foundationalist advantage of seeing basic elements as neither known nor unknown. The grounding elements, I suggest, are a kind of taking.[7] Taking is a common yet commonly overlooked epistemic attitude. In ordinary life we take to be the case, we take for granted, many things such as that we have hands, that we have ancestors and that the sun will rise tomorrow. We do not question these items or doubt them. We rarely verbalize them. Indeed verbalized takings in contrast to unverbalized ones commonly show reservations or include explicit assumptions as when we say, for example, "I take it that you want me to accompany you" when it is not altogether clear that that is what you want. Taking, like irreversibly believing, is something upon which or in accordance with which we act and against which we test our beliefs, assumptions and knowledge claims. Yet taking is not believing, irreversibly believing, even dispositional believing. If I were asked, out of the blue, if I believe that I have hands, I wouldn't know what to say. It would be an odd question. I don't believe it and I don't disbelieve it either. Taking is different from knowing. If one knows something, it has to obtain, while if one takes something to be the case, it may or may not obtain. Taking is like believing in this respect. Our attitudes and actions show what we take to be the case, what is fundamental in this way.

Pace BonJour's claim that the only justification for empirical beliefs is other empirical beliefs, I believe that it is quite all right, even necessary at times, to move in justification into a different area. Epistemic justification rarely proceeds *via* formalized premises and conclusions. Doubts about epistemic claims are often resolved, grounds for them given, in practice, by moving into a different category, say by doing something. For example, I do not justify my claim that I have cannas in my garden by noticing the premises from which I infer this, or for that matter by citing my visual and tactile sensations caused by a certain red bloom and tuber. I may, rather, try to get you, the botanist, to come over and see for yourself. Many knowledge claims get tested by seeing and doing. There the justification occurs, although our looking at the flowers is not something which is known (or unknown), true or false. Even BonJour is willing to depart from his coherentist account of justification by endorsing a correspondence view of truth, another kind of category switch, so it is not clear why he criticizes Quinton for making the same move to the external world. One has to deal with the world sooner or later if one's account is to be empirical.

Why start and stop our epistemic enquiries with what we take to be the case? What grounds these grounds? Does not this kind of purported foundation, like so many others, lead easily to a charge of not being genuinely foundational? There is no perfectly uncriticizable beginning. Skepticism is always a possibility. But, as Aristotle says, it is a mark of ignorance to ask for a proof of everything. There are at least two advantages to recognizing what we take to be the case as foundational. First, while we may very well quibble and change our minds about what particular items are basic, the idea that there are at any given time quasi empirical bases reflects common practice. We support our knowledge claims, when pressed, with reasons and argument, and if pressed further we may notice what just about all of us take for granted and cannot support empirically in the usual ways. But the justification does come to an end. There is no infinite regress. We may simply act upon what we take to be the case. At any rate the starting place is not there by stipulation or postulation as it is, say, in the foundationalism of Roderick Chisholm.[8] The starting place of taking is not arbitrary. Second, there fails to be anything more certain than what we take to be the case that we can enlist as grounds. We have emphasized with Wittgenstein the failure of one's trying to use one's sighting of one's hands as grounds for taking it that one has them. If one tries to resort to sense-data or Russellian purported knowledge by acquaintance, that fails. One does not and cannot enlist knowledge or truth, for they are what need grounding and establishing.

A foundationalism that begins with what we take to be the case is no guarantor of knowledge. But it does remove us from a coherentist circle of belief and from that very remote concern of BonJour's, one's whole system of beliefs. I doubt that there are such systems. This view of foundations just may reflect characteristically how we do ground knowledge.

NOTES

1. *The Structure of Empirical Knowledge*, part 1, hereafter SEK.
2. Lehrer (1986), 20-21.
3. *The Nature of Things*, ch. 5, hereafter NT; "The Foundations of Knowledge,", hereafter FK in Williams and Montefiore (1986), repr. in Chisholm and Swartz (1973), 542-570.
4. Moore (1939); Wittgenstein (1969), hereafter 'OC', followed by section numbers.
5. *Philosophical Investigations*, 150.
6. I discuss this notion in Black (1983), 66-75.
8. *Theory of Knowledge*, ch. 2.

REFERENCES

Black, Carolyn. "Obvious Knowledge." *Synthese* 56 (1983), 373-385.
----- . "Taking." *Theoria* 40 (1974), 66-75.
BonJour, Laurence. *The Structure of Empirical Knowledge*. Cambridge, Mass.: Harvard University Press, 1985.
Chisholm, Roderick. *Theory of Knowledge*. 2nd ed., New Jersey: Prentice-Hall, 1977.
-----, and Robert Swartz eds. *Empirical Knowledge*. New Jersey: Prentice-Hall, 1973.
Lehrer, Keith. "The Coherence Theory of Knowledge." *Philosophical Topics* 14.1 (1986), 5-25.
Moore, G.E. "Proof of an External World." *Proceedings of the British Academy* 25 (1939).
Williams, Bernard and Alan Montefiore. *British Analytical Philosophy*. London: Routledge, 1966.
Wittgenstein, Ludwig. *On Certainty*. G.E.M. Anscombe and G.H. von Wright, eds., translated by Denis Paul and G.E.M. Anscombe. Oxford: Blackwell, 1969.
-----. *Philosophical Investigations*. G.E.M. Anscombe, tr.. 2nd ed. Oxford: Blackwell, 1958.

iv. focus: coherence and related
epistemic concerns

The Unattainability of Coherence

Hilary Kornblith
University of Vermont

Coherence theorists of justification hold that an agent should accept beliefs which cohere with those he already holds and reject beliefs which fail to cohere with those he already holds. The processes of belief acquisition and rejection must therefore be sensitive to coherence and incoherence. Some theorists believe that this sensitivity should operate at a conscious level: if an agent is to be justified in his belief, he must hold it in virtue of recognizing that it coheres with his other beliefs. Other theorists hold that it is sufficient for justification that an agent's beliefs be acquired in virtue of the fact of their coherence with the agent's other beliefs; the agent need not be aware of this fact for his beliefs to be justified. In either case, an ideal of belief acquisition is proposed which crucially depends on determinations of coherence: in one case these determinations are made by the agent, whilee in the other these determinations are made by subconsciously operating processes of belief acquisition. I do not believe that such determinations can be made. The ideal of processes of belief acquisition which are sensitive to coherence is unattainable, whether this sensitivity is supposed to reside in the agent himself or in his processes of belief acquisition.

In Section I, I examine Laurence BonJour's defense of the coherence theory. On BonJour's internalist account, an agent must be able to determine, by introspection, whether candidate beliefs cohere with beliefs currently held. I argue that agents cannot do what BonJour requires of them. Moreover, I argue that this is not merely a fault with BonJour's version of the coherence theory, but rather a problem for any internalist version of the coherence theory. The coherence or incoherence of an agent's beliefs is simply not internally available.

This may suggest that the coherence theorist's difficulty can be resolved by rejecting internalism. In Section II, however, I argue that an externalist version of the coherence theory fares no better. Gilbert Harman's view is examined here, according to which subconscious processes of belief revision are sensitive to coherence and incoherence. I argue that no such processes can exist. The difficulty here is not merely with Harman's account, but with any externalist version of a coherence theory. In sum, I argue that no version of the coherence theory is workable. A problem remains, however, for those who would deny that beliefs may be accepted or rejected in virtue of their coherence or incoherence with beliefs already held. There is an argument which is Quinean in inspiration and which has recently been offered by Jerry Fodor which seems to force a choice between a coherentist account of belief acquisition and skepticism. Since the focus of this paper is the rejection of the coherentist account of belief acquisition, and since I do not wish to be seen as offering an argument for skepticism, I take up Fodor's dilemma in Section III. I sketch an account of belief acquisition which is neither coherentist nor skeptical, yet is true to the Quinean spirit which, I believe, moves not only Fodor but many other coherence theorists as well.

I.

Laurence BonJour defends an internalist version of the coherence theory in his recent book, *The Structure of Empirical Knowledge.* BonJour writes,

> According to a coherence theory of empirical justification, as so far characterized, the epistemic justification of an empirical belief derives entirely from its coherence with the believer's overall system of empirical beliefs and not at all from any sort of factor outside that system. What we must now ask is whether

J.W. Bender (ed.), The Current State of the Coherence Theory, 207–214.
© *1989 by Kluwer Academic Publishers.*

> and how the fact that a belief coheres in this way is cognitively accessible to
> the believer himself, so that it can give him a reason for accepting the belief.
> (101)

What makes BonJour an internalist is this claim that the coherence of one belief with others is "cognitively accessible" to an agent, and that it is for this reason that coherence may provide an agent with justification. This requirement of cognitive accessibility, however, is not an easy one to meet. As BonJour notes, ". . . if the fact of coherence is to be accessible to the believer, it follows that he must somehow have an adequate grasp of his total system of beliefs, since it is coherence with this system which is at issue."(102) One very important part of BonJour's book thus concerns the extent to which an agent's beliefs are cognitively accessible to him.[1] Ironically, BonJour never discusses the extent to which coherence itself is accessible to an agent. It is this issue I wish to discuss. I argue that coherence is not sufficiently   accessible to an agent to serve an internalist theory of justification.[2]

One necessary condition for the coherence of a body of beliefs is that they be consistent. (95) To what extent, then, is the consistency of a body of beliefs accessible to an agent? Consider, for example, the axioms of Frege's Basic Laws of Arithmetic. Frege thought long and hard about these axioms. After extraordinarily careful consideration, he adopted them as the foundation of his system. He clearly believed each of the axioms to be true and, of course, he believed them to be jointly consistent. Frege was, famously, mistaken. As Russell demonstrated in a letter to Frege, the axioms of the Basic Laws were inconsistent.

Now it is clear that Frege was not simply being careless. We are not considering an agent who arrived at his beliefs haphazardly, or even the case of an agent who carefully arrived at his beliefs but then failed to consider the question of their consistency. I think it is safe to say that Frege arrived at his beliefs in the axioms of the Basic Laws as carefully and self-consciously as an agent can. Nevertheless, the fact of their inconsistency eluded him.

According to BonJour, the coherence or incoherence of a set of beliefs is cognitively accessible to an agent. Since coherence requires consistency, the consistency of a set of beliefs must also be cognitively accessible to an agent. Thus, according to BonJour, the inconsistency of the axioms of the Basic Laws was actually cognitively accessible to Frege from the very beginning. What does BonJour mean by this claim of cognitive accessibility? What reason, if any, is there to think that BonJour is correct?

Before addressing these two questions, I want to introduce two more examples, each of which demonstrate the difficulty of determining whether a set of beliefs is actually coherent. Although BonJour is certainly not committed to the claim that coherence is easy to determine, I do not believe that the difficulty of determining coherence is irrelevant either.

In a famous criticism of the coherence theory, Moritz Schlick[3] claimed that fairy tales and novels satisfy coherentist requirements for justified belief. Although I do not wish to endorse Schlick's criticism, I do wish to appropriate one of his examples. Let us consider the case of a short novel, and let us ask whether the sentences of the novel satisfy BonJour's criterion of coherence. First, of course, the novel must not be internally inconsistent. As the Frege example should alert us, determining consistency is no easy task. Frege was working with a small number of axioms. Even a short novel of two hundred pages is likely to contain somewhere in the neighborhood of five thousand sentences. If the inconsistency of the Basic Laws could elude Frege, it does not tax the imagination to suppose that inconsistency could arise in a short novel without coming to the attention of even the most careful reader. Now consider how many times this problem is magnified when we move from the five thousand sentences of a short novel to the corpus of an adult's beliefs. The problem of hidden inconsistency is highly non-trivial.

Finally, let us consider cases involving inference to the best explanation. BonJour believes that the coherence of a body of beliefs has a great deal to do with the explanatory relations among them. (98) Cases involving inference to the best explanation may involve huge bodies of data and theory directly; of course, on any coherentist account, such inference will indirectly involve all of an agent's beliefs. In actual practice, there is typically a social dimension to inference to the best explanation: potential explanations are proposed to colleagues and tested against their reactions. The mechanism of publication assures that potential explanations are widely aired. On BonJour's account, however, the coherence of a set of beliefs is supposed to be "internally available" and "cognitively accessible" to an agent. Introspection alone should suffice, on BonJour's account, for determining the best explanation of a set of beliefs. There can be little doubt that inference to the best explanation can often be astoundingly difficult. BonJour seems to endow the faculty of introspection with remarkable abilities.

Given how difficult coherence is to determine, and given how easily even careful and insightful agents can go wrong about coherence, what could BonJour mean in claiming that coherence is cognitively accessible to an agent? One clue to answering this question can be found in BonJour's criticism of reliabilism. Reliabilists hold that a belief is justified just in case it is produced by a reliable process.(See Goldman 1979,1986) BonJour describes a number of cases (37-57) in which a belief is in fact reliably produced, and yet, intuitively, we would say that the agent has excellent reason to reject his belief. BonJour concludes that although the belief is clearly unjustified, reliabilists are committed to claiming that the belief is justified. Reliabilism is thus shown to be mistaken. BonJour's explanation of the reliabilist's error, however, is extremely revealing.

> ...these cases and the modifications made in response to them also suggest an important moral which leads to a basic intuitive objection to externalism: external or objective reliability is not enough to offset subjective irrationality. If the acceptance of a belief is seriously unreasonable or unwarranted from the believer's own standpoint, then the mere fact that unbeknownst to him its existence in those circumstances lawfully guarantees its truth will not suffice to render the belief epistemically justified... (41)

Justification may not be explained in terms of objective reliability because a belief may be reliably produced and yet "seriously unreasonable or unwarranted from the believer's own standpoint." Reliability is thus too distant from the agent's point of view. It is not cognitively accessible to the agent.

But how is coherence supposed to differ from reliability in this regard? Is it impossible for the objective facts about coherence to differ from their appearance "from the believer's own standpoint"? Even if we choose a believer as careful and insightful as Frege, there may be substantial gaps between the appearance and the reality of coherence. Coherence may be just as external to an agent's point of view as reliability. The very argument which BonJour uses against externalism is thus equally successful in application to his own theory of justification. Since BonJour's requirement ofcognitive accessibility seems to require that there be no gap between the appearance and the reality of justification, and since the difficulties involved in determining coherence open just such a gap, BonJour's coherentist account of justification fails to live up to the very standards which BonJour himself lays down.

The fact that the reliability of belief forming processes is, in some sense, a factor external to the agent's system of beliefs, while coherence is, in some sense, internal to that system of beliefs does not in any way show that coherence is cognitively accessible or appropriately available to the agent. It is only by implicitly making the traditional Cartesian assumption that what is internal to the mind is wholly transparent to the agent that BonJour may slide from the claim that coherence is internal to an agent's beliefs to the claim that it is cognitively accessible to the agent in a way that objective reliability is not. Even if one endorses the traditional Cartesian claim about the special accessibility an agent has to the contents of his own mind, however, the claim of special access to relations among belief contents remains wildly implausible. The objective difficulty of determining coherence is simply undeniable.

This creates a problem not only for BonJour, but for all internalist versions of the coherence theory. The motivation for internalist accounts, as BonJour clearly states, is to give an account of what is justified from the agent's own point of view. The objective coherence of an agent's beliefs, however, may be unavailable to an agent, and thus the dictates of coherence may fit the agent's point of view no better than the reliability of his processes of belief acquisition does. An internalist account of justification simply cannot be elaborated in terms of coherence.

II.

The difficulties involved in developing a coherence theory of justification cannot be resolved by giving up internalism. Consider the externalist version of the coherence theory proposed by Gilbert Harman in *Thought*. In discussing the nature of inductive inference, the only kind of inference Harman believes occurs, Harman rejects the view that such inference

> ...is a matter of going from a few premises we already accept to a conclusion one comes to accept ... the suggestion that only a few premises are relevant is wrong, since inductive inference must be assessed with respect to everything one believes. A more accurate conception of inductive inference takes it to be a way of modifying what we believe by addition and subtraction of beliefs. Our "premises" are all our antecedent beliefs; our "conclusion" is our total resulting view. (1973, 159)

The principle of such modification, according to Harman, is just inference to the best explanation. On Harman's view, this is not only a description of how we actually arrive at our beliefs; it it is also a description of how we ought to arrive at our beliefs. Harman does not have BonJour's internalist scruples. It can thus be no objection to Harman that the coherence or incoherence of an agent's beliefs is not transparent to the agent. It would be sufficient for Harman's account were human beliefs the product of subconsciously operating mechanisms which are sensitive to features of the entire body of beliefs. There can, however, be no such mechanisms. Since coherence requires consistency, let us consider once again the problems involved in determining the consistency of large numbers of sentences. The problem discussed in Section I involved the difficulty human beings have with determining consistency. The problems involved, however, are not limited to human beings. Consider a device which checks a set of sentences in the propositional calculus for consistency by drawing up a truth-table. The number of lines on this truth-table will grow exponentially with the number of atomic sentence letters contained in the formulae to be tested. If there are only two atomic sentence letters, the truth-table will be four lines long; if there are five atomic sentence letters, the truth-table will be thirty-two lines long. In general, for n atomic sentence letters, the truth-table will be 2^n lines long.

It should be clear that any such device runs into difficulties involving computational complexity quite quickly. As Christopher Cherniak notes,

> Given the difficulties in individuating beliefs, it is not easy to estimate the number of logically independent atomic propositions in a typical human belief system, but 138 seems much too low-- too "small-minded". Yet suppose that each line of the truth table for the conjunction of all of these beliefs can be checked in the time a light ray takes to traverse the diameter of a proton, an appropriate cycle time for an ideal computer. At this maximum speed, a consistency test of this very modest belief system would require more time than the estimated twenty billion years from the dawn of the universe to the present. (1984, 755-6)

It is not simply that human beings have difficulty in determining the consistency of large sets of sentences. It is simply beyond the powers of any possible computational device to determine the consistency of a large set of sentences. Insofar as coherence requires consistency, we can be sure that our beliefs are not the product of mechanisms which determine coherence because such mechanisms are fundamentally impossible.

The suggestion then that we ought to arrive at our beliefs by means of processes which recognize coherence proposes an ideal which human beings cannot meet and, indeed, which cannot be met by any possible computational device whatsoever. Nor is the problem simply one of determining consistency. The problem of computational complexity seems bound to arise for any holistic relation whatever operating over large fields of belief. It thus seems quite safe to say that not only Harman's version of the coherence theory, but all versions of the coherence theory propose an ideal which is very far out of our reach.

III.

My argument thus far shows that the ideal which coherentists propose is one which cannot be reached; it is impossible for human beings, or any information processing device, to accept beliefs in virtue of their coherence with others, so long as the field of beliefs over which coherence must operate is tolerably large. Jerry Fodor, however, has recently offered an argument which suggests that the only alternative to a coherentist account of the fixation of belief is skepticism. Since I do not wish to see the first two sections of this paper taken along with Fodor's argument as a proof of skepticism, I address Fodor's dilemma here.

Like many coherence theorists, Fodor takes his inspiration from Quine.

> ...confirmation in science is isotropic and it is Quineian. It is notoriously hard to give anything approaching a rigorous account of what being isotropic and Quineian amounts to, but it is easy enough to convey the intuitions. By saying that confirmation is isotropic, I mean that the facts relevant to the confirmation of a scientific hypothesis may be drawn from anywhere in the field of previously established empirical (or, of course, demonstrative) truths. Crudely: everything that the scientist knows is, in principle, relevant to determining what else he ought to believe. In principle, our botany constrains our astronomy, if only we could think of ways to make them connect...(1983,105)
>
> By saying that scientific confirmation is Quineian, I mean that the degree of confirmation assigned to any given hypothesis is sensitive to properties of the entire belief system; as it were, the shape of our whole science bears on the epistemic status of each scientific hypothesis...(1983,107)

...I shall take it for granted that scientific confirmation is Quineian and isotropic. (Those who wish to see the arguments should refer to such classic papers in the modern philosophy of science as Quine, 1953, and Putnam,1962.) Moreover, since I am committed to relying upon the analogy between scientific confirmation and psychological fixation of belief, I shall take it for granted that the latter must be Quineian and isotropic too... I propose, at this point, to be both explicit and emphatic. The argument is that the central processes which mediate the fixation of belief are typically processes of rational nondemonstrative inference and that, since such processes of rational nondemonstrative inference are Quineian and isotropic, so too are central processes. In particular, the theory of such processes must be consonant with the principle that the level of acceptance of any belief is sensitive to the level of acceptance of any other and to global properties of the field of beliefs taken collectively. (1983, 109-110)

Quine's views about the nature of confirmation are thus given psychological reality on Fodor's view. For Quine, confirmation is a holistic affair; for Fodor, this shows that the fixation of belief is holistic as well.

It is not hard to see the attraction of this view. Suppose that one believes, with Quine, that any statement may in principle bear on the epistemic status of any other. One will then believe that positive epistemic status requires the appropriate interrelations among an agent's beliefs. Since many agent's beliefs have this positive epistemic status, these holistic interconnections must frequently, if not typically, be exhibited in agents' belief systems. Belief fixation must therefore be holistic. All that seems to be required to get from the Quineian premise about conirmation to the holistic conclusion about belief fixation is the rejection of skepticism. Those who are anti-skeptical must thus believe that belief fixation is as holistic as confirmation. Thus, if confirmation is radically holistic, as Quine claims, then belief fixation must be radically holistic as well. Or, to put the point slightly differently: if Quine is right about confirmation but belief fixation is not radically holistic, skepticism must be true. Since I accept the Quineian view of confirmation, this argument presents me with a special challenge. It is, moreover, a deceptively attractive argument. In response, I sketch an account of how belief acquisition might proceed without violating the constraints of computational complexity. Belief acquisition, on this account, is not holistic; but neither is this account an elaboration of skepticism. What I want to suggest is that the mechanisms of belief fixation are computationally quite simple, and their simplicity is achieved by operating on very small sub-systems of belief. These mechanisms are, for the most part, reliable; they are well suited to operation in a certain range of environments, and these are the environements in which we tend to find ourselves.

The advantage of having such mechanisms of belief acquisition are straightforward. Indeed, the advantages here are simply those of having beliefs over not having beliefs, for, as we have seen, the constraint on inferential processes that they be computationally tractable requires that they operate over small fields of beliefs. Computational tractability thus requires severe informational encapsulation. Any attempt to draw on very much of the vast resources of an individual's body of beliefs all at once will run into the problem of combinatorial explosion. So inferential mechanisms must work over small fields of beliefs.

This constraint on inference brings with it a second constraint: many of the inferential mechanisms we have must be specifically tailored to the environments in which we tend to be found. The necessity of this constraint is not hard to see. Consider the alternative: imagine a system of inferential principles all of which are environment-neutral; i.e., they work as well in any one environment as any other. The principles of logic, for example, are just such principles, and there may be others as well. Now many philosophers have suggested that belief acquisition proceeds in accord with just such environment-neutral principles. In order to make these proposals plausible, however, they have all had to assume computational access to a very wide range of beliefs simultaneously. No content-neutral inductive principle can work even tolerably well without access to a very wide range of an agent's beliefs. Hence, inductive logic is said to be guided by a "principle of total evidence". But the postulation of just this kind of computational mechanism ignores the problem of combinatorial explosion. Once we recognize the limitations imposed by the requirement of computational tractability, we see that the broad access which content-neutral principles of belief acquisition would require are not possible. So in order for us to be able to perform inductive inference successfully, our inferences cannot be content-neutral. What this means is that our inferences must, in effect, build in certain substantive assumptions about our environment; they are tailored, as it were, to the environments in which we tend to be found. We must assume, at least, that they are so tailored if our inductive inferences are to be at all successful.

One of the side effects of inferential mechanisms of this sort is that they will produce some internal incoherence in an agent's body of beliefs. Even if we assume that these mechanisms operate reliably, it is perectly clear that they are not going to be entirely error free. And since the operation of these mechanisms is largely informationally encapsulated, the output of any one such mechanism may well be inconsistent with the output of another. The resulting inconsistencies which crop up in an agent's beliefs need not be detected by the agent. A system which could detect all internal inconsistencies would have to operate holistically. The operation of individually reliable but informationally encapsulated systems of belief acquisition will thus lead, as BonJour has suggested, to "a set of conflicting sub-systems." (93) There is but a grain of truth, however, in Bonjour's claim that non-holistic belief acquisition will result in a set of conflicting sub-systems. The amount of internal inconsistency should not be exaggerated. There are a number of factors working to keep the amount of inconsistency down. First, there is the fact that the individual mechanisms of belief acquisition tend to be reliable. Since truth is, of course, internally coherent, the beliefs produced by individually reliable mechanisms will not consist of vast numbers of wildly incompatible sub-systems. Second, social factors in cognition tend to put a damper on cognitive individuality.[4] Finally, human beings do tend to monitor their beliefs, so that when inconsistencies are discovered, they may often be weeded out. This last point itself should be carefully circumscribed, for these mechanisms of inconsistency detection must themselves operate locally. They are no more capable of operating holistically than the primary mechanisms which govern unselfconscious belief acquisition. Nevertheless, the fact remains that inconsistency may be removed after the fact through self-conscious monitoring.

On the view I am defending then, belief acquisition is the product of individually reliable mechanisms which are tailored to environments in which we tend to be found. These mechanisms operate locally rather than holistically; they operate over small fields of belief. A product of this kind of belief acquisition is the inevitable appearance of internal incoherence in human bodies of belief. This does not mean, however, that belief systems will consist of massively inconsistent sub-systems, for the pressures under which belief acquisition operates tend to keep down the amount of inconsistency.

I began this section with a brief but important argument for holism: if we are to reject scepticism, belief fixation must be as holistic as confirmation; since Quine has shown us that confirmation is radically holistic, we must conclude that belief fixation is radically holistic as well. In light of my rejection of holism, this argument presents a special problem for my view. How is it possible to reject holism without embracing scepticism?

The short answer to this question is that the very factors which insure that inconsistency is kept down - reliability of individual mechanisms, social factors in cognition, and local monitoring of one's beliefs - also insure that our beliefs are kept in reasonable touch with the world. It is by means of these features that our informationally encapsulated mechanisms of belief acquisition may simulate a holistic system to a sufficient degree to ward off scepticism. Just as digital devices may simulate the output of analog devices to any given degree, non-holistic systems may simulate the output of holistic systems. The greater the reliability of the individual belief-acquiring mechanisms, the greater the coherence of the resulting body of beliefs. Of course there are other means by which greater coherence may be acheived, but I focus on the feature of reliability precisely because the argument for holism seems to force a choice between holism and skepticism. This dilemma is a false one, however, precisely because the advantages of holistic belief acquisition may be acheived by other means.

Our contact with the world is thus assured by the reliability of our belief-acquiring mechanisms. Instead of being equipped with some kind of central processing device which holistically adjusts our beliefs, the various mechanisms of belief acquisition are specially tailored to the environment in which we live. It is only in virtue of this pre-existing harmony between ourbelief acquisition mechanisms and the environment that these mechanisms may be computationally simple. And it is only in virtue of the possibility of such computationally simple mechanisms that we may have beliefs at all.[5]

NOTES

1. I discuss BonJour's treatment of this problem in Kornblith (1988).
2. I presented an overly brief version of this argument in Kornblith (1986).
3. Schlick (1934), 215.
4. I have discussed this aspect of belief acquisition in Kornblith (1987).
5. I have received helpful comments on an earlier draft of this paper from David Christensen and Derk Pereboom.

REFERENCES

BonJour, Laurence. *The Structure of Empirical Knowledge* . Cambridge: Harvard University Press, 1985.
Cherniak, Christopher. *Minimal Rationality*. Cambridge: Bradford Books/MIT Press, 1986.
Fodor, Jerry. *The Modularity of Mind* . Cambridge: Bradford Books/MIT Press, 1983.
Harman, Gilbert. *Thought*. Princeton: Princeton University Press, 1973.
-----. *Change In View: Principles of Reasoning*. Cambridge: Bradford Books/MIT Press, 1986.
Goldman, Alvin. "What is Justified Belief?," in *Justification and Knowledge* , George Pappas, ed., Dordrecht: Reidel, 1979, 1-23.
-----. *Epistemology and Cogntion* . Cambridge: Harvard University Press, 1986.
Kornblith, Hilary. "Naturalizing Rationality," in *Naturalism and Rationality* , Newton Garver and Peter Hare, eds., Buffalo: Prometheus Books, 1986, 115-133.
-----. "Some Social Features of Cognition," *Synthese* 73 (1987), 27-41.
-----. "How Internal Can You Get?," *Synthese* 74 (1988), 313-327.
Schlick, Moritz. "The Foundation of Knowledge," (1934) in *Logical Positivism* , A. J. Ayer, ed., New York: The Free Press, 1959, 209-227.

Epistemically Justified Opinion

Bruce Aune
University of Massachusetts

The theories of epistemic justification advanced in recent years are commonly offered as contributions to an adequate conception of knowledge and are, perhaps in consequence, either foundational or coherentist.[1] I take exception to such theories here, arguing that they exaggerate the importance of knowledge for an adequate epistemology. I claim that an adequate epistemology requires a central concept of epistemic justification not subordinate to the concept of knowledge and that the needed concept (which I attempt to identify) should presupppose a new theory of empirical justification - one that is neither foundational nor coherentist. Since the theory I accept has interesting affinities with the coherence theory recently developed by Laurence BonJour,[2] I comment freely on his theory in supporting my alternative.

1. Knowledge and Rational Uncertainty

Ever since the Gettier problem captured the attention of philosophers in the early 'sixties, the task of providing a satisfactory definition of "s knows that p" has assumed a central role in epistemology. In spite of the exceptional effort and ingenuity expended on the task, no generally accepted account has yet (unfortunately) appeared, and some of the most interesting recent discussion has been largely critical rather than constructive.[3] However one may wish to explain the lack of consensus here, twenty-five years of proposals and refutations make one conjecture difficult to resist - namely, that if any definition of "s knows that p" is ever accepted as immune to counterinstances, it will be sufficiently demanding in its requirements that many (if not most [4]) of the well-founded opinions particularly important to us in science and common life (and such subjects as ethics, politics, and history) will not count as knowledge. I stand behind this conjecture, and believe it has important consequences for a reasonable epistemology.

Anyone who is enough of an empiricist to believe that most of our well-founded opinions about the world have some kind of inductive or experimental [5] basis should agree that these opinions are significantly uncertain. To put it positively, they are more or less probable. The claim that our empirical knowledge, in a strict sense of "knowledge" excluding uncertainty, is very limited should not, therefore, be controversial. The tendency to think otherwise may be owing to the practice, begun under the influence of the late Wittgenstein, of attacking that Peck's Bad Boy of philosophy, "the" skeptic. As I see it, skeptics really do deserve refutation if they claim that no substantive opinions about the world, however tentative, are reasonably held; but if they merely insist that, in a strict sense of the world "know," much or even most of what is commonly believed about the world is not really known, then they may deserve applause - depending on what their sense of "know" actually is. Since strong claims about the extent of our common-sense knowledge have recently been made, I want to make a brief case for epistemic uncertainty before proceeding with the constructive argument of my paper.

Speaking generally and a bit loosely, we can agree that our rationally founded beliefs about the world are either observational or inferential. As far as empirical science is concerned, inferential beliefs - particularly those of quantum mechanics, molecular biology, and cognitive science, which are distinctive of a scientifically up-to-date view of the world - are much too loosely related to their evidence to represent knowledge in the strict sense that epistemologists are trying to pin down. The inferential beliefs of common sense are characteristically, if not invariably, equally poor candidates for knowledge so understood. To support this last claim, which many would question, I want to say something about a

215

J.W. Bender (ed.), The Current State of the Coherence Theory, 215–230 .
© *1989 by Kluwer Academic Publishers.*

representative inferential belief I have and also outline the reasoning (the inferences) that led me to it. I regard the belief as practically certain (I have absolutely no doubt about its truth), but I think it is easy to show, in the spirit of recent counterexampling over "s knows that p," that it is actually too uncertain, theoretically, to count as knowledge. After commenting on this commonsensical inferential belief, I shall say something about noninferential, observational beliefs and the respects in which they, too, are theoretically uncertain.

I arrived at the inferential belief in question by a line of reasoning reminiscent of Sherlock Holmes. The problem prompting the reasoning arose at the end of a lecture to new group of undergraduates. As I was preparing to leave the lecture hall, a young woman I had never seen before came up to the lectern and presented me with an unlabeled wine bottle containing a pale yellow liquid, saying "Someone you know made this wine and wants to know if you can figure out who he is." I expressed my surprise, but thanked her for the bottle, which I later took home and opened. My curiosity moved me to undertake the case of Holmesian detection.

As it happens, I am an amateur winemaker, and I suspected that the person sending the bottle is a member of the winemakers' club to which I belong. As soon as I opened the bottle, I detected a familiar smell - one that I associated with wine made from Muscat grapes. I poured a little of the liquid into a glass, looked at it carefully, and cautiously tasted it. "There is no doubt," I thought, "this is Muscat." But who made it? Another taste convinced me that the wine was excellent - very well made. "Who makes wine like this?" One name immediately came to mind: "J.B.". Though I had not seen him in more than a year, J.B. is particularly fond of Muscat, and makes it just like this: dry. (Muscat is usually made sweet.) So J.B. must have made it. As Hume said, "From like effects we may infer like causes."

Of course, J.B. is not the only person I know who is capable of making a dry Muscat like this one; so I couldn't be certain that it was made by him. Did I have any other relevant evidence? Yes: J.B. was the only person I knew who not only made dry Muscat, but was very fond of it, knew that I am also fond of it, and was a particularly warm friend who was apt to send me a surprise bottle of it. This additional evidence made my belief much stronger. I then happened to notice the cork. There was a name printed on it, "Callaway." This made me utterly certain that J.B. was the maker because I recalled sending him a bag of corks from the Callaway Vineyard, which I had visited a couple of years earlier when I was in California . Who else in western Massachusetts would have corks from Callaway Vineyards, a small winery located not in the famous Napa or Sonoma valleys but in out-of-the way Temecula, an unlikely oasis of winemaking off the road between Riverside and San Diego? At this point I picked up the telephone, called J.B., and thanked him for the bottle. He replied that he wondered if I could still recognize his wine. He said that the young woman who gave me the bottle was a neighbor of his who said she was taking a philosophy course at the university and, in reply to his "Who is your teacher?", mentioned my name. It occurred to him that it would be fun to see if I could recognize a bottle of his latest Muscat.

Did I, when I heard J.B. tell me on the phone that he had made the wine, actually know) that he had made it? I have absolutely no doubt that it was he, and I am confident that any intelligent nonphilosopher aware of the evidence I have cited would reply "Of course: all the circumstantial evidence you have and the corroboration of the telephone call place your belief beyond any shadow of a doubt." Yet my evidence is clearly consistent with rival hypotheses that can account for all the facts available to me, and I have no other information that conclusively rules them out. My belief is epistemically far too uncertain, therefore, to count as a case of knowledge.

Consider this possibility. J.B. and his brother Elbert are bottling wine, sampling a little in the process, and talking about winemaking. Their conversation turns to the distinctive qualities of this or that person's wine. Elbert, who has decided that dry Muscat is not worth making, observes that J.B. is the only one he knows who actually likes it. J.B. says "Aune certainly likes my Muscat;" to which Elbert replies "He only says he likes it to make you feel good: he couldn't tell your Muscat from mine." (Elbert used to make a dry Muscat and still has some on hand.) They decide to test my discernment, recorking a bottle of Elbert's Muscat with one of J.B.'s corks. Since J.B., as part of a bargain with Elbert, might well be willing to tell me that he sent the wine and also deceive me about the young woman who is really Elbert's neighbor, not his, the evidence at my disposal is compatible with either hypothesis. I think the probabilities strongly favor my hypothesis, since J.B. is not the sort of person (I believe!) who is apt to deceive one this way. But these favorable probabilities are not so great that I satisfy a counterexample-resistant definition of "S knows that p."

A careful look at the reasoning by which I arrived at my belief indicates that it is, or can be reconstructed as, a complex inference to the best explanation. Although the acceptability of such inferences has recently been attacked (or at least questioned) by very able philosophers,[6] I believe and shall later argue that, properly understood or reconstructed, they are as acceptable as any other form of nondemonstrative inference. The instance I have used is particularly strong: I think that an ordinary person would regard it as yielding a practical certainty. This sort of certainty is representative, I believe, of the highest-grade of inferential certainty that we can achieve in science and everyday life. Yet it does not amount to knowledge in a strict sense of the word whose definition is resistant to plausible counterexamples.

I now turn to observational beliefs. Most philosophers would agree, I think, that if any empirical statements are minimally doubtful in a theoretical sense, they are statements representing observations or first-person reports. Yet the acceptability of such statements as true or probably true is not a consequence of the mere fact that they are made with confidence or that the speaker has no doubts about the beliefs they express. A little reflection shows, in fact, that their acceptability is properly assessed by considerations of four different, though interrelated, kinds. The first concerns the sort of object, event, or state supposedly observed or reported on. What is the nature of the thing? What are its distinguishing features? How is it identified? The second concerns the observational process, or the subject's access to the object. Was it seen, heard, or perhaps felt? The third sort of consideration concerns the observer's current state of mind - his or her attentiveness, rationality, sanity, suggestiveness, and the like. The fourth concerns the conditions under which the observation or avowal occurred. Was it noisy, frightening? Was there adequate light? How close was the observer to the observed object?

When I say that the acceptability (the truth or degree of objective probability) of an observation is "properly assessed" by considerations of these four kinds, I mean that all four must be taken into account (at least tacitly) in deciding whether the statement, or report, is apt to be true. Any verdict we reach will then relate particular facts (or presumed facts) of four kinds to the claim at hand. In doing this it will presuppose *general* beliefs (ordinarily called "knowledge") about the relations involved. Thus, if Jones claims to see a needle in a haystack or if, on awakening at dawn, I think I am seeing an old lady hovering before my bedroom window, the claim or thought is properly evaluated by general) knowldge or beliefs about the visibility of needles in haystacks, the likelihood of old ladies floating in the air,[7] and the conditions under which "apparitions" or momentary hallucinations are apt to occur. In some cases such general knowledge or general beliefs is obtained or arrived at by inference from higher-level knowledge or beliefs. In his *Human Knowledge: Its Scope and Limits* Russell formulated what he thought were the highest-level assumptions tacitly used, at least at the time, in evaluating assertions in theoretical science. He said that these assumptions, which he described as "postulates required to validate scientific method," could be reduced to five. They concern such things as objectual permanence, spatio-temporal continuity, separability of causal lines, and structural similarity [8].

If the acceptability of *any* observation statement or psychological report is determined by general beliefs about epistemically pertinent features of the observer, the means of observation, the nature of the observed object, and the conditions of observation, we should certainly want to know how the acceptability of those beliefs is determined. As the example of needles in haystacks makes clear, it is absurd to say that such beliefs are analytically true, or evident *a priori*. A pragmatist answer reminiscent of William James is "By the success we have in using them"; but this answer, though suggestive, does not tell us how the "success" of the beliefs is determined. If we are to ascertain this success by observational "test" statements, our determination of acceptability would appear to take us in circle.

Laurence BonJour would say that these general beliefs are ultimately acceptable (if, indeed, they really are) for the same reason that our observational beliefs are ultimately acceptable (if, indeed, *they* really are) - namely, that they belong to a coherent system of beliefs satisfying certain input and other constraints. I say "ultimately acceptable" and insert the parenthetical qualifications because BonJour evidently holds that, for a belief to be justified in a way that does not require some other belief to be "more or less taken for granted,"[9] it must belong to a system of beliefs that is "globally justified" by virtue of its coherence and its ability to remain coherent over the "relatively long run."[10] In my terms, a belief so justified is "ultimately acceptable." Since, in BonJour's view, the general beliefs and observational beliefs I spoke of are thus acceptable only if the system to which they belong is now coherent and will continue to be coherent "in the relatively long run," my parenthetical qualification is appropriate. Evidently, only time will tell if these beliefs really are globally justified.

BonJour's strategy here is ingenious and tempting, but it raises problems of its own. One concerns the relatively long-run coherence of a system of beliefs. Can we be sure that our current system of beliefs is coherent and will remain so in the "relatively" long run? How do we estimate this long-run coherence? BonJour does not adequately deal with this problem; in fact, he tacitly brushes it aside. In arguing for the likely truth (or correspondence to reality) of an appropriately coherent system of beliefs, BonJour makes the "Doxastic Presumption" that it does so cohere. The presumption can be accepted for the sake of BonJour's argument, but he does nothing to show that it is actually true given the requirement of long-term coherence, nor does he indicate how (with this requirement in mind) one might attempt to defend it. Obviously, some inductive step is required, and this will reduce the certainty of any unconditional epistemic justification. Another problem raised by BonJour's coherentist strategy concerns his global argument that an appropriately coherent system of beliefs probably corresponds to reality. His argument is an "inference to the best explanation" - one to the effect that the collective truth of the cohering beliefs provides the best explanation of their presumed coherence and their long-term stability under the impact of persistent sensory inputs.[11] As I mentioned earlier, I do not object to this kind of inference; but BonJour's use of it in a global context like this one does not, in my opinion, succeed.

Since I shall be discussing the logic of inferences to the best explanation at a later stage of my argument, I shall not develop my objections to BonJour's use of it now.[12] Instead, to support the claims I have been making about the ultimate uncertainty of most rational beliefs, I want to emphasize that an inference to the best explanation provides a theoretically very uncertain basis for accepting an hypothesis. The hypothesis we accept as providing the "best explanation" for a phenomenon can be shown to do so only in the sense of providing a better explanation than the alternatives available to us at the time we draw our inference. We have no way of surveying all possible hypotheses and no way of knowing that the hypothesis we accept is not inferior to a hypothesis that will occur to us (or someone else) tomorrow, next week, or a dozen years from now. As a consequence of this, accepting an hypothesis on the ground that it provides the best available explanation for some phenomenon is reasonable, if at all, only when its theoretical uncertainty is appreciated. (This theoretical uncertainty is compatible with the practical certainty, or certainty beyond "the shadow of a doubt," that I have about the identity of the maker of the wine I received, which could conceivably turn out to be made of something other than Muscat grapes.) As I shall argue a bit later, appreciating this theoretical uncertainty also requires, at least in theoretically significant and practically important cases, that the relevant conclusion be accepted *tentatively* - in a critical, experimental spirit. Closing one's eyes to further evidence or the critical observations of others would show that one's acceptance of a hypothesis is fundamentally unreasonable and unjustifiable.

An important limitation to our epistemic predicament is brought to mind by BonJour's discussion. This is that all justification or certification of acceptability is inescapably conditional. BonJour acknowledges this for what he calls local justification, but it is evident in his strategy of basing a correspondence hypothesis on a doxastic presumption. To justify or certify one thing, we have to assume (or presume) something else. As a result of this, we cannot possibly justify everything unconditionally and at once. Thus, while we may evaluate and even justify our acceptance of a psychological report or observation statement by reference to general beliefs of the four sorts I have mentioned, we must accept or presume that these general beliefs are true or probable. We may proceed to "test" them by conjoining them with other beliefs and making predictions whose success or failure we can ascertain by further observations; and we can justify them to some extent by establishing their "coherence" with other similarly tested general beliefs. In principle, there is no end to this. But this sort of conditional justification - this intellectual bootstrapping, as Glymour has called it [13] - cannot yield theoretical certainty, and it can constitute only part of the process of vindicating our claims. Another part must concern the manner) in which our assumptions, beliefs, and opinions are formed or held: the key idea, as I have indicated, is tentativeness. We must avoid dogmatism, allowing for the possibility of error even in simple cases; and we must be willing to consider arguments against even favorite hypotheses, taking alternatives seriously and listening to what can be said in their favor. We must, in short, adopt the critical attitude towards our conclusions that J.S. Mill discusses so perceptively in his epistemically classic second chapter of *On Liberty* . [14]

The points I have just made apply to a number of familiar issues relating to epistemic uncertainty. For one thing, although the general beliefs or assumptions needed to evaluate psychological reports and observation statements are as fallible as a hypotheis accepted by an inference to the best explanation, they often lie in the background of our thinking and their degree of rational uncertainty is hardly ever considered explicitly. Since justification is, as I have claimed, inescapably conditional - one thing justified or certified as acceptable by something assumed or presumed - many psychological reports and observation statements justifiable only by reference to general beliefs may seem intrinsically credible or patently true. They will continue to appear this way so long as the credentials of the general beliefs necessary for their epistemic evaluation are not identified and examined.

The failure to do this sort of thing helps explain why a claim like "That's scarlet" may seem incorrigible when made by a suitably trained and conscientious observer. Yet background beliefs about the nature of what is observed - in this case, a scarlet or, more generally, a colored object - are clearly relevent to the truth of such a claim, and these beliefs might possibly be rejected, on theoretical grounds, as false. This sort of rejection of general common-sense beliefs about color could conceivably prompt the claim, "Strictly speaking, objects in physical space are not really colored in the way ordinary people believe: such objects do not even reflect light of a constant wavelength. We see spatial objects as scarlet, magenta, or whatnot; but this process of seeing an object as determinately colored is an extremely complex response on our part to a surprisingly varied physical stimulus - one in which no simple physical property corresponding to the color can actually be found."[15]

I should emphasize that common-sense assertions criticized in this way need not be rejected for common-sense purposes. Not all the implications of our assertions are important for or even relevant to our everyday concerns, and when they are not, they are generally ignored. This point is often missed or neglected by philosophers who argue that common sense assertions should be evaluated by common sense criteria and not by their supposed relations to purely theoretical concerns.[16] It is also missed, or at least ignored, by Davidson when he argues that we must regard most of a person's beliefs as true.[17] His idea, roughly, is that we must make this assumption to make sense of a person's speech and that we can offer no coherent argument to the contrary. I have criticized his argument elsewhere, explicitly disputing this last point.[18] My principal claim was that we can interpret other people's words by assuming that they are adequate to their surroundings in much the way that our common-sense words are adequate. This sort of adequacy does not require that the majority of claims made in such words (or in ours) have no technically false implications and are actually true in a strict sense of the word.

2. Epistemic Justification and Rational Uncertainty

The claims I have been making about the uncertainty of our rationally considered assertions have important consequences for the theory of epistemic justification. Perhaps the most important is this. Since a large proporition (I believe most) of our carefully considered opinions in science and everyday life are, strictly speaking, uncertain in ways I have indicated, those opinions are not epistemically justified in the strong sense required for knowledge. We are, nevertheless, reasonable in holding those opinions - though our holding them may fall short of firm belief. Since we are reasonable in holding them - since they are carefully considered and evidentially supported - *we are epistemically justified* in holding them.

In making this last claim I am not contradicting myself, for I have two conceptions of epistemic justification in play here. One applies to assertions, statements, and beliefs; the other applies to people. I have not attempted to clarify the first concept, the one applying to assertions and beliefs; I have merely supposed that it is the concept required for knowledge. (I can allow that this concept can be relativized to a person and a time, as when a philosopher wishes to speak of an assertion, statement, belief, or proposition as justified *for a person at a time* .) I haven't attempted to clarify the second concept either; my claim is merely that such a concept is needed in epistemology, that it is weaker, less stringent or demanding than the first one, and that it applies primarily to persons: according to it, Jones may be said to be epistemically justified in tentatively accepting the proposition that p.

It is worth noting that if epistemic justification is defined, as BonJour defines it, in relation to a coherent set of beliefs that includes scientific beliefs (about molecular reactions, the behavior of light, and so on) then such justification is bound to be too weak to serve as a plausible "third condition" for a definition of knowledge. The reason is simply that the included scientific beliefs, at least, involve too much uncertainty: as members of a coherent set of beliefs, they may epistemically justified, but they are too uncertain (now and in the foreseeable future) to count as knowledge if they happen to be true. To make things a bit more complicated, I might add that a concept of epistemic justification defined, as BonJour defines his, in relation to a coherent set of beliefs that are apt to be true (or whose long-term coherence is conducive to their truth) is too strong for a suitable weak concept of epistemic justification, the kind that is associated with reasonable tentative opinion.

How can an appropriate weak sense of epistemic justification be defined, explicated, or characterized? The explication I favor and have sketched elsewhere is particularly suitable for a concept applying to people rather than beliefs, assertions, or propositions.[19] Accepting or holding an opinion is, broadly speaking, an action or doing, and those who do what (according to certain standards) they are entitled to do, or may do, are justified (according to those standards) in doing it. Since to do what one may do is to do what is permissible, an appropriate weak sense of "epistemic justification" would be tantamount to a sense of "epistemic permissibility." Since, generally speaking, one is permitted to do anything one is not forbidden to do, we could also say that a person is epistemically justified in accepting an opinion, principle, or rule - with a certain degree of tentativeness, we might add - just when he or she is not epistemically forbidden from doing so.

Although I am after an appropriate weak sense of epistemic justification, epistemic permissibility could be very strong, presupposing very stringent standards. W.K. Clifford espoused standards of this kind in his famous "ethics of belief": they require us, he said, to withhold assent to anything for which we have "insufficient evidence" - to guard ourselves from such things "as from a pestilence." [20]   These standards are far too strong for life in an uncertain world where science without induction is impossible. To get an appropriately weak sense of epistemic justification we must relativize it to appropriately weak epistemic standards.

But how are such standards to be identified or defended? The general strategy is, I believe, clear. Since we are concerned with epistemically permissible behavior, the standards we seek are standards for behavior. Such standards relate behavior to ends of some kind. If there are epistemic standards, they are related to epistemic ends. What ends are these? BonJour says that there is just one fundamental end that is relevant here: "we want our beliefs to correctly and accurately depict the world". [21] In his view:

> It is only if we have some reason for thinking that epistemic justification constitutes a path to truth that we as cognitive beings have any motive for preferring epistemically justified beliefs to epistemically unjustified ones. [22]

As I see it, this view is too strong and too simple. It is too strong because we cannot actually know that the inductive methods we use will bring us to the truth in the short run that is the life of our species; and it is too simple because truth is not our sole epistemic value.

Philosophers who say that our principal epistemic end is that of discovering "the truth" mistakenly suppose that there is such a thing as (the) truth. Plato's Socrates seemed to suppose such a thing when he spoke of the philosopher or dialectician aiming to carve reality "at the joints,"[23] and it is implicit in the medieval view that God created natural things in accordance with His Divine Ideas, thus bringing about a system with a right because divinely intended structure. It is also implicit, perhaps, in the ontology of Wittgenstein's *Tractatus* - according to which "Die Welt ist die Gesamenheit der Tatsachen, nicht der Dinge." [24] I am not attempting to saddle BonJour with such a view; but it seems implicit in well known claims by highly respected contemporary philosophers.[25] I think it is a mistake partly because I think it is clearly up to us - human beings - to create kinds or sorts (to specify nature's joints) by our classificatory practices. The world may or may not contain instances of these kinds; or to put it another way, distinguishable regions of the world may not satisfy our kind-criteria. When such criteria are satisfied, a belief, assertion, or proposition is true, but its truth is scheme-relative. Since alternative conceptual schemes are, in my opinion, possible and sometimes even equivalent, [26] there is no unique system of truths that every rational being wants (let alone intends) to discover. The alethic *want* of such a being (if a single basic want could be identified) would be something like discovering what is true, or approximately true, about the world relative to a conceptual scheme of some special kind. The being's epistemic *intention* would have to be weaker than this, for rational beings cannot intend to do what they know, or believe, is not in their power. (Truth is something we have to hope for: given inductive uncertainty, we can't count on getting it - at least to the desired extent.)

I have spoken vaguely of a "special kind" of conceptual scheme here because even partly rational beings have a number of distinct epistemic values, and different rational beings actually rank such values in different ways. Some, like Descartes, appear to be primarily interested in certainty and impatient with mere probabilities; others, like me, have almost the opposite attitude. And then some are interested in the big picture while others are obsessed with details. Even among philosophers there are, as Gustav Bergmann once remarked, both blueprint theorists and sketch theorists.[27] An ideally rational being with ideal interests (supposing we can make sense of such a thing) would no doubt possess a scheme that is more catholic than those of even the wisest actual people, but it would embody several distinct epistemic values.

The values I am thinking of here are reminiscent of a coherence theory. One is *simplicity of conceptual apparatus* - meaning, roughly, minimal redundancy of concepts and explanatory principles. Another value is *comprehensiveness*: the whole world should be covered by the scheme, extensively and intensively. These first two values are united in a third, which might be called "*systematic unity*." The ideal, somewhat vaguely expressed, is to achieve a conceptual picture of the world that is maximally comprehensive and yet unified by a minimal set of explanatory principles (ideally, the smallest set compatible with the desired intensive and extensive comprehensiveness). A final value is *fidelity*. This is not simply truthful representation but something more qualified - perhaps minimal error compatible with the realization of other epistemic values.[28] A highly comprehensive, well systematized view of the world that is only approximately true is no doubt preferable (at least for many thinkers) to a less comprehensive, less well organized view whose truth is less approximate.

Supposing that an appropriate epistemic end can be constructed on the basis of such epistemic values, the next question to face is "How, in relation to such an end, can the epistemic standards we are seeking be identified?" As I have implicitly indicated, BonJour thinks that "the basic role of justification is that of a *means* to truth." [29] I have rejected this idea, vague as it is, because the fundamental riskiness of all known inductive methods make it unrealistic to suppose that we will, in fact, reach the truth (even "more often than not") by complying with some plausible set of epistemic standards. We must admit that we can justifiably adopt opinions and methods without any assurance that the opinions are true and the methods will actually bring us closer to it. I hasten to add, of course, that adopting an opinion or method under such conditions is reasonable only if it is tentative, open-minded, and the like.

If an epistemic aim ideal for a human being is something like getting a maximally comprehensive yet maximally simple conceptual scheme that one can reasonably hope to be minimally erroneous, two sorts of epistemic standards for cognitive behavior can be identified. Standards of the first sort can be described as positive; they identify policies or objectives that actively promote the ideal end. Thus, to obtain the intended comprehensiveness in one's conceptual scheme, one should seek "causes" or explanations for observed or conjectured phenomena; and to obtain the intended simplicity and systematic connection in the scheme, one should minimize redundancy, attempt to subsume disparate phenomena under common principles, eliminate nomological danglers, and so forth. Conceptual activity will be epistemically permissible only when it accords with such policies. Standards of the second sort may be described as negative in aim, for they promote the ideal end indirectly - by prohibiting things that will frustrate it. The key policy here is consistency, deductive and inductive. This policy is particularly important and deserves extended treatment.

3. Consistency and Probability

Deductive consistency is related to the ideal epistemic end in a way that is often misunderstood. If P entails Q, then Q is certain to be true if P is. Philosophers who think of the epistemic end as that of discovering "the" truth often suppose that valid entailments require one to accept the deductive consequences of one's beliefs.[30] But such a requirement is absurd: every belief has infinitely many such consequences, and no one can be expected to accept all of them. The correct requirement concerning acceptance is actually negative: If P entails Q and you accept P, then don't accept ~Q because doing so will introduce inconsistency into your belief set - and this is incompatible with an acceptable epistemic end. Inductive consistency is a related requirement best described by reference to inductive rules. On first approximation it may be identified by the injunction that one should not accept inductive rules that singly or jointly permit mutually incompatible conclusions to be drawn from a consistent body of evidence.

Inductive consistency is a particularly important notion because it is arguable that we may identify acceptable inductive rules solely on the basis of it. The argument in question involves two basic contentions pertaining to the probability calculus, the underlying assumption being that conclusions obtained by inductive rules (or, more generally, by "experimental" methods) are probabilistic in character. The first contention, supported by such writers as Frank P. Ramsey and Bruno de Finetti, is to the effect that any probabilistic conclusion inconsistent with what is inferable according to the probability calculus is inductively inconsistent, or incompatible with a coherent inductive policy. [31] The other contention, suggested by Wesley Salmon among others, is that intuitively plausible inductive methods can be reconstructed within the probability calculas as applications of Bayes' theorem.[32]

The inductive method that I have mentioned in earlier sections of this paper is Inference to the Best Explanation. If we think of an explanation as a relation between statements - an explanans, or explaining statement, H, and an explanandum, or statement of what is to be explained, E - and agree that when an explanation is a good one, the explanandum is inferable from the explanans, then we can regard an inference to the best explanation as an application of the so called hypothetico-deductive (or H-D) method. The application involves the deduction of the datum to be explained, E, from an explanatory hypothesis, H, and acceptable background assumptions, A. (Such background assumptions are a tacit part of the explanans in inferences to the best explanation.) Since the E, deduced from H and A, is true, H is to a degree confirmed; but H is accepted as "the best hypothesis" for additional reasons that users of the H-D method have always taken into account: it is preferable to alternative hypotheses that are also confirmed to a degree by E. [33] (It is simpler or inherently more credible than alternative hypotheses; it fits in better with other assumptions we accept; and the like.) Both confirmation by deduction here and the relevant additional considerations can be accommodated by Bayes' Theorem:

$$P(H_i/E) = \frac{P(H_i)P(E/H_i)}{\sum P(H_j)P(E/H_j)}$$

where Hi is a particular hypothesis belonging to the set of alternatives H1,...,Hj.

One way of seeing the relation of this formula to the H-D method is to note that when evidence E is explainable by a hypothesis H1, the so called likelihood P(E/H1) normally equals 1. When this equality holds, we can decide whether H1 is the "best" hypothesis covering E by employing Bayes' theorem. We do this by considering the prior or antecedent probability of H1 and the relation of this probability to that of the ascertained evidence E computed in relation to the alternative hypotheses H1,...,Hj. These latter considerations are appropriate for H-D inferences because those who make such inferences normally assume that experimental data is most likely explainable by antecedently likely hypotheses and that the occurrence of antecedently unlikely data adds particularly strong support to any hypothesis that, in contrast to plausible alternatives, allows us to predict it. Users of the H-D method also assume that the relative simplicity of a hypothesis is relative to its acceptability, and this too is arguably understandable in probabilistic terms.[34]

Although I shall not attempt to argue the point here, it seems to me that, pragmatic considerations aside, the inferential structure of inferences to the best explanation and (as Salmon says) reasonable applications of the H-D method really can be captured by the probability calculus. But to apply this probabilistic machinery to the subject of epistemic justification, we must consider how the relevant notion of probability is to be understood and, equally important, how the prior probabilities needed to compute the probability of an explanatory (or other) hypothesis are to be ascertained.

Statisticians and others who hold that legitimate inductive (or experimental) methods can be derived from the notion of inductive consistency interpret probability statements as expressing degrees of belief in the relevant propositions. For such people, the probability calculus represents conditions of consistency on such belief. A formula like Bayes' theorem indicates (for them) the degree to which one may consistently believe one thing if one believes certain other things with indicated degrees of firmness. Although this approach to the probability calculus (and to the conceptual foundations of nondemonstrative inference) is very attractive to me, it prompts an important question that requires some discussion. The question is, "What accounts for the reasonableness of the basic beliefs (or the prior probabilities) in relation to which the reasonableness of other beliefs are assessed by the theorems of the probability calculus?"

Statisticians of the so called Bayesian school give an answer to this question that is very exciting for anyone who is highly critical of foundationalism and thinks, as I do, that reasonableness is ultimately a property of one's cognitive procedure rather than of one's belief in some distinctive set of propositions (perhaps those that cohere in a special way). Their answer is that the beliefs in question may ultimately be arbitrary, not reasonable at all: If one forms new beliefs in accordance with the requirements of the probability calculus, taking new information freely into account, one will ultimately obtain an acceptable result no matter what (with one reservation) one's initial beliefs may have been. The reservation is that the degree of one's initial beliefs be positive, not equal to 0. The result attained will be rationally acceptable because it will be in general agreement with the result attained by others who, starting with different initial beliefs, proceed in a similar manner.[35]

To appreciate the basis for this last claim, it is helpful to consider a concrete example. The example I shall present concerns an unscrupulous gambler who has two coins, one fair and the other biased towards heads. Having thrown the latter many times, the gambler believes that the probability of its turning up heads is 0.6. Looking for a game, he takes one of the coins from his pocket; but before he has a chance to see what coin it is, another player snatches it from his hand and announces that the gambler's coin is almost certainly biased: the chances are 8 to 2, he says, that the coin is unfair. The gambler, by contrast, thinks the chances are about equal that the player has the biased coin. Assuming (i) that the gambler and the player are willing to use Bayes' theorem to correct their opinions about the coin on seeing it thrown and (ii) that it is thrown ten times with the outcomes H,H,T,H,H,H,H,H,T,H, we might ask, "What opinions would they have after the first five flips, and again after the second five?" They agree, we may assume, that the probability of getting a single head is 0.6 for the biased coin and 0.5 for the fair one.

In describing the required calculations I shall employ some standard terminology. An antecedent degree of belief is called a *prior,* the probability of a certain outcome given a certain hypothesis is called a   likelihood), and a corrected or updated degree of belief (the probability of a hypothesis given the experimental data) is called a *posterior.* The following tables give the key probabilities for the case at hand, the posteriors calculated by Bayes' theorem.

Here are the gambler's probabilities for the first five flips, which are, again, H,H,T,H,H:

Hypotheses	Priors	Likelihoods	Priors times Likelihoods	Posteriors
Fair	0.5	$(0.5)^5$	0.015625	0.38
Biased	0.5	$(0.6)^4 (0.4)$	0.02592 Sum = 0.041545	0.62

For readers new to the subject, the first likelihood listed here, which can be denoted by "P(HHTHH/fair)," is $(0.5) + 5$ because the probability of each outcome on a fair coin is 0.5, and there are five such outcomes, each independent of the others. The second likelihood, denoted newpage by "P(HHTHH/biased)," is $(0.6) + 4 (0.4)$ because the sequence of outcomes contains four heads, each with a probability of 0.6 on the hypothesis the coin is biased, and one tail, which has a probability of 0.4 on that hypothesis. Here are the player's probabilities for the first five flips:

Hypotheses	Priors	Likelihoods	Priors times Likelihoods	Posteriors
Fair	0.2	$(0.5)^5$	0.00625	0.13
Biased	0.8	$(0.6)^4 (0.4)$	0.041472 Sum = 0.047722	0.87

The initial disagreement was 0.3, the gambler thinking the probability that the coin is fair is 0.5 and the player thinking it 0.2. The first five flips changed this disagreement, for the gambler now judges the probability to be 0.38 and the player 0.13, a difference of 0.25. The gambler's probabilities for the next five flips (H,H,H,T,H) with a revised assessment of his hypotheses (his revised priors) are:

Hypotheses	Priors	Likelihoods	Priors times Likelihoods	Posteriors
Fair	0.38	$(0.5)^5$	0.011875	0.27
Biased	0.62	$(0.6)^4 (0.4)$	0.032141 Sum = 0.044016	0.73

Here are the player's revised probabilities for the next five flips:

Hypotheses	Priors	Likelihoods	Priors times Likelihoods	Posteriors
Fair	0.13	$(0.5)^5$	0.004062	0.08
Biased	0.87	$(0.6)^4 (0.4)$	0.045101 Sum = 0.049163	0.92

Here, after ten flips, the disagreement about the probability of the coin being fair amounts to 0.199, or 0.27 - 0.08. If further data were collected, further revision of the priors would bring the gambler's and the player's opinions even closer. The Bayesian's claim is that if enough data were considered, the opinions of the two people would eventually become indistinguishable. [36]

This outcome, if it can stand without qualification, would be extremely exciting for epistemology. Given the Bayesian claims that I mentioned earlier, we could then say (i) that epistemically permissible inductive methods can be identified and characterized wholly by reference to the consistency conditions for degress of belief; (ii) that we do not have to infer our derivative, posterior probabilities from priors that are either inherently certain and foundational or ultimately inferable from such, but that (iii) we may start with priors that are, to a large extent, epistemically arbitrary (they must not take the values 0) and work our way to intersubjectively acceptable results (or posteriors) by sound inductive methods. What could be epistemically nicer than this?

Unfortunately, things are not (they never are) as nice as they might seem. The convergence of posterior opinion emphasized by Bayesians and illustrated by the example is real, all right, but it is not ultimately inferable by mere rules of consistency from ultimately arbitrary (or largely arbitrary) priors. This is easily seen by reference to the computations involved in the example. As the entries I have included indicate, these computations are based on important assumptions or beliefs that the gambler and the player share. At the lowest level, they agree on the outcomes of the ten flips of the coin; they are, in fact, wholly certain about these outcomes, taking the information as a "given" that they do not express probabilistically.[37] They also agree on the relevant likelihoods and how they are to be computed. This latter agreement is particularly significant. It includes agreement on the possible variety of the outcomes (either heads or tails) and on their probabilistic independence) - on the fact, for example, that later flips are not influenced by the results of earlier ones. (These assumptions about variety and independence are needed if we are to conclude that the likelihood of getting four heads and one tails on the fair coin is $(0.5)^5$ but $(0.6)^4 (0.4)$ on the biased one.) The agreement about likelihoods also includes a specification of the precise degree to which the unfair coin is biased (60% in favor of heads). These points of agreement are not only extensive; the progressive convergence of the new posteriors is fundamentally dependent upon it.

It may be an analytic (or purely verbal) truth that every coin is either fair or biased and that a fair coin is one that ideally turns up heads as often as it turns up tails. But it is certainly not analytic that a biased coin will turn up heads sixty per cent of the time. On the face of it, there are infinitely many ways in which a coin can be biased; if a given coin is either fair or biased in a special way, this is a factual assumption that, if reasonably made, requires some justification. The same is true of the other assumptions I mentioned in the last paragraph: they are factual and, when reasonably made, require some sort of justification. This is always the case with an application of Bayes' theorem: factual assumptions must be made.[38] A particularly important, nontrivial assumption that must always be made when (as in the example) more than one hypothesis is considered concerns the exclusive and exhaustive character of the alternatives. Pure logic will allow us to select "~(The coin is fair)" as an alternative to "The coin is fair," but the former will not allow us compute a determinate likelihood comparable to those in the example.

4. Concluding Remarks

What is the import of all this for the subject of epistemic justification, which led me to discuss Bayesianism in the first place? The answer, I believe, is this. We may be able, as the Bayesian says, to reduce our conception of acceptable inductive reasoning to a set of consistency conditions for degrees of belief, but such conditions will not enable us to achieve any absolute assurance that a particular belief, however weak, is actually true or even close to the truth. As in the case of unqualified belief, consistency conditions merely enable us to identify things we should not believe or accept (to such and such a degree) given that we believe or accept certain other things (to such and such a degree). They also, indirectly, enable us to identify the value (the truth, falsity, or acceptable degree of belief) of one proposition given that other propositions have this or that value. We may appeal to such conditions in the endeavor to justify our acceptance (to an appropriate degree) of some belief or opinion, but we have to acknowledge that any propositional justification we may achieve by this means is inescapably *conditional*: we are showing one belief or opinion to be justifiable given that something else is.

Does this outcome push us back to one of the traditional means of avoiding a regress of propositional justification, a foundational or coherentist theory? I think not. Having argued that the acceptability of even a observation statement or a psychological report is conditional on the acceptability of general beliefs about observers, observation, observable objects, and conditions of observation, I have undermined (at least to my satisfaction) the basis for a foundational theory. There is not even probabilistic bedrock. A coherentist theory of probabilistic justification - something appropriately weaker than a coherentist theory of *knowledge* - might seem more promising, but it is not satisfactory either. If our beliefs (individually more or less firm) are probabilistically consistent, they are, of course, coherent in one important sense - but they are not thereby epistemically justifiable. The difficulty is not that many or even most of the propositions in which we believe strongly may actually be false: this possibility must be accepted merely on grounds of inductive uncertainty. The real difficulty is that many of our mutually consistent opinions may be held uncritically and protected from possible refutation by fanatical attitudes, superstitious fears, institutionally entrenched interests, etc. Such attitudes, emotions, and interests may contribute to *delusive views* that may be probabilistically consistent with accepted opinions, allowed investigations, and entertained conjectures.

This sort of objection is only partly applicable to BonJour's coherence theory, for a system of beliefs coherent in his sense must satisfy his Observation Requirement, the condition that any ingredient belief not justified *a priori* "should in principle be capable of being observationally checked, directly or indirectly, and thereby confirmed or refuted." [39] BonJour no doubt hopes this condition will protect a coherent belief set from the sort of delusion I mentioned, but it does not actually do so as he formulates it. It is not enough that every belief in the system be capable in principle of observational confirmation or refutation; the believer must have the right critical attitude: the will to criticize, to listen to objections, to put even cherished opinions to the test - and, to parody Hume, to proportion one's degree of conviction to the quality and quantity of the available evidence. One cannot prove that a coherent system of beliefs formed in response to sensory input and guided by the right critical attitude will actually correspond to the world, [40] but one can do one's best to undermine the suspicion of delusion and to be a good Quinian sailor on the epistemic sea.

Earlier in the paper, when I spoke of the ideal epistemic ends that acceptable epistemic standards presumably serve, I claimed that such ends are unified by the ideal of getting a maximally comprehensive yet maximally simple conceptual scheme that one can reasonably hope to be minimally erroneous. It is obvious that the idea of such a conceptual scheme is very close to BonJour's idea of a coherent set of empirical beliefs. The fundamental difference between us is that he regards an empirical belief as ultimately justifiable if it belongs to such a coherent set, while I doubt (certainly have no confidence) that such a set of beliefs will ever come into existence. Also, though we both appeal to our respective ideals - our ideal scheme or belief set - in justifying empirical beliefs, we do so in very different ways. For me, beliefs are epistemically justified if they are not inconsistent with such an end and may help toward its realization; for him, beliefs are epistemically justified only if they satisfy a much stronger condition. Since I am confident that the totality of my beliefs do not now, and never will, comprise an ideally coherent set (or anything like one), I am convinced that my position is more realistic than his. On my view, we are epistemically justified in holding an opinion with a given degree of confidence if doing so is not epistemically forbidden (given reasonable epistemic aims). This is not the strong sort of justification required for knowledge; it is the weak sort I have been concerned with in this paper.

NOTES

1. See, e.g., BonJour (1985), chs. 1 & 5.
2. *Ibid.*
3. I am thinking of Saul Kripke's unpublished lectures critical of Robert Nozick's proposed definition of "s knows that p "
4. Anyone who is worried that the number of these opinions is infinite can interpret me as saying that, for every finite representative sample of these opinions, most may not count as knowledge.
5. When I speak of induction in this paper, I am referring not just to enumerative induction (or inductive generalization) but to the whole family of generally accepted methods in which a conclusion is supported by evidence. A better word here might be Hume's "experimental inference." As I shall explain, I intend "induction" to cover inferences to the best explanation and applications of the hypothetico-deductive method.
6. I heard Bas C. van Fraassen attack it in his talk for the Colloquium on Sellarsian Philosophy held at University of Pittsburgh in the fall of 1987. (For a hint on how the inference about the wine can be subsumed under a simple version of Bayes' theorem, see footnote 38 below.)
7. I actually had the experience of "seeing" the hovering old lady. It was far from an ordinary experience; in fact, it appeared to be a perfect example of what is sometimes called "experiencing an apparition." I regard it as clearly hallucinatory, but I can't claim to know how it is best classified scientifically.
8. See Russell (1948), 439-527. Russell (1959), 190-207, made some helpful retrospective remarks on these postulates, indicating how he arrived at them. It is interesting to note that his third postulate (of spatio-temporal continuity) has subsequently been disconfirmed by the experimental verification of Bell's theorem, which implies that interactions in reality may be "non-local." For an excellent discussion of the matter, see Herbert (1987), ch. 12.
9. See BonJour,   91.
10. *Ibid.*, 169.
11. *Ibid.*, 80-82 and 157-188.
12. See footnote 40 below.
13. See Glymour (1980), ch. V.
14. Mill (1859), ch. 2.
15. For a very illuminating discussion of color, see Hardin (1987).
16. Schiffer (1987) makes this assumption is squaring his sentential dualism with his ontological physicalism; see especially   172.
17. See Davidson (1984),   197.
18. See Aune (1988).
19. See Aune (1981).
20. W.K. Clifford (1859), cited in Castell (1963),   63.
21. BonJour,   7.
22. BonJour,   8.
23. Plato, *Phaedrus*, 265E.

24. Wittgenstein (1922), 1.1.
25. I think it is implicit in the so called Putnam-Kripke interpretation of natural-kind terms. See Putnam (1975), 215-271.
26. For a discussion of this last point, see Aune (1987) and Aune (1985), 125f.
27. Bergmann (1954), 89.
28. Some interesting conflicts between fidelity and other epistemic ends are perceptively discussed by Catherine Elgin (1988).
29. BonJour, 7.
30. See Binkley (1965).
31. See Ramsey (1926) and de Finetti (1937) in Kyburg (1964), 61-92 & 93-158.
32. See Salmon (1966), 108-132.
33. See my discussion in Aune (1970), 153-178.
34. See Rosenkrantz (1977), ch. 5.
35. See Phillips (1973), ch. 4.
36. *Ibid.*, 77, where the example I have presented is given.
37. If the occurrence of the relevant outcomes is not taken as certain, a more complicated rule for calculating the relevant posterior probabilities is required. On this see Skyrms (1975), 195-198.
38. This assertion requires some qualification for the simple version of Bayes' theorem in which $P(H/E) = P(H)P(E/H)/P(E)$. This version is useful in cases like that of the mystery wine in which the occurrence of antecedently unlikely evidence (e.g., getting a bottle with a Callaway cork from a western Massachusetts winemaker) may strongly support a hypothesis (e.g. that J.B. made the mystery wine) without explicit reference to alternative hypotheses. I should add that, as I see it, a conclusion can be reasonably accepted on this basis only by someone who is willing to consider further evidence and to modify or reject the conclusion in the light of that evidence.
39. BonJour, 141.
40. My argumentation in the previous section supports this assertion, and it is not undermined by BonJour's global inference to the best explanation. At best, BonJour's inference warrants no conclusion that is not warranted collectively by lower-level inferences for beliefs in the system: the conclusions of both are, in any case, subject to significant uncertainty. At worst, his global inference, in not presupposing empirical beliefs, leaves us no firm basis for identifying rival hypotheses and rejecting them as inferior to the correspondence hypothesis. This last point stands out when BonJour relates his inference to Bayes' theorem (see 181). In comparing the correspondence hypothesis, C, and a skeptical hypothesis, S, with the evidence of coherent beliefs, E, BonJour notes that the numerator in $P(H,E) = P(H)P(E/H)/P(E)$ can be neglected since they will be the same in both cases, i.e. when $H = C$ and $H = S$. We thus need to show that $P(E/C)P(C) > P(E/S)P(S)$. But since the likelihoods here are both 1 or close to it, the comparison has to be based on the values of the priors alone, i.e. $P(C)$ and $P(S)$. But in the case of this global inference no evidence remains to rank these priors.

REFERENCES

Aune, Bruce. *Rationalism, Empiricism, and Pragmatism*. New York: Random House, 1970.
-----. *Metaphysics: The Elements*. Minneapolis: University of Minnesota Press, 1985.
-----. "Epistemic Justification," *Philosophical Studies* 40 (1981), 419-429.
-----. "Action and Ontology," *Philosophical Studies*, forthcoming (1988).
Bergmann, Gustav. *The Metaphysics of Logical Positivism*. New York: Longmans, Green, & Co.,1954.
Binkley, Robert. "A Theory of Practical Reason," *Philosophical Review* 74 (1965), 423-448.
BonJour, Laurence. *The Structure of Empirical Knowledge*. Cambridge, Mass.: Harvard University Press, 1985.
Clifford, W. K. "The Ethics of Belief," (1859), cited, in part, in A. Castell (1963), 62-64.
Castell, Aubrey. *A Modern Introduction to Philosophy*. second edition, New York: Macmillan, 1963.
Davidson, Donald. "The Very Idea of a Conceptual Scheme," in Davidson, *Essays into Truth and Interpretation*, Oxford: Clarendon Press, 1984, 183-198.
de Finetti, Bruno: 1937, *Foresight: Its Logical Laws, Its Subjective Sources*. trans. by H.E. Kyburg, in H.E. Kyburg & H.E. Smokler (1964), 93-158.
Elgin, Catherine. "The Epistemic Efficacy of Stupidity," in Nelson Goodman and Catherine Elgin (1988), 135-152.
Goodman, N. and C. Elgin. *Reconceptions in Philosophy*, Indianapolis: Hackett, 1988.
Glymour, Clark. *Theory and Evidence*. Princeton: Princeton University Press, 1980.
Hardin, C.L. *Color for Philosophers*. Indianapolis: Hackett, 1986.
Herbert, Nick. *Quantum Reality*. New York: Doubleday, 1987.
Kyburg, H.E., and H.E. Smokler. *Studies in Subjective Probability*. New York: Wiley, 1964.

Mill, John Stuart. *On Liberty*. (1859). Many editions.

Phillips, Lawrence, D. *Bayesian Statistics for Social Scientists*. London: Nelson, 1973.

Putnam, Hilary. *Mind, Language, and Reality: Philosophical Papers, Vol. 2*, Cambridge: Cambridge University Press, 1975.

Ramsey, Frank P. "Truth and Probability," in Kyburg and Smokler (1964), 61-92.

Rosenkrantz, Roger. *Inference, Method and Decision*. Dordrecht: Reidel, 1977.

Russell, Bertrand. *Human Knowledge: Its Scope and Limits*. London: Allen and Unwin, 1948.

-----. *My Philosophical Development*. London: Allen & Unwin, 1959.

Salmon, Wesley. *The Foundations of Scientific Inference*. Pittsburgh: University of Pittsburgh Press, 1967.

Schiffer, Stephen. *The Remnants of Meaning*. Cambridge, Mass.: MIT Press, 1987.

Skyrms, Brian. *Choice and Chance: An Introduction to Inductive Logic*. Encino, Calif.: Dickinson, 1975.

Wittgenstein, Ludwig. *Tractatus Logico-Philosophicus* trans. W.K. Ogden, London: Routledge & Kegan Paul, 1922.

The Multiple Faces of Knowing:
The Hierarchies of Epistemic Species

Hector-Neri Castañeda
Indiana University

1. Local vs Holistic Relativity of Justification to Background

Claims, and attributions, of knowledge or justified belief are made against varying backgrounds of assumptions or takings for granted, which are not themselves known or justifiedly believed. Offering an account of the constitution of epistemic backgrounds and an elucidation of their roles are the main parts of a Theory of Epistemic Coherence. This study belongs to the foundations of such a theory. We examine some data and discuss certain theoretical alternatives.

The relativity of knowledge and justified belief to background assumptions is a local relativity. It must not be confused with the *holistic relativity* epistemologists discuss in connection with an infinite regress in the total chain of knowledge. The idea that to know requires total linear justification clearly leads to an infinite regress or to the postulation of some absolutely non-justified or self-justified justifiers that start justification running through a system of beliefs. Those non-justifiers are called foundations. There must certainly be an *entry ramp* into justification questions and knowledge. It does not matter whether we call it foundation or not. At the moment, however, our topic is not holistic relativity or foundationalism, but local relativity or, let us create a verbal contrast, *(local) foundationism*. This is compatible with absolute foundationalism as well as with its denial. To illustrate (local) foundationism consider the following datum:

The Meeting. The Chair of the Department has called a departmental meeting for Friday afternoon two weeks hence. Given the normal background of information about departmental meetings, the Chair, etc., we, after reading the Chair's memo, are justified in believing that the departmental meeting will take place at the appointed time. We assume, rather *take it for granted*, that the Chair will not cancel the meeting or postpone it. Are we also justified in *believing* this? For us to be so further justified we must be certain of acts beyond the present situation: facts outside the issue at hand, which is the date of the meeting, given a certain historical background about the Department. Likewise, we take it for granted that the Dean or the President of the University will not unexpectedly call a general faculty meeting that will automatically cancel our departmental meeting. Nor do we take it as a viable alternative that the University will be closed again because of snow drifts, or the failure of the heating system. Nor do we consider it a relevant alternative that the President of the United States will declare war, or there will some riots. These we merely assume, rather, since we do not even think of them, we take for granted as standard background conditions that make up the justificatory framework for the belief that there will be a departmental meeting a fortnight hence.

Those takens-for-granted - as well as the countless others we cannot specify, except by saying collectively that our corner of the world is as usual or *normal* - are local non-justified justifiers. An absolutist will say that non-justified beliefs or takens-for-granted do not justify anything. This route may lead to skepticism; nonetheless, it is by my lights perfectly respectable. Let's, however, experiment with the other fork of the road.

Clearly, (local) foundationism does have one initial advantage. It accommodates our ordinary talk of being justified in believing this or that, even though we are unable to place our claim in a chain of absolutely justified beliefs. Nevertheless, before adopting this view we must garner more data. We must also be satisfied with the nature of the view.

2. The Manifold Species of Knowing

An immediate consequence of the local relativity of claims and attributions of

231

J.W. Bender (ed.), The Current State of the Coherence Theory, 231–241.
© *1989 by Kluwer Academic Publishers.*

knowledge or justified belief is this:

> (Mult.K*.1)   Knowledge and justified belief are multifarious in their   species and types.
>
> (Mult.K*.2)   The species or types of knowledge and justified belief are determined by the background takens-for-granted.
>
> (Mult.K*.3)   Perhaps the types are determinables in that they are not really definable, but can be exhibited in definitional schemata each capturing a family of species.

(Mult.K*.1)-(Mult.K*.2) are straightforward. Clearly, variations in the networks of background assumptions and takings for granted determine different types of epistemic claims and attributions. An important datum that would favor foundationism are those situations, if any, in which epistemic claims and attributions seem both true and yet are inconsistent. Consequently, if this is the case in daily life we do not use a monolithic concept of knowledge, but utilize a family or perhaps families of concepts of knowing and doxastic justification.

3. Epistemological Multiple-Deontology: Conflicts of Doxastic and Epistemic Duties

Foundationism, with its multiplicity of species of knowledge and justified belief, provides the basis for an application of my comprehensive deontic logic to epistemology. The richness of this deontic logic is due to a fundamental distinction between deontic circumstances and deontic foci. This distinction is needed also in epistemology, as between epistemic circumstances and epistemic foci.[1] In fact, the model I would propose for epistemology is the threefold deontic structure I have found in the structure of the institution of morality.

Morality as I see it is composed of three deontic systems: (i) the *euergetical* system, which proposes moral obligations for the solution of the interpersonal conflicts outside institutions and urges charity (Greek eu+ergeteo = to do good); (ii) the *ethical* system, which ranks morally non-moral institutions and proposes solutions to institutional conflicts, whether personal or interpersonal; (iii) the *metathetical* system, which in special circumstances urges changes (Greek metathesis = change) in the moral code, the ongoing conception of the ideal moral point of view. The pivotal intuitions have been, first, that conflict of wants, of duties, of persons, or institutions is at the core of life, and, second, that morality aims at furnishing a systematic and uniform point for the solution of all conflicts for all occasions and for all agents. A conflict of duties is a reality, not a contradiction, and is a situation in which minimally truths of the following form hold: Obligation$_i$ to A, obligation$_j$ to B, $i \neq j$, and the agent cannot perform A&B, but can perform A&~B and alternatively ~A&B. The subscripts signal the systems of duties involved[2].

Epistemology should, in my opinion, be modeled in the above structure of morality. A network i of evidence or doxastic justification yields a certain *prima facie* duty to believe, a doxastic ought$_{di}$. The doxastic duties conflict without contradiction, and we seek everything-considered doxastic solutions. In accordance with certain principles - constitutive the main field of epistemology - doxastic oughts yield epistemic oughts. These also enter, without contradiction, in conflicts: Ought$_{ei}$ to believe that p and ought$_{ej}$ to believe that q, but p&q&B is a contradiction, where B is the background of takens-for-granted. The conflict is to be solved from an everything-considered epistemic perspective, which urges its acceptance through an epistemic ought$_e$. There are also metathetic epistemic duties to change our living epistemic point of view, our ongoing working conception of the ideal of rationality. Changes in epistemic outlook have been required by advances in scientific theorization, technological progress, even political developments.

The modeling of epistemology on the above conception of morality is the major advantage of (local) foundationism and its multifarious species of epistemic justification. We cannot pursue this here.

4. Local Foundationism and the Standard Basic Epistemology

The foregoing theses of foundationism, (Mult.K*.1)-(Mult.K*.3), cut across the differences between coherentism and foundationalism. Typically basic epistemologists work according to a clear-cut plan: each counter-examples his colleagues' proposals in order to justify his own proposed analysis of *the* meaning of 'X knows that p', where this is built on a lemmatic definition of *the* meaning of 'X is justified in believing that p'. Sometimes the proposed analyses are typically not even recursive or dovetailing: they are linear analysantia offering one single monolithic concept of knowledge and justified belief. A recursive or dovetailing definition of knowing actually delivers a tightly organized family of species of knowings. A recursive definition is not really an analysis, that is, a reduction of the concept of knowing to the concepts entering in the definiens. Thus, basic epistemologists who operate under a presupposition of conceptual reductionism have a good reason for staying away from recursive characterizations of knowing or of justified belief [3].

The clearcut program followed by most basic epistemologists requires the *refutation* of the analyses proposed by others. Thus, the field as a whole - seen so to speak from above - is one of adversarial cooperation: all practitioners cooperate by constructing proposals which asymptotically approach the single meanings of 'know' and 'justified belief'. This is of course an idealization from the outside. Each basic epistemologist may build on others' work, but his aim is to produce *the* final analysis of 'knows'. The disputes about this final analysis have reached a very sophisticated stage: each of the examples and of the proposed analysantia is a masterpiece of complexity. The situation seems to be one of invincible impasse.

Foundationism urges an interpretation of the situation of basic epistemology. Given the three theses (Mult.K*.1)-(Mult.K*.3) it is quite in order to suppose that the debates over *the* analysis of 'knows' and 'is justified in believing' may include disputes that slide past each other. The writers involved may fasten to different species of knowledge, or of justified belief, and argue against the opponent's different species - from the presupposition of a monolithic conception of knowledge.

This is a prediction from foundationism that can be put to the test.

5. A Most Educational Joust Between Keith Lehrer and Alvin Goldman

Keith Lehrer has invented an endurable character named Tom Grabit, who originally lived with a crazy father but lately has turned out to have also an insane mother. Fortunately for epistemology, neither Tom nor either of his parents is our epistemic agent. The original doxastic agent was that paragon of rationality, Keith Lehrer himself. Lately, however, other believers have dislodged Lehrer.

Tom Grabit's doxastic adventures have been variegated and variously informative. Let us unreel some of those early adventures woven around Tom Grabit, as depicted by Lehrer (here and in later citations I introduce capitals to signal my own added emphasis):

> Suppose I see a man, Tom Grabit, with whom I am acquainted and have seen often before, standing a few yards from me in the library. I observe him take a book off the shelf and leave the library. I am completely justified in believing that Tom Grabit took a book, and, assuming he did take it, I know that he did. Imagine, however, that Tom Grabit's father has, [(B)] QUITE UNKNOWN TO ME, told someone that Tom was not in town today, but his identical twin brother, John, who he himself often confuses with Tom, is in town at the library getting a book.

> HAD I KNOWN that Tom's father said this, I would not have been completely justified in believing I saw Tom take the book, for if Mr. Grabit confuses Tom for John, as he says, then I might surely have done so. Imagine further that John is nothing more than a figment of the demented imagination of Mr. Grabit who had a neurotic desire to have twin sons because his older brother has twin sons. Moreover, ... but for this quirk ... Mr. Grabit is quite reliable and truthful man, indeed, more so than the rest of us. ... Surely, if I had known just the latter truths about Mr. Grabit, I would not ... believe that there is a better chance that Tom took the book than that John took it. ... I would fail to know that Tom took the book. [(L)] ... the reason I know is not merely my good fortune at missing out on the speech of Mr. Grabit; it is the consequence of two other important features. First, if I knew not only Mr. Grabit's words but also the truth about these words, to wit, they are neurotic lies, I would remain completely justified in believing that Tom took the book. Second, the beliefs ... that make me completely justified in believing that Tom took the book do not include any beliefs about Tom's father and what he might or might not have said.
>
> (Lehrer 1974, 221f; labeling and capitals are mine.)

Here we have the most exceptional case in the exemplary literature of a believer. This one sees possible conflicts of evidence, weights the different pieces, and explains at (L) why he is justified in believing what he believes. But other epistemologists disagree. For instance, Alvin Goldman holds a much more stringent view:

> ... consider the case in which you apparently see Tom Grabit steal a book from the library. [(B.1)] UNBEKNOWNST TO YOU, Tom's mother has said that Tom is miles away while his twin brother, John, is in the library. This may be ENOUGH TO DEFEAT [(C)] ANY claim on your part to know that *Tom* stole the book, even if it is true. My explanation of this case is that [(G)] you cannot discriminate this truth from *John's* stealing the book. Furthermore, the latter alternative seems to be relevant, as long as Mrs. Grabit says what she says. When it transpires, however, that there *is* no twin - he's only a figment of Mrs. Grabit's demented imagination - this ceases to be a relevant alternative, and you can be credited with knowing. In this fashion, the no-relevant-alternatives element of my account seems able to handle Gettier and post-Gettier examples.
>
> (Goldman 1986, 55; labeling and capitals are mine.)

Palpably, these authors disagree concerning the meaning of the locution 'knows that'. Their disagreement is *not* as philosophical as one might think at first sight. They do not differ in philosophical objectives or in the analytic methodology suitable for achieving those objectives. It is not that they agree on the analysandum and then propose different analysantia. They differ on the analysanda themselves: they use the words 'knows that' differently. Each one has been analyzing, and perhaps revising, the meaning of that locution in his own idiolect. Their meanings differ; hence, astute philosophers as they are, they come up with different analysantia. Each - Lehrer in his passage I have labeled (L) and Goldman in his labeled (G) - explains very clearly how he uses the locution.

What, then, should *we* do?

6. The Slippery Slope of Relevant Alternatives

Not being a native-born speaker of English I dare not intrude by myself alone in the Lehrer-Goldman dispute. Thus I have consulted with ten native speakers. All of them have sided with Lehrer. They agree that in the case both start with, the case in which the observer does not know anything about Tom's parent's statement, the speaker is justified in believing Tom Grabit stole the book. My informants think that asking the speaker to consider whether Tom, with whom he is "acquainted," has a twin, even though he has never heard of him, is excessive. Students in a small class, acquainted with each other and knowing their names, were somewhat bewildered; some, after the example, thought that it be would too demanding to ask them to wonder whether they would ever be justified in their beliefs about what they perceive their classmates do, giving that they have never considered whether those classmates have twins, much less whether unbeknownst to them their classmates' parents have said that their children's twins are now on campus.

Goldman says that before it transpires that John Grabit does not exist the veto power of Tom's father stands over those who perceive Tom act. His reason: because otherwise the relevant twin alternative remains unrejected, *regardless* of whether one knows that it exists or not. To many this is an excessive constraint. It seems excessive even merely as requirement for asserting that one is justified in believing, or that one knows.

My native informants held that an unknown statement such as Grabit's father's cannot have such an epistemic veto power even if it is not refuted, much less if it is utterly false. Even if Mrs. Grabit has a twin son, and even if Lehrer hears her say that John has been with her in the library and Tom is in another town, Lehrer can be justified in believing that Tom stole the book, indeed, he may be in a position to refute, internally so to speak, Mrs. Grabit's claim by the very mass of his perceptions: Lehrer saw Tom's characteristic mole on his left hand, and before he stole the book Tom responded to Lehrer's "Hi, Tom, working hard again!," etc. Yet nothing Lehrer could use to identify Tom as the one who he has seen steal the book secures a logical uniqueness for Tom. A demented mother, or father, or anybody else with some minimal right to claim to know Tom, could, on Goldman's statement, simply by making a statement far away, veto Lehrer's justification. To be sure, there is the point about the alternative being relevant. Is it relevant if Tom's parent lives in a neighboring state and makes his remark to somebody in town on the telephone? Is it still relevant it the remark is a written note he mailed the day before? an oral remark to his neighbor? in Davis, California? In Manila?

Just ponder a skeptic Lehrer asking to himself: "Oh my God! Is that really Tom Grabit - stealing a book? Oh! No! Could it be that he has a hitherto wholly unmentioned twin brother and it is this brother who is stealing the book? But why a twin brother? Why not one of triplets? ... It must be a clone. A look-alike cousin. Well, perhaps a space visitor pretending to be Tom."

Obviously, here we are on a slippery slope. Goldman sees this and claims that many an alternative "is not *relevant*." This is certainly right, and it opens the major topic of epistemology. Yet Goldman quickly adds: "(I do not, however, have a detailed theory of relevance.)" (55) This leaves the issue unresolved.

7. The Internal and External Epistemic Requirements of Normality: Rebuttals and Contra-
     rebuttals

Some informants have asked, "What could have Lehrer done to show that Tom's parent was lying, given that he did not know *anything* at all about Tom's parents or their remarks?"

The situation seems to be very much of the kind I described in a battery of examples called *The Cheater Series* (Castañeda 1980). These examples were intended to establish, among other things, that in claims and attributions of knowledge an *assumption of normality* enters twice over. First, it enters *externally*, not so much as an explicit claim made by those who attribute knowledge, but as a deep-seated taken-for-granted that the world is normal: this has to do with the realistic condition that what is known must be true. Second, the normality condition enters *internally* in that the person who believes that p takes it for granted - even if he or she is incapable of articulating what exactly normality is - that the situation is normal. By normality of the situation I mean that either there were no respects that could make that p false or doubtful, or every respect has been canceled by an opposite respect, hence, has restored certainty and has defeated the falsity-making character of the former respect. The illustrations were made in terms of mechanisms disrupting an established (normal) order - e.g., the contract to cheat on a lottery - and of mechanisms defeating that disruption - e.g. a play of lights and mirrors that made the lottery officer see a different number from the one he was bribed to select. The word 'normal' is not entirely appropriate; it could suggest to a reader the normative idea of normality in which we speak of persons with normal intelligence or eyesight[4].

Perhaps we should speak of *standard epistemic situations* as those situations S in which the believer acquires the belief that p in entrenched reliable ways, and either (i) there is no truth that q about S that casts doubt upon that p, i.e., that q would falsify that p if all the propositions in a set $N(q)$ of propositions about S are true, or (ii) for every truth that q satisfying condition (i) some propositions in the corresponding set $N(q)$ are false, so that the truth of that p is not imperiled by that q. Each proposition that q that satisfies condition (i) will be called a *rebuttal*, and the denials of the propositions in the set $N(q)$ that undermine the refuting force of that q will be called *contra-rebuttals*.

Let us return to Lehrer's belief that Tom Grabit stole the library book. The statement by Tom's parent that he was in another town and it was his twin brother who visited the library is a rebuttal of Lehrer's belief. The statement that the parent was lying is a contra-rebuttal. Here the refuting mechanism and the balancing mechanism are part of the standard (normal) background situation within which Lehrer acquires his belief. This is my requirement of *external normality* or standardness. Lehrer has no idea of the rebuttal. Hence, he need not be concerned with any contra-rebuttal. For him it is enough to conform with the requirement of *internal normality (standardness)*: simply to take it for granted that things in the library and in the town are standard, as usual. This he does. Hence, he knows. The Tom Grabit Case subsumes under The Cheater Series.

8. The Hierarchy of Species of Knowing and Justified Belief

Is, therefore, Goldman mistaken as to how English speakers use sentences of the form "X knows that p"? Is he misconstruing his own idiolect? Perhaps, but very unlikely, or not entirely.

The crucial question is this: Are there examples in other speakers' idiolects handled in the stringent way described by Goldman's analysandum?

There certainly are situations that require stronger uses of 'knows'. Consider, for instance, the case of a criminal detective. He is bound by the rules of his profession to go all out of his way, not merely to investigate unknown relevant alternatives, but to create alternatives. The detective *qua* detective would see Tom, or John, steal the book, and may put him into custody. It does not matter whether the man is Tom, or John. Clearly, the detective's perceptions start him off with a dominant weight. As long as the man remains in custody the identification by name is secondary. If the detective has only statements to go by, still Lehrer's witness' testimony will have a great weight. He will not be faulted by his declaration that he believes that Tom stole the book: he will offer his justification for his belief. Since he doesn't know about Tom's parent's statement about him, he certainly has the *right to say* that he knows. In his role as a detective he must, however, be more cautious before making an apprehension.

Teachers give grade-school students history tests to show what they have learned and know about certain events; yet that knowledge may not be enough for those students to pass the later tests in high-school, and the knowledge these latter tests demand merely qualifies those students as ignorant in college tests - not to mention contributions to the appropriate history magazines.

There are some very strict types of knowledge. Radical skeptics of different stripes are specialists in the most strict types of knowledge. Efforts at meeting, or confuting the skeptic on the assumption of one monolithic type of knowledge is generally self-defeating. The defeat does not merely consist of the loss of an argument; it is the self-defeat of depriving oneself of understanding the dynamics of one's belief acquisition and the coherence of one's own beliefs.

The Lehrer-Goldman disagreement concerning Lehrer's belief that Tom Grabit stole the library book is at an unresolvable impasse. Each has zeroed in on a species of knowledge and has offered a decent characterization of it. Their dispute brings out forcefully the foundationist theses (Mult.K*.1)-(Mult.K*.3), that justified belief and knowledge are multifarious and are determined by varying networks of background assumptions, especially deep-seated and even inarticulable takens-for-granted. The (local) foundationist agrees with their claims about Lehrer's knowing that Tom Grabit stole a book and finds them only apparently contradictory. They are studying two different types of knowledge within the family of knowings.

9. Some Morals from the Lehrer-Goldman Disagreement

It may not be amiss to record some important morals that issue from the preceding discussion:

C1. On most types of knowing$_i$ at issue in most daily proceedings, whenever there is no conflict of evidence confronted by a believer S and S's evidence in support of a proposition that p is as strong as it normally or standardly can be, and S has no idea of a rebuttal lurking around, then S is (internally) justified$_j$ believing that p - where 'j' signals the relevant background assumptions and takings for granted.

C2. If a believer S conforms to the conditions of C1, but unbeknownst to him there are some rebuttals and each rebuttal is voided by a contra-rebuttal, then S is still justified$_j$ in believing that p.

C3. If a believer S faces a conflict of evidence between her own perceptions and another person's testimony, there is no *a priori* reason for S always to assign to the testimony an epistemic veto power to be overridden by additional evidence that transcends her perceptions for S to be justified$_j$ in believing that p.

C4. Sometimes there are *two* sets of criteria for claiming that X knows that p. Since the criteria conflict, and they are equally entrenched in the idiolects of English, it is hard to judge some uses substandard. Thus, it seems reasonable to hold that in such situations we confront a conflict of *two different species i and j of knowing*: believer S knows$_i$ that p, without knowing$_j$ that p. As an example we have Lehrer's both knowing$_L$ and not knowing$_G$ that Tom Grabit stole the library book, where 'knows$_L$' and 'knows$_G$' denote the types of knowing described, respectively, in the passages I labeled (L) and (G) in Lehrer's and Goldman's quoted texts.

10. Species of Knowing Relative to Interrogative Epistemic Powers

Moral C4 is of the utmost importance. It deserves elucidation and further motivation. We arrived at it from the general relativity of doxastic justification and knowledge to background assumptions and takings for granted. Then we found the helpful example furnished by Lehrer and Goldman. We need more empirical corroborative data. We must investigate whether for some situations a person, let us call her Helen, and a proposition that p:

(11) At time t Helen knows that p;

(12) At time t Helen does not know that p;

(13) There is no contradiction between (11) and (12);

(14) The common words in sentences (11) and (12) seem to have, on all fours, the same sense or meaning.

This would provide us with a puzzle to be solved. Doubtless, many local theories can be invoked to solve the puzzle. As always, we want our theories to be capable of being snugly embedded in more comprehensive theories. We already have data urging us to distinguish different species of knowing. Thus a simple theoretical move is to postulate that the word 'knows' has the same meaning in (11) and (12), denoting a generic type of knowing, but the puzzle arises from the tacitness of the different species of knowing predicated in (11) and in (12). The situation is analogous to a child's puzzle that two things are blue, yet the color of one is not the color of the other. Once more, this account is *not* a deductive consequence of the data (11)-(14): it is only at this juncture the simplest theoretical posit.

One crucial caveat. In a situation like the one depicted in (11)-(14) we may say that the *sentence* 'Helen knows that p' occurs ambiguously in (11) and (12). But we must *not* conclude from this that the word 'know' is ambiguous[5].

A datum that fits our situation like hand and glove has been provided by Lawrence Powers in his magnificent essay (Powers 1978). He reports having asked Helen [6] :

(Q) Is there an English four-letter word that ends in EE, ENN and WHY?

[The reader new to (Q) may want to investigate the answer before continuing reading.] The fact is that Helen went through the English dictionary in her memory and could not find a word answering to the description in (Q). After a pregnant pause Powers asked Helen mischievously:

(R) Is the word 'deny' an English four-letter word that ends in EE, ENN and WHY?

Helen laughed with an expression of having been taken in for a ride. Her laugh and her feeling are also part of the data. The situation was this:

(D)   Helen said "No, I don't think so" as an answer to question (Q); but she, laughing *knowingly*, said "Yes, of course there is an English four-letter word ending in EE, ENN, and WHY," when confronting question (R).

Let the proposition that P be "There is an English four-letter word ending in EE, ENN, and WHY." Helen's laugh suggests that she already knew that P when Powers asked her question (Q), but that she didn't know that she knew, yet she ought to have known. Since believing and knowing are dispositional states Helen does not commit a howler by suggesting that she has known that P all along. Yet she failed to exhibit that knowledge when she was asked question (Q). When she attempted to answer this question she tested her doxastic dispositions, and she failed the test. Thus, it seems literally true that she both knows and does not know that P. Hence, there are two species - and perhaps also two types[7] - of knowing involved. Then (D) may be exegesized as suggesting that questions (Q) and (R) and Helen's powers to give the answers she gave are connected with her knowing that P. I propose to go further and theorize that (D) illustrates how justified belief and knowledge are relativized to powers to answer questions, which are, for this reason, hereafter called *epistemic powers*. Thus, in this case we have:

(11.a)   Helen knows$_R$ that P;
(12.a)   Helen does not know$_Q$ that P.

11.   An Interesting Local View and Two False Empiricistic Principles

One structural remark may not be out of place. In their typical uses 'know' and 'believe' denote dispositional states, referring to the storage of information, their retrieval, and the connection to the world and other pieces of information the believer has. Coming to believe is generally conceived to be a way of acquiring information to store in oneself; coming to know is generally conceived to come to possess what one has (believes), can retrieve it, and can connect it to reasons (other beliefs) that guarantee its truth. This is the general intuition or model on which I developed the Multiple-Species Indexical Theory of Knowledge. To accommodate this we may interpret datum (D) as showing how *rehearsals* of believing can be *caused* by different episodes of asking questions; and also how rehearsals of knowledge can be prompted by certain episodes of asking questions.

If we take beliefs as stored information, whatever the structure and the mechanisms of their storage may be, then Helen has at any time of her life certain doxastic systems, which she may amplify through different experiences, including the experience of being asked questions. This allows of another account of Helen's predicament. It might be said that at the time she was asked question (Q) Helen did not know [presumably in one monolithic sense of 'know'] that there is an English four-letter word ending in EE, ENN, and WHY, but her very episode of understanding question (R) provided her with this knowledge. This is a good local account. It seems to me, however, to leave Helen's special laugh and sense of having been taken in unaccounted for. This local account would, certainly, fit a doxastic version of the old Lockean principle of concept empiricism:

(Conc.Emp) *Nihil est in intellectu quod non fuerit in sensu.*

Its doxastic counterpart runs as follows:

(Dox.Emp) Nobody believes any proposition he or she has not thought.

According to this alleged principle, Helen wouldn't believe that 'deny' is a word ending in EE, ENN, and WHY, if she has never thought of this, regardless of how many times she has uttered and written 'deny'. But both forms of empiricism seem to me to be mistaken. An operational view, in consonance with experience, recognizes that persons have concepts they have acquired without perception of instances as much as have beliefs that were somehow unconsciously wrought out without having to have been rehearsed in episodes of thinking. Thus, this local account of datum (D) about Helen above does not seem to blend well with other facts and accounts of the mental phenomena. I hasten to explain that I am not in sympathy with the local view that Helen was caused to believe and know that P when she was asked question (R), but this type of account may be perfect in other cases. Surely Mary's asking Helen a question, even question (R) or (Q), may cause Helen to know about Mary's state of mind, about the condition of her larynx, about the topic uppermost in her mind at the time, what she thinks of Helen, and so on[8].

12. Parameters at the Core of Epistemic Justification

Doxastic and epistemic justification constitutes a hierarchy of species and degrees. This hierarchy is in part determined by the powers to answer questions which in their turn follow the hierarchies of the questions that are their contents[9].

The powers to ask questions are just one parameter. Understood broadly the power to answer a given question is itself a bundle of powers: to understand the question, to retrieve, derive, or construct an answer from the information stored in oneself, to do so in accordance with the appropriate methodological requirements. Thus, a crucial doxastic and epistemic sub-parameter submerged in the powers to answer questions is the manifold of powers to draw inferences and to propose hypotheses. Yet it is worthwhile to stress the powers to draw inferences as a special parameter.

The powers to answer questions and to draw inferences are of extreme importance. They allow us to have a broader view of doxastic and epistemic justification than is customary: they take us out of the circle of beliefs, within which epistemologists tend to remain. They bestow a dynamic quality upon justification and knowledge.

The dynamic character of epistemic justification allows it to be subordinated to different epistemic purposes. Here is another fundamental respect in which we must abandon the monolithic view of justification and knowledge. It is easy to suppose that in the pursuit of epistemically justified belief there is just *one* indivisible purpose: to attain truth. However, this is not quite right. Given the limitations of our nature some truths cannot be attained but only approached, and this imposes methodological constraints. Furthermore, the purpose of seeking for truth is to live in accordance with certain general plans, including the struggle for basic survival and the mastery of the environment. Knowledge and epistemic justification are at the service of the knower and of the *whole* of the community of knowers, they include the establishment of varying limits of approximation to truth and of useful patterns of truths. We saw both the methodological constraints and the degree of approximation of belief in the above example of children's increase in knowledge along their educational career. We also saw these same types of constraints operating in the case of police charges, court indictments, and jury decisions [10]. We also saw some stringent methodological requirements present in Alvin Goldman's preferred species of justification, and some more manageable methodological requirements promote Lehrer's belief that Tom Grabit stole the library book to the status of knowledge, in Keith Lehrer's preferred species of knowledge.

Let's sum up the discussion of parameters that distinguish between the types or species of knowledge and justified belief by making explicit the parameters we have seen function in our exegesis of examples. These are:

    (i)   a belief condition;

    (ii) a methodological relevance condition, which includes methodological constraints, individual epistemic goals, and social objectives;

    (iii) an epistemic power condition;

    (iv) an inferential power condition;

    (v) an external stability or standardness (normality-abnormality cancellation) condition about the environment surrounding the believer, and an internal standardness condition: the believer takes it for granted that the world is stable or that he or she is justified in believing that every rebuttal he is cognizant of is undermined by a contra-rebuttal;

    (vi) an evidence condition.

These parameters deliver a more complex view of knowledge than most epistemologists with reductionist proclivities would like. Yet it seems to me that a wide-ranging canvassing of cognitive experiences, with detailed phenomenological exegesis of diverse examples, may very well show that we must reckon with other *further* parameters for a fuller understanding of our epistemological situation.

NOTES

1. For data urging epistemic paradoxes analogous to the well known paradoxes of (actional) deontic logic, see Castañeda 1988. The appendix contains a second-order two-sorted quantificational deontic logic. For a discussion of the deontic paradoxes see Castañeda 1975 Chapter 7, and Castañeda 1980b. See also Tomberlin 1988b and other materials mentioned in its bibliography.
2. See Castañeda 1974 Chapters 1 and 8.
3. Anil Gupta has done admirable work on circular definitions. He has in fact proposed to interpret them as providing schemata for "revising" the extension of the defined predicate. See Gupta 1989. I want to interpret his work as the study of families of properties: the circular definitional schema introduces the generic property, each step of revision introduces the extension of a species. Thus, the circularity is an important treatment of a major generic-specific ambiguity. In any case, his work generalizes on recursive definitions. We may use it in epistemology to capture the varieties of types and species of knowing. He is not pleased with this interpretation.
4. Robert Shope proposed this interpretation in his comments at the 1986 Brown University Symposium in Epistemology in Honor of Roderick Chisholm. Shope's criticisms of my "reliabilist analysis" of 'knows' in Shope 1983 do not take into account the Multiple-Species thesis of my Indexical View of knowledge proposed in Castañeda 1980a.
5. Boër and Lycan 1986 makes this objection. For responses see Castañeda 1986 and Kapitan 1989.
6. I have been recently told by Helen Cartwright that she is the Helen of the Powers's story.
7. Boër and Lycan 1986 take issue with my Multiple-Species view. They speak, however, of tacit knowledge. This seems to me to be a type I want to recognize. Hence, the species captured by my definition schema in Castañeda 1986 are species under the type *operative knowledge*. Lehrer 1983 and Boër and Lycan 1986 object to distinguishing knowledge species by the powers to answer questions. See the comments on the former by Hilpinen 1988 and on the latter by Kapitan 1988.
8. For further discussion of alternative views see the Lehrer 1983 and Castañeda 1983, as well as Boër and Lycan 1986 and Castañeda 1986.
9. For more of these constraints see the exchange between Boër and Lycan 1986 and Castañeda 1986.
10. Castañeda 1983, develops an account of the *answer*-relationship between a question and a proposition that is answer to it. Castañeda 1986 develops a theory of interrogative content that is the content of epistemic powers, i. e., the powers a person puts into action when she knows operatively-Q that p when asked Q?

REFERENCES

Boër, Stephen E., and Lycan, William G.. "Castañeda's Theory of Knowing," (1986), in Tomberlin 1986, 215-235. This is a detailed critique of Castañeda 1980a.
Castañeda, Hector-Neri. *The Structure of Morality*. Springfield, Ilinois: Charles Thomas Publisher, 1974.
-----. *Thinking and Doing: The Philosophical Foundations of Institutions*. Dordrecht: Reidel, 1975.
-----. "The Theory of Questions, Epistemic Powers, and the Indexical Theory of Knowledge," (1980a), in *Midwest Studies in Philosophy* 5, (1980), 198-237.
-----. "The Paradoxes of Deontic Logic: The Simplest Solution to All of Them in a Fell Swoop," (1980b), in Hilpinen 1980.
-----. "Knowledge, Probability, and Certainty (Reply to Keith Lehrer)," in Tomberlin 1983, 451-458.
-----. "Reply to Stephen E. Boër and William G. Lycan," in Tomberlin 1986: 350-370.
-----. "Knowledge and Epistemic Obligation," in Tomberlin 1988.
Goldman, Alvin I. *Epistemology and Cognition*. Cambridge: Harvard University Press, 1986.
Gupta, Anil. "Truth." *Aristotelian Society Proceedings*, 86, 1989.
Hilpinen, Risto, ed., *Deontic Logic and the Foundations of Ethics*. Dordrecht: Reidel Publishing Company, 1980.
-----. "Review of Tomberlin 1983." *Nous* 22, (1988).
Kapitan,Tomis, "Review of Tomberlin 1983." *Nous* 23, (1989).
Lehrer, Keith. *Knowledge*. Oxford: Oxford University Press, 1974.
-----. "Coherence and Indexicality in Knowledge," in Tomberlin 1983, 253-270, a critique of Castañeda 1983a.
Powers, Lawrence, "Knowledge by Deduction." *Philosophical Review* 87, (1978), 337-371.
Shope, Robert. *The Analysis of Knowing*. Princeton: Princeton University Press, 1983.
Tomberlin, James E., ed.. *Agent, Language, and the Structure of the World*. Indianapolis: Hackett Publishing Company, 1983.
-----. ed.. *Hector-Neri Castañeda*. Profiles Volume No. 6. Dordrecht: Reidel Publishing Company, 1986.
-----. ed.. *Philosophical Perspectives: 2. Epistemology*. (1988a). Atascadero: Ridgview Publishing Company, 1988.
-----. "Obligation, Conditionals, and the Logic of Conditional Obligation," (1988b). *Philosophical Studies* 73 (1988).

Equilibrium in Coherence?

Ernest Sosa
Brown University

The method of reflective equilibrium aims to maximize two factors in one's beliefs: harmonious coherence, and plausibility of content.[1] Analytic philosophy has long paid deference to these factors, for instance in its use of the counterexample, which attacks a principle as *incoherent with the plausible* (by one's lights). A critique of this tradition has recently appeared, and it shall be my main objective here to assess its merits. An appendix will apply our results to issues of moral relativism and rationality.

A. Epistemologies in Conflict
Radical methodism is opposed to narrow reflective equilibrium. Karl Popper champions such methodism, Nelson Goodman such equilibrium. This opposition leads to a more moderate equilibrium, wide rather than narrow, in a sense to be explained.

1. Methodism
"Science is justified by means of induction on the basis of observation and experience." This has been widely accepted and is widely accepted today. According to Popper, nevertheless, to think thus is a grave error, for as Hume showed, no supposed inductive reasoning is of any value. Popper reasons that "...theories can never be inferred from observation statements, or rationally justified by them." For "...induction cannot be logically justified." (Popper, 42). That is to say, the fact that a theory T has been induced from certain data does not justify accepting T, since it does not ensure that T is true. Even if induced correctly from true data, it is still possible that the theory be false.

That is why Popper opposes induction and favors appeal to falsification. Unlike induction, falsification is a deductive process. A datum D falsifies a theory T only if it entails the negation or falsity of T. If the negation of a theory follows by deductive logic from certain data, then the theory must be false. For Popper, corroboration consists *not* in inducing a theory on the basis of experience but in submitting it to tests: i.e., in trying to falsify it by means of observational data. (And a statement is scientific only if it is at least falsifiable.)

But how do we respond to the Duhem-Quine objection? "No matter how experience turns out," says the objection, "it is always possible to retain any given commitment, even if this requires drastic changes in the rest of our beliefs." In other words, no statement is strictly falsifiable, scientific statements included, especially those which are highly theoretical.

Against this objection, Popper offers a twofold defense:

> (a.) To derive a testable prediction from a scientific theory it is often necessary to make use of auxilliary suppositions which are numerous and complex, and many of them implicit. "If we do make auxilliary assumptions, then of course we cannot be certain whether one of them, rather than the theory under test, is responsible for any refutation. So we have to guess."[2]
>
> (b.) We "...can always immunize a theory against refutation. There are many such evasive immunizing tactics; and if nothing better occurs to us, we can always deny the objectivity - or even the existence - of the refuting observation." But such evasion puts an end to any science worth pursuing.[3]

Popperian methodology is intricate when displayed fully, yet it seems incoherent for the following reasons.

J.W. Bender (ed.), The Current State of the Coherence Theory, 242–250.

First of all, it rejects induction *for not being deductively valid* , yet accepts a method of falsification no more valid than induction, since strictly speaking falsification takes us only so far; beyond that we cannot proceed except by guessing and by rejecting abhorrent immunizing tactics; but neither such guessing nor such rejection can be deduced from perceptual experience or observation.

One can of course immunize a scientific theory against all refutation, if only by denying the objectivity or even the existence of any contrary observation. But to immunize thus is a ridiculous evasion. About that Popper is clearly right. How ironic that he should scorn his message in his own practice! What motive could there be to deny that certain predictions and expectations are justified (as, for instance, that normally a pen held aloft will fall if released), or at least better justified than others (as it is more reasonable to expect the pen's fall than its metamorphosis into an elephant)? Whatever may be Popper's motive, the effect of his practice is to immunize a certain theory derived from Hume. Apparently, for neither philosopher is any belief reasonable unless formed by an infallible process: no fallible form of reasoning can yield justified beliefs.

This Hume/Popper epistemology is incompatible with many data: its truth would preclude justification for the simplest and most common expectations that guide our daily lives. Consequently, only immunizing it can we sustain our belief in such a theory; only denying that our common expectations are a whit more reasonable than their respective denials, no matter how insensate or even insane.

In sum. Popper accepts an exclusively deductive methodology: only deductive proof can justify belief. It follows that almost nothing of what we believe ordinarily can be justified, which applies both to science and common sense. Popper defends his method by denying that we could possibly be justified in our beliefs of science or daily life. Ironically, this immunizes a theory of justification uncritically accepted from Hume and Descartes.

2. Narrow Reflective Equilibrium

These most recent observations are in close harmony with an influential methodology of philosophy expounded by Nelson Goodman as follows:

> How do we justify a *de*duction? Plainly by showing that it conforms with the general rules of deductive inference. An argument that so conforms is justified or valid, even if its conclusion happens to be false. An argument that violates a rule is fallacious even if its conclusion happens to be true...Analogously, the basic task in justifying an inductive inference is to show that it conforms to the general rules of *in*duction...
>
> Yet, of course, the rules themselves must ultimately be justified. The validity of a deduction depends not upon conformity to any purely arbitrary rules we may contrive, but upon conformity with valid rules. When we speak of *the* rules of inference we mean the valid rules - or better, *some* valid rules, since there may be alternative sets of equally valid rules. But how is the validity of rules to be determined? Here...we encounter philosophers who insist that these rules follow from some self-evident axiom, and others who try to show that the rules are grounded in the very nature of the human mind. I think the answer lies much nearer to the surface. Principles of deductive inference are justified by their conformity with accepted deductive practice. Their validity depends upon accordance with the particular deductive inferences we actually make and sanction. If a rule yields unacceptable inferences, we drop it as invalid. Justification of general rules thus derives from judgments rejecting or accepting particular deductive inferences.
>
> This looks flagrantly circular. I have said that deductive inferences are justified

> by their conformity to valid general rules, and that general rules are justified by their conformity to valid inferences. But this circle is a virtuous one.... *A rule is amended if it yields an inference we are unwilling to accept; an inference is rejected if it violates a rule we are unwilling to amend.* The process of justification is the delicate one of making mutual adjustments between rules and accepted inferences; and in the agreement thus achieved lies the only justification needed for either.
>
>   All this applies equally well to induction. An inductive inference, too, is justified by conformity to general rules, and a general rule by conformity to accepted inductive inferences. (Goodman 1973, 63-64).

Foundationism with regard to a certain domain is the project of legitimizing that domain by showing how it may be founded on a certain basis. Descartes's radical foundationism tries to show how all our beliefs, both the scientific and the quotidian, may be founded by means of deduction on a basis of intuitive reason. But ethical foundationism need not be so radical. Having adopted as basis some theory of practical reason, or about the meaning of moral language, ethical foundationism may then try to derive principles of ethics from the given basis. Recent foundationist projects have elicited less than universal agreement, however, and many have turned to the alternative method used for example by John Rawls in his *Theory of Justice*. It is not Rawls's objective to appeal beyond ethics in search of some external foundation. On the contrary, one may proceed in the way pointed out by Goodman. Specific moral judgments about actual or imaginary situations may be justified by means of moral principles or rules, and these in turn may be justified by their agreement with the specific judgments accepted. This is the method of *narrow reflective equilibrium* . But one may also appeal to a wider reflective equilibrium, as follows.

3. Wide Reflective Equilibrium

    Let us distinguish our moral philosophy from our enclosing body of knowledge and wisdom. And let us distinguish further between (i) philosophical reflection aimed at formulating moral principles, (ii) philosophical reflection aimed at explicating how one justifies acccepting particular moral views or principles, and (iii) the knowledge or wisdom in general possessed by one who reflects in either of the two ways just distinguished. Having drawn these distinctions, we turn next to the "starting points" of the knowledge or wisdom of the thinker who reflects. In such philosophical reflection we may begin with intuitions and beliefs about matters of morality, of causation, of knowledge, of perception, *et cetera*; which does not imply that our knowledge and wisdom must begin with our philosophical reflection.

    Starting points of the process of philosophical reflection need not be original sources for the justification or aptness of the resulting beliefs. Our attention may be drawn to certain beliefs or attitudes about morality, causation, perception, knowledge, *et cetera* , as a way of launching philosophical reflection, and we may reach various conclusions and form various hypotheses on the basis of such beliefs or attitudes. Such beliefs or attitudes would then be psychological starting points of reflection and occasionally even grounds for the *results* of such reflection. However, that does not deny them a source in turn of their own aptness or justification. Nor need that source of their own justification have been some further inference or reflection. For example, epistemological reflection *might* give rise to the conclusion that perception and memory are ultimate sources of aptness or justification and our initial basis for philosophical reflection *might* have as its own basis some perception and memory. Thus, reflection might begin with things that one reads (perception) or remembers (memory). Yet this part of our initial basis of perception or memory for philosophical reflection might never have been inferred from anything, not by the subject who reflects. Accordingly, even though they serve as starting points for philosophical reflection, such beliefs might still have a source for their own aptness or justification through their origin in perception or memory.

The method of *narrow reflective equilibrium* in any domain is restricted to the end of securing harmony between specific judgments and general principles in that same domain. This is the method expounded and defended by Goodman. The method of *wide reflective equilibrium* seeks harmony between the beliefs and principles accepted in the given domain, but it seeks harmony also with beliefs and principles in any other pertinent domain. Clearly, the narrow method cannot be fundamental. Narrow reflection must be supplemented by wider reflection, at least to the point where we are satisfied that there is no other domain relevant to the topic under reflection.[4]

B. Critique of Reflective Equilibrium

The use of reflective equilibrium has been attacked as serving only to organize and protect conservative orthodoxy. This objection has some weight when directed against the narrow equilibrium favored by Goodman, the sort of reflection that encloses itself in a particular ambit - say, induction, or normative ethics - and aims for the best coherence of one's views*within* that ambit. More defensible is the method of wide equilibrium, however, since it does not isolate itself from any knowledge or wisdom, no matter how far afield, but takes into account *everything* that may seem pertinent.

Wide equilibrium seems equivalent to a pure coherentism which at any juncture would always opt for the most harmoniously and comprehensively coherent view available. If a conflict pits the intuitive pull of an example against the tug of a familiar principle, we seek to remove or revise one or the other, so as to remove the tension. Sometimes the particular intuition(s) will win, but sometimes the tug of the principle must prevail. In any case, our aim in dealing with the problem is to remove the tension and restore harmonious coherence while retaining as much as we can of our views (thus the comprehensiveness desideratum).

Equilibrium coherentism has been a target of repeated attacks. Most recently a spirited critique has been published by Stephen Stich,[5] who warns against supposing that mere reflective equilibrium, and the comprehensive coherence involved, can rationally justify one's beliefs and attitudes.

Actually, Stich takes aim at "the tradition of analytic epistemology," defined as "... any epistemological project that takes the choice between competing justificational rules or competing criteria of rightness to turn on conceptual or linguistic analysis" (405). But I doubt that there is any such tradition.

Not since Moore's "open question" attack on the "naturalistic fallacy" has normative ethics or epistemology been thought by many (if any) to turn on conceptual or linguistic analysis--except in an outlandish sense of "turn" which makes *every* choice among sentences "turn" on such "analysis" by "turning" on what the terms involved mean, on what concepts are thus involved.

Stich offers two exhibits as evidence for his conception of analytic epistemology: (A) some quotations from Alvin Goldman's *Epistemology and Cognition* (1986) and (B) a reference to Robert Shope's *The Analysis of Knowing* (1983).

Concerning exhibit A, Stich argues that much of what Goldman says

"...suggests that, on his view, *conceptual analysis* or *conceptual explication* is the proper way to decide among competing criteria of rightness. The correct criterion of rightness is the one that comports with the conception of justifiedness that is "embraced by everyday thought or language" (58). To test a criterion we explore the judgments it would entail about specific cases, and we test these judgments against our "pretheoretic intuitions." "A criterion is supported to the extent that implied judgments accord with such intuitions, and weakened to the extent that they do not" (66). [6]

It is puzzling to argue thus when writers in normative ethics and epistemology have long distinguished emphatically between mere linguistic or conceptual analysis and substantive theorizing. To use exhibit A as above, in the teeth of that widely shared distinction, must depend on some such assumption as this: "Unless one has some pretty strange views about intuitions, it is hard to see what we could hope to gain from capturing them apart from some insight into the concepts that underlie them" (411). But the required views about intuitions are not strange in contemporary ethics and epistemology.

As for exhibit B, Shope's book is about the analysis of propositional knowledge or of 'S knows that p', in response to the Gettier problem. *This* may well fall properly within the ambit of conceptual or linguistic analysis, and has widely been thought to do so. But theories of justification are quite another matter.

Besides, Stich's main point against so-called "analytic epistemology" can be disentangled from his unusual views about the place of linguistic or conceptual analysis. What he highlights in his whole discussion is, after all, the simple fact that the prevalence of certain "intuitions" is no sure guide to theory or practice, that such consensus cannot function as a fundamental criterion in epistemology or ethics. And *this* valuable point deserves emphasis. Agreement can still remain a relevant factor, moreover, with *some* proper weight in one's formation of ethical or epistemic views. If we find ourselves in *dis*agreement with others, it would lend us plausibility and coherence to have a theory of error explaining why and how others go wrong - especially if our position turns out to be solitary.

There are hence *two* versions of reflective equilibrium and coherentism: (a) the individual version, which requires reflective equilibrium and coherence in one's own views, even if these turn out to disagree with those held by others, and (b) the social version, which requires reflective equilibrium and coherence *across* persons in a group, even for the justification of individual members in the group. The individual version seems more plausibly defensible, especially since it would still admit social considerations in the way already suggested - through the increment of coherence that may derive from knowing oneself in agreement with others.

Perhaps Stich's arguments could be applied even against our individual version of reflective equilibrium. Stich himself does not do so, even in his claim about a "...guru who is as bonkers as he is charismatic," that "...we certainly don't want to say that the followers of such a guru would be rational to invoke whatever wild inferential principle might be in reflective equilibrium for their leader" (410). For there is here no *explicit* suggestion that the guru himself cannot be rational (though bonkers).

If the argument is *not* extended even implicitly to the individual version, however, then analytic epistemology can easily meet the critique, simply by opting for that individual version of reflective equilibrium. It seems to me that this is anyhow the best position open to analytic epistemology, and that the appeal to "common sense" or to "ordinary intuitions" should be considered accidental. As epistemologist (or moral philosopher) one is primordially concerned to elaborate one's *own* coherent view. One's primary project is thus first person, though normally one takes one's own situation to be more or less widely shared in relevant respects, and one hence offers one's (first-person) results to others in the familiar style of Descartes. And if one's pertinent intuitions seem widely enough shared, they may then be labelled "common sense intuitions," though it is not their being common that really matters. For that is after all just an accidental feature which both relieves one from the burden of a theory of error and also makes one's results seem of interest to others.[7]

Again, Stich's arguments might be applied even against our individual version of reflective equilibrium; and here we must make a stand, or so I will argue. Nevertheless, even here Stich's reasoning retains the merit of highlighting the value of a distinction important for epistemology, that between rational justification and wider intellectual virtue.[8]

C. Defense of Reflective Equilibrium

Admonished to recall that by the test of equilibrium a coherent madman or fanatic would count as rational, we need to distinguish two forms of madness or fanaticism. On one side is the madness or fanaticism that weaves systems of impressive complexity, systems that satisfy the requirements of deductive logic, and even probability theory, statistics, and inductive logic. Such a madman or fanatic is willing to postulate hypotheses heavy with epicycles, if they will only preserve the beliefs or attitudes favored by his madness or fanaticism.

But there is also a madness or fanaticism which needs no aid of epicycles. For it relies rather on selective or even illusory perception or memory. Whatever incoming data may clash with the favored beliefs are ignored or forgotten. And whatever suits the system - presto! - appears. Nor need that result from premeditated policy. Rather, it may simply express the subject's nature. Such an unfortunate can develop a coherence as perfect as that of the best scientist, philosopher, lawyer, or police detective. Having attained thereby a reflective equilibrium of the greatest width, must he not be granted rational justification?

It might be alleged that the perception or memory of such a madman or fanatic is too defective, that it gives him a view of things too unrepresentative of reality and that so large a cognitive defect is incompatible with rational justification. To test this hypothesis, we perform a thought experiment. Suppose yourself a victim of the Cartesian evil demon. Your inner life is then just as it has been in every nonrelational detail, yet you are in broad and deep error about your surroundings. But are you guilty of irrationality? Are you not on the contrary as rational and as rationally justified as you are now in actuality?

It might be responded, on the basis of an externalist account of the content of our thoughts and experiences, that the example is incoherent, since someone so detached from their external world could not so much as form beliefs or have experiences pertaining to it. One's access to propositional content may derive from a normal childhood and adolescence, however, if one becomes a victim of the demon only as an adult. I see no incoherence here, even granting the externalist account of content.

Our question was what to say of the madman or fanatic whose *data* are defective through some defect in his memory or perception. If he reasons admirably or even brilliantly on the basis of such data and achieves wide equilibrium, we have indeed no choice but to grant him rational justification. But such a concession is as correct in his case as it would be in ours were we now victims of a Cartesian demon.

And just how broad are the concepts of rationality and of rational justification? This seems in large measure a matter of terminology and convention. If only to fix ideas, let's give them the widest allowable breadth. Even so, we must still distinguish rationality and internal justification from a broader intellectual virtue which derives from pertinent cognitive faculties, perception and memory among them.

The most that philosophical reflection can give us is rational justification. Broader intellectual virtue is not attainable just by reflection, not even by the deepest, most wide-ranging and intense reflection. Broader virtue requires faculties other than reason, such as perception and memory. And this distinction between rational justification and broader intellectual virtue makes it possible to accept wide reflective equilibrium as a way to rational justification, without conceding that coherent madmen or fanatics are not only rational but also more broadly virtuous.

Conclusion: Philosophical reflection enhances rational justification through wide reflective equilibrium. But it is philosopher's arrogance to suppose mere reflection the source of all intellectual virtue. Perception, in particular, be it of nature or of values, is not derivable from reflection alone. It requires instead the formative influence of God, or evolution, or a good upbringing. What is more, such a virtue is virtuous only relative to appropriate surroundings, which are not the product of any reflection.

D. Appendix: An Application to Issues of Moral Relativism

Relativism emerges through disagreement in deep conceptions or beliefs irresolvable through any shared procedure, as in Phillippa Foot's example of two cultures or races that disagree on what it takes to be good looking. (Foot, 1970). In the spirit of that example, consider also disagreement as to what is good music, or a fine meal, or as to what does or does not taste good. On matters of taste, we should often just agree to disagree, since there is no such thing as the truth *period* . There is instead what is true for me and what is true for the other, or at most what is true for us and what is true for them.

What it is to be good looking for us or to taste or sound good for us may not have a similar status for others. If there is such disagreement, then, who is in the right? This seems as bogus as asking who is in the right when the pygmies disagree with the watusi over what it takes to be tall. Such disagreement is only apparent and is removed by the introduction of a pertinent index. A Pygmy is equally tall *as a Pygmy* for the Watusi as for the Pygmies.

Real disagreement lies beyond preferences of facial appearance, taste, or music, for opinions on such matters are objectivized and absolutized more or less in the way of opinions on height, as above.

May we extend that train of thought to cover morality as well? That depends on what we include in morality, for 'moral' and its cognates are a slippery crew. Parts of moral doctrines shared by large groups and even civilizations have aspects so subjective and relative as the phenomena of taste preference. Often it is the fact of *custom* that makes the corresponding conduct morally correct for the group involved, even though another group may have an incompatible custom.

The interesting question is whether *all* of morality is based thus fundamentally on the customs in force, *and nothing more* . And that is closely related to the question of whether there is any conduct that it would never be correct to permit, that is *impermissible* , even if the customs of some society in fact allow it. This would mean that some concept of the permissible is absolute and distinct from the concept of the *permitted* in a given society S. For such impermissible conduct would of course be "permitted-relative-to-S" if S does permit it. The more fundamentally interesting question is hence whether there are any such absolute moral concepts *in addition* to the relative ones, since the relative ones are there for all to see.

Absolute moral concepts are often alleged to be illusory and unacceptable as objective categories, given the absence of any rational procedure for the resolution of deep disagreements. But just what may be meant by such "rational procedure"? Suppose there is a disagreement as to whether a contradictory proposition could ever be true. If someone opts for the affirmative, there is no procedure to refute him which does not already presuppose the negative. Hence there is no noncircular logical procedure to defend elementary logic against such a dissenter.

It may be said that by definition of 'rational,' elementary logic cannot be rejected *rationally*, whereas even the most basic moral disagreement need not involve any failure of reason on either side. If the term 'reason' is to be reserved so categorically, however, we would just need some other vocabulary for the objectivity of morality, perhaps the vocabulary of "intuition," or of "perception," or of "sensibility," or that of inferential or ampliative reason. The main point is anyhow this. Not only in fundamental morality, but also in basic epistemology, and in elementary logic, there will be a circle of principles each defensible only by appeal to itself and the others. In logic there is at least the principle of noncontradiction. In epistemology there would be principles of perception, perhaps, of memory, of intuitive reason, of inferential reason, of coherence, etc., none of which we could defend without leaning on itself or others. Is not morality subject to the same logical phenomenon? May there not be principles of justice and of general welfare defensible only circularly or at least through appeal to more particular moral intuitions? May it not be so even if the intuitions require coherence with moral principles for their own full justification? Of course anyone who rejects all principles and opinions to which one might appeal cannot be answered without petitio. But that would apply not only to morality but also to epistemology and logic. It remains to be seen, therefore, what idiosyncrasy of basic moral principles may distinguish them from their epistemic or logical counterparts, subjecting them to a correspondingly idiosyncratic relativity.

What is distinctive of morality, it may be replied, is the extent and depth of actual disagreement. It is not enough that there be *some* disagreement: some disagreement there is in any ambit. More important is the question whether or not there is any fundamental disagreement which cannot possibly be resolved by any conceivable procedure yielding something more than *just* a third opinion. Many opposing preferences are thus irresoluble, of course, neither preference being superior to the other. Are all moral disagreements like that: opposing preferences, neither objectively superior?

It may be replied that the spread of history and the diversity of cultures must hold many disagreements of maximum depth. Supposing some at least of these turn out to constitute irreconcilable opposing preferences, just what procedure might we invoke to declare winners and losers?

In a way the problem is not so much the lack of procedures as their excess. Each party to a disagreement could appeal to their own deepest principles for a resolution, and would of course emerge victorious. Still, it is a popular error to think such circularity *necessarily* vicious. This error forces one to view even the most elementary logic as necessarily relative, for even its defense must in the end come full circle.[9] To give logic the prestige label of 'rational' cannot conceal this fact.

The error of believing circularity irremediably vicious may simply overlook that criteria of rational thought for a person or group need not be criteria for correct and rational interpersonal dialogue - an oversight abetted by the ancient notion of thought as inner dialogue. Nevertheless, we have seen already how reflective equilibrium might lead to a circular coherence which yields rational justification - even if a circular *petitio* is always a fault in dialogue or debate (which seems less than obvious anyhow).

NOTES

[1] Comprehensiveness has occasionally been added as well, insightfully in my view, but we leave this aside in the present context. Reflective equilibrium has been adopted by John Rawls in ethics, and Roderick Chisholm has long defended a closely related view in epistemology: critical cognitivism, which answers the "problem of the criterion." See Rawls (1971), esp. section 4, "The Original Position and Justification"; also Chisholm's *Theory of Knowledge,* the chapter entitled "The Problem of the Criterion."

[2] Karl Popper, "Replies to my Critics," in Schilpp (1974), 998.

[3] *Ibid.,* 983.

[4] Rarely, if ever, could a domain lie in total epistemic isolation. Is there some citadel of reason hermetically sealed and protected from other theoretical and empirical concerns?

5 Stich (1988). (Parenthetical page references will be made to this article.) Earlier work on reflective equilibrium in ethics includes, in addition to that already cited in footnote 1 above, Rawls (1974-5); Daniels (1979); and DePaul, (1986).

6 Stich, *op. cit.*, p. 404. The references in brackets are to *Epistemology and Cognition.*

7 Being thus relieved from a theory of error does not entail that one can ignore the question of how and why others know rather than err. But presumably this question can now be answered by appeal to the same theory of knowledge that one would apply to oneself.

8 That we must distinguish similarly between *justified* and *apt* belief is the main burden of my "Methodology and Apt Belief," (1988).

9 Its defense would be circular or at least, "spiral," in the sense given in Sosa (1985).

REFERENCES

Chisholm, Roderick. *Theory of Knowledge.* Englewood Cliffs: Prentice-Hall, 1st ed., 1966; 2nd ed., 1977; 3rd ed., 1988.

Daniels, Norman. "Wide Reflective Equilibrium and Theory Acceptance in Ethics," *Journal of Philosophy* 76 (1979), 256-82.

DePaul, Michael. "Reflective Equilibrium and Foundationalism," *American Philosophical Quarterly* 23 (1986), 59-69.

Foot, Phillippa. "Morality and Art," Henrietta Hertz Lecture, *Proceedings of the British Academy* LVI, 1970.

Goldman, Alvin. *Epistemology and Cognition.* Cambridge: Harvard University Press, 1986.

Goodman, Nelson. *Fact, Fiction, and Forecast.* 3rd edition. Indianapolis: Bobbs-Merrill, 1973.

Rawls, John. *Theory of Justice.* Cambridge, Harvard University Press, 1971.

-----. "The Independence of Moral Theory," *Proceedings and Addresses of the American Philosophical Association,* (1974-75), 5-22.

Popper, Karl. *Conjectures and Refutations.* London: Routledge and Kegan Paul, 1969.

-----. "Replies to my Critics," in *The Philosophy of Karl Popper,* Paul Schilpp, ed., Illinois: Open Court. 1974, Vol. II.

Shope, Robert. *The Analysis of Knowing.* Princeton: Princeton University Press, 1983.

Sosa, Ernest. "Methodology and Apt Belief," *Synthese* 74 (1988).

-----. "The Coherence of Virtue and the Virtue of Coherence," *Synthese* 71 (1985), 3-28.

Stich, Stephen. "Reflective Equilibrium, Analytic Epistemology and the Problem of Cognitive Diversity," *Synthese* 74 (1988), 391-413.

v. coherentists respond

KEITH LEHRER

LAURENCE BONJOUR

Coherence and the Truth Connection: A reply to my critics*

Keith Lehrer
University of Arizona
and
University of Graz

I. Summary of the Coherence Theory

To reply to the interesting articles in this volume, I shall need to supply a brief summary of my views specifically designed to meet the objections contained in these articles. I defend a coherence theory of justification which I have modified and, I believe, improved since the publication of *Knowledge,* though the main ideas have remained constant. I define a notion of justification based on a background system, what I now call an acceptance system of a person at a time. To say that a person accepts that p, crudely reformulated, is to say that he is in a certain kind of functional state which typically arises when a person reflectively judges that p with the objective of judging that p if and only if p. The functional role of the state is manifested in thought, inference and action. Though such a functional state may arise from reflective judgment, it most often arises unreflectively. I shall say more about what acceptance amounts to subsequently when discussing the article by Bender and Davis.

The acceptance system is a set of statements affirming that a person accepts at a given time what the person, in fact, accepts at that time. The objective of the requisite kind of acceptance is to obtain truth and avoid error in each thing one accepts, that is, to accept something if and only if it is true. Thus the acceptance system of S at a time t is a set of statements of the form, S accepts p at t, S accepts q at t, and so forth. A person, S, is personally justified in accepting that p at t if and only if p coheres with the acceptance system of S at t. Coherence is the central notion.

The notion of coherence is defined in terms of a notion of comparative reasonableness. We use this notion when we say that it is more reasonable for a person to accept one thing than another. Although I think it is possible to give an interesting account of this notion of reasonableness in terms of the comparative expected epistemic utility of accepting one thing rather than another measured in terms of our epistemic objectives, no such account, including ones I have articulated, strikes me as quite adequate to my purposes. Moreover, for the purposes of applying the theory, I think that the notion of comparative reasonableness is clearer and more useful than the notion of comparative epistemic expected utility. Judgments of comparative expected epistemic utility will, I think, be derived from judgments of comparative reasonableness rather than *vice versa* . We decide that the expected epistemic utility of accepting one thing is greater than that of accepting another by deciding that it is more reasonable to accept the first than the second rather than the other way around. An account of reasonableness in terms of expected epistemic utility would, of course, be of considerable theoretical interest, but we do not require such a theory to decide whether it is more reasonable to accept one thing than another. I shall return to this topic in reply to Feldman.

I shall give the key definitions below, but it may be more useful here to explain the intuitive idea behind my analysis of coherence with an acceptance system than to dwell on the technical details. The idea is this. We can imagine various sorts of objections a critic or skeptic might raise to what a person accepts. These objections might directly contradict what the person accepts or they might, while being logically consistent with the thing accepted, shed doubt on the reasonableness of accepting the thing accepted. An example of the first sort of objection to a perceptual claim arises when a skeptic says something entailing you are deluded, that you are hallucinating, while an example of the second sort of objection is when a skeptic says you cannot tell when you are deluded or not, that you cannot tell whether you are hallucinating or not. These objections, which I call competitors, pose a threat of incoherence because what the skeptic says conflicts with what you accept.

J.W. Bender (ed.), The Current State of the Coherence Theory, 253–275.
© *1989 by Kluwer Academic Publishers.*

Coherence results when the objections are met and all threat of incoherence is removed.

If it is more reasonable for you to accept what you do than to accept the skeptical objection, the objection is met by being beaten, and the threat of incoherence is removed. That is not the only way to remove a threat of incoherence posed by a skeptical objection, however. Another way to meet an objection is to neutralize it by appeal to some reasonable consideration which removes the skeptical or competitive force of the objection. The neutralizing consideration must, however, be as reasonable to accept in combination with the objection as the objection alone, or the threat of incoherence remains. When all threats of incoherence to what one accepts can be removed by beating or neutralizing all competitors on the basis of a system, then what one accepts coheres with the system. Technical considerations aside, that is my idea.

It is easy enough to see that what coheres with one system might not cohere with another. Different kinds of justification arise from different systems. Personal justification is coherence with an acceptance system of a person. Such justification may be defeated, however, by some error one has made in what one accepts. When one or more errors in the acceptance system of a person are corrected, a new system is formed, what I call a member of the ultrasystem of the person. A person may fail to be justified in accepting something on the basis of such a corrected system even though she was personally justified in accepting on the basis her acceptence system. In that case, her personal justification is defeated.

An omniscient critic, who would be in a position to correct errors in a person's acceptance system, could generate a set of different systems, the members of the ultrasystem, from the original acceptance system of the person. What such a system contains will depend on how many errors the critic corrected and how she corrected them. Suppose my acceptance system includes the statements that I accept p1, p2 and so forth to pn. Suppose that p2 and p3 are false. The critic might correct my acceptance system by deleting the statement that I accept p2, or the statement that I accept p3, or both. These I call weak corrections. If the statement that I accept pj is deleted, then if the statement that I accept pk is also included in my acceptance system and pk entails pj, then simultaneous deletion of the statement that I accept pk is also required. The reason for the requirement is I may wrongly accept pj because I wrongly accept pk which entails pj. The critic might, however, correct my errors by replacing the statement that I accept p2 or that I accept p3 by the statement that I accept not-p2 or that I accept not-p3 respectively. These I call strong corrections and again require the simultaneous replacement of acceptance in accord with entailment as in the case of deletion. The resulting one or more weak or strong corrections yields a system which I call a member of the *ultrasystem* of the person.

When what a person accepts fails to cohere with one of these systems, even though it cohered with his acceptance system, I say that her personal justification is defeated. The reason such justification is defeated is that failure to cohere with the systems contained in the ultrasystem of the person shows that her justification was based on some error contained in her acceptance system. Whatever one accepts with personal justification is converted into knowledge by being undefeated. In a logical nutshell, that is my coherence theory of knowledge.

For those who prefer a more exact formulation, I offer now a set of definitions which reduce all the epistemic terms to reasonableness, acceptance and truth. Those who dislike definitions, however, may choose to rely on the foregoing account and skip the definitions.

> D1. A system X is an acceptance system of S if and only if X contains just statements of the form - S accepts that p - attributing to S just those things that S accepts with the objective of accepting that p if and only if p.

D2. S is justified in accepting p at t on the basis of system X of S at t if and only if p coheres with X of S at t.

D3. S is justified in accepting p at t on the basis of system X of S at t if and only if all competitors of p are beaten or neutralized for S on X at t.

D4. c competes with p for S on X at t if and only if it is more reasonable for S to accept that p on the assumption that c is false than on the assumption that c is true, on the basis of X at t.

D5. p beats c for S on X at t if and only if c competes with p for S on X at t, and it is more reasonable for S to accept p than to accept c on X at t.

D6. n neutralizes c as a competitor of p for S on X at t if and only if c competes with p for S on X at t, the conjunction of c and n does not compete with p for S on X at t, and it is as reasonable for S to accept the conjunction of c and n as to accept c alone on X at t.

D7. S is personally justified in accepting that p at t if and only if S is justified in accepting that p on the basis of the acceptance system of S at t.

D8. S is justified in accepting that p at t in a way that is undefeated if and only if S is justified in accepting p at t on the basis of every system that is a member of the ultrasystem of S at t.

D9. M defeats the personal justification of S for accepting p at t if and only if S is personally justified in accepting p at t, but S is not justified in accepting p at t on system M at t where M is member of the ultrasystem of S at t.

D10. A system M is a member of the ultrasystem of S at t if and only if either M is the acceptance system of S at t or results from eliminating one or more statements of the form - S accepts that q - when q is false, replacing one or more statements of the form - S accepts that q - with a statement of the form - S accepts that not-q - when q is false, or any combination of such eliminations and replacements in the acceptance system of S at t with the constraint that if q logically entails r which is false and also accepted, then - S accepts that r - must be also be eliminated or replaced just as - S accepts that q - was.

These definitions yield the following definition of knowledge:

DK. S knows that p at t if and only if (i) S accepts that p, (ii) it is true that p, (iii) S is personally justified in accepting that p at t and (iv) S is justified in accepting that p at t in a way that is undefeated.

Condition (iv) implies condition (iii), and interpreting it so that it implies (i), it will imply (ii) as well. So, we may obtain the following reduction of the analysis:
DK*. S knows that p at t if and only if S is justified in accepting that p at t in a way that is undefeated.
Hence, knowledge becomes undefeated justification.

In *Knowledge,* I defined knowledge in terms of complete justification, which resembled the current notion of personal justification. I now think that the notion of defeated justification suffices for the definition of knowledge and that the notion of complete justification is of less importance for an analysis of knowledge. For whatever residual interest might attach to the notion of complete justification, however, I would propose that we define it in such way that it turns out to be a more objective notion of justification than mere personal justification, which seems more in accord with the ordinary notion, though not sufficient for knowledge, since it falls short of undefeated justification. We may do this by basing complete justification on a system in which all errors in the acceptance system are deleted. Proceding by first defining verific justification in terms of a verific system, the definitions are as follows:

> D11. A system V is a verific system of S at t if and only if V is a subsystem of the acceptance system of S at t resulting from eliminating all statements of the form - S accepts that p - when p is false. (V is a member of the ultrasystem of S.)
>
> D12. S is verifically justified in accepting that p at t if and only if S is justified in accepting that p on the basis of the verific system of S at t.
>
> D13. S is completely justified in accepting that p at t if and only if S is personally justified in accepting p at t and S is verifically justified in accepting p at t.

This notion of complete justification is discussed by Bender and Davis.

I shall expand on the coherence theory in the process of replying to my critics. To provide some unification of my discussion of various alleged counterexamples, I note here that the theory has a built in internal prophylactic against a popular sort of counterexample. It is one in which a person lacks knowledge because, contrary to what the person accepts, the person is in a position where she is likely to err, though, in fact, she does not. Such examples are not going to be effective against my analysis. I prove this by proposing a dilemma for my critic. Either the person in the counterexample does not accept anything within her acceptance system to meet the objection that she is likely to err, in which case the competitor that she is likely to err will remain an unbeaten and unneutralized competitor with the result that she is not personally justified, or she will accept something within her acceptance system implying that she is not likely to err, in which case she will be personally justified, but the justification will be defeated when her mistake concerning her likelihood of error is corrected. My critics valiantly attempt to find cases in which the acceptance system of a person yields coherence and, therefore, personal justification which remains undefeated even though the personal justification is isolated from truth. This is the heart of what they call the isolation argument.

The strategy is doomed, however. If the coherence and justification based on the acceptance system is isolated from truth, then the person will err in accepting that she is not isolated or something implying this. She must accept some such thing in order to meet the objection, the competitor, to the effect that the isolation obtains. In short, either the person accepts the she is not isolated from truth in the way they imagine her to be, in which case, contrary to their claims, she accepts something erroneous which defeats her justification, or she fails to accept that she is not isolated from truth in this way, in which case she is not personally justified because the competitor to the effect that she is isolated is not met. Thus, any relevant kind of isolation must be rejected by the person to provide personal justification, and, if the isolation in fact obtains, then the rejection will be transformed into a defeater. I call this the *transformation argument* as it will arise often in reply to my critics. Of course, some fine tuning of technical details might be required to insure the strength of the prophylactic against the wear and tear of ingenious counterexamples, but such difficulties are not fundamental. To show that no such counterexamples are effective, however, I consider them in detail below.

The foregoing reflections illuminate the connection between skeptical objections, justified acceptance, Gettier counterexamples, and undefeated justification. The connection is this. Gettier counterexamples are ones in which justification depends on some error. Skeptics suggest hypotheses in which our justification depends on error. To avoid skepticism, we must reject the skeptical hypotheses, which include those that would generate Gettier counterexamples. If we do not reject those hypotheses, we lack justified acceptance. If we do reject them but they are true, then, though we may have justified acceptance, our justification is defeated by our mistake concerning the skeptical hypotheses. Coherence enables us to escape from the clutches of skepticism *if* we are right in rejecting skeptical hypotheses and not otherwise. That is exactly what we should require of coherence and no more.

A second advantage of this coherence theory distinguishes it from others. Bonjour and other defenders of the coherence theory have been inclined to introduce material conditions, ones concerning introspective or perceptual beliefs, for example, to insure that the coherence theory would suffice for our epistemic purposes, most notably, to insure the right connection between coherence and truth. We need not add such constraints. The reason will be apparent from the argument above. Any objection to the coherence theory based on the idea that coherence is not connected to truth in the appropriate manner will amount to an objection to effect that what we accept, what is contained in our acceptance system, is not connected with truth in the appropriate manner. But such an objection will be a competitor to anything we accept. This means that we must accept that we are connected to truth in the appropriate manner, or the competitor will not be met. Thus, the additional constraints some defenders of the coherence theory are inclined to add on to the coherence theory in a somewhat *ad hoc* manner to insure that coherence is appropriately connected to truth, are things we must already accept for coherence to arise, in which case there is no need to add them. I prefer to look upon the formulation of such conditions as Bonjour proposes as an attempt to explicate what a person must actually accept for something to cohere with her acceptance system. Nevertheless, as I analyze coherence, it suffices to yield a sort of justification which, when undefeated by any error in what a person accepts, converts to knowledge. Coherence is the foundation of epistemic conversion.

With this brief sketch of my form of the coherence theory and its implications before us, I turn to reply to my acute critics. I shall take a certain liberty in replying to what they have written, namely, I shall appeal to my most recent formulation of the coherence theory, one which is now in print and to which they have had access, in replying to them. In so doing, I ignore the question of whether their objections may be effective against earlier versions of the theory. They may well be effective, but I assume that the reader is interested in whether a coherence theory of the sort I defend can meet the objections raised rather than with the question of whether some earlier version of that theory contained a technical defect. It is my intention to take the objections seriously by examining the question of whether they are fundamental rather than concentrating on some imaginary dialectical scorecard of the discussion.

I shall argue that the objections of critics can be met, but I think that all of them present important examples and arguments to test any epistemology. All of the articles contain important reflections on my work and many of them contain refutations of earlier formulations. I am deeply indebted to their authors for their valuable criticism which has caused me to refine and reformulate my version of the coherence theory of knowledge. I hope that I have succeeded in improving upon what I had formerly written and, to the extent that I have, these articles are responsible.

II. Reply to Moser

Moser, like other of my critics, presents what he calls an isolation argument against the coherence theory backed by an ingenious example. This argument is of fundamental importance, and it provides a basic test, a kind of crucial experiment, to test the adequacy of a coherence theory of justification. His claim is that there are experiences, sensory experiences or sensations, for example, that might undermine justification even though a person accepts nothing false that could defeat the justification. My reply is a dilemma related to the transformation argument. Either we have some representation of the experience or we do not. If we have no representation, then, though it may cause us to accept something which undermines our justification, it does not defeat our justification because we are as ignorant of it as we are of events in remote galaxies. If we do have some representation of the experience, either we accept the representation, or we do not. If we do accept the representation, then it becomes part of our acceptance system and is no objection to the coherence theory.

The remaining possibility is that the experience is represented but the representation is not accepted or, for that matter, rejected, in which case the experience is, in effect, ignored. Suppose the experience is relevant information against what a person accepts, as it is in the sort of example Moser imagines. Consider the competitor to what the person accepts to the effect the person has ignored relevant information against what she accepts. If the person is personally justified in accepting what she does, then something in her acceptance system must imply that she has not ignored such relevant information. But that is an error, and when it is corrected in some member of her ultrasystem, her justification will be defeated. So the coherence theory does explain how the represented experience can generate defeat of the personal justification. That is the way in which the isolation argument is handled by the transformation argument.

Consider the precise formulation offered by Moser. His counterexample runs as follows. California Jones, CJ for short, hears a lecture by Paul Churchland defending a version of eliminative materialism incorporating the thesis that there are no throbbing pains. CJ accepts what Churchland says, presumably regarding him as a trustworthy expert in the matter, but CJ has no explanation for the apparently throbbing pain experience he undergoes when he bites on a bolt and breaks a tooth. Moreover, in spite of the character of the experience, Moser asks us to assume that CJ neither believes nor accepts that he is experiencing a throbbing pain, or, for that matter, that he is even apparently experiencing a throbbing pain. Finally, Moser asks us to assume that eliminative materialism is true so that CJ has made no error that could be corrected. Moser then apparently thinks that CJ is neither justified in believing that there are no throbbing pains nor does he know that there are no throbbing pains even though CJ has made no error. What am I to say to this?

I find the example bizarre, but I agree with Moser that CJ does not know that eliminative materialism is true or that there are no throbbing pains. I do think CJ considers that he has a pain or seems to have a pain, but I would have to agree with Moser that if CJ is strongly convinced that Churchland is correct, he might not accept what he thus considers. It is acceptance, moreover, that is relevant to my present account of coherence. It important, however, to realize that this case is one in which the experience is represented, indeed, represented as pain, though the representation is not accepted. The question, then, is why doesn't CJ know that there are no throbbing pains if he accepts this conclusion from Churchland and Churchland is right?

Moser suggests that the reason is that CJ has no explanation for the apparently throbbing pain experience in that CJ is a neophyte materialist and does not know how an eliminative materialist would explain such things. Thus, according to Moser, the experience is negative evidence that CJ cannot explain away. I do not think that is the reason that CJ fails to know. Consider the case of someone quite ignorant of astronomy, DK, for short, who meets an astronomer he *knows* to be trustworthy about the astronomy of the earth and sun. The expert astronomer informs him that the earth revolves around the sun and, when DK shows surprise, informs him that this is established beyond any doubt. If DK accepts what the astronomer has told him, I think he knows that the earth revolves around the sun even though he has no explanation for his apparent experience of the sun moving across the sky while the earth remains stationary. The fact that DK cannot explain the experience that provides negative evidence does not deprive him of knowledge of the motion of the earth around the sun when he knows that he has obtained this information from a trustworthy expert.

The reason that CJ does not know is connected, I think, with the choice of Churchland. Though Churchland is an admirable philosopher, as I am sure Moser agrees, Churchland is not someone we know to be trustworthy about the truth of eliminative materialism, however brilliant his speculations. Thus, CJ does accept something false, to wit, that his source of information about materialism is trustworthy and knows what he says is true. I think Moser used Churchland because he could assume that the reader would not consider Churchland to be as reliable an expert about eliminative materialism as the astronomer is about the motion of the earth - even if Churchland is, in fact, correct. No one, Churchland included, has scientific knowledge and expertise about our nature comparable to scientific knowledge and expertise about the motion of the earth.

If we consider a system in which CJ's error is corrected by deleting the assumption that Churchland is trustworthy about the truth of eliminative materialism with the assumption that he is not, for no one is, we will find that CJ is not justified with respect to that system. Thus, though CJ is personally justified in accepting eliminative materialism, his personal justification is defeated. As I use the notion of acceptance there is no doubt from Moser's description of the case that CJ accepts that Churchland is trustworthy about eliminative materialism.

What if Churchland is as trustworthy about eliminative materialism as the astronomer is about the motion of the sun and earth? In that case, CJ knows what Churchland has told him, the evidence resulting from the experience of the injured tooth notwithstanding. CJ like DK accepts something that conflicts with the sensory information he receives. If, however, the experts are knowledgeable and trustworthy, CJ and DK know what they have been told even if they have no explanation for the conflicting sensory information. The example of CJ and Churchland poses a severe test for the coherence theory, but the theory passes the test and is, I believe, strongly confirmed thereby.

III. Reply to Russell

This paper is an examination of many interesting examples that Russell alleges pose difficulties for the analysis of knowledge that I have proposed, including my most recent proposals. These examples provide important test cases for the analysis and, once again, the opportunity for the analysis to either suffer refutation by failing to handle them or strong conformation by handling them satisfactorily. We may divide the difficulties that Russell raises into two sorts. The first sort concerns the relationship between acceptance and justification. The second sort concerns the relationship between justification and the relationship to external circumstances.

The first example is a well known one in which Jones believes that someone in his class owns a Ford because he is deceived into believing this by a student in the class, Mr. Nogot, who convinces Jones on the basis of false evidence that he, Mr. Nogot, owns a Ford, which he does not, though, unknown to Jones another student in the class, Mr. Havit, does own a Ford. Jones has a justified true belief that someone in his class owns a Ford, but he does not know this to be the case because Mr. Nogot does not own a Ford. This was the example I introduced in my first paper on the Gettier problem; it is a minor modification of the original Gettier example. I claim that the solution to the problem is to say that Jones's justification for accepting that someone in his class owns a Ford depends on his accepting that Mr. Nogot own a Ford, which is false. The falsity of this defeats the justification. Now Russell, in the grand tradition of Gettier counterexampling, introduces a modification into the example so that Jones's justification does not depend on his accepting anything false. The modification is that, though Nogot has forgotten it, he does own an old Ford which is back on the farm. Moreover, his wife, asked by Nogot to produce some fake papers to trick Jones into thinking that Nogot owns a Ford, finds the papers for the old Ford, leaves them on the table, and Mr. Nogot, thinking they are the false papers, shows them to Jones. Russell concludes that it is obvious that Jones does not know that Mr. Nogot owns a Ford and, therefore, does not know that someone in his class owns a Ford.

My immediate response to this example was that it is very unclear whether Jones knows that someone in his class owns a Ford. The reason I think that Jones may know is that he has adequate evidence, the legal papers concerning the old Ford, and the epistemic joke is on Mr. Nogot. In fact, I would expect intuitions concerning the example to be quite divided. Those who lay great emphasis on Mr. Nogot's deceptive intentions will be inclined to say that Jones does not know. Those who lay great emphasis on Mr. Nogot's evidence concerning the legal ownership papers will be inclined to say he does know. I think the example is, therefore, borderline and is not decisive. Moreover, I think that my analysis explains why it is borderline.

Does Jones accept that Mr. Nogot is not trying to deceive him about owning a Ford? That depends on Jones, but it seems likely to me that his thoughts, inferences and actions would not differ from what they would be had he reflectively judged that Mr. Nogot was not trying to deceive him about this. Suppose Jones does accept that Mr. Nogot is not trying to deceive him. Then, on the account I have offered, Jones must remain justified in accepting that someone in his class owns a Ford when we correct what he accepts about Nogot and suppose Jones accepts that Mr. Nogot is trying to deceive him. Is he still justified in accepting that Mr. Nogot owns a Ford? Notice that he would continue to accept that the ownership papers that Mr. Nogot showed him are authentic, since that is true. Now I think that explains why we should be inclined to say, contrary to Russell, that Jones does know that Mr. Nogot owns a Ford. It is because, whatever he accepts about Nogot's intentions, he continues to accept that the papers are authentic.

The reason the example is borderline concerns the claim that Mr. Nogot has deceived Mr. Jones about the authenticity of the papers. That is a skeptical objection, what I call a competitor, and it must be more reasonable for Jones to accept that Mr. Nogot owns a Ford than that Mr. Nogot has deceived Jones about the authenticity of the papers, even when Mr. Jones accepts both that the papers are authentic and that Mr. Jones is trying to deceive him. For such acceptance will occur in some member of his ultrasystem. But is it more reasonable? I am inclined to answer in the affirmative, but I appreciate the opposite reply. To wit, that since Jones accepts that Mr. Nogot is trying to deceive him, he might be deceiving him about the authenticity of the papers, and therefore, it is no more reasonable for Jones to accept that Mr. Nogot is not deceiving him about the authenticity of the papers than to accept that he is deceiving him. The example is borderline, and the analysis explains why this is so.

The second example that Russell appeals to is the case of Tom Grabit which Paxson and I introduced. Smith, who knows Tom, see him steal a book from the library. Mrs. Grabit, Tom's mother, has said that Tom was not in town on the day of the theft and that his identical twin, John, was in town that day. However, she says this while sitting alone in a mental institution caught up in fantasy, and Smith knows nothing about Mrs. Grabit, not even that she is alive. The question is whether the fact that Mrs. Grabit has said what she has deprives Smith of knowledge. Paxson and I assumed that the information Smith lacks concerning what Mrs. Grabit said does not deprive him of knowledge. We assumed that Smith knows that Tom Grabit stole the book. I assume that Smith does not accept anything about Mrs. Grabit, for example, that she did not say what she did about Tom having a twin. I think that this is unproblematic. Smith is not in a functional state equivalent to one that would arise from reflectively judging that Mrs. Grabit did not say that Tom was not in town on the day of theft and so forth. Smith does not think, infer or act in a way that would result from such a functional state.

Russell affirms that there is a problem about affirming that Jones accepts that Nogot is not trying to deceive him while denying that Smith accepts that Mrs. Grabit says that Tom was not in town and so forth. I see no grounds for thinking there to be a problem. The problem arises only from a defective account of what is required for someone to assume that p in believing that q, namely, that if she believed the denial of p, then she would not believe that q. Since I do not employ the account of assuming offered by the author, I leave him to extricate himself from difficulties to which it leads.

There are, however, a pair of examples Russell discusses on which I will comment without discussing Russell's remarks about assuming something to be the case. The first is the example in which someone accepts that the dusky sea sparrow is extinct because he has read it in all the newspapers. Russell says that the person falsely assumes that no eminent ornithologist thinks otherwise and has good grounds for assuming this. There is, in fact, an eminent though remote and concealed othnithologist who thinks the bird is not extinct, but no one is aware of his opinion. This example strikes me as being like the Grabit case and the answer is the same unless if we imagine that the subject accepts that no eminent ornithologist believes the bird is not extinct. If the person accepts that, then the question of whether the person knows that the sparrow is extinct becomes a rather subtle matter where intuitions would differ.

On my theory, the question of whether the person knows depends on whether the skeptical force of the objection that there is such an eminent ornithologist can be neutralized. To neutralize the objection that there is such an ornithologist, it must be as reasonable for the person to accept that objection and the neutralizing observation that the dissenting ornithologist is in error as to accept just the objection. Given the person has, as Russell said, read in all the newspapers that the sparrow is extinct, I think the neutralization succeeds even when the person's acceptance system is altered, as it will be in some member of his ultrasystem, to contain his accepting that there is an eminent ornithologist who believes the sparrow is not extinct. The background evidence concerning what he read in all the newspapers suffices to neutralize the competitor. Someone with less trust in newspapers might, however, object that the neutralization is ineffective. Such a person will, I conjecture, have the intuition that the person does not know. Again, I expect intuitions to divide. It is a virtue of my theory that it explains why.

Finally, let us consider an example offered by Bender and cited by Russell. Johnny's mother believes correctly that Johnny is not taking drugs. She believes this on the grounds that if he were she would know it and be aware of the evidence of it. But Johnny is hiding drugs at home for a friend, and his two sisters have discovered the drugs. They are worried that the drugs belong to Johnny, though they have not communicated any of the information to Johnny's mother. Bender says that in this case Johnny's mother does not know that Johnny is not taking drugs, because her daughters do not know this, and they know more than she does. The difference between this case and the Grabit example is that the misleading evidence is not in the public domain in the Grabit case but is in the present example. Russell says that Johnny's mother does know that Johnny is not taking drugs. To me the example is again a borderline case. Russell maintains, moreover, that the coherentist cannot account for either intuition. On the contrary, the coherentist can account for both and explain why the intuitions differ.

The claim that Johnny has drugs in his possession competes with Johnny's mother's belief that he is not taking drugs on the basis of her acceptance system. Relative to her acceptance system, it is more reasonable for her to accept that Johnny is not taking drugs than that he has drugs in his possession. Is her justification undefeated? This is a more difficult question to answer because it depends on what she accepts. It is natural, for example, to suppose that she accepts that Johnny does not have any drugs in his possession. If she does accept this, then in one member of her ultrasystem, she accepts that Johnny is in possession of drugs. The statement that Johnny is in possession of drugs competes with the claim that Johnny is not taking drugs. The competitor cannot be beaten in the member of the ultrasystem containing acceptance of it. Can it be neutralized? That really depends on what we imagine Johnny's mother's evidence concerning him to be like. If she has strong enough evidence that he is not taking drugs, the claim that Johnny has drugs in his possession may be neutralized by adding the claim that they are not for his own use. My intuitions, which I do not take to be decisive, are that the neutralization fails. If Johnny's mother accepts in some member of the ultrasystem that Johnny has drugs in his possession, it is more reasonable for her to accept just that on the basis of the member than to accept the conjunction of that claim with the neutralizer to the effect they are not for his own use. If the competitor cannot be beaten or neutralized in the member of the ultrasystem in which she accepts that Johnny has drugs in his possession, then she does not know that Johnny does not take drugs. I think intuitions will differ depending on whether one imagines Johnny's mother to have strong enough evidence to neutralize the claim that Johnny has drugs in his possession.

Russell says that the coherentist cannot account for the role of negligence or luck. This would only be the case if we suppose that people accept nothing about luck or negligence. But, in fact, people do accept that they have not been negligent and that they have proceeded in a trustworthy manner. It is, moreover, essential to their justification that they accept such things or they would fail to be even personally justified in what they accept. Consider the case of negligence. I accept that p. Am I justified in accepting that p? A competitor for the claim that p is that I have been negligent in considering evidence against p. If I accept that I have not been negligent in considering evidence against p, then this competitor will be beaten. Suppose then that I am personally justified accepting that p in that all the competitors, including the one about negliglence, have been beaten or neutralized on the basis of my acceptance system. Suppose further, however, I have, contrary to what I suppose, been negligent in considering evidence against p. This claim of negligence will then defeat my personal justification because some member of my ultrasystem will contain my accepting that I have been negligent in considering evidence against p which is a competitor of p that cannot be beaten or neutralized on the basis of the member of my ultrasystem. It is clear that this reply is an instance of the transformation argument.

IV. Reply to Mattey

Prof. Mattey has provided a very accurate historical account of the development of my views and reveals a deep understanding of them. He presents an argument that constitutes a well grounded and profound challenge, one at first considered unanswerable. Upon considerable reflection, however, I have hit upon an answer that satisfies me. Mattey says he is concerned with the isolation problem. He interprets this as being the problem that an internal system of justification, resulting in personal justification, for example, fails to provide any guarantee that that justification is connected with truth or that justified beliefs are not isolated from any external reality. I agree that internal relations do not guarantee truth about the world. The connection between justification and truth arises when we turn from personal justification to undefeated justification. The reason is that our acceptance system contains not only what we accept about the external world but what we accept about our relationship to that world, including what we accept about the conditions under which we are reliable or trustworthy. Error concerning those conditions may defeat our justification for accepting what we do about the world. If, however, we are not in error, then such justification may go undefeated, and we obtain knowledge. It is this required match between what we accept and what we correctly accept that generates the truth connection. Accepting that we are reliable in certain ways is essential to personal justification and being correct in accepting it is essential to undefeated justification.

Mattey correctly sees that starting with *Knowledge* I was a sort of metareliabilist arguing that we must estimate that we have a propensity to be correct in what we accept in order to be justified. We must, moreover, be correct, or nearly so, in those estimates for the justification to be undefeated. The theory is a kind metareliabilism in that it makes justification depend on what we accept about our reliability and on the correctness of what we thus accept, that is, on our reliability itself. Mattey argues that the attempt to shoestring reliabilism into a coherence theory is unsuccessful, and he concludes that we should distinguish between an externalist conception of knowledge, reliabilism, for example, and another internalist account of knowledge, reflective knowledge. This would amount to the claim that there are two conceptions of knowlege, one based on a reliabilist conception of knowledge built on a connection between belief and truth, genuine information processing, and another conception of knowledge, reflective knowledge, based on evaluation of information in terms of a system.

I have nothing against this sort of division and, indeed, suggested something like it in a paper Mattey cites. I prefer to call the latter knowledge and the former possession of information, but that is largely a verbal matter. At any rate, I am largely in agreement with Mattey's proposal that we should distinguish between information received at the level of automatic processing by an input system and information processed at a higher level of central processing where it is evaluated in terms of the background system. I disagree with Mattey about whether the coherence theory is successful, however.

My basic argument against Mattey is again a form of the transformation argument. One competitor for any claim is the objection that I am untrustworthy about what is claimed. That competitor must be beaten or neutralized on the basis of my acceptance system, and this will only result, I contend, if I accept that I am trustworthy in the matter or something that implies this together with other things I accept. If I am wrong in accepting that I am trustworthy, then my personal justification will be defeated. Hence, undefeated justification for accepting something will result only when I am trustworthy about the matter, and this yields the truth connection. Trustworthiness implies at least a propensity to be right. So I argue.

Let us consider Mattey's counterargument. Mattey formulates his objection first in terms of my earlier views and then in terms of my more recent writing, but the objection is the same. It is that a person may consider herself to be generally trustworthy, though not accept anything about how trustworthy she is in the present circumstances, and, as a result, possess an undefeated personal justification for what she accepts even though, in the circumstances, she is quite unreliable. As Mattey develops the objection, she has no views about her reliability in the present circumstances and, therefore, does not accept anything false about her reliability that would defeat her justification for what she accepts based on her acceptance of her general reliability.

Here is an example Mattey adapts to his purposes from my own writing. A person, whom I shall call Tina to blend with an example from Bender and Davis, is looking at a wall on which she sees red spots. She believes that she sees a painted red patch which she does. In fact, however, there are many red spots on the wall resulting from a red light shining on on a white wall which, from where she is standing, are indistinguishable from the painted red patch she is looking at. Now Mattey argues that she is personally justified in accepting that she sees a painted red patch but that there need be nothing false that she accepts that defeats her personal justification. She might not have reflected on her special circumstances and, hence, not accept anything false about them. She might only have a general conviction about her reliability, that, in general, she tell a painted red patch when she sees one. The general conviction would suffice for personal justification and at the same time free her from any defeating error. That is the crux of his objection.

It is an important objection, but I do not think it quite works. The reason is that the claim that she cannot tell a painted red patch from other things in her present circumstances competes with her claim that she sees a painted red patch. For her to be personally justified in accepting the latter, the former competitor must be beaten or neutralized. It seems clear to me that this will only be the case if she accepts that she can tell a painted red patch from other things in her present circumstances or something that directly implies this together with other things she accepts. But then she accepts something false which will defeat her personal justification. I think my strategy should be clear by now. You must accept that the circumstances are not deceptive, or something immediately implying it, to beat the competitor claiming that the circumstances are deceptive and obtain personal justification. But then you accept something false which defeats your justification. Thus, when Mattey says that it is far from clear that the theory of justification requires that a person accept that they are reliable and not deceived in the circumstances, I think he overlooks the fact that the claim to the contrary is a competitor that must be beaten or neutralized, and the latter seems to require that the person accepts that she is reliable and not deceived in the circumstances.

Mattey has a reply which I seem committed to from my writings, to wit, that it suffices that the person think that she is probably reliable and not deceived in the circumstances. Does her accepting that enable her to cope with the competitor that she is not reliable in the circumstances? Her accepting that she is probably reliable in the circumstances makes it more reasonable for her to accept that she sees a painted red patch than that she is not reliable which exhibits the force of Mattey's objection.

My reply concerns the role of erroneous probability estimates in defeating justification. It is highly probable that Tina can tell a red patch when she sees one, but, in the present circumstances, she cannot do so. That is a competitor of the claim that she sees a red patch. Can it be beaten or neutralized? One might argue that it is more reasonable for her to accept that it is highly probable that she can tell a red patch when she sees one in the present circumstances than to accept the competitor. But consider the following two claims:

> 1. It is highly probable that I am reliable in the present circumstances, but I am not, and
> 2. It is highly probable that I am reliable in the present circumstances, and I am.

It must be more reasonable for Tina to accept (2) than (1) if she is personally justified in accepting that she sees a painted red patch.

What makes it more reasonable? Tina accepts

> 3. It is highly probable that I am reliable

which yields the conclusion

> 4. It is highly probable that I am reliable in the present circumstances

as a result of ignorance about the present circumstances. That is Mattey's argument. Let us construe probabilities in the acceptance system as personal estimates of objective probabilities. In that case, however, the second claim is an incorrect estimate of the objective probability. In circumstances in which colored lights are illuminating objects one is not reliable. Hence the competitor that Tina is not reliable in the present circumstances will, in some member of her ultrasystem, not be beaten or neutralized and her personal justification will be defeated. In short, though it is personally highly probable that she is reliable in the circumstances, which accounts for her personal justification, it is not objectively highly probable that she is reliable in the circumstances, which accounts for the defeat of her personal justification.

V. Reply to Peterson

Peterson's paper contains a large number of interesting and valuable observations concerning my views which I fully appreciate. In this reply, however, I shall focus on the critical points that he raises. He criticizes my remarks concerning intuition. I said that the appeal to intuition is an appeal to consensus, and Peterson quotes me to that effect. Peterson assumed I was implying that the only way that a person could have evidence that something is intuitive would be to carry out a sociological investigation. He remarks on the absurdity of supposing that the only way someone can know that some mathematical or logical claim is intuitive is by carrying out such an investigation. This was not my intention, nor is it a consequence of my theory. The way to find out whether something is intuitive, crudely put, is to reflect on it. Reflection is, however, fallible, and *many* heads are better than one. Consensus comes in as an interpersonal check on the fallibility of personal intuition. I may be, and often am, in a perfectly good position to predict what other people will think without sociological investigation, however. If I sum five numbers and check my arithmetic carefully, I will be in a good position to predict what other people will say who sum those numbers and check their arithmetic. My prediction is social, though my evidence may be personal. The claim that something is intuitive, and not merely intuitive to me, requires social confirmation.

Let me next consider the problem Peterson raises about whether on my account a person will ever know that she knows anything. Conditions added to the analysis of knowledge to cope with the kind of examples Gettier and his followers, myself proudly included, called to our attention have led some to doubt whether we can ever know that such conditions are satisfied and, hence, whether we can ever know that we know anything. Peterson claims that on the sort of account I offer the simple condition of personal justification is one that a person would rarely and perhaps never know to be satisfied and, therefore, conditions for the Gettier problem aside, my account of personal justification would yield the result that a person never knows that she knows anything. His reasoning is that since personal justification requires that all the competitors for a given claim be either beaten or neutralized, in order to know that one was personally justified in accepting something one would need to canvass all the competitors, including ones that no one would ever think of, and decide whether each of those competitors was beaten or neutralized. Thus, he concludes, no one knows that she is personally justified in accepting anything because no one has ever canvassed all such competitors and made all such decisions.

My answer is that I denied in *Knowledge* that the conditions of my analysis of knowledge provide a recipe one applies to decide whether one knows. They are necessary and sufficient conditions for knowledge. I hope they are illuminating with respect to what cases of knowledge have in common with each other, but that is all I claim. Personal justification is necessary for knowledge on my account, but I see no reason for concluding that in order to know that one is personally justified in accepting something one needs to canvass all the competitors of what one accepts and decide whether each one is beaten or neutralized.

Consider an example. I see a computer in front of me. That is something I accept. Do I know that I am justified in accepting that? It would suffice to know that I am justified to know that my evidence is adequate to meet objections. Now I would say that I do know that my evidence is adequate to meet objections, even if I have not reflected on all such objections or how I would meet them. So why do I say that I know that my evidence is adequate? Simply because it is such good evidence. But if I know that my evidence is adequate to meet objections, then I know that I am personally justified. The notion of personal justification is a technical condition intended to illuminate exactly when my evidence is adequate to meet objections.

Thus, I would say that I knew that I was personally justified in accepting that I was a man in the sense that I knew that my evidence was adequate to meet objections to that claim before I ever thought of the technical notion of personal justification. To be sure, I did not then know that it was called "personal justification" or how it might be analyzed. The problem Peterson raised is, in short, as old as the ancient paradox of analysis. The solution is the same. A person can know that something satisfies the *analysandum* without ever having thought of the *analysans* or having thought it was the analysis of the *analysandum*.

There are many other interesting comments that Peterson has made concerning related issues, but many of them do not call for reply, though they are an important basis for further reflection and theoretical development.

VI. Reply to Feldman

Feldman has provided a series of challenges, some of them protests about lack of clarity and some of them counterexamples to my analyses. These are deep and probing objections that must be answered. Concerning lack of clarity, Feldman says that the notion of comparative reasonableness is obscure. As I noted above, though one could analyze the notion, for example in terms of epistemic expected utility and achieve some theoretical illumination thereby, that would not result in clarity of application. It may be difficult to decide in some cases whether it is more reasonable to accept one thing than another, but that is because epistemic decisions like practical ones are sometimes difficult.

Feldman also complains that the relationship between probability, reasonableness and acceptance is left unclear. I have already commented on the multiple factors that influence how reasonable it is to accept something on the basis of an acceptance system. Feldman does fairly inquire, however, how we are to decide how probable something is on the basis of a member of an ultrasystem. Suppose we consider the subject to be rational in the sense that her acceptance maximizes expected epistemic utility. When we consider probabilities on the basis of a member of an ultrasystem in which what the person accepts differs from what was accepted in the acceptance system, we should minimally alter the probabilities so that what the subject accepts on the basis of the member of the ultrasystem can also be considered to be rational in terms of maximizing expected epistemic utility.

A standard way of representing the epistemic expected utility of accepting h on the basis of a system X, $e_X(h)$, is in terms of probability of h on the basis of a system X, $p_X(h)$, the utility of accepting h on the basis of X when h is true, $uT_X(h)$, and the disutility of accepting h on the basis of X when h is false, $uF_X(h)$ as follows:

$$e_X(h) = p_X(h)uT_X(h) + p(\sim h)uF_X(h)$$

Suppose the utilities of accepting something remain stable from the acceptance system to a member of the ultrasystem of a person but what a person accepts within the two systems differ. If acceptance maximizes expected epistemic utility, then the probabilities must be different on the acceptance system from what they are on the member of the ultrasystem. The shift in probabilities should be no greater than what is minimally required for the differences in what maximizes epistemic expected utility on the two systems.

It would be useful to offer some simple rules relating what a person accepts within a system to the reasonableness of accepting one thing rather than another on the acceptance system. Any such rule, however, like simple rules of conduct on a utilitarian ethical theory, can only be considered to be a rule of thumb to estimate the outcome of utilitarian computation. The following strikes me as a useful rule of thumb, though violations result in extreme cases.

AR. If a person accepts that p within a system X, then it is not more reasonable to accept ~p than to accept p on the basis of X.

The rule might be overridden in an odd case in which a person accepts that what she accepts in a certain domain, the stock market perhaps, counterindicates truth, but the rule provides us with a useful though fallible guide.

Let me now turn to the very clearly articulated examples Feldman raises as objections. Some are similar to those raised by others and some are more unique to Feldman. The first example concerns the prediction of an election, for example, that Dukakis wins, based on an early opinion poll. Feldman suggests that there is no competitor for the prediction and hence, if correct and not based on the acceptance of anything false, would improperly turn out to be an instance of knowledge on my theory.

My reply is that the competitor for the prediction is the objection that you cannot reliably predict an election from early opinion polls. This competitor cannot be beaten or neutralized on the basis of an acceptance system of a person informed about opinion poles. Feldman suggests that a person might be able to neutralize the competitor with the reply that candidate X will win, because I said that I might neutralize the competitor that people sometimes hallucinate, when I see a monitor, by replying that I am not hallucinating. But the cases are dissimilar in a critical way. It is much more reasonable for me to accept that I am not hallucinating now than that candidate X, Dukakis for example, will win on the basis of early polls. The competitor concerning the unreliability of the poles cannot be neutralized. It is much more reasonable to accept that competitor than the conjunction of it with the claim that candidate X will win or with any other neutralizer. By contrast, it is so obviously the case that I am not now hallucinating, that it is just as reasonable for me to accept that in conjunction with the other obvious claim that people sometimes do hallucinate as to accept the latter alone.

Feldman asks us to reconsider the example in which Smith's acceptance of

1. Nogot, who works in the office, says he owns a Ford, etc., is the basis for Smith, concluding
2. Nogot, who works in the office, owns a Ford, and ultimately
3. Someone in the office owns a Ford.

Feldman asks us to suppose that in addition to accepting the foregoing claims Smith accepts

4. No one in the office other than Nogot owns a Ford.

Of course, (2) is false but (3) is true because (4) is false; someone else in the office owns a Ford.

I claimed that the falsity of (2) defeats Smith's justification because of the acceptance of the falsity of (2) in some member of Smith's ultrasystem. Feldman doubts this. He considers the system, N, in which acceptance of the false (2) is replaced by acceptance of the true

~2. It is not the case that Nogot, who works in the office, owns a Ford.

while acceptance of (3) and (4) are retained. He denies that this member of the ultrasystem defeats Smith's justification for (3). This objection is not decisive, if it were correct, which I doubt. The system, N3, consisting of the acceptance of (1), (~2) and (3) is a member of the ultrasystem resulting from replacement of acceptance of the false (2), a strong correction of his acceptance system, and deletion of acceptance of the false (4), a weak correction of his acceptance system. This system, N3, suffices to defeat Smith's justification for (3) without considering inconsistent acceptance systems.

System N3 suffices to defeat Smith justification for (3) because there are a number of competitors to (3) that cannot be beaten or neutralized on the basis of N3. The most notable is

C. The evidence that Nogot owns a Ford described in (1) is deceptive.

Now (C) clearly competes with (3). It is also very reasonable for Smith to accept (C) on the basis on N3. It is precisely (C) that makes sense of what S accepts in N3. For Smith accepts that it is not the case that Nogot owns a Ford in addition to accepting the evidence that he does own a Ford described in (1). In short, (C) provides us with the best explanation of what is going on given acceptance of (1), (~2), and (3) and, as a result, is so reasonable to accept on the basis of N3 that it cannot be beaten or neutralized.

Feldman introduces a minor modification of the foregoing example in which Nogot does, in fact, own a Ford, having just won a Ford in a lottery, but is totally ignorant of the outcome of the lottery, and his intentions are just as deceptive as in the original example. I have considered this sort of example in reply to Russell. Of course, Smith does not know that Nogot owns a Ford being ignorant of the lottery and having only the evidence supplied to him by Nogot with deceptive intentions. Feldman, like Moser, thinks that everything that Smith accepts might be true and, therefore, that Smith's justification for accepting (2) and (3) will go undefeated on my account.

The example, like Russell's, is again vulnerable to the transformation argument. Condition (C) is a competitor of (2) and must be beaten or neutralized on the basis of Smith's acceptance system for Smith to be personally justified in accepting (2). Either Smith accepts nothing implying that the evidence of (1) is not deceptive, in which case the competitor (C) will not be met, or Smith accepts something which does imply this, in which case, Smith will be justified in accepting (2), but what he accepts to meet the competitor (C) will be false. Feldman says that it is not clear that Smith must accept anything false. His claim may be based on what I had formerly written about acceptance, but I think that when acceptance is treated as a functional state, it is clear that Smith does accept something false, something required to meet competitors, and these errors will result in defeat of the justification.

Finally, Feldman thinks that my theory of undefeated justification falls victim to the problem of misleading defeaters. Feldman discusses a modification of the Tom Grabit example in which Feldman assumes that the subject, Smith again, accepts the false statement that no one who knows Tom has said that Tom did not steal the book. Feldman thinks that this claim will then become a misleading defeater.

Like the example from Moser, I find this example to be borderline and am sure that informants would have differing intuitions about whether Tom knows. Their intuitions will, I propose, depend on the details of the imagined acceptance system. The clarity of the example as an example in which Smith knows that Tom Grabit took the book depended, I think, on Smith not accepting that Mrs. Grabit or, for that matter, anyone else who knows Tom well enough to know whether he took the book, said that he did not take it. Smith's evidence that Tom stole the book did not rest on his falsely accepting that others who know Tom did not say that Tom did not steal the book.

If, as Feldman asks us to imagine, on the other hand, Smith accepts something to effect that no one who knows Tom has said that Tom did not steal the book, then people will disagree about whether Smith knows. What they think will depend on whether they think that the true competitor

K. Someone who knows Tom said he did not steal the book

of the claim that Tom stole the book can be beaten or neutralized on the basis of a member of the ultrasystem of Smith in which his error in accepting that no one who knows Tom said he did not steal the book is replaced by what amounts to the acceptance of (K). Can it be beaten or neutralized? Some will think that perception is so much more reliable than testimony that (K) can be neutralized by

N. The person who said Tom did not steal the book is in error.

Others noting that the subject has no particular reason to accept that the specific person who knows Tom and said he did not take the book was in error, will reject neutralization by (N) and deny that Tom knows. It will all depend on how reasonable a person thinks it is for the subject to accept (N), and that, in turn, will depend on how one conceives of the acceptance system of the subject.

My current account has the following advantage over other accounts of defeaters. Only things that a person actually accepts, and accepts erroneously, can produce defeat. This is a substantial advantage over accounts that permit defeat by any truth whatever, for there are many misleading truths. When something a person accepts produces a defeater by means of the correction of the person's error, I would say the person fails to know even if the correction producing the defeat is in some way misleading. Consider the following analogy. A person argues from a set of premises in defense of a conclusion. It seems unfair in such a context for a critic to criticize the argument by appealing to some extraneous truth he knows to be misleading. That is like allowing any truth to serve as a defeater. But it does not seems unfair for the critic to criticize the argument offered by pointing out that some premise of the argument is false even if the falsity of premise is misleading with respect to the conclusion. Whatever a person uses as a premise may be fairly held against his or her argument if it be erroneous, whereas the introduction of misleading extraneous truths to dissuade him or her from the conclusion seems epistemically unjust. If my replies to Feldman's perceptive objections have been epistemically just and philosophically cogent, my theory is undefeated by any error in my acceptance system.

VII. Reply to Bender and Davis

Bender and Davis claim they have revealed fundamental flaws in the coherence theory. I shall vigorously defend the coherence theory against the claim that the theory is flawed, but they do raise fundamental objections which call for a prolonged and detailed reply. The kind of objections they raise have forced me to clarify the notion of acceptance and to distinguish it more precisely from the notion of belief. This clarification has important ramifications throughout my theory, and I am grateful to them for providing the needed incentive to introduce improvement.

A number of objections Bender and Davis raised are based on their denial that a person believes what I am inclined to say a person accepts. The conception of acceptance put forth at the beginning of the present work was not in print when they wrote their essay, though my ideas were known to Bender, but it is useful, perhaps essential, for the purpose of meeting their most frequent sort of objection to the coherence theory, namely, that people do not accept what is necessary for justification to arise on a coherence theory from an acceptance system. I shall in replying ignore questions of what a person believes, conceding they may be right, and focus on the question of what a person accepts. That is the doxastic notion, a somewhat technical one, essential to my present account.

As I said above, acceptance is a functional state, that is, a state that has a functional role in thought, inference and action. A fully articulated and scientific notion of acceptance is yet to be developed, but it is easy enough to characterize the role informally assuming an understanding of considered or reflective judgment that something is the case. If we consider the question of whether something is the case, and reflectively judge it to be so, our considered judgment produces a mental state of accepting that it is the case which has the role of influencing how we think about the matter judged, what we infer about related matters, and how we act. This functional mental state of accepting something may arise without reflective judgment, indeed, it usually does, and is distinct from the judgment. The considered judgment occurs briefly and does not long exist; the acceptance arising from this ephemeral episode has lasting functionally organized effects.

Most of what we accept, for example, that 57 is an odd number, we accept without ever having considered it. The functional role of such acceptance in thought, inference and action is the same before considered assent as afterward, however. We are inclined to assent to it automatically, to draw inferences based on the assumption of it, and, in general, to act as though it were true. Of course, sometimes what we think, infer and do depends not simply on what we accept but on the costs and benefits of error as well as the probability of error. On the whole, our thought, inference and action is based on rules of thumb driven by what we accept. We have the capacity to go beyond mere acceptance and rejection to finer grained notions of utility and probability, however. The justification for introducing the notion of acceptance, which I admit to using as a term of art, is our psychology. We prefer to operate on a yes or no basis and stick with our decisions for the sake of economy of effort.

The relationship of probability to reasonableness and personal justification also plays a considerable role in the critique Bender and Davis provide. I have commented on this issue in my discussion of Feldman and add only some brief comments here. There are a number of factors that determine how reasonable it is to accept something by determining the utility of acceptance, namely, simplicity, explanatory power, and informativeness. The advantages of some of these factors can be represented in terms of our assignment of prior probabilities, the advantages of causal and naturalistic explanations, for example, but the utility of informativeness cannot be represented in this way. A more informative statement is equivalent to a conjunction of less informative ones, and conjunctions are going to turn out to be less probable than the conjuncts unless one conjunct has a probability of unity conditional on the other. It is not only informativeness but, as others have argued, simplicity and explanatory power that must be considered additional determinants of reasonableness. That is why I adopted the cautious *correspondence* principle to express the relationship between reasonableness and probability, namely, that everything else being equal, the more probable something is the more reasonable it is.

Now let me now turn to the question that Bender and Davis raise in common with my other commentators. It concerns basic beliefs. They claim, as foundationalists are traditionally wont to do, that there are some perceptual, introspective and mathematical beliefs that do not depend on inference. This I concede. They further insist that the justification for these beliefs does not depend on anything else that the person accepts. This I do not concede. On one fundamental conception of justification, the claim is in error. I have called this conception of justification a *converter* conception of justification because it has the power, if undefeated by error, to convert mere true acceptance into knowledge.

Consider the examples of alleged basic beliefs offered by Bender and Davis, for example, my seeing a brown bird. Does my being justified in accepting this depend on anything else I accept? Yes it does. It depends on my accepting that I can tell a brown bird when I see one in the present circumstances. Consider my having a headache. Does my being justified in accepting this depend on anything else I accept? It depends on my accepting that I can tell a headache when I have one. If the foundationalist did not think that a person could tell a headache when he had one, he would not contend that beliefs about headaches were basic. What makes foundationalism plausible is that we accept that we can tell whether or not certain things are true without reasoning, and so we can. But if we did not accept that we could, if we had no idea whether we were trustworthy in such matters, our beliefs about them would not seem basic.

I can anticipate only two kinds of rejoinders. Bender and Davis object to a view they attribute to Bonjour to the effect that the justification of alleged basic beliefs, introspective beliefs, for example, may be explained by our accepting general principles to the effect that beliefs of these kinds are very likely to be true. They object that such general principles are insufficient to yield justification of particular beliefs of the kind in question. They are right. More specific information is necessary to yield justification, but it is supplied by the coherence theory. My being justified in accepting that I have a headache does not directly depend on my accepting that my belief that I have a headache is an introspective belief and that introspective beliefs are likely to be true. It depends, instead, on my accepting that I can tell that I have a headache when I have one. My accepting that I can tell a headache when I have one is also justified on the coherence theory. The justification for that depends on something else I accept which I might put by saying that I would not accept that I can tell a headache when I have one unless I could. None of this justification involves using one statement as a premise for inferring a conclusion, however.

The second sort of objection Bender and Davis raise is based on their assertion that a person could know that he sees a brown bird or that he has a pain without accepting that he tell a brown bird when he sees one or that he can tell a pain when he sees one. They, like other foundationalists and their causal cousins, appeal to small children and even animals to defend their views. I have argued elsewhere that a being, whether child or animal, who lacks the ability to decide whether information it receives is correct or deceptive may have information but lacks knowledge. I would, however, not fight over a word. If someone wishes to say they have knowledge, I would reply that they do not have the sort of knowledge that is most characteristically human, namely, knowledge based on an understanding of the distinction between truth and error, between correct information and misinformation.

To see the point of this reply, one only need reflect on a brain damaged adult who believes and repeats whatever it is told without any understanding of the distinction between truth and deception and without any capacity to evaluate whether what it is told is true or false. Such a being, if able to remember what it is told about some subject, the history of the French Revolution, for example, might have more information than any of us. So might a file in my word processing program. They do not, however, know that the information they possess or contain is correct, and in that sense they are ignorant. If, on the other hand, one is in a position to evaluate the information one receives, one must have some basis for such evaluation. What one accepts is the basis. There is, therefore, no justification that converts to knowledge in those who receive information but lack the capacity to distinguish correct information from misinformation.

What about arithmetical statements and simple tautologies? Bender and Davis argue that I cannot account for our knowledge of them. Are they right? In this case, standard probability theory poses some problems if, as Bender and Davis suggest, we must assign a probability of unity to all logical and mathematical truths. The probability relevant to the sort of reasonableness that yields justification must be nonstandard. A person who is not mathematically or logically omniscient will not assign a probability of unity to every mathematical or logical truth for the simple reason that they will have some doubts about whether some of them are mathematical or logical truths. The technical solution to the problem of developing a probability theory that accomodates these results is interesting and the interest is by no means restricted to being used in the theory I advance.

The probabilities used are personal, and personal probabilities are supposed to explain our bets. I would prefer a bet that 2 + 2 = 4 to a bet on some complicated sum I computed by hand involving ten numbers each of which contained nine different digits. I would be a fool not to as there is surely a greater chance that I have erred in such a computation than in accepting that 2 + 2 = 4. So I reject the notion that all tautologies and mathematical statements are assigned a probability of unity by me or, for that matter, by Bender and Davis. Similarly, I reject the notion that all tautologies and mathematical statements are assigned a probability of unity conditional on my acceptance system. It is more reasonable for me to accept some such statements than others, depending on how sure I am that the statements are tautologies, correct sums and so forth, in short, on how probable they are. Moreover, some such nonstandard theories of probability have been developed by Popper.

In short, I do not see that logical and mathematical statements provide any special problems, other than technical problems in the articulation of a nonstandard theory of probability. I am personally justified in accepting that all men are men, to take the example from Bender and Davis, because all competitors can be beaten or neutralized. For example, the competitor that not all men are men would be less reasonable for me to accept on the basis of my acceptance system and would be beaten. The competitor that people sometimes err in their judgment that something is a logical truth is no more reasonable than the conjunction of that competitor with the neutralizer that I have not erred in this case. The reasonableness of accepting that all men are men depends, I suggest, on my accepting that I can tell whether that sort of statement is true.

Let us consider the problem of inferential justification. Here Bender and Davis contend that two people who accept the same set of statements but are such that one infers a conclusion from a subset from which the conclusion does not follow, while the other infers the conclusion from a subset from which the conclusion does follow, differ in the justification they have for the conclusion. In fact, one is justified and the other is not. They conclude that I cannot accomodate this fact within my theory and, therefore, that my theory must be incorrect. I am puzzled by their claim that my theory cannot handle this. They place emphasis on the claim that the set, S, of statements accepted logically entails the conclusion, C. So they apparently take me to assume what, in fact, I would deny, namely that if a person accepts a set of statements which entails a conclusion, then the person is justified in accepting the conclusion.

How would I handle the matter of justification by inference within my theory? The answer is rather simple. The person, call him Mr. Fallacy, who infers C, that is, (5) in the example, from a subset of S, namely, (1), from which it does not follow, differs in what he accepts from what Ms. Valid accepts, who infers C from the subset of S from which it does follow, namely, (2) and (4). Mr. Fallacy accepts that C follows from subset X of S, which it does not, while Ms. Valid accepts that C follows from subset Y of S, which it does. Now each of them may be personally justified in accepting C in terms of what they each accept. This will depend on what else they accept about their reliability in determining whether something such as C follows from such things as X and Y. It does not suffice, for example, to suppose that Mr. Fallacy accepts that C follows from X to be personally justified in accepting C any more than it follows from his accepting X alone that he is personally justified. The competitor that C does not follow from X or that he cannot tell whether C follows from X must be beaten or neutralized on Mr. Fallacy's acceptance system. We can imagine, however, that Mr. Fallacy accepts that C follows from X and the other things necessary to his personal justification in accepting that C. He is then personally justified in accepting that C. But, of course, his personal justification is defeated. If his error in accepting that C follows from X is corrected, then his justification would be defeated. That is how knowledge arises from inference. Acceptance that something follows from something else and that we can tell whether this is so is required for personal justification to arise and must be correct for the justification to go undefeated.

There are finally some problems that Bender and Davis raise which are more fundamental. One concerns the global lucky guess problem. Suppose that I have a sufficiently elaborate acceptance system which contains only guesses but ones that turn out to be entirely correct. Then Bender and Davis conclude that the person would be personally justified in accepting what he does and the justification would be undefeated. Is that a good objection? The reply is the transformation argument.

Suppose I accept that p, for example, that there is a red apple in front of me. One competitor for that claim is precisely that p is just a guess. The claim that there is a red apple in front of me is more reasonable for me to accept on the assumption that this is not a guess than that it is. Thus, any claim will compete with the statement that the claim is just a guess. Moreover, this competitor can only be beaten if something I accept implies that the claim is not a guess. But if it is a guess, then, contrary to Bender and Davis, what I thus accept implying it is not a guess must be false. In short, statements to the effect that what one accepts is a guess are competitors that must be beaten or neutralized by something in the acceptance system implying that they are not guesses. Hence, it is impossible that one should obtain undefeated justification when one's acceptance system consists simply of guesses, lucky or not.

Again the strategy against the foundationalist is clear. The foundationalist assumes that basic beliefs are not guesses. On my theory, the acceptance system must imply this or the beliefs will not be personally justified, and what implies this must be true as well or the personal justification will be defeated. This is part of the explanation for why the beliefs alleged to be basic by the foundationalist are justified. We accept what the foundationalist assumes, that the beliefs are not guesses, and, to meet other skeptical competition, we must assume more strongly that these are matters in which we can discern the truth in a trustworthy manner. Thus, once one takes seriously the consequences of supposing that all unneutralized competitors must be beaten for a person to be justified, it becomes clear that the acceptance system of the person must contain enough to rule out the competitors to the effect that one what accepts is a guess or in any other way untrustworthy. In brief, that is why I do not think it necessary to add the sort of material constraints Bonjour adds. What is needed to beat unneutralized competitors suffices to meet the objections against the coherence theory without such artifices.

I am inclined to think that Bender and Davis like other of my critics failed to appreciate the importance of the fact that the statements accepted by a person do not constitute the acceptance system of the person. If they did constitute the acceptance system, then anything accepted would be entailed by the acceptance system with the result that unneutralized competitors would be trivially beaten on the basis of the acceptance system. The system would entail their falsity. Once one notes, however, that the acceptance system is the set of statements affirming that one accepts the things one does, one requires the acceptance of something further, something implying that the acceptances are not lucky guesses for example, to produce justification.

Finally, Bender and Davis raise a technical problem connected to a fundamental doubt. I argue that a person might accept that she sees something, a painted red patch on the wall, for example, in circumstances in which there are spots on the wall illuminated by a red light which she could not distinguish from the painted ones. So even if seeing a painted red patch causes the person, Tina, who we met before, to believe that she sees a painted red patch, since she cannot tell a painted red patch from an illuminated spot, she is incorrect in thinking she can in tell a painted red patch when she sees one in the present circumstances. Thus her justification would be defeated by correction of her error.

Now, Bender and Davis reply by imagining that Tina also accepts that things are the way they appear on *this* (the spot where the painted red patch is) small part of the wall, that there appears to be a painted red patch on the wall, and that there is a painted red patch on the wall. As I am employing the notion of acceptance, I think it is natural to suppose that

Tina does accept these things in the original example I presented, so I have no objection to this supposition. But an error of Tina's defeats her personal justification. She accepts that she can tell a red patch when she sees one in her present circumstances, and this is false. If we modified her acceptance system to include her acceptance of what is true about her abilities, namely, that she cannot tell a red patch when she sees one in her present circumstances, this claim will become an unbeaten competitor, and her justification will be defeated.

In discussing this example, Bender and Davis mention a more general claim I make, one taken from Reid, to the effect that it is part of our natural constitution to accept the trustworthiness of our senses, memory and other faculties. I go on to contend that every normal person accepts not only that their faculties are trustworthy but that *they* are trustworthy evaluators of truth. This claim goes beyond Reid. What does it imply? If I am trustworthy in the sense required, this implies that my accepting something in the interest of obtaining truth and avoiding error is to be trusted to serve that interest. This in turn implies that my accepting something in this way can provide another with a reason for accepting what I do. If, moreover, my accepting something provides another with a reason for accepting it, then it provides me with a reason for accepting it as well. I have discussed this in a forthcoming paper, however, and will not rehearse my argument here.

Bender and Davis contend that the general principle of my trustworthiness, GT, is not sufficient to yield personal justification for more specific claims such as Tina's, and I agree with them. The justification of her claim, as I have noted, depends on more specific claims to epistemic competence. They also see what I took to be the role of the general principle, namely, to back up the more specific claims, to insure that they are not guesses. Moreover, they correctly understand why I thought that GT did not require backing and formulate a quite correct objection to what I said. I claimed that if I am trustworthy and accept that I am, then what I accept is not a lucky guess. They correctly object that even a person who is trustworthy, being fallible, occasionally guesses, and the acceptance that one is trustworthy might be one of those occasions. I did not say what I intended. What I intended to say was that if I accept that I am trustworthy as a *result* of my trustworthiness, then it is not a lucky guess.

Finally, they raise the question of whether I have, in effect, become a foundationalist with regard to the principle in question, the principle of my trustworthiness in matters of truth and error. They might equally have asked whether I have become reliabilist. Just as the principle seems to justify itself without depending on other things I accept, so it might appear that the justification of the principle is a simple consequence of my trustworthiness without depending on other things I accept. A superficial reply is that a person who alleged that only one statement was justified in itself or justified as a result of our trustworthiness would be a very modest foundationalist or reliabilist. I am far from affirming that foundationalism and reliabilism are entirely in error. Both contain a truth, the former that there are noninferentially justified beliefs and the latter that undefeated justification of our beliefs depends on our reliability. So I do not mind if my coherence theory contains a modest commitment to foundationalism and reliabilism.

In fact, however, the justification of the principle of general trustworthiness, GT, is not the sort of justification that a foundationalist or reliabilist would offer us. There are unneutralized competitors of the principle, for example, the competitor that I am more often wrong than right in what I accept which are beaten as a result of what I accept about my past successes and failures. Thus, just as my justification for accepting particular claims may depend on the inclusion of some general principle of my trustworthiness, so my justification for accepting the general claim may depend on the inclusion of specific claims of obtaining the truth and avoiding error in my acceptance system. Justification requires beating unneutralized competitors. No statement can beat all the competition by itself but, instead, requires allies within the acceptance system. No justified statement is an island. Coherence cycles.

Reasoning for the conclusion that one is generally trustworthy in the quest for truth from particular claims of past successes might result in circularity, though Alston and Van Cleve, critics of the coherence theory themselves, have argued convincingly to the contrary. My claim that justification depends on coherence is not intended as an argument to prove to a skeptic that we are trustworthy. It is the claim that our justification for what we accept depends on a system of acceptance containing general claims about our competence and trustworthiness as truth seekers and what results therefrom as well as a record of our successes and failures in the search. That is the stuff of which a coherence theory is made. For the justification of what we accept to go undefeated and convert to knowledge, the justification must be able to survive correction of the errors in our acceptance system. When there is an adequate match between acceptance and reality, coherence converts to knowledge. In spite of the probing and important arguments of my critics, I hope I have succeeded in explaining why I prefer my conversion to theirs.

NOTE

*I am greatly indebted to the editor of this volume for his many helpful and insightful and often brilliant comments on this article and on my earlier work. I should especially like to call attention to some of his articles on my work which are not here cited which include, "The Ins and Outs of Metaknowledge," *Analysis*, October, 1988; "Knowledge, Justification, and Lehrer's Theory of Coherence," *Philosophical Studies* (1988), 49-75; and with Wayne A. Davis, "Technical Flaws in the Coherence Theory," *Synthese* (forthcoming, 1989). I should also like to thank T. Kuys for a constructive suggestion which will occur in a paper of his forthcoming in *Philosophical Studies* which was the basis for my definition of undefeated justification.

I wish to thank the contributors to this volume who studied and reflected on my work for their exceptionally valuable and penetrating discussions. Finally, I have always had the desire to write a long article without footnotes, which I chose to indulge here, and no one should be held responsible for this feature of the present article except myself.

Replies and Clarifications

Laurence BonJour
University of Washington

I wish to express my gratitude to the authors of the foregoing essays for the impressive skill and care that they have expended on my work. They have done so well that I have not surprisingly found it impossible to deal adequately with all that they have said in the space available to me in the present volume. Thus while I have done my best to focus on the most important and potentially telling criticisms, there are some valuable points which have been omitted from the present discussion and others with regard to which I have been unable to do much more than suggest a line of response, postponing more detailed consideration and argument to other occasions. I have also confined myself entirely to discussions directed explicitly at my views, which has meant ignoring much that is of interest in the essays in the other sections of the present volume. To make things a bit less chaotic for the reader, I have adopted the organizing principle of dealing with topics in roughly the same order in which the corresponding discussions occur in *The Structure of Empirical Knowledge* [1] (hereafter SEK).

I

I begin with a brief and highly intuitive recapitulation of my basic internalist epistemological outlook, which may perhaps help to shed light on the notion of metajustification, on the charge of "level-confusion" raised by both Alvin Goldman and Mathias Steup, and on the internalism-externalism issue itself.

Suppose that I am a cognitive agent attempting to decide what to believe, which beliefs to accept, in relation to some particular subject-matter. Suppose moreover, though it will emerge later that this is inessential to the main issue, that I am initially at least in the situation, vaguely reminiscent of Descartes, of having only my own resources to draw upon. I might simply believe willy-nilly whatever strikes me as vaguely appealing, or I might select my beliefs for reasons of a non-epistemic sort, perhaps moral or religious or political in character. But if I am to be epistemically rational, I must instead seek beliefs which I have reason to think are true-or at least likely to be true.

As far as I can see, there are two and only two general ways in which I can hope to succeed in such an undertaking. The first of these appeals to the idea of self-evidence: if there are beliefs which I somehow am able to grasp or intuit to be necessary, guaranteed solely on the basis of their content to be true in any possible world, then it is epistemically rational to accept such beliefs. The second way, the only one applicable to contingent beliefs, depends on there being beliefs which can be singled out in some indirect fashion as likely to be true, even though this is not apparent solely on the basis of their content. In SEK, I formulate this point in terms of there being beliefs (a) which I have good reason to think possess some feature or characteristic F, itself not directly related to truth, but such that (b) I also have independent good reasons for thinking that beliefs possessing feature F are in fact likely to be true. In such a case, I again have an epistemically relevant reason for accepting such a belief: it has feature F, and beliefs having F are likely to be true. Whereas if a candidate contingent belief possesses no feature satisfying this schema, then I have no good reason for thinking that it is true-and hence would be epistemically irresponsible, not properly attentive to the cognitive goal of finding the truth, in accepting it.

This latter formulation still seems to me to be a reasonable way to put the point, but it is potentially misleading in that it might be taken to suggest that this second sort of reason must always take the form of an explicit metabelief; Steup at least has been thus misled. What matters, of course, is that I have a reason of some sort for thinking that a belief with a particular content is likely to be true. Such a reason need not be couched in explicitly meta-

276

J.W. Bender (ed.), The Current State of the Coherence Theory, 276–292.
© *1989 by Kluwer Academic Publishers.*

doxastic terms, though as far as I can see it would always be possible in any particular instance to recast it in such a form. Thus the demand for such a reason does not generate an infinite hierarchy of metabeliefs in the automatic and almost mechanical way that Steup suggests.

On an internalist view, being epistemically responsible, rather than irresponsible, in accepting a belief is at least a necessary condition for that belief being epistemically justified. It is natural to take it, as I do in the book, to be a sufficient condition as well, but whether this further claim is correct seems to me relatively unimportant in relation to the main issues to be considered here; and, with one brief exception, I will accordingly ignore it.

Though I will have a little to say later on about self-evident beliefs and *a priori* justification, the main concern of the book under discussion is empirical knowledge, where the reason for taking the belief to be true takes the latter of the two indicated forms. In relation to this sort of case, what I meant by a standard or criterion of justification was a rule or principle picking out beliefs possessing feature F, whatever that might be, as justified. But from an internalist standpoint, the fact that a belief meets such a standard does not in and of itself yield a complete and cogent reason for thinking that it is likely to be true: such a rule never stands on its own, but rather depends essentially for its status on the availability to the believer of a good reason for thinking that beliefs possessing feature F are at least likely to be true. This is what I refer to as a metajustification. For without such a reason, following the rule in question would not be epistemically responsible in the quasi-Cartesian situation envisaged. (It is thus perhaps misleading to refer to such a rule by itself as a standard or criterion of justification. This at least suggests, mistakenly in my view, that satisfying it is sufficient for justification, whether or not a further metajustification is available.)

Thus from an internalist standpoint, the distinction which Alvin Goldman stresses between merely being justified and being justified in believing that one is justified (or Steup's analogous distinction between being justified in having a basic belief and being justified in regarding it as basic) comes to very little in normal cases (where by speaking of "normal cases," I mean to exclude, e.g., cases where one's correct understanding of the concept of justification is itself at issue). If justification, as the internalist claims, requires that I have in my cognitive possession a reason for thinking that the belief in question is true, then merely by reflecting on that reason I will ordinarily also be justified in believing that I have it and hence in believing that I am justified; a reason which did not reveal itself to reflective scrutiny would be useless from the standpoint of the quasi-Cartesian situation. Equally, if I am not justified in believing that I have such a reason, then I do not genuinely have it, and the belief is simply not justified in the first place.

The charge of "level-confusion" accordingly has no force at all, as far as I can see, from an internalist perspective. It seems cogent only if an externalist perspective is tacitly being assumed, one in which it is possible for a belief to be justified simpliciter simply by possessing a feature which is in fact truth-conducive, even though the believer has no reason to think that this is so. In particular, since my argument against foundationalism is developed on the basis of the internalist conception of justification developed previously in chapter one, I am unable to see that there is any "level-confusion" involved in it. Applied to this more specific issue, the basic point is that it is unacceptable from the internalist perspective presupposed by the argument to hold that someone might be justified in accepting a first-level basic belief without at the same time being justified in accepting the higher level belief that beliefs having whatever feature qualifies a belief as basic are likely to be true.

II

Now, of course, if this is the dialectical situation, then my general anti-foundationalist argument in chapter two of SEK, since it presupposes an internalist perspective, obviously cannot count as an argument against externalism. Nor was it intended to. On the contrary, externalism is explicitly introduced as one possible response to this argument, not as being already ruled out by it. Indeed, as already suggested both above and in the book, I doubt very much whether there is any non-question-begging argument available on either side of the internalism-externalism controversy. There are, however, what seem to me to be overwhelming intuitive reasons favoring internalism, some of which I have attempted to display here. Since several authors (Alvin Goldman, Swain, Tolliver, Kornblith, and, to some extent, Alan Goldman) are to varying degrees advocates of externalism and since the internalism-externalism issue strikes me as perhaps the most crucial at present in the whole of the theory of knowledge, I want to say a bit more about why externalism seems to me to be a completely unacceptable response to the main problems of traditional epistemology.

I will restrict myself to reliabilist views and will initially offer only a rough formulation, which will nonetheless suffice to raise the main issues. On a reliabilist view, the main condition for justification is that I arrive at the belief in question in a way or via a process which makes it objectively likely that the belief is true. Further conditions, of the various sorts suggested by Goldman, Swain, and others, may also be required, but what is not required is that I have complete possession of any reason for thinking that the belief is true.

Some of the appeal of views of this kind is easy enough to understand. In the first place, as both Alvin Goldman and Swain point out, such views seem initially at least to agree well with our ordinary, commonsensical ascriptions of knowledge and belief, especially those involving relatively unsophisticated knowers. How strong a reason this is depends, of course, on how well competing views do in this respect and also on just how much weight this sort of consideration is taken to have. My view is roughly that an acceptable philosophical account must be able to explain why common sense makes the ascriptions that it does, but need not agree with it any more closely than that. And I believe that the kind of theory I espouse can satisfy this requirement well enough by appealing to the idea of tacit or implicit awareness of various aspects of justification together with the suggestion, which seems to me independently plausible, that knowledge is an ideal which ordinary cognitive states only loosely approximate. In particular, contrary to Goldman's suggestion, I believe that the sort of metajustification which I suggest for a coherentist account of justification appeals to nothing which is not tacitly available to ordinary knowers. But it is hard to say any more in defense of this claim in the space available here. And what is really missing, of course, is a better account than anyone has offered so far of correct philosophical methodology, in particular of the countervailing considerations which prevent the appeal to common sense from being completely decisive (as Goldman himself admits that it is not).

A second, closely related reason favoring externalism is that on such a view, many supposedly intractable epistemological problems can seemingly be provided with quite straightforward solutions. Descartes' problem of the external world, the problem of other minds, the problem of induction, etc., at least when construed as problems about epistemic justification, become relatively easy to deal with in a non-skeptical way. For example, Goldman, in his recent book, sketches a solution to the problem of induction which would, if externalism were correct, unquestionably be adequate in principle; this takes slightly more than one page in a footnote.[2] Indeed, while not wishing to minimize the difficulties of working such positions out in detail, it seems fair to say that from an externalist standpoint, the standard epistemological problems offer no real difficulties of principle. (Of course, someone might want to count this result against externalism, on the grounds that these longstanding problems cannot really be as easy to solve as that.)

In any case, these reasons are both rather extrinsic and also depend for real force on further claims or assumptions about either the status of common sense or the falsity of skepticism and about the inadequacy of competing views. What one would like is a straightforward intuitive account of why the satisfaction of an external condition of the sort in question should be thought to confer epistemic justification on a belief. Putting the point in a way which connects up with my earlier discussion, the externalist needs either to explain how the satisfaction of a merely external condition can make it rational for me to accept a belief with the aim of reaching the truth even though I admittedly have thereby no reason for thinking that the belief is true, or else to explain how such an acceptance can be epistemically justified without being thus rational. It is because I can see no plausible way of doing either of these things that externalism seems to me, despite the undoubted ingenuity of its defenders, to be essentially an evasion rather than a solution of the classical epistemological problems.

In SEK, I attempt to bring out this intuitive point by considering some detailed counterexamples, cases of beliefs which satisfy the reliabilist account of justification but which seem intuitively not to be justified. I also appeal to related, though perhaps less controversial, intuitions concerning moral justification and rational action. Goldman has discussed the counterexamples elsewhere, and Swain considers the most crucial one of them, the case of Norman, in his present paper. They both respond by appealing to further requirements, over and above the basic requirement of reliability, which are claimed to exclude the problematic cases.

Here I have time only for a brief look at Swain's modification of reliabilism.[3] The basic idea of Swain's position is to require for justification that a belief be reliable in relation to a set of what he calls "reason states" upon which it is causally dependent, i.e. that the probability that the belief is true, given that it was caused by those reason states and given the other relevant characteristics of the believer, be appropriately high. Reason states must be either belief states or other states of which the believer could become directly aware, though there need be no actual awareness of them. Thus, contrary to what the phrase might seem to suggest, a reason state need not in fact be grasped as a reason by the believer. And the relevant characteristics do not include, quoting Swain, "those which guarantee the probabilistic facts all by themselves". Thus, it is claimed, the bare fact that Norman is clairvoyant is excluded, so that his belief is not justified.

I am not as clear as I would like to be about just how this result is arrived at, but it seems to me relatively easy, if I have understood Swain correctly, to elaborate the case of Norman in such a way as to reinstate the counterexample: simply let Norman's clairvoyant beliefs possess some distinctive phenomenological character or be accompanied by some phenomenologically distinctive state, of which Norman is or could be directly aware, and let there be some unknown mechanism of clairvoyance, such that given Norman's other relevant characteristics it is objectively probable to the requisite degree that beliefs having this distinctive phenomenological character are true - even though neither Norman nor anyone else either believes or has any reason to believe that this is so. Given such an elaboration (which is in fact in no way incompatible with my original description of the case), Norman's belief seems to qualify as justified according to Swain's account, but I cannot see that the intuition that he is in fact not justified is affected at all. Speaking more generally, I have two main responses to such modified versions of externalism. First, it seems plausible to suppose that any particular counterexample to externalism can be blocked or at least mitigated by some modified view of this kind: any such counterexample attempts to exhibit some particular way in which a belief may be internally or subjectively irrational despite satisfying the main externalist requirement, and such modified views seem to me in general simply to incorporate enough of the ingredients of internal rationality to rule out some particular mode of irrationality. But it seems to me equally likely that there will always be further counterexamples of the same general sort to be found so long as the account falls short of requiring full internal rationality, i.e. so long as it remains an externalist account-though increased complexity may make these somewhat more tricky to bring out clearly on an intuitive level.

Second, and even more importantly, the intuitive motivation for these added requirements seems to me extremely unclear - unless of course the appeal is simply to the internalist intuition. Why should partial internal rationality be required for justification if complete internal rationality is not? Unless this question can be answered, it is hard to avoid thinking that what the modified externalist positions do is to provide essentially *ad hoc* counterfeits of internal rationality, both implicitly acknowledging the force of the internalist intuition and failing at the same time to satisfy it in any full or principled way. A related difficulty is that it is very hard to find any principled rationale for drawing the line as to just how much partial rationality is required, and externalists in fact often find themselves at odds on this sort of issue. It is for these reasons that, churlish though it may seem, I am not tempted by Swain's proposed compromise positions.

I want to stress one further consideration which seems to me to bear importantly on the acceptability of externalism. Though the main externalist claim is that the individual believer whose belief is justified need not have complete internal access to any reason for thinking that his belief is true, it is important to emphasize that the absence of such a reason is not somehow confined to the individual perspective. If the epistemic regress problem is solved exclusively along externalist lines, it follows for the same reasons that no group of people, however large, ever has access to a complete reason for thinking that any empirical belief is true - where by a complete reason I mean simply one which is adequate on its own, i.e. a reason *simpliciter* ; to have only part of such a reason amounts to having some of the premises of an argument while lacking others which are equally essential, and this is in fact to have no reason at all for the conclusion in question. (Thus Swain's talk of degrees of epistemic responsibility seems to me highly misleading.)

One way to bring out the force of these considerations is to suppose, contrary to what I have been suggesting, that the externalist view is somehow correct as an account of ordinary usage or of the common-sense conception of justification. If this were so, we might, if the appropriate external conditions were satisfied, be justified in believing and perhaps even know that there is an external world, that other humans have minds, etc. But we still, even if we could somehow pool our cognitive resources and even add in those of all the persons who have ever lived or who ever will live, would have access to no reason of any sort for thinking that any of these things are so - and also of course equally to no reason for thinking that the externalist conditions are indeed satisfied. Now this seems to me both a massively counterintuitive result and also one which by itself, no matter what account is given of the concepts of justification and knowledge, constitutes a very deep and troubling version of skepticism - thus suggesting once again that externalism is at best a quite superficial response to the classical epistemological problems.

III

While externalist views, whether foundationalist or non-foundationalist in structure, strike me as simply wrong-headed, as evasions of the main epistemological issues, internalist versions of foundationalism are much more appealing. Indeed, on a first approach to these issues, an internalist foundationalism of some sort appears to be the only sensible alternative. The problem with such a conclusion, as I argue at great length in SEK, is that on careful scrutiny, internalist foundationalism turns out to be incoherent: there is no apparent way in which the holder of a putatively basic empirical, contingent belief can have cognitive possession of a reason for thinking that the belief is true, as internalism requires, without the belief ceasing to be basic.

I have already dealt, in section I, with the main responses to this general anti-foundationalist argument which are contained in the present set of papers. In the present section, I want to briefly review positive suggestions in several of the papers as to how an internalist foundation might work. My thesis will be that all of these suggestions fail for basically the same reason advanced in the general argument.

Steup and Lemos offer the suggestion, putting it in Steup's terminology, that a basic belief might be justified solely by a "nondoxastic psychological state," e.g. that my belief that I have a headache might be justified solely by the non-doxastic state of my actually having a headache or that my belief that the pen on my desk is red might be justified solely by the non-doxastic state of my "being appeared to redly by the pen." Can this sort of suggestion provide the basis for a viable internalist foundationalism?

The key word in the above formulations is, of course, the word "solely." A coherentist position like my own need not deny that states of this sort can play a role in justification - if they are themselves apprehended in a justifiable way (see SEK 122, 129). Both Steup and Lemos seem to rest their claim that nothing further is required for such states to play a justificatory role solely on intuitive grounds, but I doubt that sheer intuition really speaks very strongly to this kind of point.

A way of pursuing the issue is to ask why on the view in question it is only psychological non-doxastic states which can serve in this way to justify basic beliefs. Presumably neither Steup nor Lemos would claim that my belief that there is a book on the desk can be justified solely by the non-doxastic state of there actually being a book on the desk, nor even that my belief that my leg is broken can be justified solely by the non-doxastic state of my leg actually being broken. Such a view would be merely a version of externalism and a particularly implausible one at that. But why does the psychological character of the state supposed to make such a difference?

The only apparent answer to this question is that psychological states are accessible to reflective awareness in a way that non-psychological states are not. Indeed, the natural way to think about the examples which Steup and Lemos appeal to, the headache and the book appearing red, is to include in the picture an awareness of the character of the psychological state which is somehow justified. Anyone will agree that in the cases as thus specified (and with everything else being equal), the beliefs in question are justified; but now the question of how these collateral awarenesses are themselves justified cannot be avoided, and I have argued that it must ultimately be given a coherentist answer. Whereas if it is stipulated either (i) that no such awareness is present, or (ii) that it does not extend to the character of the psychological state as specified by the belief, or (iii) that the awareness, though present, is not justified, my intuition that the belief is justified vanishes (assuming, of course, that no other sort of justification is present). Steup and Lemos may not agree. But they and other like-minded, would-be foundationalists surely owe us some account of why a non-doxastic psychological state of which the person has no justified, specific awareness can play such a justificatory role when a non-doxastic non-psychological state cannot. My conviction is that no such account is available.

I turn, rather more briefly, to two rather different foundationalist proposals. Alan Goldman suggests that a basic or foundational belief might be "self-justifying" in the sense that the explanation for the existence of the belief consists simply in the fact that it is true. Such a situation does not obtain for most beliefs, whose explanations will have to appeal to further facts as well even when their truth is part of the explanation; but it does, he suggests, obtain for a belief like the "belief that I am appeared to redly" for which the complete explanation is "simply that I am so appeared to." Thus a belief of this sort is, he suggests, self-justifying and so can play a foundational role.

There are, however, several difficulties with this suggestion, at least as it is adumbrated in the present paper.[4] In the first place, it is far from clear, to me anyway, that the occurrence of such a state of being appeared to provides a complete explanation for the belief in question; this would seem to mean that the state could not occur without the belief occurring as well, and I see no reason for thinking that this is so. More basically, however, even if Goldman is right about the explanatory situation, it is completely unclear why the presence of such an explanatory relation means that the belief is justified in an internalist sense (which Goldman seems to intend, though this is not as clear as it might be). How does the existence of such an explanatory relation give the believer in question a reason for thinking that the belief is true?; or if it fails to supply such a reason, why does it make it epistemically responsible for him to accept the belief?

Finally, Black suggests, following Wittgenstein, that a foundation for knowledge might be found in our "takings," by which she means roughly those things that we at any given time unquestioningly accept. Black holds that taking is not a kind of believing; but I am not persuaded by her ordinary language argument for this point, which seems, like so many such arguments, to assume that what we would not say in a given situation is thereby shown to be false, rather than perhaps only misleading (*via* conversational implicatures of various sorts) but still true.

If takings are viewed as a kind of belief, I think that there is some merit in Black's suggestion, but also that it plainly will not do as it stands. The obvious objection is that, whether the category of takings is delineated on an individual or a social basis, there is plainly no reason in general for thinking that a belief which has this sort of status is thereby likely to be true, and thus no reason for regarding inferability from takings as yielding epistemic justification. Indeed, it seems abundantly clear that the category of takings often includes beliefs which are flagrantly irrational and epistemically unacceptable: at least many religious beliefs, superstitions of various other sorts, ideological convictions, etc..

A rather different way of proceeding would be to treat the truth of one's takings, or some appropriately winnowed subclass thereof, as a background presumption against which issues of epistemic justification are raised. One might ask, in other words, whether a particular belief is likely to be true if the takings in question are true. The epistemic justification yielded by such an inquiry would, of course, be conditional rather than absolute, but the result in question might nonetheless be of significant epistemological interest, if the class of takings in question is carefully delineated and at least relatively small. Indeed, it might be the case that something like this is the best we can do, at least for the justification of beliefs whose content is contingent. As I will explain more fully in the next section, this sort of approach to justification underlies the status of my so-called Doxastic Presumption. But, as also explained there, I do not believe that such a view constitutes a version of foundationalism in any interesting sense.

IV

I turn then to issues and objections pertaining to my specific brand of coherentism, beginning with those pertaining to the Doxastic Presumption. I am under the impression that this is the only topic in SEK which has occasioned uncertainty and misunderstanding in a major proportion of those who have commented on the book, and it is clear to me that I must assume the major share of the responsibility for this situation. What went wrong, basically, was that I failed to distinguish at all clearly those parts of the discussion in SEK in which the nature and status of the presumption is explained from those parts which attempt to argue that an epistemological position which involves such a presumption can still yield interesting results and in particular can still speak to something like the classical epistemological issues. Whether or not this latter argument succeeds, it has no direct bearing on the nature of the presumption itself, and thus only confusion can result from running the two parts together as I unfortunately did. Thus I must begin by trying to re-explain as clearly as possible just what the Doxastic Presumption amounts to. Fortunately, this is not terribly difficult to do.

The underlying problem, of course, concerns the epistemic status of my representation of my own system of beliefs in the context of a coherence theory of empirical justification. Clearly the metabelief that I have such-and-such a system of beliefs is contingent and thus seemingly in need of empirical justification. But for a coherence theory, all empirical justification depends on the fact that the justificandum belief coheres with an overall system of beliefs, where for any plausible version of such a theory, the system in question must be the one that the believer actually holds. The inescapable consequence is that such a metabelief (or system of metabeliefs) cannot be justified along coherentist lines because any such justification would be hopelessly and unavoidably circular, dependent on the acceptability of the very representation of my system of beliefs whose justification is at issue (SEK 102). And this result threatens to undermine the whole project of a coherentist account of empirical justification.

It is this problem which provides the motivation for the Doxastic Presumption. Reduced to its barest essentials, the suggestion is that for a coherence theory, all empirical justification must be understood as relativized to or conditional on the presumption that my representation of my system of beliefs is at least approximately correct - only approximately correct because the issue of whether I have some particular belief or relatively small set of beliefs, unlike that pertaining to my whole system of beliefs, is capable of being settled on coherentist grounds (SEK 104). If P is the claim whose empirical justification is at issue, then what a successful coherentist justification shows is that if this presumption is correct, then P is likely to be true (SEK 104-106, 147).

The obvious question raised by this response is why the need to appeal to the Doxastic Presumption does not show that the justification provided by such a coherence theory is simply inadequate because it fails to show that the belief thus justified is genuinely likely to be true. My answer is that this result follows only if adequacy requires that likelihood of truth be established in a way which requires no background assumptions of any sort (or, which comes to the same thing, in a way which can meet any possible skeptical challenge). Unfortunately, however, as argued in SEK (13-15), any imaginable epistemological view is inadequate when judged by such a standard. If, as Aune suggests, all justification is "inescapably conditional" (I myself would restrict this claim to empirical justification), then it is not surprising that this is so for a coherence theory.

The foregoing should be enough to make it clear that Alvin Goldman is mistaken in his assertion (following Brueckner) that the metabeliefs which fall under the Doxastic Presumption "satisfy the characterization of basic empirical beliefs" which I offer in my anti-foundationalist argument (6; see SEK 32). The difference, of course, is that those metabeliefs are not claimed to be epistemically justified, but rather to constitute the background presumption against which issues of epistemic justification are raised. Nor, contrary again to Alvin Goldman's suggestion, can I see why the fact that one's reasons for thinking that one's beliefs are true can only be of this conditional sort should somehow be taken to open the door to externalist views in which justification requires no reasons of any sort.

What does follow from this account of the Doxastic Presumption is that there are certain versions of skepticism, those which either deny or question the truth of the metabeliefs which fall under the presumption, to which a coherence theory like mine can offer no reply. If it is true that all empirical justification is conditional, however, this is hardly a fatal objection, for any epistemological theory will face an analogous difficulty. Thus the interesting question, from my standpoint, is whether there are alternative epistemological positions, perhaps similar in structure at least to foundationalism, which can get by with weaker or otherwise less problematic presumptions and which are otherwise at least approximately as adequate as the coherentist view in question. I have argued in SEK (79-84) that there is not, but argument there is admittedly less than fully conclusive, and I await further developments with interest.

V

I consider next issues pertaining to another central ingredient of my coherentist position, the concept of coherence itself. One issue raised in several papers-those of Alvin Goldman, Alan Goldman, and Swain-concerns the requirement of logical consistency, which is presented in SEK as a necessary condition for coherence: isn't this too demanding a requirement, since it would mean that even minor inconsistencies render one's entire system of beliefs incoherent and hence, according to a coherentist view, unjustified?

I have two things to say on this point, the first of which amounts to a modification of the position of the book, though one which was anticipated by the footnote which Alvin Goldman mentions. First, it is plausible to suppose that not all sorts of inconsistency are equally inimical to coherence and thus to justification. I know of no worked out account of which are which and of why this is so, but I see no reason to think that such an account, when it is available, cannot be taken over by a coherentist view - which would mean that a system of beliefs could have a fairly high degree of coherence in spite of the presence of some sorts of inconsistency. But, second, I see no reason to doubt that any sort of inconsistency, even that involved in cases like the preface paradox, detracts to some degree from the justification of the system of beliefs in question, though perhaps not enough in a particular instance to make them fail to satisfy the level of justification required for knowledge - whatever that in fact may be.

A further issue, posed by Alvin Goldman, Aune, and especially by Kornblith, concerns the accessibility of coherence to ordinary epistemic agents and the related problems of such an agent's access to his own system of beliefs and grasp of the concept of coherence itself.

First, as regards the grasp of one's own system of beliefs, I agree with Alvin Goldman that a complete and explicit reflective grasp of one's own system of beliefs is in fact probably impossible for cognitive beings like ourselves. My claim is rather that optimal epistemic rationality would require such a grasp, and hence that, to the extent that we fall short of it, we only approximate ideal justification. In other words, our inability to fully access and compare our beliefs is a cognitive defect, one which may in some cases be very serious.

Something analogous should also be said about the ordinary person's grasp of the concept of coherence, though I do not intend this to be part of the Doxastic Presumption. I disagree with Alvin Goldman's claim that philosophically uneducated adults and even children have no grasp at all of this concept. On the contrary, I think that such persons frequently find failures of coherence intuitively objectionable (even though they of course wouldn't formulate the point in that way). But given the admitted sketchiness of my own account, I am hardly in a position to deny that even we philosophically sophisticated ones fail to have a fully explicit and adequate grasp of this concept. To the extent that this is so, I hold, once again, that even we fall short of and hence only approximate ideal epistemic justification.

The deepest and most troubling concern in this vicinity, however, is the one developed at length by Kornblith. Kornblith's claim is that, even apart from worries about the accessibility of the agent's belief system and the agent's grasp of the concept of coherence, the degree to which the system of beliefs actually is coherent is not cognitively accessible to the agent to a sufficient extent to satisfy the requirements of an internalist account of justification. And his further suggestion is that once this point is appreciated, externalists like Alvin Goldman and Kornblith himself are seen to be no worse off as regards the accessibility of their justification than is a supposedly internalist coherence theory.

Kornblith's discussion convinces me that I (along with very many others) have taken the question of the accessibility of coherence much too lightly, that it deserves a much fuller discussion than I have the space (or, very likely, the present insight) to give it here. I do not, however, believe that he has shown that the situation is as dire (from the standpoint of coherence theorists) as he claims, that "coherence may be just as external to an agent's point of view as reliability." Much of his discussion focuses on consistency, and here the concession already made earlier in this section, viz. that complete consistency is not always a necessary condition for a reasonably high degree of coherence, is perhaps of some help.[5] Beyond that, if it is conceded that the separate ingredients of coherence are individually accessible, I do not see how it can be denied that coherence itself is accessible in principle in a way in which purely external reliability is not. Nor do I see any easy way to establish just how close an estimate of the actual degree of coherence human beings may be capable of; for the moment, I can only record that my intuitions on this point are substantially more optimistic than Kornblith's. It does seem clear, however, that it must at least be conceded that a completely accurate grasp of the degree of coherence of his system of beliefs is very unlikely to be available to the ordinary epistemic agent, and hence that here once again the ordinary agent's epistemic situation is only an approximation, and perhaps a fairly distant one, to an epistemic ideal.

The remaining question is whether there is anything implausible about any of these results. My basic claim is that one who falls short of a fully explicit grasp of his system of beliefs, or of the concept of coherence, or of the degree to which his system of beliefs is coherent, thereby fails to that extent to have a complete and fully explicit reason for thinking that those beliefs are true. And this seems to me in turn to make it reasonable to say that the justification we in fact have is only approximate. But, at the same time, if the approximation is reasonably close, it is also easy enough to understand how common sense, neglectful as usual of fine distinctions, might regard our beliefs as in many cases fully justified. (Aune's discussion of his "weak" concept of justification is highly germane here, and indeed I find much of his paper quite congenial - including the suggestion that relatively few of our actual beliefs satisfy a concept of knowledge which is demanding enough to be interesting.)

VI

Bogen is also concerned with what he takes to be the implausible implications of a coherentist view with respect to the epistemic status of our actual beliefs. He offers several examples of commonsensical and scientific beliefs which seem intuitively to be cases of epistemically justified and epistemically responsible belief, but which, he claims, fail to satisfy the requirements of a coherence theory like mine [6] hereby showing, he thinks, that such theories are much too demanding.

Bogen's first example is his belief that Thelonius Monk composed 'I Mean You' after 1935. His claim is that this belief is justified and responsible in spite of the fact that he presently fails to have cognitive access to good reasons of any sort, and *a fortiori* to any good reasons of a coherentist sort, for thinking that the belief is true. Now although I obviously cannot be sure about this particular example, I think that Bogen is right that beliefs of this general sort are very often justified: any normal person is able to recall more or less at will a very large number of bits of factual information about the world, presumably acquired in various ordinary ways, but such that the person doing the recalling is at the time in question unable to summon up either a personal memory of how the information was acquired or any very obvious reason of some other sort for thinking that the belief is true. What then can a coherentist say about such cases?

Though beliefs of this sort are not explicitly mentioned in SEK, I think that the main ingredients of a plausible coherentist account of them are available there, mainly in the brief discussion of memory knowledge (155-56). (Indeed, though beliefs of the sort in question are not what philosophers standardly refer to as memory beliefs, they would often be cited commonsensically, albeit in a broader sense, as products of memory.) First, the belief about Thelonius Monk is, I presume, a cognitively spontaneous belief for Bogen, one which simply occurs when he asks or is asked the right sort of question without being arrived at via any sort of inference. Secondly, I presume that it is also the case for Bogen, as it is for most normal persons, that his cognitively spontaneous factual beliefs of this kind are highly likely to be true and also that he has checked or otherwise confirmed them often enough to have abundant evidence that this is so. (Quite possibly he, like most people, is much better at correctly recalling some kinds of facts as opposed to others, e.g. perhaps facts pertaining to the history of jazz in general or to Thelonius Monk in particular; and he may well also have evidence of a more specific sort that this is so.) But if these two presumptions are correct, then Bogen does possess a perfectly good reason, and one which as far as I can see fits well into a general coherentist framework, for thinking that the belief in question is true. And if these presumptions, or something very much like them, are not correct, then the intuition that the original belief is justified seems, to me anyway, to be severely undercut.

My suggestion would be that something along these same general lines can also be said about Bogen's other examples of non-scientific belief, his belief about his own last name and also the case of the good chef Machamer, but I will have to leave it to the reader to fill in the recipe.

Turning to the issue of scientific belief, Bogen discusses at great length the interesting historical example of Newton's argument for his law of universal gravitation from the evidence provided by the orbit of the moon. His general point is that Newton's argument on this point involves a variety of idealizations and simplifications, made largely in the interest of computational simplicity, the result of which is that several key components of the argument are either (i) false according to the best empirical evidence available at the time, or (ii) inconsistent with the very conclusion which they are supposed to support, namely the principle of universal gravitation itself, or in several cases both. Examples would include the claim that the moon's orbit is a Euclidean circle, the claim that the moon reaches its apogee in the same place, and the claim that the earth does not accelerate as the moon travels around it. Thus, Bogen argues, Newton's belief system or at least the fragment of it reflected in this argument is a coherentist's nightmare: inconsistent, probabilistically inconsistent, and potentially in violation of the Observation Requirement if the empirical evidence against these various claims is disregarded. Such a wildly incoherent set of beliefs would presumably not be epistemically justified or responsible according to my coherence theory or any position which is very much like it, and this, Bogen suggests, is surely an overwhelming reason to reject such views - especially since, as he quite correctly points out, such idealizations and simplifications are "the rule rather than the exception in good science".

Bogen considers and rejects a variety of ways in which a coherence theory might try to accommodate this sort of case. I agree that none of the possibilities he considers are acceptable. But in spite of this, I am not convinced that such cases pose an insuperable objection to a coherentist position, because I think that Bogen's analysis of the case in question is mistaken in a very simple and obvious, though also very natural and tempting way: he attributes beliefs to Newton which Newton plainly did not hold. Newton did not believe that the moon's orbit was perfectly circular; on the contrary, he believed, presumably justifiably, that it was not. What he did believe, as Bogen himself points out, was that the orbit was close enough to being circular that calculations on that basis would be acceptably close to being correct. And so also, I would suggest, for the other claims which create the problems which Bogen is concerned with: rather than believing these claims simpliciter, what Newton actually believed was some much more complicated proposition or set of propositions, involving difficult concepts like that of an acceptably close approximation, in which the claims Bogen cites are suitably embedded. This means, of course, that Newton's actual argument was much more complicated than the simple one which Bogen cites, and it raises difficult problems as to how justified his background assumptions about the degree of error introduced by such simplifications and idealizations may have been. But while I have neither the space here nor very likely the historical knowledge to give a detailed account of these issues, I can see no reason at present for thinking that such an account would reveal that the coherence of Newton's actual beliefs was significantly incommensurate with the degree of epistemic justification which would, in light of such an account, seem intuitively plausible.[7]

VII

Silvers's difficult paper raises a number of issues in the vicinity of my coherentist account of observation. While parts of his argument are still elusive to me, I hope that its main thrust is adequately captured in the following three objections.

First. Silvers argues that the sort of specification of belief content which is required to identify a particular kind of putatively observational belief cannot be derived from internally accessible ingredients but must rather depend on external causal etiology in a way which is incompatible with an internalist view of justification. I suspect that something like this view would be plausible to many philosophers, but I do not think that Silvers or anyone else has shown that it is true in a strong enough way to cause problems for my account. There can be no doubt that Twin Earth examples and similar sorts of cases have shown that there is a dimension of content, one which seems to me best conceived along indexical lines, which depends on the external context and thus is not internally accessible. But while I obviously cannot go into these issues in detail here, nothing in the discussion of such cases seems to me to show that there is not still an internally accessible specification of content which is adequate for epistemological purposes. What such examples seem to me to show is only that the identification of belief kinds and also the assessment of the various inferential and explanatory relations which contribute to coherence may well require a background presumption of a uniform context, i.e. the presumption that no shift of the sort represented by being transported from unknowingly from Earth to Twin Earth has taken place.

Second. Silvers also questions whether the sorts of generalizations (about the reliability of the beliefs of ordinary observers under specifiable circumstances with respect to various sorts of subject matter) which are involved, on my view, in the justification of a putatively observational belief can genuinely be laws of nature. His suggestion is that only "nomic properties" can figure in natural laws and that the properties explicitly specified in such generalizations are not properly nomic. Unfortunately, perhaps unlike Silvers, I am not blessed with firm intuitions as to which properties are nomic in this sense and which are not. I can see no reason, however, for denying that the kinds of generalizations cited in SEK, if otherwise acceptable, are adequate for justification, whether or not they are, properly speaking, laws of nature. Thus the issue is only whether accepting them as such opens the door to an objectionable "relativity of epistemic justification" in the way that Silvers claims. To this I can only reply that Silvers hasn't made clear in the present paper why this is supposed to be so. Since I am unable to arrive independently at any clear and compelling line of argument for such a conclusion, I can only hope that he will elaborate further at some later time.

Third. Silvers also worries about what he describes as an "ambiguity" in the idea
of cognitive spontaneity. As he notes, the claim that a particular belief is cognitively
spontaneous is supposed to exclude implicit or tacit reasoning or inference as well as that
which is fully explicit, raising the question of whether the cognitive spontaneity of a belief
is a feature accessible to the believer in the way that internalism requires. I agree that this is
a serious and important question, one which deserves substantially fuller discussion than I
was able to give it in SEK. My intuition, however, is that the line between beliefs which
are cognitively spontaneous and those which are not is relatively easy to draw in practice,
even if a detailed theoretical account is more elusive; and I cannot see that Silvers has given
any serious reason for doubting that this is so. (One could still, of course, raise a skeptical
worry as to whether beliefs which seem cognitively spontaneous might not in fact be
produced by inferential processes of some sort which are not accessible to consciousness,
thereby in effect raising anew the input objection. In SEK, I treat this version of
skepticism as basically on a par with the Cartesian demon hypothesis, to be handled in the
same way; and this approach still seems to me basically correct.)

Some further problems in the same vicinity are raised by Davis and Bender in the
course of a discussion mainly devoted to Lehrer's position. In effect, they propose some
putative counterexamples to my claim that satisfying the Observation Requirement is
adequate to meet the input problem (see SEK 139-43). Disentangling all of the issues
raised by their examples from the discussion of features specific to Lehrer's position would
take more space than I have available here, but a consideration of the following two points
will help to make clearer my construal of the requirement.

First. Suppose that a person's belief system indeed contains "laws attributing a
high degree of reliability to a reasonable variety of kinds of cognitively spontaneous
beliefs,"[8] as required by the Observation Requirement, but that the system contains no
actual beliefs which are identified as instances of those laws, so that no actual justified
input results. My response is that I intended the requirement to include the idea that the
laws apply to a reasonable variety of actual beliefs. This is perhaps somewhat clearer in
SEK than it was in the paper considered by Davis and Bender, but is also at least strongly
suggested by the stipulation that it is laws which are required. (See also the discussion of
the justification of such laws at SEK 124-26.)

Second. Davis and Bender also suggest the possibility that a spontaneous belief
produced by "random misfirings" of someone's brain, one that intuitively ought not to be
justified, might nonetheless be justifiable within the framework of my position. If such
beliefs are very rare, and normal observational and introspective beliefs are highly reliable,
then a law attributing a high degree of reliability to the spontaneous belief kind comprising
all of these beliefs taken together will be both true and (if the rest of my account is
acceptable) justifiable within a coherentist framework. But here Silver's point about
"nomic properties," discussed earlier, is surely correct: such a statement, though perhaps
true as an "accidental generalization," would not be a putative law and would not be
inductively justifiable by appeal to its instances, because the disjunctive property specifying
the "kind" in question is not nomic. Its status is distantly analogous to that of the
properties specified by Goodmanesque predicates like "grue."

VIII

I turn now to Swain's proposed counterexamples to my metajustificatory argument.
To recapitulate briefly, the main idea of that argument is that the best explanation of why a
system of beliefs remains coherent and stable in the long run, while continuing to receive
apparent observational input, is that the beliefs in the system in fact correspond to reality.
Swain accepts this claim as it applies to putatively observational beliefs and to beliefs which
are directly inferred from observation, but argues that it does not hold for the more

theoretical beliefs in the system, those whose connection with observation is relatively indirect.

His leading example here is the case of the fisherman who is able to predict the weather with extreme accuracy on the basis of barometer readings, but who at the same time accepts a wildly erroneous theory of how and why the barometer works: specifically, he believes that periodic increases in the force of gravity are responsible for both the deflection of the barometer needle and the subsequent rainfall. Swain's claim is that there is no reason why the fisherman's system of beliefs could not remain highly coherent and stable over an indefinitely long run despite the fact that its theoretical component fails utterly to correspond to reality - thereby showing that my metajustificatory argument is mistaken.

The problem with this objection, as I see it, is that it seriously underestimates the range of putatively observational implications which theoretical beliefs in a highly coherent system will inevitably have. This is relatively easy to see in the fisherman example. If we suppose that the concept of gravity which figures in the fisherman's theory is more or less the ordinary one, then the theory will have all sorts of further observational implications beyond those pertaining to barometer needles and raindrops: implications concerning the distance traveled by an object, such as a rock or a harpoon, when hurled with a specified force and at a specified angle; implications concerning the ease with which various objects can be lifted or carried; implications concerning the sagging of shelves, the pressure required in automobile tires, the depth of one's footprints in the sand, etc.; and, most obviously, implications concerning the weights of objects as measured by a scale- including, of course, the weight of the fish that he catches. Thus the fisherman is literally surrounded with potential observations which would conflict with his theory. Of course, he might not do some of the things which would lead to such conflicts (though he can hardly avoid them all), and he might fail to notice the results of others; but he would then violate the provision of my Observation Requirement which stipulates that the believer must seek out potentially conflicting observations. And if he does seek out such observations, then the coherence of his system will be quickly destroyed.

It would be possible, of course, to devise a theoretical view which had no clear-cut observational implications, but to do so would greatly reduce the degree to which the view in question coheres with the rest of the cognitive system. This seems to me what typically happens with religious beliefs, the other sort of example considered by Swain. It seems plausible to suppose that many sorts of religious belief are, as it were, relatively free- floating in relation to the rest of the person's cognitive system, possessing no definite inferential implications in relation to other parts of the system and hence more or less immune from any observational refutation. But such beliefs, though consistent with the rest of the system, do not cohere with it in any very strong way and hence will not, on my view, be justified to any substantial extent. And if this result is avoided by specifying the religious beliefs in such a way as to connect them more tightly to the system, then the possibility of observational conflict is restored; the familiar problem of evil is the most obvious example of such a conflict, but there are many other possibilities as well. Most actual religious beliefs probably fall somewhere between these extremes, cohering with the rest of the system to only a weak degree but still having some weak observational implications which are on the whole not borne out; they are thus not justified to any significant degree on my view.

There is one further issue which might be raised about this example, one which connects up with Alvin Goldman's worries about whether a coherentist view can allow for different degrees of justification attaching to different beliefs in the system. Suppose that a particular religious belief or set of beliefs fails to cohere closely with the rest of a given person's system of beliefs, either through sheer absence of inferential connection or because it conflicts to some degree with other beliefs in the system, whether observational or otherwise. Such a belief, I have suggested, is not justified according to the coherentist account. But does it not follow that the person's entire system of beliefs is incoherent to a significant degree, and hence equally lacking in justification on a coherentist account, which would surely be an implausible result?

The answer is that such a result would indeed be implausible, but that it does not follow from a coherentist view as I conceive it. Though a coherentist position is necessarily holistic, in that justification depends on the characteristics of the overall system of beliefs and on the ways in which individual beliefs fit into that system, it need not be monolithic in ascribing justification to particular beliefs, and there are many ways in which it is possible for some beliefs in a system to be more or less justified than others. One situation, which occurs in the religion example and many others as well, is where certain peripheral beliefs are only very weakly connected to a larger core system of beliefs which, considered on its own with those beliefs temporarily set aside, is highly coherent. In such a case, the core system would be highly justified if it existed on its own, and the peripheral beliefs thereby acquire some weaker degree of justification from it, depending on just how close the connection is. The presence of such peripheral beliefs may also have a negative impact on the justification of the core system, but if the connection is very loose this will not be very significant. The extreme case would be one in which a person has a highly coherent set of beliefs which by itself satisfies all of the coherentist requirements, but also has one or more additional beliefs which are entirely unrelated to the main system (and to each other). I see no reason not to say that the isolated beliefs are entirely unjustified, but also that this has no effect at all on the beliefs in the main system, which accordingly have whatever degree of justification they would have had if the others did not exist.

More generally, on a coherentist view as I understand it, the justification of individual beliefs or of small sets of beliefs is a function both of the overall coherence of the system and of the particular inferential connections which pertain directly to those beliefs. Given the background of a reasonably large and coherent system of beliefs, there is no reason why the implications of a coherentist view as regards the degree of justification of particular beliefs should not differ very widely from belief to belief or why these implications should in general depart significantly from the judgments of reflective common sense.

IX

Alvin Goldman also raises objections to my appeal, in the proposed metajustification, to the idea of *a priori* justification. He is, of course, perfectly right that the rationalist views on that subject which are briefly sketched in the appendix to the book are quite crucial to the viability of my overall epistemological position and thus that it is regrettable that I was unable to say more about them than I did. Unfortunately, however, one can only do so much in one book, especially given the unfortunate tendency of publishers to insist on brevity.

Goldman, however, does not in these comments offer a direct challenge to rationalism itself. His main objection is rather that the absence of any metajustificatory requirement for *a priori* knowledge together with the fact that *a priori* justification, on my view, involves no appeal to coherence, results in what he calls a "thoroughgoing bifurcation" in my account of epistemic justification.

I do not, however, believe that this is so. On my view, the unified concept of epistemic justification is that captured by the idea of epistemic responsibility outlined at the beginning of the present paper, i.e. the idea of having a reason in one's cognitive possession for thinking that the belief in question is true or likely to be true, and it is the property of being held with epistemic responsibility that all justified beliefs have in common. As mentioned above, this generic concept may take two specific forms. In the case of empirical justification, the appeal is to some extrinsic feature of the belief, a feature which must accordingly be shown via a metajustification to be relevant to finding the truth. But in the case of *a priori* justification, as understood by the rationalist, the appeal is to self-evidence, to the direct, intuitive grasp that the proposition believed is necessary; and since the connection with truth is thus built into the idea of self-evidence, no metajustification is required. My response to Goldman is thus that there is no fundamental bifurcation in my conception of epistemic justification, but rather a generic conception with two specific instances.

It is, of course, still possible to raise skeptical doubts, either about particular alleged instances of self-evidence or, more importantly, about self-evidence in general, and exactly what should be said about such skepticism is a difficult and dialectically complicated matter. It is clear at once, however, that it would play directly into the skeptic's hand to simply retreat from a full-fledged claim of self-evidence to a claim of apparent self-evidence and then attempt to argue one's way from apparent self-evidence to truth: since any such argument would have to depend ultimately on allegedly self-evident inferential transitions, it could never have any more force, other things being equal, than the original claim of self-evidence itself. Thus a rationalist view must hold in general that particular instances of self-evidence stand on their own feet, rather than depending, as in the empirical case, on a more general criterion or principle which is independently justified-and this is what I meant by saying that there is no criterion or standard of *a priori* justification. It would still be possible, I suppose, to regard self-evidence as the criterion of *a priori* justification, but putting it this way seems to me more misleading than helpful, since in this case the tenability of the general criterion would depend on that of the specific instances, rather than the other way around.

The last issue raised by Goldman in connection with the *a priori* is whether I would accept as a requirement for *a priori* justification that the relevant *a priori* processes or acts of intuition must be reliable. My response is that while this may well, for Gettier-type reasons, be a requirement for knowledge, it does not seem to me to be a requirement for justification. If, as I claim, all empirical justification depends ultimately on an *a priori* metajustification, then I could in general have no better reason for thinking that any belief is true than its being a clear instance of self-evidence, and hence accepting a belief on that basis exhibits the highest possible degree of epistemic rationality and responsibility, and so on my view the highest possible degree of justification, even if such beliefs should somehow still happen to be unreliable. (Of course, the story might be more complicated if unreliability manifested itself in some way in some limited range of cases, but that would not affect the main point at issue.)

X

I will conclude by mentioning very briefly a few further issues which have not managed to make their way into the foregoing sections.

First. Tolliver's discussion starts from what he regards as "a platitude about knowledge: that there would be no problem about knowledge if everything always had been, were, and always would be just as we believe it to be". The upshot of this "platitude" is that in "an incorrigible world," one in which all beliefs are true, all beliefs would also be instances of knowledge. But this is obviously inconsistent with a coherence theory like mine, for it is easy to imagine an incorrigible world in which the requirements for justification and knowledge laid down by such a theory are not satisfied. My response to this is simple enough: Tolliver's supposed platitude seems to be not only not to be a platitude but indeed to be obviously false. The easiest way in which to see this is to consider the most unlikely but still imaginable world in which there is a cognitive agent who adopts beliefs utterly arbitrarily and capriciously, indulging in wild leaps, wishful thinking, and so forth to the most extreme degree imaginable while inadvertently and fortuitously maintaining consistency, but whose beliefs by sheer coincidence and luck are all true. I can feel no intuitive pull at all toward the view that such a believer knows the things he believes.

Second. My problem with Alan Goldman's madman example is that it does not seem to me that he has even begun the job of describing the case in a way which would yield a genuinely coherent system of beliefs satisfying the observation requirement and remaining stable over the long run. (See SEK 149-51 for some discussion of what would be required.) I am not questioning that something like this case could be elaborated in this way, only insisting that until this is done in some detail, one's intuitions about whether such a madman would be justified cannot be taken very seriously.

Third. Alan Goldman also raises Gettier-type worries about the ability of a coherence theory to give a satisfactory account of knowledge. I am not convinced that, as he suggests, such considerations "indicate that a very different sort of account of knowledge [from the justified true belief account] is required." But I am also inclined to doubt that the ordinary concept of knowledge will turn out in the long run to have the sort of pivotal importance which it has usually been ascribed. (See Aune's paper for some relevant discussion.) Finally, I want to mention that I found Day's reflections on the idea of non-linear justification very helpful and basically correct.

NOTES

1. Cambridge, Mass.: Harvard University Press, 1985. References to the pages of this book will use the indicated abbreviation and will be placed in the text. All other references in the text are to the pages of the present volume.

2. See Alvin Goldman, *Epistemology and Cognition*, Cambridge, Mass.: Harvard University Press, 1986), 393-4, footnote 21.

3. See Marshall Swain, *Reasons and Knowledge*, Ithaca, N.Y.: Cornell University Press, 1981.

4. Some or all of these objections may be met in Goldman's forthcoming book, to which I did not have access while preparing this response.

5. Certainly the point about truth table determination of consistency which Kornblith makes later in his discussion of Harman (4-5) is far less telling than he thinks and indeed seems to me to have very little force at all. What it shows is only that, as was obvious enough anyway, human judgments of consistency are not normally made via the construction of large truth-tables.

6. One question raised by this response is whether cognitively spontaneous beliefs of this sort, i.e., those involved in what might be called factual as opposed to personal memory, should contribute to satisfying the Observation Requirement. I think it is clear, at least in general, that they should not, but will defer to another occasion the task of saying exactly why not or of reformulating the requirement to all for this point.

7. A rather different problem posed by Bogen (10) concerns the ability of Newton's theory to explain only idealized and simplified descriptions of the observed facts, resulting in unexplained anomalies and, on my account, lessened coherence and so lessened justification. This point seems to me substantially less serious than the ones considered in the text. To explain a simplified version of a fact is, I would suggest, to give a partial explanation of the actual fact: it is to explain why it falls within the range of approximation involved in the simplification. A degree of anomaly does remain and so a degree of lessened coherence, but this may be quite minor in comparison to the anomaly which would have been present had there been no explanation at all; thus the resulting level of justification may still be high enough to satisfy our intuitions.

8. Cited by Davis and Bender from my earlier paper, "The Coherence Theory of Empirical Knowledge," *Philosophical Studies* 30 (1976). In SEK, the phrase "kinds of" is deleted (SEK 141).

INDEX